ADVANCE PRAISE FOR *THE BILLIONAIRE RAJ*

'James Crabtree distinguished himself as the most insightful journalist writing for the *Financial Times* from India. It is not surprising therefore that he has now written a book that offers a splendid overview of the issues that have been raised concerning India's spectacular growth since the reforms began in 1991. It is bound to become a classic.'

Jagdish Bhagwati, author of *In Defense of Globalization*

'A lucid, detailed and at times epic account of the new India, opening our eyes to the economic and social transformation that has quietly occurred there in recent years, behind the facade of the headlines.'

Robert D. Kaplan, author of *Monsoon*
and *The Return of Marco Polo's World*

'Who are the Indian *nouveau riche* and what do they want? James Crabtree's *The Billionaire Raj* will prove the defining work on these questions. It is a must-read for anyone interested in wealth, inequality, India, or the evolution of capitalism.'

Tyler Cowen, economist, blogger and
author of *The Great Stagnation*

'A fascinating look into the world of the Indian business elite – the "Bollygarchs" – and their political entanglements. James Crabtree deftly explores the changing balance between big money and democratic accountability, shedding considerable light on whether the country will sustain the miracle that is the Indian democracy or go the way of populism and authoritarianism as so many others have.'

Dani Rodrik, Professor of International Political Economy,
Harvard University, and author of *The Globalization Paradox*

THE BILLIONAIRE RAJ

A JOURNEY THROUGH
INDIA'S NEW GILDED AGE

JAMES CRABTREE

ONEWORLD

A Oneworld Book

First published in Great Britain and Australia by Oneworld Publications Ltd, 2018

Hardback ISBN 978-1-78607-380-8
Trade Paperback ISBN 978-1-78607-529-1
eISBN 978-1-78607-381-5

Photographs: Dhobi Ghat © Aleksandr Zykov; Antilia © Jay Hariani; Mallya © Sajjad
Hussain/Stringer/Getty Images; Adani © Mint/Getty Images; Gujarat riot © Sebastian
D'Souza/Stringer/Getty Images; protest against demonetisation © Fotokannan;
Modi © *Hindustan Times*/Getty Images; Jayalalithaa © Nandhinikandhasamy; Jindal
© *Hindustan Times*/Getty Images; Reddy wedding © Stringer/Getty Images; IPL
protest © Manjunath Kiran/Stringer/Getty Images; Goswami © Sujit Jaiswal/Stringer/
Getty Images; Modi and Obama © Pete Souza; Aston Martin © James Crabtree

Typeset by Hewer Text UK Ltd, Edinburgh
Printed and bound in Great Britain by Clays Ltd, Elcograf S.p.A

Oneworld Publications Ltd
10 Bloomsbury Street
London WC1B 3SR
England

Stay up to date with the latest books,
special offers, and exclusive content from
Oneworld with our newsletter

Sign up on our website
oneworld-publications.com

To my parents

CONTENTS

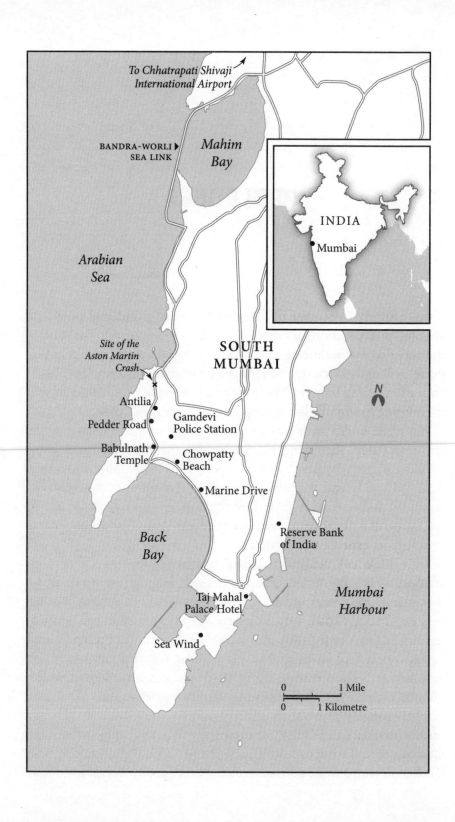

To Chhatrapati Shivaji
International Airport

BANDRA-WORLI
SEA LINK

*Mahim
Bay*

*Arabian
Sea*

**SOUTH
MUMBAI**

*Site of the
Aston Martin
Crash*

Antilia

Pedder Road

Gamdevi
Police Station

Babulnath
Temple

Chowpatty
Beach

Marine Drive

Reserve Bank
of India

*Back
Bay*

*Mumbai
Harbour*

Taj Mahal
Palace Hotel

Sea Wind

INDIA

Mumbai

N

0   1 Mile

0   1 Kilometre

PROLOGUE

It was a sunny December day when I found it, abandoned outside a Mumbai police station and draped in a dirty plastic sheet. The silhouette revealed the outline of a car, low to the ground and beaten out of shape. A chunky black tyre was propped awkwardly against the chassis. Thin white string tethered the sheet to a telephone pole, although this did nothing to stop me lifting it up and taking a peek below.

The scene underneath was a mess. A tangle of metal erupted from the driver's side. The bonnet was bent across the middle, pushed up by a violent impact. Broken tubes stuck out from the engine. Through a shattered windscreen I could see cramped rear seats, once plush red, now filthy and covered with dust. But the passenger's side was in better shape, revealing the classic lines of an Aston Martin Rapide, one of the world's most expensive supercars.

The vehicle had met its demise late at night a few weeks earlier, in an incident whose mysterious aftermath stuck long in my mind as an exemplar of the power of India's new super-rich. It had been roaring north up Pedder Road, a dual carriageway that separates two wealthy sections of the country's financial capital. To the left was Breach Candy, a plush enclave of residential towers offering pleasant views over the Arabian Sea. Narrow lanes to the right led up to Altamount Road, where colonial-era mansions hid behind high walls and iron gates.

It was roughly 1:30 a.m. when the Aston's driver lost control, rear-ending another car. Jolted by the impact, the second vehicle, an Audi A4, spun onto the opposite carriageway and clipped an oncoming bus. A collision with a third car then crushed the Aston's front end, sending it skidding across the road, where it crumpled to a halt in a whirl of smoke and glass. No one was killed, but as her Audi came to a stop, Foram Ruparel – a 25-year-old business school student, who had driven south earlier for dinner – realised she was in a fix. There were plenty of fancy cars in Mumbai, but Aston Martins remained rare. Anybody owning one had to be rich – really rich. And that meant trouble.

What happened next is fiercely disputed. Media reports said the Aston's driver first tried to flee in his crippled vehicle.[1] Realising it was too smashed-up to drive, he jumped into one of two Honda sports utility vehicles that happened to have followed him down the road.[2] 'In seconds, there was a swarm of security men around the car and they bundled the driver into one of the SUVs and sped off,' Ruparel told a local paper a few days later.[3] The security detail zoomed back down the road, racing off in the direction of a house just a few minutes' drive away.

Although not visible from the crash scene, a building came quickly into view as they raced south. A giant residential skyscraper called Antilia, it loomed high above the street, an unavoidable symbol of the prominence of its owner: billionaire Mukesh Ambani, India's richest man.

News of the hit-and-run filtered out quickly the next morning, Sunday 8 December 2013.[4] The ruined Aston turned out to be owned by Reliance Ports, a little-known subsidiary of Ambani's main Reliance Industries business, a giant conglomerate with interests stretching from oil refining and gas exploration to telecoms and television.[5] Later that afternoon, Bansilal Joshi, a portly 55-year-old driver employed by the Ambani family, presented himself at Gamdevi police station, about two kilometres from the crash site.[6] He had taken the car out for a late-night test drive, he confessed, and had been behind the wheel when it crashed. Then he fled the scene.[7]

Ruparel told a different story, at least at first. 'I could see in the rear-view mirror the car was moving at a high speed, weaving left and right. And then, in a flash, it hit my car,' she told one local newspaper. 'I had a decent look at the driver's face. He was a young man.'[8] In the days after the crash rumours spread that the young man may have been a member of the Ambani family, the country's pre-eminent business dynasty.[9] Yet over the next few weeks Ruparel had a change of heart. Towards the end of December, she signed a statement in a magistrates' court claiming Joshi had been the driver after all.[10]

The Reliance Industries account of what happened that night may very well be true. No one has been able to find out for sure. The police said CCTV footage of the moments leading up to the crash was inconclusive.[11] Pedder Road is one of Mumbai's busiest thoroughfares, teeming even late at night with roadside hawkers, pedestrians and pavement-dwellers, trying to catch a few hours of sleep on cardboard mats. Yet none of those at the scene caught a glimpse of the fleeing driver. India's usually tenacious media covered the story with caution too.[12] 'While the cops have maintained a stoic silence so have most of India's leading television channels,' a report in *Forbes* went so far as to put it later. In spite of the denials, the article even named a member of the Ambani family on the basis of rife 'speculation online' that he 'was allegedly involved in the smash-up'.[13]

Curious to find out more, I called a company spokesman in the days following the crash. He told me it was perfectly normal for Reliance Ports, ostensibly a logistics and transport business, to own a sports car with a price tag in the region of $700,000.[14] There was also nothing unusual, he said, in an employee taking such a car for a test drive in the small hours of the morning, or for him to be trailed by security vehicles. The company firmly denied that anyone other than Joshi, its driver, had been involved.[15] In private many of those I met over the following days were sceptical of elements of this story, although almost no one said anything in public. Omar Abdullah, the outspoken chief minister of the state of Jammu and Kashmir, was one exception, tweeting: 'If friends in Mumbai are to be believed, it seems the only people who don't know who was driving the fancy Aston Martin are the Mumbai police.'[16]

Not long afterwards, I went to an evening reception in the seafront Taj Mahal Palace hotel, whose Gothic stone facade and pale red dome provide one of Mumbai's most recognisable landmarks. Darkness was falling outside as corporate luminaries gathered beneath glistening chandeliers in the main ballroom. The lights of distant yachts glinted in the harbour. Talk turned quickly to the mysteries of the crash, although only after much conspiratorial glancing over shoulders. Reliance continued fiercely to deny any wrongdoing, but rightly or wrongly many of those I met seemed doubtful about the company's version of events.

Whatever the truth of the matter, the incident cast a revealing light on how billionaires were viewed in India. That evening, I found myself playing devil's advocate. Both theories about what happened seemed questionable, I argued: the Reliance account of the late-night test drive on the one hand and the vague conspiracy and cover-up theory on the other. At one point at the Taj I told the head of a local bank that the Reliance story seemed the more likely of the two. He shot me a look with which I would soon become familiar: a combination of amazement and pity at the foreigner's naivety. I realised then the mystery of who exactly had been driving was not the real issue. Such was the mystique surrounding the Ambanis, and so comprehensive was the belief in their power, what mattered was that many believed they could, if needed, make such a scandal disappear.

A few days later I went to Gamdevi police station to find out more. It was a dusty, chaotic old building, set back a few blocks from Chowpatty Beach and the Art Deco apartment blocks of Marine Drive, the city's crescent-shaped promenade. Bored-looking officers napped on plastic chairs beneath slowly turning fans, guarding rooms filled with overflowing piles of paper. The inspector was out, one told me. He returned eventually and granted a cautious interview.

'Where is the car now?' I asked.

'It has been impounded. For tests,' he said.

'And when will those tests be finished?'

'It will take some time.'

As we spoke, my mind conjured up a scene from the television series *CSI*, in which the Aston's ruined body had been carried to a spotless warehouse somewhere on the edge of town, where experts in overalls and white gloves were conducting a careful forensic examination. It was only when I emerged blinking back into the sunlight that a silhouette wrapped in a grey sheet caught my eye, parked a short distance down the street. No, I remember thinking. It can't be.

Over the next year, I would stop by from time to time to see if the car was still there. It always was. The sheet got progressively dirtier, its top more deeply encrusted with bird shit. But the car beneath never seemed to have been touched. Sometimes I would stop by the police station and ask the officers how the investigation was progressing. 'Ongoing,' they told me, a code word we both understood to mean nothing whatsoever was happening.

Here was one of the world's most expensive cars belonging to one of the world's richest men: a tycoon whom no sensible person would want to cross; a man whose power and influence, while enigmatic, was considered an inescapable fact of modern India. And so the car itself – an awkward reminder of events that early December morning – just sat there, ruined, fully wrapped and half forgotten, as if all involved hoped they might wake one morning and find that a passing magician had whisked off the sheet, and made the wrecked vehicle conveniently disappear.

The Dhobi Ghat, a sprawling open-air laundry in Mumbai where as many as half the population live in slums.

INTRODUCTION

Nothing symbolises the power of India's new elite more starkly than Antilia, the residential skyscraper Mukesh Ambani built for himself, his wife and their three children. Rising 160 metres in height, the steel and glass tower has a floor area roughly two thirds the size of the Palace of Versailles, although it stands on a plot of barely an acre.[1] A grand hotel-style ballroom takes up most of the ground floor, fitted with twenty-five tonnes of imported chandeliers.[2] Six storeys of parking house the family's car collection, while a staff complement in the hundreds caters to their needs.[3] The upper levels feature opulent apartments and hanging gardens. A top-floor reception room, encased on three sides in glass, leads onto a giant outdoor terrace offering sweeping views down over the city. Somewhere below there is a health club with gyms and yoga studios. An ice room, a kind of sauna in reverse, offers escape from Mumbai's fierce summer heat.[4] Further down, in sub-basement 2, the Ambani children have a recreation floor, including a football pitch and basketball court.

Mumbai has long been a place of divisions: a tightly packed metropolis where the homes of tycoons and financiers cram in next to shanties, with corrugated sheets and tarpaulins for roofs. Antilia seems only to magnify this segregation, as if the building's very excesses were designed to add yet greater stratification to a city already famed for its extremes of wealth and poverty. Even so, I came to feel a strange connection with the building, which provided a backdrop to my time there, right from the day I landed. My employer's driver picked me up that morning in November 2011. We began the slow crawl south through blaring traffic, driving past slums leaning up against the airport fence and then down along the Sea Link, a short stretch of eight-lane motorway running alongside the city's western flank. After an hour or so we crossed onto Pedder Road, passing the spot where the Aston Martin would later crumple to a halt. Seconds later my driver pointed excitedly through the windshield, as Antilia loomed out of the haze up ahead.

Over the next five years the tower became part of the grammar of my daily life. Home to around twenty million people, Mumbai is a thin, teeming peninsula, a little like Manhattan in shape, with a series of arterial roads running up its west side. Beginning along the seafront at Marine Drive, these snake north along the coast, passing roadside shacks and elegant mansions along the way. My work as a journalist often took me along this route as I headed out around the city, passing twice beneath the shadow of Antilia: once on the drive north and once coming back south. In time I even warmed to its unusual cantilevered design, defending it to horrified visitors as if afflicted by an architectural variant of Stockholm syndrome. Much like New York's Empire State Building, the tower provided a helpful landmark above the city's choked streets, as well as a public testament to its owner's extraordinary wealth, which at the last count stood at $38 billion.[5]

This fortune made Ambani comfortably India's richest person, but he was far from alone. In the mid-1990s just two Indians featured in the annual *Forbes* list of the world's wealthiest, racking up $3 billion between them.[6] That number then ticked up slowly, reaching five by the time Ambani took over his family's businesses after his father's death in 2002. But then an explosive expansion began, adding dozens more names over the remainder of the decade. Some transformed old family-run conglomerates into global multinationals. Others were first-generation entrepreneurs, accumulating billions in sectors from software to mining. *Forbes* ranked forty-nine Indians as billionaires by 2010, the year in which Antilia's four-year construction finally wrapped up.

Today, India's most exclusive club has ballooned to over one hundred, more than in any other country bar America, China and Russia.[7] Together its members owned assets worth $479 billion in 2017.[8] One level below them the country has 178,000 dollar millionaires.[9] If you take billionaire wealth as a proportion of national output, the super-rich do best of all in Russia, whose powerful oligarchs are renowned for their lifestyles and business dealings.[10] But India now often ranks close behind, with a new super-rich business class sometimes jokingly dubbed the 'Bollygarchs', for their ability to bring together much the same mixture of industrial might and intimacy with power.

The rise of the super-rich was propelled at first by domestic economic reforms. Starting slowly in the 1980s, and then more dramatically against the backdrop of a wrenching financial crisis in 1991, India dismantled the dusty stockade of licences and tariffs that had protected its economy for a generation or more. Strict industrial rules controlling what could be made and by whom – a convoluted system sometimes known as the 'Licence-Permit-Quota Raj', or just 'Licence Raj' for short – were scrapped. A clear-out began of companies cosseted under the old regime, via deregulation, foreign investment and heightened competition. In sector after sector, from airlines and banks to steel and telecoms, the ranks of India's tycoons began to swell.

Yet this growth was also intimately bound up in larger global story. The early 2000s were the heyday of the 'great moderation', a moment when world interest rates stayed low and industrialised nations grew handsomely. China entered the World Trade Organization in 2001, kicking off one of the most remarkable expansions of any country in history. Booming Chinese exports, along with the demand for commodities they fuelled, boosted other developing economies, including India's. Bullish investors flooded the emerging world with cash, spreading the fruits of what some dubbed a new era of 'hyper-globalisation'.

It was in the mid-2000s that the fortunes of India's tycoons really began to change. For all its drama, only a handful of sectors took off in the decade after 1991, including generic pharmaceuticals and software outsourcing. Over that ten-year period India's economy also barely grew faster than it had in the previous one. But in the early years of the new millennium the twin impact of liberalisation and hyper-globalisation became impossible to ignore. Pumped up by foreign money, domestic bank loans and a surging sense of self-belief, industrialists like Ambani dumped billions into projects from oil refineries to steel mills. Others rushed to build toll roads and power stations, or spent heavily on Airbuses and broadband networks. Stock markets boomed. From 2004 to 2014 India enjoyed the fastest economic expansion in its history, averaging growth of more than eight per cent a year.

These boom years brought undoubted benefits, helping over one hundred million escape from poverty. Just as importantly they began to reintegrate India with the rest of the world. The Indian subcontinent had been the planet's largest economy for most of the last two millennia.[11] Three centuries of colonial rule ruined that legacy, as the East India Company suppressed and plundered southern Asia. In the late seventeenth century, when Britain controlled just a handful of coastal cities, India's Mughal Empire presided over close to a quarter of global gross domestic product. That figure stood at four per cent when the last British troops left, not long after Independence in 1947, the final battalion marching out through the grand basalt arch of Mumbai's Gateway of India, just down the road from the apartment in which my wife and I would later live.[12] Yet even under the yoke of imperialism local merchants still sent plentiful cargoes to Liverpool and Manchester, while Indian capital coursed through the exchanges of the City of London. It was only after Independence that Jawaharlal Nehru, a cerebral Cambridge-educated lawyer and the nation's first prime minister, began to abandon a heritage as a trading power that stretched back two thousand years.

The point is that these decades of self-imposed quarantine were the exception. India is now a remarkably globalised nation once more. Rather than struggling to scrape together foreign exchange, it holds hundreds of billions of dollars in reserves. It is on some measures a more open economy than China, which began to liberalise roughly a decade earlier. India now trades more goods and services as a proportion of GDP than its larger Asian neighbour, and far more than America. The value of that trade has rocketed from just seventeen per cent of GDP when its economic reforms began 1991 to around sixty per cent today.[13] It attracts as much foreign direct investment as China did at the peak of its growth in the mid-2000s.[14] Not far off half of all the freely traded shares on Indian stock markets are owned by foreigners.[15]

India's leading companies have spread out around the world too, buying up everything from African mines to British steel makers. Its citizens remain instinctive internationalists, boasting the world's largest diaspora population and sending home more than $60 billion in remittances each year.[16] The fear that India would reject the arrival of foreign companies and global investment, viewing them as akin to a new form of colonialism, has been handily disproved. Indeed, globalisation remains strikingly popular. More than four in five Indians currently view it positively, among the highest rates of any country, reflecting the sharp improvements in basic living conditions most of its people have experienced since reopening.[17]

Rather than fearing the world, India has embraced it. Yet for all their benefits, these decades of whirlwind growth have proved to be economically disruptive, socially bruising and environmentally destructive, leaving in their wake what novelist Rana Dasgupta has described as a sense of national 'trauma'.[18] Those benefits have also undeniably been shared unevenly, with the greatest portion of India's new prosperity flowing to its top one per cent, or, more specifically, the top fraction of that one per cent. For nearly a century prior to Independence, India was governed directly by the British under a system commonly known as the Raj, a term that takes its origin from the Sanskrit word *rājya*, meaning 'kingdom' or 'rule'. Then for the best part of the half-century after 1947 there followed the Licence Raj, with its perverse edicts and myriad restrictions. Now, in the quarter century after liberalisation, and set against the backdrop of a world in flux, a new system has grown up in their place: the Billionaire Raj.

THE BILLIONAIRE RAJ

This book charts three critical elements in India's recent history, beginning with the rise of the super-rich themselves and the associated problems they bring of inequality and entrenched corporate power. India has long been a stratified society, marked by divisions of caste, race and religion. Prior to Independence the country was subjugated by imperial administrators, as well as myriad maharajas and the feudal monarchies they led. Yet in the decades after 1947 it at least grew economically more equal, with an elite that lived modestly by the standards of the industrialised West.

This changed rapidly from the beginning of the 2000s, as wealth flowed first to an educated, globally connected elite. A newly prosperous class emerged in major cities, giving birth to 'islands of California in a sea of sub-Saharan Africa', in the words of economists Jean Drèze and Amartya Sen.[19] The wealth accumulated at the very top was most eye-catching of all. In 2008, as the scale of India's new billionaire fortunes became clear, economist Raghuram Rajan, the future head of India's central bank, asked: 'If Russia is an oligarchy, how long can we resist calling India one?'[20]

A sense of perspective is needed about such claims. India remains a poor country. The average citizen earns less than $2,000 a year. To be counted among its richest one per cent required assets of just $32,892, according to research from investment bank Credit Suisse in 2016.[21] But that same one per cent now owns more than half of national wealth, one of the highest rates in the world. The International Monetary Fund (IMF) suggests that India, alongside China, now ranks as Asia's most unequal major economy. Thomas Piketty, the French economist famous for his work on global inequality, has shown the share of Indian national income taken by the top one per cent of income earners to be at its highest level since tax records began in 1922.[22]

On these measures, India should now rightly be viewed alongside South Africa and Brazil as one of the world's least equal countries. Yet a strange intellectual consensus has often downplayed this conclusion. In the decades since liberalisation, many thinkers on the right of the political spectrum have argued that rapid rates of growth matter more than its eventual distribution. Those on the left, by contrast, have focused more on conditions at the bottom, worrying about India's poor progress on indicators of social development, such as child mortality. For both groups the gap between rich and poor has been secondary. Yet there are good reasons to be worried about it. Recent IMF research has challenged the consensus that inequality does little economic harm, showing that unequal nations tend to grow more slowly and be more prone to financial instability. Countries riven by internal divisions are also less likely to build the kind of broad social consensus that makes it easier to introduce tough structural reforms, of the type that India itself now badly needs if it is to continue to develop economically. There is also every reason to believe that, without intervention, the gap between India's rich and the rest will keep widening.

The rise of the super-rich, then, ties into a second issue: crony capitalism, meaning collusion between political and business elites to capture valuable public resources for themselves. India's old system of central planning and state controls created fertile ground for graft, forcing citizens and businesses alike to pay myriad bribes for basic state services. Yet these problems of retail corruption were trivial compared to those that emerged during the go-go years of the 2000s. Scarce assets worth billions in sectors like telecoms and mining were gifted to big tycoons, in a series of scandals known as the 'season of scams'. Giant kickbacks helped businesses acquire land, bypass environmental rules or win infrastructure contracts. Soaring commodity prices prompted a boom in the mining of minerals such as iron ore, leading to rampant corruption in extractive industries. Headlines filled up with scandals, from fraudulent public housing schemes to dodgy road-building projects.

Those who pushed India's reforms in 1991 expected that a more free market economy would lead in turn to better and more honest government. This proved optimistic, to put it mildly. Instead rapid growth and globalisation placed huge strains on the country's rusty state machinery. Even if they themselves were honest, over-burdened bureaucrats, judges and regulators failed to set boundaries within which the market could develop. But often they were indeed corrupt, and many extravagantly so. Crony capitalism infiltrated almost every area of national life. There were furores over mining rights and land allocation and public food distribution schemes. Cash-for-access scandals hit the media. Allegations of cronyism even besmirched cricket, the beloved national sport. 'Hundreds of billions of dollars' were siphoned away in megascams, according to one estimate.[23] India's old system of retail corruption went wholesale.

Many politicians became astoundingly rich in this process, and would rightly have taken a place on the *Forbes* list had their holdings not been hidden in shell companies and foreign banks. More generally, rapid economic growth increased the value of holding political power, in terms of what could be extracted from it. Political parties spent more to win elections, requiring them to raise more money, both to fight campaigns and to fund the patronage that kept them in office. Much of the monies parties raked in was donated illegally by favoured tycoons, in exchange for unknown future favours. Politics in the world's largest democracy no longer comes cheaply. One estimate suggested that India's last election, in 2014, cost close to $5 billion.[24] The contest was won handily by the Hindu nationalist Bharatiya Janata Party of current Prime Minister Narendra Modi, in large part because Modi managed to tap public anger about corruption, promising both economic renewal and an end to graft.

The third focus of this book – the boom and bust cycle of India's industrial economy – came as a consequence of the first two. Over the last two decades China has conducted the largest infrastructure building spree in history, almost all of which was built and funded by state-backed companies. By contrast, India's investment boom was dominated by the private sector. The Bollygarchs borrowed huge sums from local banks and invested it all – with gleeful abandon – in one of the largest deployments of private capital since America built its railroad network more than a century and a half earlier. But then India's good times came gradually to an end, beginning in the aftermath of the global financial crisis. The tycoons' earlier hubris was rudely exposed, leaving their businesses over-stretched and struggling to repay debts. In 2017, ten years after the financial crisis began, India's banks were left holding at least $150 billion worth of bad assets.[25]

This cycle of boom and bust followed a pattern familiar from other emerging economies, as when tycoons in Malaysia and Thailand gorged on cheap credit and splurged on speculative investments in the run-up to the 1997 Asian financial crisis. But India's wider story was still global. In America and Britain, two decades of hyper-globalisation ultimately overwhelmed the financial system, taking down once-mighty banks and insurers in New York and London. In India, the same surging global forces swamped the industrial system instead, battering the conglomerates that had long formed the backbone of the industrial economy. And just as the reputations of financiers in London and New York were ruined, so the image of the swashbuckling tycoons of Mumbai and New Delhi took a hit from which they have still not entirely recovered.

My interest in these topics – the super-rich, cronyism, and the travails of the industrial economy – was born partly of circumstance. Working as a foreign correspondent I saw all three up close. Travelling around India, I became fascinated above all by the empire builders: those who grew powerful in politics and business during the mid-2000s boom and were then forced to grapple with their aftermath, especially as the tide began turning after Modi's election victory in 2014. These were people who dealt with India as they found it, not as they would have liked it to be. They displayed ambitions on a scale that no longer seemed possible in the sanitised capitalism of the West. Even the vocabulary used to describe them was dredged up as if from a different era: baron, boss; magnate, mogul; titan, tycoon.

If this all sounds familiar, that is because it is. India is far from the first country to enjoy a period of rampant cronyism and wild growth, and to emerge changed fundamentally in its aftermath. In Britain the onset of the Industrial Revolution kicked off such a moment in the mid-nineteenth century, commemorated in the novels of Charles Dickens and Anthony Trollope. But the more obvious parallel is with America, and the era that ran from the end of the Civil War in 1865 to the turn of the twentieth century: the Gilded Age, or the era of 'the great corporation, the crass plutocrat [and] the calculating political boss', as one historian put it.[26]

Mid-nineteenth-century America viewed itself as a rural, egalitarian idyll: a nation of yeoman farmers governed by gentleman politicians. It was a vision that would have been shared by Mohandas Gandhi, the monastic civil rights leader whose philosophy of non-violence helped India win its independence, and who believed firmly in the spiritual superiority of village life. Yet just two generations later the United States stood transformed, after a whipsawing period of booms and busts in which its economy grew faster than at any point before or since.[27] Industrial centres like Chicago and Pittsburgh absorbed millions who left their land and millions more immigrating from Europe. What had been a nation of isolated smallholders turned into a giant continental economy and the world's leading industrial power.

Just as in India, this growth gave birth to a new generation of pluto-crats, from oil magnate John Rockefeller and banker John Pierpont Morgan to railroad tycoons Jay Gould and Cornelius Vanderbilt. These men sat atop a new 'millionaire class' known for its extravagant houses and vulgar displays of wealth. Then they acquired another name: the 'robber barons', for the speed at which they built their fortunes and the lack of conscience they displayed while doing so. From the clifftop mansions of Newport, Rhode Island, to the splendour of New York's newly minted millionaires' row on Fifth Avenue, it was the wealth these tycoons accumulated that defined their era. The phrase 'Gilded Age' came from a novel by Mark Twain, describing a period that glittered on the surface, as if painted in gold, but was decaying underneath.[28] That decay was to be found in politics above all, as the expansion of the franchise in the early 1800s gave birth to the rampant corruption of the 'spoils' system.[29] Powerful urban political machines traded bribery and patronage for jobs and votes. Most famous of all was New York's

Tammany Hall, which controlled the US financial capital for much of the nineteenth century.

I first came across the notion that India might be going through a similar stage of development via an article published in the *Financial Times*, just before I moved to the country. Written when controversy about corruption was at its height, authors Jayant Sinha, a venture capitalist, and Ashutosh Varshney, an academic, argued for firm action to limit the power of their country's new tycoon class. 'In its rot and heady dynamism, India is beginning to resemble America's Gilded Age,' the duo argued.[30] Their headline read: 'It is time for India to rein in its robber barons'.

Many in India bristled at this comparison, as if insulted by the idea that their country, with its unique heritage and complexities, might be following a path others had taken before. Nineteenth-century America, the critics protested, was a sparsely inhabited young nation, with a vibrant private sector and a minimal state. India, by contrast, is an ancient civilisation, heavily populated and cursed with over-mighty government. Still I found the comparison illuminating, and it stuck with me as I came to know more about the country's own tycoons and Tammany Hall-style politicians. India's economic situation was strikingly similar too. In 2013 its GDP per capita, adjusted for the cost of living, was $5,200. The US hit that same level at the height of the Gilded Age in 1881.[31]

Whatever happens, India is set to grow in economic might and political power for the remainder of the twenty-first century, as America did during the nineteenth. By some accounts it has already overtaken China as the world's most populous nation; by others the baton will pass during the next decade or two.[32] By mid-century more than 400 million Indians will have moved from villages to cities, in one of the largest ever human migrations, while New Delhi and Mumbai are projected to become the world's two largest cities, with fifty million residents apiece.[33] Today, India's $2.3 trillion economy is slightly smaller than Britain's.[34] Barring something unforeseen it will surpass America in size by mid-century, and then, perhaps, China too.[35]

Ultimately what follows is an optimistic story. In a country changing this quickly, it is always possible to imagine reinvention. The American philosopher Richard Rorty once alluded to what he called the 'romance of a national future', or the sense of hope that infuses powers on the rise.

'We rich, fat, tired North Americans must hark back to the time when our own democracy was newer and leaner,' he wrote, 'when Pittsburgh was as new, promising and problematic as São Paulo is now.'[36] Irving Howe, the socialist essayist, talked in the same way of 'the American newness' of the nineteenth century, a time when 'people start to feel socially invigorated and come to think they can act to determine their fate.'[37]

The coming century will be told as a contest between a trio of continental giants: America, China and India. Of the three, it is India whose journey is at the earliest stage, and thus whose potential to change remains greatest. This process of change is often far from virtuous. 'They were careless people,' F. Scott Fitzgerald wrote of his characters in *The Great Gatsby*, his classic novel of post-Gilded Age excess. 'They smashed up things and creatures and then retreated back into their money or their vast carelessness or whatever it was that kept them together, and let other people clean up the mess.'[38] But in discovering similar characters in India I have tried to steer clear of moralising, telling instead a story of a nation at a critical moment of national remaking, in which a brighter future is partially visible but far from secure.

The decades that followed America's Gilded Age were known as the Progressive Era. This era had a lasting and positive effect, both at home and abroad. Anti-corruption campaigns cleaned up politics. Monopolies were broken up. The middle classes exerted control over government. Prosperity was shared more broadly. Today, India stands at the crossroads of what sort of superpower it will become. As democracy falters in the West, so its future in India has never been more critical. Will India's Gilded Age blossom into a Progressive Era of its own, in which the perils of inequality and crony capitalism are left decisively behind? Or will the excesses of the last decade gradually re-emerge, presaging a future scarred by graft and deformed by inequality; a saffron-tinged version of Russia? India's ambition to lead the second half of the Asian century – and the world's hopes for a more democratic, liberal future – depends on getting this right.

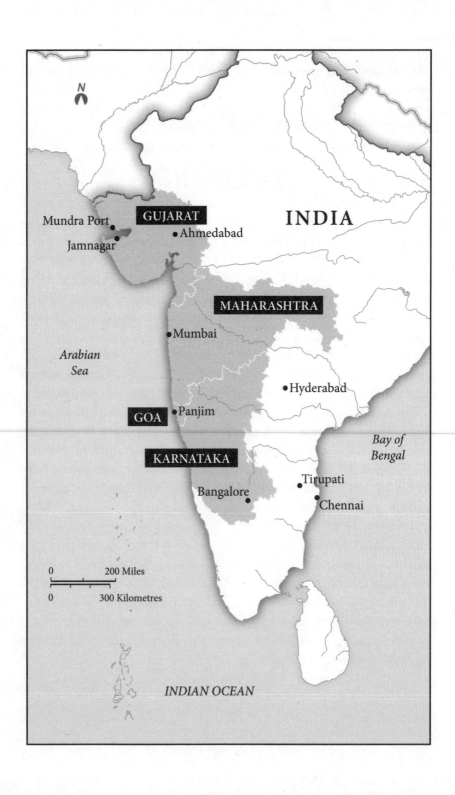

PART 1

TYCOONS

Antilia, Mukesh Ambani's 160-metre-tall skyscraper and a symbol of India's new super-rich, is often dubbed the world's first 'billion-dollar home'.

CHAPTER 1

THE RICHEST MAN IN INDIA

UPWARD MOBILITY

Talk that Mukesh Ambani would build a magnificent new house began drifting through Mumbai in the early years of the new millennium, not long after his father died.[1] The business magnate bought a plot of land on Altamount Road and quietly launched an architecture competition. Early designs showed a soaring 'eco-tower' with lush green plants spilling down the sides.[2] Residence Antilia, as the structure was first called, quickly became known as the world's most expensive private home.[3] It was to be a vertical palace with a rumoured price tag of $1 billion, towering over a city where half the population still live in slums.[4] As gossip it was irresistible. A petrol pump attendant turned industrial titan, Dhirubhai Ambani's was corporate India's most celebrated rags-to-riches story. Now the scale of his son's plans hinted at the grandeur of his own ambitions, not simply to run his father's business but to seize his mantle as the nation's pre-eminent tycoon as well.

For those who knew the Ambani clan the building carried still deeper symbolism. Dhirubhai Ambani passed on without leaving a will, assuming that his sons – Mukesh, then forty-five, and Anil, two years his junior – would go on to control Reliance together. The pair had contrasting reputations: the elder unflashy, introverted and well organised; the younger a flamboyant financial wizard. They worked together amicably enough under the old man's gaze. But relations soured quickly without him, and a ferocious battle for control began. Over three acrimonious years their feud gripped India, playing out first in the press, then in the courts.[5] Associates of the two men still refer to this period as 'the war', a corporate Cain-and-Abel battle so fierce it appeared as if the country itself was being forced to take sides.

Back then both brothers lived in a fourteen-storey residential tower called Sea Wind, a thin, white structure with a helipad on the roof, about a fifteen-minute walk from my own apartment in southern Mumbai. The Ambanis had the whole building, with each brother living on separate floors. During their feud, the two men co-ordinated their entry and exit, to avoid running into one another in the lifts.[6] The intimacy of these arrangements gave their squabbles an added frisson, replicating the plots of Indian soap operas in which members of big business families plotted against one another under the same roof. Their mother, Kokilaben, lived in the building too; her early attempts at detente went nowhere. India's most powerful business family was tearing itself apart. And if Mukesh Ambani planned to leave Sea Wind and build a new home of his own, there was no clearer signal that it would not come back together.

Dhirubhai Ambani grew up in a poor village in the western state of Gujarat, before moving in his late teens to seek work in Aden, a British imperial port in what is now Yemen. He tended a Shell petrol forecourt at first, then worked as an office clerk. On the side he learned to trade in the souks.[7] Eight years later, having married and had his first son, he moved back home to start a business in Bombay, as Mumbai was known before its name changed in 1995. Dhirubhai founded what would become Reliance Industries in the late 1950s, trading yarn, importing polyester and exporting spices. It was profitable work, but money remained tight. Mukesh Ambani spent much of his early childhood living with his three siblings in a two-roomed *chawl* or tenement house, in a poor midtown area packed with belching mills.

Reliance began to grow even when entrepreneurs remained shackled by the restrictions of the Licence Raj, all set up in the name of Jawaharlal Nehru's 'scientific socialism'. Dhirubhai Ambani proved masterful at navigating these rules, learning both to work the system and to work around it.[8] He realised the value of favours in New Delhi, where he befriended politicians and coaxed information from bureaucrats.[9] 'His philosophy was to cultivate everybody from the doorkeeper up,' as his unofficial biographer Hamish McDonald put it.[10] Regulations or licences helpful to Reliance appeared mysteriously, aiding Ambani's move into textiles manufacturing, then enabling him to open a giant polyester plant.[11] At the time Mukesh was living in America, studying for an MBA at Stanford University; his father told him to end his studies early and return home to Mumbai to run the facility.

Styling himself as a populist, Dhirubhai Ambani floated Reliance Industries on the stock market in 1977, becoming an icon to India's first generation of retail investors and addressing giant crowds at shareholder meetings held at football grounds and cricket pitches.[12] As his businesses grew so the tycoon moved his family as well, first taking an apartment in a prestigious residential high-rise, then buying the entire Sea Wind block. Yet for all his ability to work India's system, he still chafed against its limitations. Arun Shourie, a former newspaper editor and otherwise staunch critic of the tycoon's business style, gave a speech not long after his death, praising him for exposing India's failing bureaucracy. 'The Dhirubhais [of this world] are to be thanked, not once but twice over,' Shourie argued. 'They set up world-class companies [and] by exceeding the limits in which those restrictions sought to impound them, they helped create the case for scrapping those regulations.'[13]

The 1991 reforms began that clear-out, giving Indians a taste of a new world of mobile phones, multi-channel television and foreign consumer goods. For business leaders like Ambani it meant the ability to import freely and expand into deregulated sectors. By the time Mukesh Ambani took over, Reliance had spread out into many of these new areas, using its connections and commercial heft to build an industrial behemoth with divisions stretching from petrochemicals and oil refining to energy and telecoms. The company's growing powers were once captured in a joke, emphasising the shift from state-dominated socialism to a rapacious market economy: the history of independent India, the joke went, could be charted in the shift 'from self-reliance to Reliance'.

Yet even this rich legacy was not enough to hold the company together. After years of feuding, confirmation that Reliance would be partitioned arrived in June 2005. Kokilaben, the matriarch, finally hammered out a peace accord, concluded with a ceremony at the family's temple. 'With the blessings of Srinathji, I have today amicably resolved the issues between my two sons, Mukesh and Anil, keeping in mind the proud legacy of my husband,' she wrote in a statement.[14] The younger sibling would get half of the company, including its telecoms and power divisions. The elder would keep the energy and petrochemicals operations. Both would use the name Reliance. The armistice did not end the brothers' bad feeling exactly. Instead a kind of cold war began, in which the duo scrapped over the terms of their separation. Nor did it reassure those who viewed Reliance as the epitome of a more worrying trend: the growing concentration of corporate wealth in India, and its corrosive effects on political power.

At first both brothers fared well during India's mid-2000s boom. But as the decade wound on it was the elder man who prospered, building projects that were bold in scale and ruthlessly well managed. He finished the company's giant oil refinery and set up a new energy exploration arm. His operations, which were mostly set up early in his father's career, easily outperformed the newer concerns inherited by his sibling. Mukesh grew wealthier too. In 2005 he ranked third on the *Forbes* India Rich List, one place ahead of his brother.[15] But over the next few years he powered upwards, taking the title of richest Indian that he has never since relinquished.[16] At the time of his death Dhirubhai Ambani was placed 138th in the *Forbes* global billionaire rankings. By 2008 his son had elbowed his way into the top five.[17] Mukesh Ambani rarely spoke in public and cloaked his ambitions in bland corporate language when he did. But those who knew him told a different story. 'Isn't it obvious?' a friend from his university days once told me. 'He wants to be the richest man in the world.'

THE MYTHICAL ISLAND

Antilia's terraces faced west towards the sea, but visitors arrived at the entrance at the back, the only one on Altamount Road, where heavily armed guards stood outside on the street. An imposing three-metre-high rust-and-gold-coloured gate slid slowly from right to left to let guests inside, revealing a short driveway up towards the lobby. Inside, the building doubled as an opulent private hotel, foyer festooned with cut flowers and garlanded images of Dhirubhai Ambani. The ground floor's ballroom hosted Reliance corporate functions, as well as the many gatherings the family threw for local charities and dignitaries. Its ceiling was covered almost entirely in crystal chandeliers. A giant golden Buddha statue stood in the garden, surrounded by elegant water features. 'It's all very bling,' an occasional guest once told me. 'Lots of chandeliers. The chandeliers have chandeliers.'

Part of the building's grandeur came from its adaptability, allowing Mukesh Ambani to host private events on almost any scale within his own court walls. Those invited back noticed how the fixtures would change from one gathering to the next. His wife Nita often took charge of remodelling the space, adding or removing walls and staircases as the occasion demanded. Catwalks and foreign DJs were brought in for fashion shows. Stylish interior canopies appeared at wedding receptions thrown for favoured relatives. The cast of Broadway musicals flew in for special one-night performances. The grander the gathering, the greater the throng of Bollywood stars, celebrity cricketers, bigwig politicians and fellow tycoons, at a venue whose very exclusivity marked out membership of India's new aristocracy. Smaller and more intimate soirées were hosted higher up, where the truly elect were whisked upwards by express lift to the sky terrace on the roof. On Diwali, the annual festival of lights, there was no grander spot than Antilia's top terrace from which to watch fireworks explode out over the skyline.

When not used for entertaining, the building provided a more basic function: a sanctuary and place to retreat. It doubled as an office, with facilities for video conferences with executives in distant Reliance divisions. There were places to relax, from the temple on the upper floors to the basement sports courts in which Ambani's eldest son Akash invited friends to play football, handing out free pairs of Nike trainers to anyone who did. Rather than go out, the family often hosted small events for friends, hiring in musicians or stand-up comics. There was a home cinema too, in which the tycoon could indulge his taste for late-night Bollywood movies. A gated community in the sky, the building provided a sense of privacy for a man whose fame made it complicated to appear in public, and whose shyness meant he rarely wanted to do so. It was a tension the building itself could never quite resolve: an oasis designed to keep India at bay, but one that succeeded only in attracting more attention to its reclusive owner.

Controversies dogged the place too. There was a court case about the land upon which it was built, acquired from an Islamic trust that had originally planned to use the plot to establish an orphanage.[18]

Not long after construction wrapped up in 2010, a local journalist managed to get hold of Antilia's monthly energy bill. It came to roughly seven million rupees ($109,000), causing a minor outcry in a country where hundreds of millions lived without power of any sort.[19] There was more intrigue the next year: although Antilia was already being used for entertaining it emerged that the Ambanis themselves had not actually moved in. Rumours swirled about problems concerning *vastu shastra*, a Hindu theory of harmonious architecture, similar in some ways to *feng shui*.[20] In a rare 2012 interview with *Vanity Fair*, Nita Ambani confirmed that the family had by then finally taken up residence, although she declined to give reasons for their delay. Such was the family's desire for privacy that the article's author talked of months of 'nuclear-treaty-level negotiations' before their meeting, most of which were designed to stop any questions relating to Antilia at all.[21]

The building's lavish interiors – and the life of untouchable privilege that went with them – caused fascination and resentment in equal measure. Visitors whispered details of specially shipped-in artworks along the driveway, or lavish parties in which acrobats from Cirque du Soleil spun from triple-height ceilings. One friend attended an event in which guests were taken up in lifts with live butterflies fluttering around inside, caged in cylindrical glass walls. Antilia hinted at an existence that was part burlesque fantasy, part oligarch mansion, part Bond villain lair: a city within a city, and a barrier against the chaos below. Even the mysterious name seemed to hint at a deeper, epochal change. The Ambanis never did explain their choice, but before they adopted it the word 'Antilia' was used to describe a mythical island on the far side of the Atlantic. Similar to Atlantis, it embodied the idea of territory yet to be discovered, serving as a target for sea-faring explorers in the fifteenth century. In the words of historian Abbas Hamdani, Antilia was a 'motivation for exploration' – a new beginning; a fresh chapter in history.[22]

Mukesh Ambani's home embodied India's brash new style, but also an underlying clash of cultures. The old commercial elite were English-speaking and cosmopolitan, with accents polished at foreign schools and family fortunes dating back to imperial times. For them, liberalisation had been at once thrilling and unnerving: a font of opportunities but also a source of raw new competitors muscling their way in from unfamiliar parts of India, of whom the Ambanis were merely the most forceful. Thousands thronged the streets when Dhirubhai Ambani died in 2002, a sign of the affection with which he was held by shareholders and ordinary citizens. While many criticised his buccaneering methods, they also admired the way he bulldozed his way into a closed business elite. His son, however, was viewed with less warmth and just as much suspicion. One exemplary member of the old establishment, Ratan Tata, patriarch of the Tata conglomerate and perhaps the only man to rival Mukesh Ambani's stature in business, hinted as much in a 2011 interview. 'It makes me wonder why someone would do that,' he said when asked about Antilia. 'That's what revolutions are made of.'[23]

'You walk around the streets of this city, and the amount of rage at Antilia has to be heard to be believed,' Meera Sanyal, a former international banker turned local anti-corruption campaigner, told me a few years later.[24] Sanyal had spent three decades working in finance, rising to become head of Royal Bank of Scotland's India operations. During the 2009 general election she ran as an independent candidate, angered by the incompetent government response to Mumbai's terror attacks the year before, when gunmen attacked prominent targets, including the Taj Mahal Palace hotel. But as time wore on she found a new target: not so much the incompetence of the state but the venality of its business class, amid a welter of multi-billion-dollar scandals, ranging from corruption during the 2010 Commonwealth Games to the handing out of valuable coal and telecoms licences on the cheap. Almost all involved allegations of collusion between politicians, bureaucrats and business titans – the basic definition of crony capitalism.[25]

When we met in 2014, Sanyal was again trying to become a member of parliament in south Mumbai, standing, again unsuccessfully, for the new anti-corruption Aam Aadmi ('Common Man') party, in the same national election that would sweep Narendra Modi to power. One warm spring evening not long before the poll, I found her on a busy roadside next to a well-known Hindu temple, not far from Antilia. Cars honked as they streamed past, while the smell of marigold blossom hung in the air. A ragged holy man dressed in black sat cross-legged on the pavement, selling lotus flowers to worshippers. Sanyal wore an orange and yellow sari, along with the white peaked side cap often adopted by Aam Aadmi party workers, in a conscious echo of the 'Gandhi cap' worn by nationalist activists during the fight for Independence.

A few dozen supporters tagged along as we walked through the neighbourhood, banging drums and brandishing the brooms that symbolised their plans to sweep away dirty politics. Not long after we set out, a cheer went up. Over the next junction stood a Reliance jeweller's shop, part of Ambani's ever-expanding retail operations. Sanyal's band waved their brooms cheerfully at the staff, who stared back bemused behind displays thick with gold watches and rings. Around the next corner we walked past Gamdevi police station and the group stopped to pose for pictures next to a busted-up Aston Martin, hidden beneath a dirty grey sheet.

Later that week I watched Sanyal try to win over a late-night gathering of dozens of young professionals, crammed into a cavernous living room in the south of the city. There was an energy among the crowd, with people sitting five deep on the floor. The audience were well to do and liberal, although mostly disengaged from mainstream politics. In India, unlike in the West, wealthy neighbourhoods tend to have lower voter turnouts while poor areas stream to the polls, in the hope that loyalty to some local politician or other might improve their lot. The upper middle classes view their politicians as they view their tycoons: as operators of dubious machines fuelled by graft and patronage. Even so India's anti-corruption movements – which began around 2011, and a few years later resulted in the launch of Sanyal's party – have raised hopes of change. In 2014 the troubled state of Indian capitalism was a central electoral theme, and Mukesh Ambani found himself decried frequently by politicians on the stump as an exemplar of how private financial might was corroding democracy.

Sanyal perched at the front of the room on a tall thin stool, white cap affixed, her voice cracking as she tried to be heard. 'I stood for election but I lost,' she explained, referring to her earlier 2009 run.[26] 'The paradigm in India was "good people can stand but you can never win". You can't win without a war chest of money, without being the son or a daughter of a politician, or a criminal.' Sanyal went through the problems India faced, returning often to the entrenched power of business. These were people she knew, she said. As a banker she warmed to entrepreneurs and had no problem with profits. Still the power of families like the Ambanis, and what she described as their ability to bend the rules in their own interest, now embodied the frustrations middle-class Indians felt over their corruption-riddled economy. Some tycoons now behaved like the 'robber barons of America or the oligarchs of Russia', she said. Antilia was a particular bugbear. 'At first I just thought of it as a terribly ugly structure, a blight on the face of Mumbai, but you see what people say about it,' she explained. 'It's not good for the country when you have crony capitalism of that nature.'

A NEW GILDED AGE

Speaking in 1916, Mohandas Gandhi warned that India faced a pernicious new kind of commercialism. 'Western nations are groaning today under the heel of the monster god materialism,' he told students at a college in the heartland state of Uttar Pradesh. 'Many of our countrymen say that we will gain American wealth, but avoid its methods. I venture to suggest that such an attempt, if it were made, is foredoomed to failure.'[27] Gandhi's views were rooted in his own era, chiming with the theories of anti-colonialism and non-violent protest that earned him the title 'Mahatma', or 'great soul' in Sanskrit. Almost a century later, his warnings seemed prescient.

From the Colosseum in Rome and the church steeples of medieval Europe to the gleaming modern skyscrapers of New York or London, the spirit of an age is often captured in its grandest buildings. Rising high above Mumbai, it was hard not to view Antilia as a symbol of the country India was becoming. Although conspicuously modern, by turns it also harked back to earlier eras when India had been more familiar with lavish fortunes. 'Bombay has always had a history of ostentatious homes of the very rich,' I was once told by Mustansir Dalvi, a professor at the city's JJ School of Architecture.[28] The building reminded him of the mansions of this merchant class, and the maharajas' palaces before them. 'In the nineteenth century, several of the wealthiest, like Sir Jamsetjee Jeejeebhoy and the Tata family, built large town houses, heavily ornamented and very well appointed. They were also the great philanthropists of the city and are now remembered as city fathers. Mr Ambani's efforts are simply the latest example.'

Antilia's excess also carried echoes of an earlier era in America, and another celebrated business dynasty: the Vanderbilts. Like Dhirubhai Ambani, Cornelius Vanderbilt grew up modestly. The son of poor Dutch immigrants, he was born in a wooden house on Staten Island in 1794, working on his father's boat as a boy and learning to take goods over the bay to New York. In his teens he pestered his mother to lend him $100 to buy a vessel of his own, earning the nickname 'Commodore' for his fearlessness on the water.[29] He went on to build a small fleet, only to find his expansion plans blocked by local rivals whose businesses were protected by exclusive government licences and charters, which were controlled in turn by pliant politicians. 'When Vanderbilt became a steamboat operator in 1817, the mercantile economy was controlled by an elite circle,' according to historian Steve Fraser.[30]

As in socialist-era India, this patrician commercial class dominated America's pre-industrial economy. They were especially powerful in river transport, handing out valuable monopolies for ferry routes to their own members. The Commodore took them on, cramming his fleet with more boats than the rules allowed and pushing them to their limits, risking workers and passengers alike. Some competitors were taken out with ruthless price wars, others via aggressive legal suits. Vanderbilt styled himself as a populist, penning rabble-rousing articles against his rivals and christening his Hudson ferry service 'The People's Line'. He expanded first into shipping and then into rail. As the first true railroad tycoon his style embodied America's new, bare-knuckle capitalism. In 1871 Vanderbilt built the original Grand Central station, New York's most prominent public building. When he died six years later he was America's wealthiest citizen, passing on an unheard-of fortune of more than $100 million.

For all of his wealth, Vanderbilt lived frugally, hoarding money and keeping modest houses. After his death his children found themselves cut adrift from the city's elite, unable to shake their father's ruffian image. Just as Ambani did more than a century later, they crafted an answer to these delicate social problems in concrete and steel, beginning a series of fabulous residences just south of the city's new Central Park. William Henry, Cornelius's eldest son, spent a good portion of his inheritance on a 'triple palace' – a trio of adjoining sandstone mansions on Fifth Avenue. The Commodore's grandson William Kissam Vanderbilt, along with his wife Alva, commissioned an even grander project: a Renaissance-style castle known as the Petit Chateau, complete with fairy-tale turrets and gables. 'Alva wasn't interested in another home,' as one account put it. 'She wanted a weapon: a house she could use as a battering ram to crash through the gates of society.'[31] In the spring of 1883 the couple celebrated its completion by throwing a lavish costume party, welcoming more than a thousand guests into the grandest private ballroom New York had ever seen.

Vanderbilt's legacy divided America just as the Ambanis' divided India. His admirers saw in the Commodore a new kind of American promise: a low-born scrapper whose guile and cunning had pushed him to the very top. To his detractors Vanderbilt was an unprincipled figure, with a weakness for fistfights and infidelity. As his empire grew, newspapers compared him to the historic robber barons of Europe, so called because they extorted payments from travellers crossing their lands. One family descendant wrote a memoir recalling the patriarch's worst habits: a man who spat 'tobacco juice on his hostess's rugs and pinched the bottoms of which[ever] of the pretty maids caught his fancy'.[32] Vanderbilt was even less popular among the liberal elite, those east coast Brahmins who worried about the growing power of their nation's new industrial giants. Mark Twain, perhaps the most famous public figure of the age, once wrote him an open letter, mocking what he described as Vanderbilt's ceaselessly acquisitive instincts, even as he stood unchallenged 'upon the pinnacle of moneyed magnificence in America'.[33]

The idea that India's problems of crony capitalism echoed those of America's was one I heard later from economist Raghuram Rajan, by then the head of the country's central bank. Rajan was a man known for questioning orthodoxies. Back in 2005, during his time as chief economist at the International Monetary Fund, he gave a speech predicting important elements of the coming financial crisis, earning him a reputation as a minor prophet of the calamities of global capitalism. Born in southern India, he spent most of his adult life as an academic in the US, teaching economics at the University of Chicago. But in 2012 he moved home to take a position as a government economic adviser, and a year later he was appointed as governor of the Reserve Bank of India (RBI). It was a position traditionally held by cautious technocrats. At first Rajan looked the part, with his circumspect manner and professorial habit of arguing both sides of a point. Soon enough it became clear he had bigger ideas, however, not just about India's problems of inflation but also about the troubling ties that had grown up between its tycoons and politicians.

Rajan's intellectual curiosity shone through in speeches that strayed far outside the normal remit of his job, including one delivered about a year after he joined the RBI, laying out 'a hypothesis on the persistence of crony capitalism'.[34] India's public services were threadbare, he argued. Social welfare programmes meant to help the poor worked badly. State schools and hospitals were typically dismal, while the state failed to provide basic services like running water and reliable power. 'This is where the crooked but savvy politician fits in,' Rajan said. 'While the poor do not have the money to "purchase" public services that are their right, they have a vote that the politician wants.' In return the politician developed systems of patronage, helping constituents to find government jobs or receive welfare payments, or simply handing out cash. And to get the money to do this, as well as to fund election campaigns, the politicians needed the kind of cash that only very wealthy business-people possessed.

A few months later Rajan explained the theory to me in more detail, as we sat on the eighteenth floor of the RBI's headquarters, a boxy white concrete tower close to the southern tip of Mumbai. The meeting room had large windows offering sweeping views down over the narrow streets of the old city and the pink dome of the Taj hotel beyond. Dozens of container ships idled in grey harbour waters on the far side of the Gateway of India. Rajan was dressed in a dark suit, with wire-framed glasses and thick black hair greying slightly around the temples. Portraits of previous RBI governors covered the wall behind him. On the left were serious-looking British men in old-fashioned suits. Towards the right the tableau turned Indian, their sombre faces set off by blue turbans or high-collared Nehru jackets. Rajan often pressed his fingers together as he talked, as if to emphasise the precision of each point. He had a reputation as an orthodox economist, with expertise in the intricacies of finance and a moral belief in the fairness of free markets. He tried to be balanced but it was obvious enough as we spoke that he disdained the extravagances of India's rapacious new Bollygarchs and the style of business they represented.

Rajan's inspiration on cronyism came from *The Age of Reform*, a book by the liberal historian Richard Hofstadter explaining how the US overcame its own robber baron era. In the early stages of America's Gilded Age, as in India's, an alliance grew up between tycoons and politicians, with the former funding patronage controlled by the latter. 'Obviously, to do some of this, some of these guys need resources,' he told me. 'And where do you get resources from? You get resources from business.' Breaking this system of collusion was hard. In America it took a generation or more, beginning with new populist movements at the end of the nineteenth century, which gave birth in turn to the political and social reform of the Progressive Era. But it culminated only in the New Deal of the 1930s, when improvements in state welfare broke the system of clientelism that kept America's urban political machines in power. 'It's sort of an unholy nexus,' Rajan said of India's situation. 'Poor public services? Politician fills the gap; politician gets the resources from the businessman; politician gets re-elected by the electorate for whom he's filling the gap; and electorate turns a blind eye to the deals done with the businessman.'

Tens of thousands of middle-class protestors began to take to the streets as evidence of these relationships became ever more brazen during 2011. Although egged on by campaigning television news anchors, these anti-corruption movements were mostly sparked by a new wave of activists: Anna Hazare, the ageing ascetic who led the movement at first, then Arvind Kejriwal, an irascible tax inspector turned graft crusader who founded the Aam Aadmi party a few years later. Much of their ire was directed at the failings of the Congress, the once-proud party of India's liberation struggle, whose illustrious Nehru-Gandhi family dynasty had ruled India for most of its independent history.

The season of scams took hold as a succession of corruption scandals hit the then Congress-led government, denting the reputation of party president Sonia Gandhi, the Italian-born widow of Rajiv Gandhi. Rajiv was Nehru's grandson and the third family member to become prime minister, following his mother Indira Gandhi, who first took the position in 1966 and went on to dominate Indian politics for the best part of two decades. Although Sonia Gandhi chose not to be prime minister herself, handing the role to Manmohan Singh, she was understood to control his government behind the scenes, making her in effect the fourth member of the dynasty to rule India since 1947. (The Gandhi family are not related to Mohandas Gandhi.) At times during her tenure the Congress seemed to have ditched entirely its socialist heritage and become instead a tawdry, scandal-plagued machine. The same basic problems of political funding identified by Rajan were also true of every other major political party, however, including the more centre-right Bharatiya Janata Party (BJP). And lurking behind all these scandals lay the tycoons, the only people with funds sufficient to bankroll India's increasingly expensive democracy.

More than anything it was public disgust at corruption that lay behind Narendra Modi's electrifying election victory in 2014. Voters turned to Modi, the self-described son of a poor tea seller, hoping that his record of clean governance and rapid economic growth when he was chief minister of his home state of Gujarat could be transferred to New Delhi. For decades Indian voters had grudgingly tolerated venality among their politicians. But now the sheer scale of the kind of cronyism Rajan described had pushed the public to breaking point. 'It really is a remarkable change, which has happened mostly over the last ten years or so,' I was told a short while before Modi's electoral triumph by Ashutosh Varshney, the academic who, back in 2011, had made the comparison between contemporary India and America's Gilded Age. 'Any economy that grows as quickly as India's is bound to generate enormous human temptations. These very rich people have started buying politics, and the great churning in India you see against corruption is essentially about the purchase of politics by the wealthy.'[35]

INDIAN VERTIGO

Even the briefest appearance by Mukesh Ambani had an air of fleeting excitement. I met him first in a plush Mumbai hotel at a private lunch for a few dozen business leaders in 2013. He arrived late, dressed in his usual dark trousers and a rustic white cotton short-sleeved shirt, and seemed thoroughly ill at ease throughout. Then in his mid-fifties, he was shorter and chubbier than I expected, with dark black hair swept back with oil. Armed guards stood by the door, a reflection of his status as the only businessmen in India to have what was known officially as 'Z-list' security protection, a status normally reserved only for the most senior of politicians and civil servants.[36] There were other speakers that day but I noticed that most of those attending spent more time glancing furtively over at the chief guest than listening, as if suddenly starstruck in the presence of corporate royalty. Towards the end Ambani stood up and gave brief remarks, talking in bland, uneasy clichés about his faith in India's future and his belief in the exciting possibilities of new technology. He seemed nervous and his head nodded back and forth awkwardly as he spoke. After the meal he waited around only briefly, before emptying the room as he and his guards headed for the exit.

To see Ambani in more relaxed mood I used to go along to each year's Reliance Industries annual general meeting, one of the great displays of Indian corporate theatre. Although not as boisterous as his father's football ground jamborees, Ambani's gathering in July 2015 still packed thousands of shareholders into the Birla Matoshree auditorium, a grand colonial-era hall a few blocks from Mumbai's main cricket stadium and about fifteen minutes from Antilia. Paintings of political leaders lined the walls: Chhatrapati Shivaji Maharaj, a seventeenth-century warrior king who fought against the British; Nehru, icon of the Congress party; and Gandhi, national father figure, anti-capitalist and a man who, implausibly enough, had been born into the same business-minded Bania caste as Ambani himself. A sense of history hung about the meeting, the company's forty-first since its foundation. The twelve-member board sat on stage at a long table next to two giant images of Ambani's father, the larger of which was framed and draped with pink and white flowers.

Applause broke out at 10:51 a.m. as Ambani appeared at the front of the room, sporting the lucky red and white checked tie he favoured for big occasions. He moved into the crowd, shaking hands and smiling, surrounded by cameras but seemingly enjoying himself. 'Hello, hello, you are all welcome,' I heard him say from my seat a few rows from the front, as he slapped bystanders on the back and waved to familiar faces across the room. He grinned widely from the podium as proceedings got under way. Shareholders asked fawning questions and clapped as their chairman's achievements were read out. The hubbub gave proceedings a rowdy air, more like an American revivalist meeting than a sombre business gathering. Ambani's speech was workmanlike, mixing platitudes and lists: Reliance accounted for twelve per cent of national exports that year; it had invested more, and paid more income tax, than any other Indian company too.[37] He talked in particular about Reliance Jio, a bold and exorbitantly expensive new telecoms business he soon planned to launch, to replace the one lost a decade earlier to his younger brother in their divorce agreement. 'Along with a new India, a new Reliance is taking shape,' he said.

Up on stage, though, the old Reliance was still easy enough to spot. Nita Ambani had that year taken a seat on the board. Dressed in a glamorous traditional pink outfit she brought a dash of colour to a dais otherwise dominated by grey-haired men, many of whom were old family loyalists. Various relatives sat in the front row, including the tycoon's elderly mother and three children. Mukesh Ambani described Reliance as a modern, digital enterprise rather than the lumbering industrial giant of old. But the company still had a clannish and conspiratorial feel, in which loyalty to the boss mattered above all. 'It is a politburo type of culture,' a rival tycoon once told me. One of Reliance's most powerful employees was a somewhat mysterious executive named Manoj Modi.[38] A short man with a thin moustache, he was a classmate of Ambani's from the time when both men studied chemical engineering. Officially Modi ran Reliance's retail operations, although his name appeared nowhere in that year's annual report. Unofficially he was Ambani's confidant and co-architect of the company's ambitious new telecoms plans, which the duo had been planning for a decade or more.[39] Once a year, as the shareholder meeting droned on, Modi would appear quietly at the side of the hall to brief journalists, before leaving just as quickly.

By this time Ambani had led Reliance for more than ten years, and had taken steps to soften his murky public image. He made donations to good causes, attended Davos and sat on the board of an American bank. His Reliance Foundation set up a hospital in southern Mumbai and founded the Dhirubhai Ambani International School, to which the city's well-to-do clamoured to send their children. He bought a television station and began fashioning himself as a media magnate. Ambani had largely patched up the earlier feud with his younger brother too, with the two men striking deals between their respective businesses. His wife Nita had also grown into a public figure, becoming a member of the International Olympic Committee, running the family's charitable arm, and zealously sculpting her husband's image. She managed the Mumbai Indians too, the cricket franchise Reliance had snapped up at the launch of the glitzy Indian Premier League tournament in 2008. Invites to the company's corporate box at the Wankhede stadium became especially prized, in a town that counted commerce and cricket at its two pre-eminent obsessions. Yet even there, among tens of thousands of delirious fans, the Ambanis often sat apart, watching the match from a large, blue sofa positioned on the pitchside next to the player's dugouts, and reserved only for them.

Such things were a sideshow next to the tycoon's defining obsession with his new Jio telecoms operations, however. Mostly he pushed the project from Reliance's headquarters in southern Mumbai, working from the same old-fashioned office his father used, and which the son was said to keep largely for sentimental reasons. But on at least one morning a week his armour-plated BMW 7-series would slip quietly out of Antilia's rear gate, turn left down Altamount Road, and head towards the horse-racing track that doubled as the city's downtown heliport. From there a corporate chopper would whisk him off to Reliance Corporate Park, the company's suburban campus in Navi Mumbai, a satellite city with a population of more than one million just off the eastern side of Mumbai's peninsula.

I took the same ride early in 2016, arriving at the racecourse one sunny morning, having been granted a rare foray into the heart of Ambaniland. The helicopter had golden seat belts, and the letters VT-NMA stencilled on its side, which an aide told me stood for 'Nita and Mukesh Ambani'. I had been given a boarding pass before clambering aboard, with my name scribbled in blue ink. In the cabin I found another discarded on the floor, bearing the name Manoj Modi, who had taken the same chopper earlier that day. We took off in a whirl of dust, climbing straight up before accelerating off to the east, leaving the corrugated outline of Antilia behind in the hazy middle distance. For all of his influence Ambani had never managed to persuade India's navy, which controlled the city's airspace, to let him use the helipad on his own roof.

Competitors viewed Ambani's re-entry into telecoms with thinly disguised dread. One told me Jio's launch would be akin to the bloody battles of the *Mahābhārata*, an ancient Sanskrit epic poem whose main characters tended to perish in combat. Thousands of engineers worked for years to perfect the service, which promised inexpensive smart-phones and super-fast data connections, in a country used to basic mobile devices and crawling internet speeds. Various executives explained its scale as I walked around the Reliance campus that day, a 500-acre site filled with modern glass buildings and huge dusty car parks. Reliance had laid hundreds of thousands of kilometres of fibre optic cables across India, one told me, as well as erecting ninety thousand new mobile phone towers. I was shown a desk in an open-plan area at which Ambani himself was said to sit, although it showed no sign of having actually been used. His elder son Akash had one nearby with a more lived-in feel: a Rubik's cube sat discarded next to a framed photo of the Ambani family, while a pink poster of Andy Warhol was tacked to the desk's backboard. The poster's slogan read 'The idea of waiting for something makes it more exciting', which I took to be a tongue-in-cheek reference to Jio itself, given its launch had been delayed for the best part of five years.

Ambani funded Jio with spare cash built up through his lucrative oil-refining operations, and liked to present the new telecoms venture as an almost public-spirited exercise in national digital development. This was just as well, given how few analysts thought he was likely to make back its estimated $31 billion in costs.[40] 'It is madness, complete madness, what this guy is trying to do,' the head of another telecoms group told me back in 2015, as the momentous scale of Ambani's plans began gradually to leak out.[41] Ambani himself talked about his aims in plainer language, promising a service at a price that ordinary Indians could afford. Indeed, when it did finally launch later that year, he offered it for free, beginning a violent price war with rival operators, who accused him of unfairly cross-subsidising the new business with funds drawn from elsewhere within his empire. The free offer was a classic Reliance gambit, mixing naked populism with a willingness to endure hefty losses, so long as their competitors took a beating along the way. The deal proved understandably popular, winning Jio more than 100 million subscribers in just six months.

I met Ambani on only one other occasion, a few years earlier, sitting in his father's old office in Maker Chambers, the old-fashioned down-town office building in which Reliance kept its headquarters. At the time his enthusiasm for Jio's technological possibilities seemed almost boyish, as he demonstrated early test models of its handsets, showing off their ability to stream cricket matches and movies in high definition. The technical complexities of building the network seemed to excite his engineer's imagination. Over the years his advisers badgered him to focus on his energy operations, using acquisitions abroad to turn Reliance into a global giant in the mould of Shell or Exxon. Ambani ignored them, spreading his business into ever more sectors and investing most of his money at home.

This was partly a bet on India's changing economy. The country was on 'a journey from $2,000 to $5,000 per capita', Ambani once explained, entering a new stage of economic development as a lower middle-income nation, in which selling goods to a rising consumer class would become even more lucrative than building grand industrial projects.[42] But more than anything the tycoon seemed to lust after the status of digital pioneer, and with it the uncomplicated plaudits won by the entrepreneurs of Silicon Valley. 'I believe in the next twenty years as human civilisation we will collectively achieve more than what has been achieved in the last 300 years', he said at Jio's launch in 2016, in a rather clunky attempt to echo the tech visionaries whose ranks he hoped to join.[43]

Yet, try as he might, Ambani could never quite escape the questions that had hung over Reliance since his father's time. A draft report from India's government auditor, leaked to the press in 2014, examined how he had managed to get hold of the valuable telecoms spectrum he used to run Jio.[44] The licence had been won at auction initially by a tiny and previously little-known outfit called Infotel Broadband, which bid $2 billion, despite the company itself being worth just a fraction of that amount. Reliance then bought Infotel soon after the announcement of its auction success. Ambani's company denied wrongdoing, but the auditors still raised questions about the process.[45]

Anti-corruption activists also attacked the company. 'Reliance bid through a *benami* bidder', as political campaigner and lawyer Prashant Bhushan later put it, using the Hindi word *benami* to describe a transaction in which the ultimate buyer disguised its interest through a proxy.[46] Reliance vigorously denied this too, arguing that it had broken no rules in buying Infotel Broadband. Bhushan launched an unsuccessful legal case to have the auction scrapped. Separately, the same auditor accused Reliance of enjoying a $500 million windfall when the government changed the rules governing how that same licence could operate,

allowing Jio users to make and receive voice calls on a network originally designed for data.[47] For Ambani's critics, both were examples of
the way the tycoon maintained an unusual gift for getting what he
wanted in New Delhi, just as his father had done before him.

Such controversies were not limited to Ambani's telecoms ventures.
There were rows too about his energy drilling operations in the Bay
of Bengal, where Reliance fought various battles over the regulated
price at which it was allowed to sell gas.[48] Government auditors also
accused the company of claiming to spend more on capital expenditure than it actually had done, in order to win more favourable terms
as part of the energy exploration contract it signed with the government.[49] Reliance denied wrongdoing on this issue too, but that did
not stop its owner facing further attacks during the 2014 election, as
anti-corruption campaigners painted Ambani as the unacceptable
face of Indian cronyism. Modi's election proved no less complicated
for the tycoon, as the new prime minister, fearful of accusations of
favouritism, cut out much of the kind of insider access enjoyed by
senior industrialists.

Ambani tacitly admitted his company's heritage of influence-
peddling in a *New York Times* interview back in 2008. 'We de-merged
all of that,' he said half-jokingly, when asked about what the article
called the 'network of lobbyists and spies in New Delhi' established at
first by his father – the implication being that these activities had been
left behind when the business was split in two during the 2005 divorce.[50]
The suggestion prompted Anil Ambani to sue both his brother and the
newspaper, although unsuccessfully.[51]

Mukesh Ambani wanted to be viewed as the head of a modern,
global enterprise; a professionally managed national champion and
asset to India's economic development. Some respected observers
backed this view too. 'Reliance Industries, once legendary for garner-
ing political favours, has now moved to a higher plane,' economist
Swaminathan Aiyar wrote a few years later.[52] But the broader perception remained that Ambani wielded extraordinary political power. In
private, competitors claimed to detect his hand in almost any regulatory misfortune that might befall them. Reliance did little to help its
own cause, with a secretive culture and convoluted corporate structure designed to make its dealings impenetrable.[53] In Mumbai I spent
many unhappy hours trying to make sense of it all, sifting through

the various shell firms and smaller businesses that circled around Reliance Industries – the company that owned that shattered Aston Martin, Reliance Ports, being just one example. Ambani paid eye-catching salaries to hire in high-profile foreign executives. But these global transplants tended not to last when the executives discovered the inner workings of an entity dominated by old family retainers. The company board was stacked with Ambani friends and relatives; 'not a national champion but an embarrassment,' as *The Economist* once put it.[54]

For all the suspicion he attracted, there was still something undeniably thrilling about Ambani's ambitions. Around the time I watched his AGM speech the tycoon was midway through ploughing the best part of $20 billion into new refining and petrochemicals plants. Reliance's energy operations alone – which shipped crude oil into its giant facility in Gujarat and sent everything from diesel to kerosene back out – were among the most important engines for India's new globalisation, typically accounting for a tenth of the value of national exports each year. Yet it was the scale of Jio that remained especially striking. Here was the largest private sector investment in Indian business history, as well as perhaps the most cavalier in its disregard for future profits or shareholder returns. The business itself did well at first, as customers snapped up its early offer of smartphones with free super-fast connections. But Jio's ambition posed a more profound question, namely: what was the point of being a tycoon if not to take just the kinds of wild risks that would intimidate more conventionally minded businesses – and perhaps, in the process, bring seismic change to industries or countries? The careers of the Vanderbilts, Rockefellers and Carnegies had invited similar questions more than a century earlier, as they built the canals and railroads and steamships through which America grew. In their own eras all were pilloried as corrupt and avaricious. Over time, all have gradually been rehabilitated as masters of new technology and pioneers of industrial change rather than robber barons – the embodiment of what economist Joseph Schumpeter would later call 'the perennial gale of creative destruction.'[55] In time Ambani and his fellow Bollygarchs may come to be viewed in this way too, as the details of their methods fade but the scale of their achievements remains.

Yet behind this boldness there was also an unmistakable sense of fear. Ambani built his reputation above all on 'execution', meaning his ability to construct complex industrial projects quickly and cheaply. But with Jio he turned cautious, holding back the launch year after year. He tinkered to ensure the service was technically flawless, adding billions in expense at every stage. 'He is obsessed with the idea that it should all work perfectly, on day one,' one executive told me during my visit to the Reliance campus. As far as anyone could tell, these delays hid deeper concerns about his own legacy, and also his relationship with his father. It was often remarked that Mukesh Ambani's most successful businesses – in oil-refining and petrochemicals – were inherited. Those he built himself, in areas like retail and energy, largely flopped. Leaving his own mark required that he launch a grand new project that was entirely his own, and one delivered at a scale fit to change the nation, just as his father had done before him. 'People just don't understand that for him this *has* to work. This is the big roll of the dice,' one adviser who worked closely with Reliance told me, not long before Jio's launch. 'So you almost have to expect him to behave irrationally, to spend any kind of money. Because he can't afford to lose.'

This was the special sense of vertigo that came from being the richest, most powerful and most feared tycoon in India. 'Money means nothing to me,' Ambani told an interviewer in 2017, at a moment when his personal fortune had recently soared above $31 billion. 'My father used to tell me: "If you start anything just to make money, you are a fool. You will never make money and you will fail. All of us eat the same dal-roti." '[56]

Yet the risk of being surpassed remained real. Many of Ambani's fellow billionaires saw their fortunes plunge as India's once-booming economy slowed after the global financial crisis, and worries about graft paralysed New Delhi. Some found themselves under investigation for corruption; a handful either went to jail or left the country. Nothing of this kind threatened Ambani, although on a few occasions he did come close to losing his own place atop the *Forbes* rankings. The more obvious and chastening example was his brother Anil, whose debt-saddled empire struggled in the decade after their split, pushing the younger man down into the lower ranks of also-ran billionaires.[57] Some thought the elder Ambani a relic from an earlier era, and predicted his decline, as happened to America's Gilded Age tycoons before him. Yet Ambani seemed determined to fight this very possibility, from the Pharaonic scale of his investments to the over-the-top grandeur of his family home. No one embodied so clearly the power of India's new super-rich. And looking down from Antilia's roof terrace – his own 'pinnacle of moneyed magnificence' – no one else could grasp quite how far there was to fall.

India's 'King of Good Times', flamboyant airline magnate Vijay Mallya, poses beside Bollywood film actress Preity Zinta (left) at the launch of his Kingfisher Swimsuit Calendar in 2007.

CHAPTER 2

THE GOOD TIMES BEGIN

EXILE ON BAKER ST

Smoke curled up as Vijay Mallya lit a fourth cigarillo, took a drag, and tapped the ash into a large white ashtray. It was a damp Friday afternoon in late spring 2017. Drizzle fell outside, obscuring the view of Regent's Park over the road. Inside Mallya sheltered behind a grand wooden table, a gold lighter and two mobile phones lined up in front of him. On the surface he seemed every bit the ebullient tycoon of old: a bulky man in a red polo shirt, with gold bracelets on each wrist and a chunky diamond ear stud sparkling against his long greying hair. But he grew downbeat as the afternoon wound on and our conversation turned to his business troubles and the state of his homeland. 'India has corruption running in its veins,' he told me with a sigh. 'And that's not something one is going to change overnight.'

We were seated on plush leather chairs in the study of his home, a Grade I-listed mansion on a terrace of Greco-Roman town houses, just a short walk from Baker Street tube. It was the kind of place only the impossibly wealthy could afford, its interiors a vision of crystal chandeliers and ornate period furniture, with ceilings and staircases splashed in gold leaf. Qatari royals had bought a house at the end of the terrace for something close to £80 million a few years before.[1] Various Rolls-Royces and Bentleys were parked along the mews at the rear. As I walked up earlier, a fat silver Maybach with the number plate VJM 1 idled outside Mallya's back door. The door opened to reveal a guard watching a bank of security monitors fitted awkwardly into what appeared to be the old hallway cupboard.

The study was large and panelled in dark wood, to match the table at which Mallya sat, checking messages on both phones as we talked. A glass of water stood next to him at first. A little later he pressed a white button next to his Café Crème cigarillo tin to summon the butler and order whisky; the rear wall contained a drinks cabinet concealed behind a white and gold facade. Symbols of a rich man's pastimes were scattered all around. A trio of supercar magazines lay on the desk by the window, alongside a series of model Formula 1 cars from the Force India team, which Mallya still owned. At one point I asked to be excused to visit the toilet. A flunky ushered me into a golden bathroom, with a shiny gold seat to match its golden taps and loo roll holder. Only the fluffy hand towels were white, although each still came embossed with the letters 'VJM' in gold thread.

Yet for all its opulence a sense of loss hung over the place, reflecting its owner's status as an involuntary exile, the 'Fugitive Vijay Mallya' as the *Times of India* often called him.[2] A one-time billionaire brewer and airline magnate, Mallya revelled in his image as India's 'King of Good Times', a slogan he adopted for himself from the labels of his Kingfisher beer brand. In his pomp he was ringmaster of his own circus: a bon vivant and hard drinker; a man of coteries and Gatsby-style parties and famously ill-disciplined timekeeping. Though his phones still buzzed often, the home seemed empty bar the staff: the security guard, personal assistant, butler and chauffeur snoozing out the back. He seemed to have time on his hands too: only modestly late for our meeting, he chatted engagingly for the best part of three hours, rebuffing the various charges against him as he went.

For a fugitive Mallya lived well. He spent his weeks in the city, running what remained of his businesses or holding court at the nearby Dorchester Hotel. On the weekends he drove up to Ladywalk, a country estate about an hour out of town, bought for a reported £11 million from the father of Lewis Hamilton, the F1 driver. Even so, his newly straitened circumstances were often in the news, with properties seized and sports cars confiscated. Even his 95-metre super-yacht, the Indian Empress, which he typically moored on the French Riviera, was later impounded after a dispute with its crew over hundreds of thousands of dollars worth of unpaid wages.[3] Even his trademark haircut – a flamboyant mullet of the kind sometimes described as 'business at the front, party at the back' – seemed forlorn, as if no longer quite appropriate for a man hitting hard times in his early sixties.

Then there were the signs of the home to which he was no longer able to return. A pile of newspapers sat next to him on the table with the *Asian Age* at the top, its headlines filled with shenanigans in New Delhi. A crystal clock with two faces sat on the desk: the right showed British time, the left Indian. Two grand homes in Britain might seem plenty, but Mallya once split his time between a dozen or more: five in India, along with a private South African game reserve and places in Monaco, California and New York's Trump Tower.[4] Just as Mukesh Ambani built Antilia to tower over Mumbai, so Mallya had built a grand new residence in Bangalore, where his businesses were based. Some years before he had knocked down his family's old bungalow and replaced it with a garish skyscraper named Kingfisher Tower. This was partly a commercial venture, with apartments for sale in the lower levels. But perched at the top on a slab of white concrete was a 40,000-square-foot 'sky bungalow' for Mallya's own use, said to be worth $20 million. India's most conspicuous McMansion looked vaguely like the White House, albeit 400 feet further up in the air. Given his refugee status it was unclear whether its owner would ever actually get to live in it.[5]

'It's not going to happen for a few generations. I mean, it's a very deep-rooted system of corruption,' he went on, his shoulders hunched, talking about faltering government attempts to cut graft. The revenue authorities were particular offenders, he claimed, demanding bribes many times higher than the value of the tax they were meant to collect. 'You can't weed corruption out of the system completely. In India it's almost inbred. They [tax inspectors] are asking for ten times the money. Otherwise, fine, they'll put you behind bars.' For Mallya these were hardly academic concerns. Until a few years earlier he had been one of his country's most celebrated industrialists, a man whose wealth and flamboyance embodied the spirit of a newly confident nation. But then in early 2017 India's authorities filed corruption charges against him relating to the collapse of his Kingfisher airline, which went bust in spectacular fashion five years earlier, leaving behind mountainous debts and thousands of irate, unpaid staff.[6]

Mallya paused, flicked open the lighter, and lit another cigarillo. 'In India all this kind of jazz happens. You know, they throw you in jail and say "sit there",' he went on, his voice gravelly but suddenly serious. 'Why should I put myself in risk? Why should I not be entitled to a fair trial? . . . So I'm stuck here.'

'Here' was London, home to troubled Russian oligarchs and Indian Bollygarchs alike. In March 2016 Mallya took a first-class seat on a scheduled flight and left New Delhi for the last time. At the time he denied flatly that he had fled. But as we talked, a little over a year later, he admitted he was unlikely to return any time soon. Once a member of the Rajya Sabha, the Indian upper house of parliament, his diplomatic passport had long since been cancelled. As a long-time UK resident he was permitted to stay in the country. But without a passport he was unable to travel abroad, curtailing almost entirely his notorious jet-setting lifestyle and leaving him effectively stateless.

To make matters worse, just a month before we met Mallya found himself arrested by British police on charges of money-laundering, relating to the same set of investigations back home.[7] He protested his innocence and walked free the same day, having been granted bail. At the time he was defiant, standing on the street outside Westminster Magistrates' Court and telling a scrum of cameras they could 'keep dreaming about the billion pounds' he might one day repay to his creditors.[8] Sat in his study, however, he seemed circumspect. He now faced many years paying expensive UK legal fees to beat back extradition proceedings from Indian authorities that wanted him to face questions about loan defaults and allegations of fraud.

'It's a matter which will just play out in court over God knows how long. I mean, it's a complete witch-hunt,' he told me. Such was the political furore over his case that a fair trial would be impossible back home, he claimed; as soon as he landed he risked being tipped into New Delhi's notorious Tihar prison. '[The media are] whipping up sentiment. Defaults. Stolen money. Mallya-gate. Theft.' As he spoke, he raised both hands in exasperation to emphasise each point. 'It became not just difficult to go back, it became unwise for me to go back . . . My lawyers said: "Look, you'll be stupid if you come back. Because you'll be expecting a one-way ticket to Tihar."'

Mallya's complaints about a media frenzy were real enough. India's newspapers and TV talk shows charted enthusiastically each new stage in his downfall, splashing stories about the $2 billion he was said to owe his bankers, suppliers and former employees.[9] Initially forgiving, his lenders grew gradually more irate too, moving to seize his mansions, planes and cars. At one time it was common for the press to hail him as the face of a vibrant new Indian consumer economy: the 'Branson of

Bangalore' as magazine profiles often put it. Now TV pundits called him a debt defaulter, painting him as the epitome of a new kind of unscrupulous tycoon, whose recklessness had torpedoed India's banks and besmirched the name of its business community. The evident luxury of his exile, even as his creditors and ex-employees went unpaid, merely compounded his disgrace.

Mallya remained phlegmatic in the face of all this; a likeable rogue and raconteur, although one with more business nous than his playboy image might have suggested. Facts about loan default rates and details of old contracts tumbled out as we talked, as he tried to set records straight. Clearly frustrated with his position, his tone veered between defiance and self-pity, with just the occasional flash of the insouciant self-confidence of old. The next day would be the Monaco Grand Prix, the highlight of each year's circuit. Mallya had previously hosted a glittering annual soirée aboard his yacht. This year he would watch on television at his place in Hertfordshire, in the company of his five dogs and a few invited friends.

More than anything his critics attacked Mallya for his departure, as if that act alone was a *prima facie* indication of guilt. 'They decided very quickly that I should be the poster boy of loan default, and only because I attracted maybe the maximum media attention,' he said at one point, referring both to his press accusers and to his former friends in politics who now pilloried him as the unacceptable face of Indian capitalism. He had never been India's richest tycoon – others ran larger and more profitable businesses – but Mallya came to personify both the brash optimism of India's mid-2000s boom and the unedifying corruption and corporate debt scandals that followed. If Mukesh Ambani stood at the pinnacle of the Billionaire Raj, it was Vijay Mallya, more than anyone, who knew what it felt like to clamber up towards the peak, only to slide ignominiously down again.

Towards the end of our conversation he took a call from a friend in the motor sport world and gossiped knowledgeably for five minutes about racing drivers and their form. When the call was over, and just before he left to rouse the chauffeur and head up to his country estate, he turned reflective. 'I've lived here since '92. My mother is here. My son is here. My daughter's flying in from New York very often ... So yeah, I've a comfortable life here. It's a little frustrating that I cannot be at the Grand Prix. That's the price I have to pay.'

THE COURT OF KING VIJAY

Mallya in his pomp was a creature of the night, and few nights were more spectacular than 18 December 2005. That evening the tycoon welcomed friends to Kingfisher Villa, his mansion in the sunshine state of Goa on India's west coast, for the third day of a lavish four-day fiftieth birthday celebration. Guests drove up to imposing front gates designed to look like a Buddhist pagoda, with large 'VM' initials carved on the pillars. Then they were ushered past the Ferraris and swimming pools (one featured an underwater treadmill) and down towards the lawns by the sea. Leggy models mingled with Bollywood stars and an assortment of Mallya's fellow industrialists, many of whom had made the trip down by private jet. Others were ferried in on two Airbuses the tycoon borrowed from his own airline. At some point later in the evening Lionel Richie turned up to entertain the crowd and sing 'Happy Birthday' to the host, before the two airliners performed a fly-by over the beach.[10]

The year 2005 had been good to Mallya. That spring he wrapped up a long-awaited deal to buy Shaw Wallace, a rival spirit maker. The acquisition transformed his United Breweries group into one of the world's largest liquor companies, cementing its dominance over the domestic booze trade. Then in May Mallya launched Kingfisher Airlines, a daring attempt to tap into India's growing taste for domestic air travel. At that year's Paris air show he splashed out $3 billion to buy a dozen new Airbus planes, including five giant A380s, a clear signal of his plans to launch an international carrier too.[11] Such ambitions were expensive but they did his bank balance little harm. *Forbes* published its annual Rich List a few weeks before his fiftieth birthday, showing Mallya's fortune creeping up to $950 million.[12]

That year had been good to India too. Its previous government, led by the Hindu nationalist Bharatiya Janata Party (BJP), had lost power the year before, as voters spurned its optimistic 'India shining' slogan and elected a new Congress-led coalition government, which promised to do more to help farmers and the poor. As new prime minister Manmohan Singh settled into office, India's circumstances looked promising. The economy purred along at around nine per cent growth per year, an unheard-of level in a country that had long endured what was mockingly called the 'Hindu rate of growth' – in the low single digits prior to liberalisation in 1991.

A new optimism took hold, which Mallya himself seemed to embody. India's commercial elite had long been dominated by cautious, discreet industrialists. Even Dhirubhai Ambani, the most aggressive of the generation that rose in the decades either side of liberalisation, dressed in plain white shirts, spent with restraint and carefully guarded his privacy. Mallya was different: rich, powerful and not inclined to hide it; a bolder breed than those who had come before.

The tycoon's rise began more than two decades earlier in 1983, when his father died suddenly of a heart attack. Vittal Mallya was a canny, low-key businessman who bought United Breweries cheaply just after the Second World War, when he was only in his mid-twenties. The company made its name serving inexpensive local beer to British imperial soldiers, doing away with the need to import India pale ale from the UK. A precise and orderly man, the elder Mallya expanded his business methodically, buying out rival breweries, building his own, and learning to navigate the convoluted web of regulations that soon settled over India after 1947. The company he left behind made for a handily profitable inheritance, albeit one his only son was not remotely prepared to take over.

Vijay Mallya grew up in the eastern city of Kolkata, living with his mother while his father worked in Bangalore in the south. His flashy tastes began early. As a kid he drove a child-size Ferrari around his home; in his later teens he took to the streets in a turbocharged Porsche 911.[13] After college he joined the family firm, working first in sales, then moving to New Jersey to intern briefly at a US division. By the time his father died the younger man had achieved little beyond a clipping book of racy tabloid stories, mostly involving women and cars.

Mallya's early days in charge were marked by incoherent expansion. He launched a pizza chain, a cola brand and a telecoms manufacturer, as if trying to prove right those sceptics who thought him too young and ill disciplined to run his father's businesses. He spent a portion of the year in Sausalito, just across the Golden Gate Bridge from San Francisco, where his wife and children lived for much of the year. There he bought a vineyard, a craft beer maker and a newspaper, in the waterfront office of which he parked his growing classic car collection.[14] But in the end these various flirtations mattered little so long as his beer and spirits businesses prospered, which they did, especially as Mallya began to show a flair for promotion that his father lacked. Over time he learned to focus, shutting or selling ventures from pharmaceuticals to fast food and focusing mostly on drink.[15] Most importantly, he resuscitated Kingfisher, a moribund beer brand, turning it first into India's dominant lager, then a global curry-house staple.

Sitting in London, Mallya seemed relaxed about his youthful excesses. 'I became the darling of the media. It was all to do with lifestyle. My parties. My fast cars,' he told me. 'If I took charge at the age of 27, I behaved like a 27-year-old. But they started comparing me to Dhirubhai Ambani . . . A 27-year-old wants to drive a red Ferrari, a 50-year-old might not be interested in a red Ferrari. So I just lived my age.' Conspicuous though it was, he claimed a clear commercial logic behind his antics too. With alcohol advertising banned in India, drinks companies had to scramble to reach customers in other ways. Some gave away samples. Mallya promoted himself.

'I did what Branson does,' he told me. 'I lived the brand.' Newspapers wrote about his parties at Kingfisher Villa, or carried photos of models from his annual Kingfisher swimsuit calendar. The move into airlines was partly driven by a love of flying: like Branson, Mallya had long lusted after the glamour of airline ownership. There was an element of opportunism too; the sector's liberalisation in 1993 meant that Indian aviation remained relatively open terrain. But above all the plan was part of a longer-term strategy to launch everything from Kingfisher cruise ships to luxury trains, a move that clearly mimicked Branson's proliferating family of Virgin brands. Mallya denied it, but some industry observers wondered wryly if the tycoon had actually launched his airline as the ultimate form of brand extension, using his planes merely as expensive product placement opportunities through which to promote beer sales. Others compared the brash tycoon to another celebrated self-promoter: 'Mallya is more like an Indian version of Donald Trump,' his biographer wrote. 'He not only lives as The King of Good Times, but he is working overtime to persuade others to live the high life too.'[16]

With his shoulder-length hair, earrings and taste for bling, Mallya honed an image as the most piratical of entrepreneurs, striding into his own parties late in the evening, often many hours after his guests had arrived. When mobile phones became common it was said he walked in trailed by flunkies carrying his devices on a silver platter.[17] A specially kitted-out Boeing 727, its bar filled with his own products, whisked him between parties and business meetings, a distinction that in any case was often hazy to all involved. One ex-board member at a Mallya company told me: 'I remember being told to come for a board meeting at 10 a.m., so we flew down the night before, and the meeting did happen at ten – just ten in the evening . . . It was all a bit ridiculous. He had homes in every country, he never travelled with a suitcase because he had extra clothes in different places . . . in the end you have to think this excessive lifestyle was part of the reason he made mistakes.'

Despite the theatrics Mallya still made serious money. In 2006, he entered the *Forbes* list as a full billionaire and bought his prized super-yacht, one of the world's largest. The next year he bought Whyte & Mackay, the Scotch whisky maker, for £595 million. His ambitions began winning attention abroad. 'Mr Mallya personally is the sort of unfettered corporate czar that many American boardrooms have not seen in at least half a century,' the *New York Times* said, as he pushed on with plans to take Kingfisher global. 'He surrounds himself with a close group of long time advisers, wears copious diamonds, holds business meetings at his house until five in the morning, winks at female jour-nalists and flaunts the "good times" corporate motif.'[18]

For all the cartoonishness, Mallya was also a complex figure, with a precise and controlling side. He vetted the hiring of even lowly airline stewards and demanded staff text him whenever his planes landed. The outward flamboyance disguised a man with apparently sincere religious beliefs, a faith that grew stronger when he escaped from a helicopter crash in 2003. A showman in public, he befriended spiritualists in private, donated gold to their temples and disappeared into seclusion for many weeks each year, readying himself for a pilgrimage to a south-ern Indian hill shrine. Each new Kingfisher plane flew down to the temple town of Tirupati, close to the Sri Venkateswara Temple in the eastern state of Andhra Pradesh, to be blessed by priests on the tarmac.

The tycoon's relationship with India's establishment was double edged too. Mallya revelled in playing the rule breaker. 'I am flamboy-ant . . . and why not?' he once said. 'I am in the alcohol business. Whether people like it or not, I drink and I will continue to drink, because I enjoy it.'[19] In private, many business leaders disparaged his antics, viewing him as dissolute and more than a little unscrupulous. Yet Mallya also yearned for acceptance as a visionary and serious busi-ness leader, to rank alongside the lauded software billionaires of his adopted home town of Bangalore. He asked to be addressed as 'Dr Mallya', despite holding just an honorary doctorate from a US distance learning college. His hard-drinking lifestyle had little in common with an ascetic like Gandhi. But in 2009 he spent nearly $2 million to buy various of the Mahatma's effects at auction in New York, including a pocket watch and a pair of his iconic rounded glasses. The purchase allowed Mallya to paint himself as a patriot; a respectable man who used his fortune to serve the nation.

This tension between Mallya's exuberance and his desire for acceptance played out most obviously in politics, an area well suited to his talent for schmoozing. 'Alcohol was always kind of looked down upon. The bureaucracy looked down upon it. They thought that it was bootlegging,' he told me. 'The whole business was hugely politically intertwined.' Liquor gave politicians much-needed tax revenues, as well as under-the-table cash to fund election campaigns. But many took against it nonetheless, currying favour with female voters in particular by pledging to introduce prohibition. Alcohol was regulated at the state level too, so brewers needed friends all around India. Industrialists in other sectors won easy favours, Mallya told me. 'If they want to license or get things done, you'd just knock on the door of someone in Delhi,' he said. 'For me, it was like operating a business in what is now twenty-nine different countries.'

India's booze trade was heavily regulated and known for corruption, as businesses strived to keep powerful politicians and civil servants happy. Yet such was Mallya's facility with power that he took things a stage further. Just as he had once revived Kingfisher beer, in 2003 he took over a dormant political party and launched a quixotic effort to become chief minister of Karnataka, the southern state where he had based his headquarters, in the business hub of Bangalore. Ever the showman, on the stump he took to brandishing a sword that once belonged to Tipu Sultan, the eighteenth-century ruler of the southern Indian kingdom of Mysore, and something of a modern-day icon for his frequent battles against imperial British forces.

Karnataka's voters were ultimately not impressed, so the tycoon contented himself with a berth in parliament instead, taking a place in the upper house, whose seats are sometimes handed out to celebrities and commercial bigwigs. Mallya rarely asked questions when the Rajya Sabha was in session. But he did host the odd glamorous soirée in his

New Delhi home, while using his position to cosy up to powerbrokers. 'I think it is clear that they thought it would be better to rub shoulders with politicians as one of them, to approach them in the lobbies as an equal,' one ex-government minister once told me, reflecting on India's growing band of parliamentarian-tycoons, of whom Mallya was merely the most prominent. Even in a country where the dividing line between business and politics is often blurred, he raised eyebrows by taking a seat on the civil aviation committee, a position from which he was free to lobby against laws affecting his own airline, most obviously via a push to allow beer to be served on domestic flights.[20]

As his businesses expanded so the man-child extravagances did too. First came the F1 team, then a cricket franchise in the glitzy new Indian Premier League, which Mallya named the Royal Challengers Bangalore after his own brand of Royal Challenge whisky. But for those peering up from the bottom rungs of the social ladder his excesses held out promises of the good life, in a country long denied it. After the long, joyless decades of socialism, India's young population, and especially its men, warmed to the tycoon's promise of an uninhibited, booze-soaked lifestyle. Few industries also embodied that same sense of aspiration more clearly than aviation, as Air India, the scruffy state-owned carrier, was eclipsed by hungrier private sector competitors offering the glamour of air travel to a rising middle class.

Even today researchers disagree on exactly how large that middle class has become. Some generous estimates put the number in the low hundreds of millions. Others peg it lower, at perhaps just fifty million.[21] Certainly the number meeting near-Western standards – car and home owners with college degrees, financial savings and frequent-flier numbers – is tiny. In the years after liberalisation this group was tinier still: '99% of the Indian population have never flown in a plane,' as *Wired* put it a few years after Kingfisher's launch.[22] For those outside this narrow circle, Mallya's airline finally brought trappings of the global consumer class within reach for the first time.

I boarded my first Kingfisher plane back in 2007, taking a two-hour flight back to Mumbai from the southern state of Kerala. By then budget carriers were common in the West, turning air travel into a cheap but somewhat unpleasant experience. Mallya's airline was different. The tickets were indeed remarkably inexpensive, but his planes were shiny and new, with wide seats, extra legroom and fancy entertainment systems. As we readied for take-off Mallya's face appeared on the screen in front of me. 'Each member of the cabin crew has been hand picked by me, and I have instructed them to treat you as a guest in my own home,' he said. The aircraft were dubbed 'fun liners', and passengers were invited to email him with any complaints. The food was good. I recall being handed a free ice cream as we began our descent.

In a country with barely a decent motorway and whose city roads were riddled with potholes, Kingfisher seemed like a miracle of modernity. 'Holy shit!' the American management thinker Tom Peters wrote at the time, having just taken his first flight, praising in particular the 'butlers' who helped business-class passengers with their luggage.[23] Kingfisher's combination of the previously impossible – world-class service at rock-bottom prices – hinted that India itself might do the same, quickly leaving behind problems of poverty and inefficiency to become a world-leading economy. When Vijay Mallya took over from his father, that economy was manacled by rules, starved of capital and dominated by the state. By the time his airline launched, those rules were being undone, kicking off a period of booming growth and raising hopes for national renewal. In the same way as the country's gleaming software parks, the seeming success of Mallya's airline fed a deep hope within India – that the country might be able to leap in a single bound from the old world of sclerotic socialism to a bold new future of modern, competitive and incorrupt Western-style capitalism. It was a moment, for both Mallya and India, in which everything appeared possible. At times it seemed as if the good times might be too good to be true. And, in the end, they were.

THE GREAT REOPENING

Back in London, Mallya recalled clearly when he first began rethinking his business: the run-in to the economic crash of 1991. Over a few dramatic months India plunged into its most perilous crisis since Independence. Facing a balance of payments crunch, and with barely a few weeks of foreign currency reserves in hand, then finance minister Manmohan Singh rushed through a series of emergency reforms, tearing up controls on business and removing barriers to foreign capital. Yet even a few years before the crash it was clear the game was up for socialist planned economies. China's long boom was well under way. Even the nations of communist eastern Europe were pushing market reforms. India looked ever more like a laggard and its tycoons were preparing for the moment when all those licences, quotas and permits would finally disappear.

'I'm talking about, what, the late eighties? Because before that foreign investment in India didn't exist,' Mallya told me, sitting in his study. Back then his UB Group had at least thirty businesses. 'We used to make automotive batteries, we used to make paint, we used to make polymers, so we were in petrochemicals. We used to make food. Snacks, pizzas, soft drinks. You name it,' he added with a smile, as if recalling fondly the commercial indiscipline of his youth. 'I looked at each business and I said to myself, you know, how can we compete with the Nestlés and the Unilevers of this world? Either we have to come up with a huge bunch of resources or we're going to die.'

The 1991 crisis had roots going back more than half a century and the battle against colonial rule. In 1947, just when Mallya's father bought UB Group, a fierce debate raged among India's national founders. On one side stood Gandhi, with his vision of a future agrarian utopia, dotted with prosperous villages and free of commercial exploitation. On the other was Nehru, who became prime minister of a newly independent India at the stroke of midnight on 15 August 1947. Inspired in equal measure by British Fabian socialism and the apparent successes of Soviet communism, Nehru and his supporters envisioned a bold new planned economy, dotted with towering steel mills and hydro-electric dams. 'Their primary objectives were industrialisation, the liquidation of illiteracy and superstition, and the mitigation of India's material poverty,' *The Economist* wrote in 1948, shortly after Gandhi's assassination. 'They regarded Gandhi's glorification of the simple life as reactionary.'[24]

Nehru's vision ultimately won out, but for all their disagreements he and Gandhi remained united in their suspicion of private enterprise, which both viewed as an artefact of colonialism. 'Right through history the old Indian ideal did not glorify political and military triumph and it looked down upon money,' Nehru explained in his autobiography. 'Today the old culture is fighting against a new and all-powerful opposition: the *bania* civilisation of the capitalist West,' he added, using a Hindi word for 'traders' which implied dishonesty.[25]

Nehru's ideas set India on a path that rejected free markets for nearly half a century.

Whatever the beliefs of its founders, the violence of Partition proved the most challenging backdrop possible for India's economic rebirth. Britain's colonial rulers rushed to divide the subcontinent in two, creating a new border that brutally and arbitrarily split people and businesses. Their decision, announced in haste barely a month before Independence, kicked off a blood-soaked period of social dislocation and ethnic violence.[26] Hindu and Muslim refugees streamed in their millions between India and Pakistan, with damaging economic consequences for both. India's young government struggled to manage the cost of refugee camps, produce food or curb rampant inflation. To regain control Nehru strengthened the already impressive array of state controls he inherited from the British, launching the first of many Soviet-style five-year plans in 1951. Under his rule a new and alien set of beliefs took hold: self-reliance in economics, non-alignment in geopolitics and a sense of India not as a global power, but a leader of aggrieved third-world nations, struggling to escape the legacy of colonialism.

India's economy was handed over entirely to the state from those earliest days, as sector after sector was taken into public ownership. In 1953 Nehru brought together all eight of India's private airlines, creating two state-owned carriers in their place: Indian Airlines for domestic flights and Air India for those lucky enough to travel abroad. Industries that remained in private hands were soon enmeshed in the labyrinthine dictums of the Licence Raj. Strict rules controlled what companies made, the technologies they used and the workers they hired. Hundreds of categories of goods – from pickles and matches to padlocks and wooden furniture – were reserved for smaller and generally less productive companies, a Gandhian hangover that helped 'Made in India' become a byword for poor workmanship. Spared the rigours of foreign competition, larger businesses were inefficient too. Rather than making better products, entrepreneurs learned to win favours from bureaucrats. The more successful expanded wherever rules allowed, hence why, in his early days, Mallya decided to take a beer and spirits business and move it into making petrochemicals and telecoms equipment.[27]

Few industries were more marked by the Licence Raj than alcohol. State governments controlled where Indians bought drink and what they paid for it. Import tariffs made foreign booze many times more expensive than local brands like Kingfisher. Regulators even controlled molasses, the sticky treacle that made up the base ingredient for Indian rums and whiskies, setting the prices at which it could be sold or the quantities in which it could be traded across state borders.[28] Meanwhile, breweries and distilleries were hit with high taxes and hundreds of complex local rules – hence why it was vital for tycoons like Mallya to keep in the good graces of regional politicians.

The grip of the state only extended further when Indira Gandhi, Nehru's daughter, became prime minister in 1966, nationalising banks, insurers and coal mines. The tighter the government's grip became, the more ordinary Indians suffered goods shortages, and the further businesses retreated from international trade. The shift was profound. In 1947, Nehru inherited among the world's most globally integrated economies. Within two decades he and his daughter built one of the most rigidly closed.[29] In retrospect these policies proved to be little more than a national catastrophe. India's tryst with statism produced four decades of lacklustre growth, watched over by an over-mighty state that to this day has only partially been dismantled. Nehru's sincere concerns for the condition of the poor did little to improve their condition. Instead India idled as Asia's other powers – Japan, South Korea and finally China – first moved out of poverty and then gradually grew rich.

Today more than half of Indians are under twenty-five, meaning relatively few even remember the restrictions their compatriots once faced. Those who do mostly recall an era of petty frustrations, as was the case with chess grandmaster Viswanathan Anand, whom I met in 2013. Then forty-three, Anand was nerdy and talkative. We were meant to be discussing an upcoming match in which he would defend his world chess title for the third time, but our conversation drifted. Over a few hours in his home on a tree-lined street in the southern city of Chennai, he recounted stories of his upbringing in what was then known as Madras and how India's long era of autarky had shaped his youth.

Anand began playing chess in Indira Gandhi's time, taught first by his mother, then coaches at a nearby chess club, housed in the city's Russian Cultural Centre. Named after Soviet grandmaster Mikhail Tal, the institution itself reflected the close Cold War-era ties that grew up between New Delhi and Moscow. 'They [the Russians] allowed people to have a chess club there, as a way of promoting chess, and that's kind of how I got my start,' Anand told me.[30] Then as his career blossomed – he became India's first ever grandmaster in 1988 – he started to need to travel to Europe for tournaments. This meant trips to government offices for permission letters to leave the country, then long train rides to Mumbai or New Delhi, from where almost all international flights left.

At the time Air India ran relatively few flights. Prices were fixed by the state, meaning that they were the same whether you bought tickets many months or the day before travel. But the airline also had few planes, and they were often full. Restrictions on foreign exchange meant taking money abroad was hard. 'You needed to get a [government] sanction, and your allowance was something pitiful like $20 a day,' Anand told me. 'If you didn't have more money, then you had to live within those $20 . . . Most Indians used to stay with their relatives and then eat in the cheapest joints.' Later he tried to buy a primitive chess computer only to find that import duties increased its cost threefold. Its arrival was then delayed for months as the grandmaster visited various bureaucrats to get the permission slips you needed to import any piece of foreign technological equipment. 'It was just a different era,' he said. 'Even if I explain this to Indians today, it sounds very North Korean. But in those days, that's how it was.'

Similar restrictions were found across India's shrunken consumer economy. Sky-high tariffs made almost all imports expensive. Many foreign items were simply banned. Shortages were common: the waiting list for a scooter stretched out for the best part of a decade. Clothes were basic and made by local tailors, while telephones were a luxury that required bribery and patience to acquire. One Indian friend told me that when his father died in the mid-1990s he left the family's two landline phones in his will. Almost no homes had televisions, which in any case played just a single government-run channel. Almost no Indians owned a car either, while those who did were restricted to a handful of models, from the stately Hindustan Ambassador – a rehashed British Morris Oxford – to the boxy Maruti Suzuki 800 hatchback. Photographs of New Delhi or Mumbai in the 1980s show empty streets little changed from a century before. Owning an imported foreign car, especially a fancy one – like the teenage Vijay Mallya and his Porsche – was unusual given ruinously expensive import duties. Another friend who grew up in Mumbai in the 1980s told me that, as a child, he knew the names of almost every family in the city wealthy enough to own a Mercedes or a BMW, simply because there were so few of them.

India's 1991 crisis arrived at a time not just of economic turmoil, but of social dislocation too. Violent protests erupted the year before against controversial plans to give more public sector jobs to those from the lower rungs of the caste system. Dozens of students set themselves alight. Communal tensions simmered as the BJP launched a series of national agitations. Their focus was the Babri Masjid, a mosque in the heartland state of Uttar Pradesh. Protestors claimed the site marked the birthplace of the Hindu deity Ram and eventually demolished it in 1992, causing further nationwide riots. Then barely a month before the 1991 crisis began, Rajiv Gandhi, Nehru's grandson, and the third member of his family to serve as prime minister, was assassinated. A youthful, reform-minded politician, Gandhi's election in 1984 raised hopes for economic revival, as he began loosening some of the restrictions of the Licence Raj. His first term ended in electoral failure, however, mired in a corruption scandal involving the Swedish arms company Bofors. Gandhi hoped that victory in 1991's poll might restore his reputation. Instead his murder on the campaign trail near Chennai by a suicide bomber linked to Sri Lanka's Tamil Tigers made him the second member of his family to fall at the hands of an assassin, following the death of his mother in 1984.

It was mostly external events that pushed India's crisis to the fore. Soaring oil prices during the Gulf War hit an already yawning fiscal deficit, itself the legacy of undisciplined state spending over the previous decade. Inflation was rampant. A balance of payments crisis looked certain unless emergency funds could be found. Just as important, however, was an internal intellectual revolution, led by a band of policy advisers and economists, including future prime minister Manmohan Singh. For a decade or more this group had concluded that India needed to leave behind its statist heritage. For Singh, the crisis of 1991 provided the excuse he needed, as he devalued the rupee and launched a secretive plan to rescue the country from impending calamity.

India's position was precarious throughout the first half of 1991, but never more so than one morning in July, as a convoy of goods vehicles idled on the side of a highway in Mumbai, and Singh's rescue plan threatened to unravel. Cars streamed past, their drivers unaware that the trucks were laden with a clandestine cargo: gold bars, picked up that morning from the vaults of the Reserve Bank of India (RBI). The trucks had then moved north through the city, their destination – the cargo area of Mumbai's international airport – known only to a handful of anxious politicians and bureaucrats. Secrecy was essential. So there could hardly have been a worse moment for one truck to blow a tyre. Yaga Venugopal Reddy, at the time a senior official in the finance ministry in New Delhi, and subsequently head of the RBI, later recalled the drama. 'Guards had to be positioned all around,' he told me later, sitting one afternoon in his home in the southern city of Hyderabad, waving his hands as if to show armed personnel moving along the side of the kerb. 'When people took positions on the road in Mumbai, you can imagine the attention it caused.'[31]

These fears of loss of secrecy were well founded. Earlier in July an enterprising journalist named Shankkar Aiyar had caught a previous convoy unloading its cargo. Acting on a tip-off, he raced to Mumbai airport one Sunday afternoon and watched pallets being loaded onto an aircraft with the words 'Heavy Lift Cargo' written on the side. The plane was due to fly first to Dubai, he discovered, and then onward to Stansted airport in London. 'Secret sale of gold by RBI,' screamed his front-page headline in the *Indian Express* the next day, describing a 'highly hushed up operation' to send the metal abroad.[32] An outcry duly followed. 'It was a shock for people, it brought home the severity of the crisis,' Aiyar told me later. 'It made India seem like a family that was forced to pawn its jewels. This was felt directly and emotionally, because in India, your gold is your savings. If you sell your gold, it means you are in serious trouble.'

Still, on its own terms, this supposedly secret operation was a success. Roughly fifty tonnes of gold were dispatched abroad that month in four consignments, winning crucial breathing room. Singh stood up in parliament on 24 July and delivered a budget packed with reforms. Import tariffs and limits on foreign investment were cut. Hundreds of fiddly licences were junked. Industries long closed to private competition, from iron and steel to telecoms, were suddenly opened up. Restrictions on goods such as molasses were decontrolled too, allowing spirits makers like Mallya to increase production. Just as a physical wall had fallen in Europe, so the economic walls that kept India enclosed were being torn down. From the dispatch box Singh justified his reforms by quoting Victor Hugo's famous words: no power on earth can stop an idea whose time has come. 'Let the whole world hear it loud and clear,' he said as he concluded his speech, his thin, reedy voice rising briefly. 'India is now wide awake.'[33]

BAD TIMES

On 1 March 2016, Vijay Mallya, the man who often travelled without luggage, left New Delhi airport carrying half a dozen bags.[34] It was more than a decade after the launch of Kingfisher Airlines and four years since its collapse. In between Mallya borrowed heavily to build what was briefly his country's most popular airline. Early on he said he would break even in twelve months. But in seven years of operation Kingfisher never turned a profit. Instead stories filtered out about planes unable to take off, because the company had not paid its fuel bills, or passengers going without meals, because caterers' charges had not been met. Wages were handed out erratically, even as executives enjoyed big bonuses. Cheques bounced and plane orders were cancelled. A jump in oil prices in 2012 proved damaging. Towards the end of that year the business fell apart, as regulators grounded its fleet and revoked its licences. For the King of Good Times, time finally ran out.

Mallya's rise and fall is in many ways an allegory for modern India's own progress. A child of liberalisation, the tycoon sensed new ambitions rising in his country. 'We have broken the shackles of conservative socialism,' he once said. 'Indians are no longer going to remain subdued and live in a simple fashion . . . Young Indians want to be like me.'[35] But he rose to prominence in a particular moment in Indian history, namely the economic boom of the mid-2000s. In the consumer economy, millions of Indians bought cars, built houses and took flights for the first time. What was called the global commodity 'super-cycle' – driven in particular by rising demand in China for minerals like coal, bauxite and iron ore – kicked off a dash for natural resources across India too. Stock markets roared ahead, creating a bulging new billionaire class. It is hard to pick an exact date, but at some point between the time of Manmohan Singh's election victory in 2004 and Mallya's fiftieth birthday party the following year, something in India changed, and a new gilded age began.

The effect of this roaring growth was seen most clearly in the corporate sector. Investments by foreign companies jumped, while domestic
businesses began expanding rapidly abroad. In 2006, steel billionaire
Lakshmi Mittal, at the time the world's third richest man, announced an
unprecedented $34 billion plan to buy Arcelor of Luxembourg, creating
one of the world's biggest steel makers.[36] Tata, the biggest Indian
company of all, began snapping up British household names like Jaguar
Land Rover and Tetley Tea. Newly flushed with confidence, big-name
Indian industrialists began turning out at Davos, the annual Swiss
alpine forum favoured by the global elite. In 2006 the nearby mountain-
sides were blanketed with adverts paid for by India's government,
promoting what they called the world's 'fastest-growing free market
democracy'. Mukesh Ambani was named the event's co-chair and an
array of fellow tycoons, including Mallya, turned up to cheer him on.

India's apparently miraculous rebirth prompted an intellectual
re-evaluation. American economist Larry Summers, at the time a senior
adviser to US President Barack Obama, gave a speech in 2010 floating
the idea of a 'Mumbai consensus' to replace the 'Washington consensus',
the set of ideas that had long dominated Western thinking about international development. Until the mid-2000s fast-growing east Asian
'tiger' economies like Taiwan and South Korea had been the stars of
globalisation. These were often labelled as 'developmental states', meaning those whose governments used industrial protection and public
investment to build up export industries, before gradually opening
them up to global competition. Instead, Summers argued that India
could now become a new 'democratic developmental state', pushed not
by the brute force of manufacturing, but by technology and youthful
demographics, as well as 'growing levels of consumption and a widening middle class'.[37] Behind this lay a more radical thought. Perhaps it
would be democratic India, rather than autocratic China, that became
the model other emerging economies looked to follow?

India lapped all this up. Its long decades of humiliation and isolation
seemed to be receding. At least at first Singh's government appeared
able to combine major economic reforms with rising investment in
ambitious social programmes. Poverty rates fell while urbanisation
accelerated. Briefly, it looked as if India might be able surpass China's
growth rate while improving the lot of its poorest citizens at the same
time. 'It was a strange experience for us. Never since Independence did

we have the problem of plenty,' Y. V. Reddy, the former central bank head, told me. Foreign money gushed in, pushing up the value of the rupee. 'Domestically, we had euphoria,' Reddy added. 'That is the time when my fellow economists began to mention double-digit growth. I used the word "over-heating".'

As Reddy feared, it was not to last. India rode out the 2008 global financial crisis more easily than most, but its aftershocks still dented domestic growth. The commodity boom ebbed. An array of corruption scandals emerged, many linked directly to the excesses of the boom years. A public outcry over cronyism began, in turn sparking a period of political stasis in New Delhi. Disenchantment with Singh's Congress government grew. Growth sagged. The rupee came under pressure. Analysts who had recently lauded India's untapped potential focused again on its flaws. Talk of a new 'Mumbai consensus' quickly disappeared.

Of all of the flaws that came to light during that period one stuck to Vijay Mallya above all: bad debts. Public sector banks lent freely during the 2000s boom to industrialists and airline owners alike. Most then generously restructured those same loans when economic conditions turned sour. Mallya was far from the largest borrower, but he was among the highest profile. 'Mallya is a child of bank nationalisation,' as the head of one large business house put it to me. 'He didn't get loans from almost any private sector banks, and there is no way he could have got all that money without the state sector.' For a few years he weaved this way and that, trying to raise funds and keep his creditors at bay. He sold United Spirits, his liquor business, for nearly $2 billion, only to become locked in a bitter feud with its new owners. More than anything it was debt that caused his downfall, as a consortium of more than a dozen banks began to try to recover more than $1 billion in loans and interest.

When we met in London, Mallya blamed his various misfortunes on an array of outside forces and unfortunate circumstances, from oil at $140 a barrel to the Indian government's unwillingness to cut taxes on airline fuel or airport duty. Investment rules meant Kingfisher Airlines was also barred from finding a foreign airline to rescue it. Captured by special interests, politicians and bureaucrats favoured Air India, he claimed, pumping the failing state carrier full of subsidies. 'They allowed Kingfisher to die and spent 30,000 crores [$3.6 billion] of public money bailing out Air India,' Mallya told me. Most of all he denied fleeing the country, a charge which clearly still rankled. His plan had been to return to India just a few days after leaving for London in early March 2016, and he claimed to have said as much to various senior politicians he had met with in India's parliament during the days prior to his departure. 'I told [them] personally, face to face, that I'm going to London tomorrow, I've a meeting in Geneva on Friday and I'll be back on Sunday,' he said, looking suddenly downcast. 'And now the narrative is: "He fled India. He ran away."'

Ultimately Mallya blamed politics for his predicament, and in particular the election of Narendra Modi and his early attempts to rid India of its spate of corruption scandals. 'Three years ago, four years ago, in comes Modi. And he realises very quickly that the Indian banking system, particularly the government-owned banks, have a huge bad debt problem,' Mallya said. 'They go on the warpath and say public sector banks will recover money from borrowers, come hell or high water.' This sealed his fate in India's system, where public banks are controlled by political masters in New Delhi, attracting attention from tax authorities and the police too. He made various offers to repay, he said, but these were rebuffed. 'These guys will just show up and make life miserable. Enter your house. Search it in a rather uncouth way,' he said. 'They say, fine, either you pay us so much or we'll take you with us.'

Despite these extenuating circumstances, it was hard not to conclude that much of the blame for Kingfisher's downfall lay with Mallya himself. Partly this was down to poor judgement. In the liquor business, Mallya's exuberant style of self-promotion made good sense. But the same trick was less appropriate in an aviation industry with the thinnest of margins, where success meant a fanatical focus on cost. Mallya by contrast bought up rivals at rich valuations and spent lavishly on new planes.

When we met, Mallya denied that he had cajoled or misled anyone into lending to him. The heads of India's state banks were sober, serious public servants, he argued. 'I couldn't have gone there like a cowboy, wielding a gun, put it in some chairman's head and said "Give me money!"' But it was equally true that he was the beneficiary of generous loan restructurings which were hard to justify in retrospect given the state of his business – part of a pattern of what was known as 'evergreening', in which Indian bankers often provided new money to borrowers who were unable to repay existing loans, in order to cover up problems at the banks themselves. Then there were allegations of creative accounting, which Mallya also strongly denied. Diageo, the company that had bought United Spirits, sued the tycoon in 2017, claiming that he had used money from his profitable liquor operations to prop up other parts of his empire.[38] Earlier that year, accusations that he had diverted funds prompted a six-month stock trading ban from India's securities regulator.[39]

Mallya had a point when he complained that cabals of politicians and bureaucrats would continue to funnel cash into state-backed Air India, despite its dismal financial reputation. But he was also a beneficiary of a similar system of bureaucratic favours, especially in Kingfisher's early days. 'Mr Mallya has turned a potential enemy, India's powerful aviation bureaucracy, into an ally,' as *The Economist* put it in 2005. 'Envious competitors wonder aloud how he achieved such a remarkable thing.' The same was true in liquor, an industry whose incumbents enjoyed extensive state protection. 'Fixing provincial politicians; negotiating a series of local taxes and state-level entry and exit levies; getting permission for new breweries; lobbying to get politicians to deny permission to rivals; influencing policy to keep taxes on imports high – this is part of the architecture of the industry,' journalist Ashok Malik wrote around the time of Kingfisher's collapse.[40]

Fittingly, perhaps, it was a party that proved Mallya's final undoing. A decade after his triumphant fiftieth, he again gathered friends at Kingfisher Villa in Goa to toast his sixtieth birthday in December 2015. The affair was not quite so lavish, lasting just a couple of days. But the Spanish singer Enrique Iglesias was still flown in as entertainment, ensuring write-ups in gossip columns and an angry reaction from critics. 'If you flaunt your yacht [and] massive birthday bashes, even while owing the system a lot of money, it seems to suggest that you don't care,' RBI governor Raghuram Rajan told an interviewer a few weeks later, standing against a snowy backdrop at Davos. 'If you are in trouble, you should show that you care by cutting down your expenses.'

Rajan's attack marked a shift. For years, the authorities made only token efforts to pin Mallya down. Even after Modi's election in 2014, India's toothless bankruptcy laws and timid banking culture ensured that only half-hearted attempts were made to seize assets, as would have happened in many other countries. But after Mallya left the country, and especially after Rajan's attack, the political mood changed. The authorities decided to make an example of him, forcing him to resign as an MP and rescinding his passport. It was only then that the police filed charges of fraud, charges which he denies. Mallya's personal plane was put up for auction, along with much of his car collection, while Kingfisher Villa in Goa was seized by creditors.

One misty early October morning, about six months after Mallya had left the country, I walked up the road behind his beachside mansion, to see what remained of his pleasure empire. The sun was barely up and shopkeepers along the road were only just opening their stalls. I found a long, thin rectangle of a property, running back a kilometre or more from the sands of Candolim Beach. There was a closed-up liquor store next door, with a Kingfisher advertising hoarding propped up against its grill. Two black cows wandered slowly down the road. The initials 'VM' were still there on the gates, although the cheery yellow paint of old was now peeling off the pillars. A trio of elderly guards in scruffy blue uniforms rested on red plastic chairs just inside the entrance, where celebrities and tycoons had one once arrived.

Inside, the main swimming pool was half-filled with greenish water and watched over by three more guards. The garages, once packed with cars, now stood empty barring a solitary, classic red Ferrari, its elegant rear end poking out from beneath a white sheet. Out on the beach, at the far end of the property, four tall wooden poles stood in the sand, with their tattered Kingfisher flags flapping in the sea breeze. And at each entrance, from the modest back gate leading down to the beach to the imposing front entrance on the main road, there were the same peeling white posters, announcing 'This property is in the possession of SBICAP Trustee Company LTD', an arm of State Bank of India, the public sector bank to which Mallya owed more money than any other.

Mallya's successes marked the high point for a certain kind of Indian capitalism, in which businesses thrived on debt and their owners proved untouchable. His departure for London signalled the beginning of the end of that same system. Ultimately it was not just the scale of his business dealings that did him in, but the unrepentant manner of his failure. Many tycoons borrowed much more, using cheap loans from public sector banks to build vast industrial empires. Some even ended up with larger piles of unpaid debts too. But as the boom years petered out most of them kept a low profile, while the King of Good Times refused to go quietly. His behaviour proved shameful precisely because his ventures

– in their ambition and indiscipline, in their capacity to innovate but also their willingness to cut corners – seemed so closely to resemble India itself. But if Mallya's methods of debt-fuelled growth and canny political connections came to define the hubris of India's boom years, there were plenty of others who played the same game.

Billionaire Gautam Adani, one of India's new breed of industrialists, had a close relationship with future prime minister Narendra Modi during Modi's tenure as chief minister of Gujarat.

CHAPTER 3

RISE OF THE BOLLYGARCHS

PORT IN A STORM

We sped along an immaculate dual carriageway from the airstrip, passing oil storage tanks and yards stacked with oblong boxes. The landscape was eerie and flat, with barely a bump out towards the horizon. Half a dozen gigantic blue and yellow container cranes loomed into view as the port drew closer. Inside the gates, one of them picked up a large metal box from the deck of a waiting container ship and swung it down delicately towards the harbourside, as if its contents weighed nothing at all. The vessel, the *Mol Solution* – built in Japan, registered in Panama, its hull a towering wall of steel painted in cheery sky blue – took 66,000 tonnes fully laden. A mechanical claw reached inside a second vessel a little further down the quayside, its belly filled with coal. Moving gradually back towards land, the claw opened suddenly in mid-air and disgorged itself with a roar into a waiting truck. The tarmac all around was black with dust.

Goods of all descriptions were stacked up around the port. Giant industrial pipes stood in triangular piles. Thick tree trunks lay in rows, stripped of leaves and branches. Thousands of colourful Maruti Suzuki cars were lined up in nearby yards, ready to be driven into containers and stacked ten deep on a waiting ship. Orange excavators crawled over small mountains of recently arrived coal, preparing to shift it into waiting wagons. I searched for stevedores as the cranes whirred overhead, but found the dockside almost entirely empty of people. The tall red and white striped chimneys of a power station rose up further along the coast, fuelled with coal from Indonesia and built by migrant Chinese workers.

There are many places you might visit to see the changes brought by India's new era of globalisation, from the software parks of Bangalore, where Vijay Mallya also based his businesses, to the banks and stock markets of Mumbai. But few offered sights as dramatic as the long, jagged coastline of Gujarat, the state that juts out sharply from the country's western flank. Bordering Pakistan on one side, its proximity to the Persian Gulf had long provided a natural landing point for merchants and migrants. Zoroastrian refugees arrived here from Iran as early as the seventh century, forming what became the Parsi community, one of the India's more commercially successful minorities. In 1608, in the southern coastal town of Surat, the East India Company established its first 'factory', a trading post of fortified warehouses packed with silk, indigo and saltpetre, waiting for galleons to carry it back to Britain. More modern factories, in what had since become a bustling city, now imported, cut, polished and re-exported almost all of the world's diamonds. In the meantime the surrounding region had once again become India's gateway for global commerce, and host to some of the grandest endeavours of its tycoon class.

It was here at Jamnagar, just over the waters of the Gulf of Kutch, that Mukesh Ambani's Reliance Industries built its gigantic petrochemicals and refining complex, by some measures the largest of its type in the world. Another refinery stood just next door, built by the billionaire Ruia brothers of Essar, while the Jindals, another storied business dynasty, ran power plants and steel mills further south. The Gujarati coast was dotted with facilities to welcome container ships, oil tankers and liquefied natural gas carriers. More than anyone, however, commerce in the state had come to be associated with the extraordinary rise of one man: Gautam Adani, perhaps the most aggressive of India's new generation of tycoons.

I had squeezed into the plush leather seats of one of Adani's private jets earlier that morning in mid-2013, ready to visit Mundra, an isolated coastal town about 350 kilometres to the west of Ahmedabad, the commercial capital. The surrounding area was little more than scrubland before Adani, at the time merely an ambitious local businessman, got his hands on it about a decade earlier. Now it was the crown jewel of his business operations, including India's largest private port, a giant coal-fired power station and a sprawling special economic zone spread out over more than 30 square miles. Reaching the port took eight bumpy hours by road, the pilot told me, looking over his shoulder and yelling over the noise of the engines. In the twin-engine eight-seater we touched down in less than one.

Adani's own background was modest. A college drop-out from a middle-class family of textile merchants, he began his career in Mumbai's diamond markets, before returning home to Gujarat to work in a small plastics factory, run by one of his brothers. Eventually he set up his own commodities trading business. Then, expanding at a pace that often looked reckless, he launched successive new ventures spanning ports, infrastructure, power, mining and property. At the start he was a minor figure, unknown outside his home state. But fuelled by quantities of debt that easily outstripped those built up even by adventurous tycoons like Vijay Mallya, Adani became one of India's most successful self-made industrialists in less than ten years.

The pace and scale of Adani's expansion was comparable with those of industrial giants of earlier eras. Unable to rely on India's ramshackle infrastructure, he built his own private railways and power lines. Lacking easy access to domestic coal, he bought mines in Indonesia and Australia, and took their contents back home through his port. In the process he built 'a vertically integrated global supply chain reminiscent of when Henry Ford once owned Brazilian rubber plantations to supply his car factories', as the *New York Times* put it.[1] More to the point, his was an expansion that closely mirrored India's own. As the country enjoyed its fastest ever growth in the mid-2000s, so Adani undertook one of its most extravagant investment sprees. In 2002, Adani Enterprises, his main holding company, was worth barely $70 million.[2] A decade later he claimed to have built assets worth $20 billion, while the value of his companies had jumped more than one hundredfold.[3] By the time of India's most recent election in 2014, *Forbes* listed his fortune at $7 billion.[4]

Above all, Adani's controversial reputation rested on a final factor: his friendly ties to Narendra Modi, the man who would go on to become India's prime minister. Adani's businesses began taking off in the years following Modi's arrival as Gujarat's chief minister back in 2001. Under Modi the state grew into a vibrant industrial hub, with a particular strength in export-focused manufacturing, even being compared with the Pearl River Delta, the region around Hong Kong that powered China's transformation into a global trading giant.

The two men enjoyed symbiotic careers. Modi's pro-business policies helped Adani expand. Adani's own companies, meanwhile, built many of the grand projects that came to symbolise Modi's 'Gujarat model', with its emphasis on infrastructure investment, attracting foreign capital and export industries. There were temperamental bonds too: both were self-made men with little formal education; both were traditional in their tastes, guarded their privacy and were distrustful of outsiders; both spoke in halting English; both, in general, avoided talking to the press. Where other Gujarati industrialists like Mukesh Ambani often settled in Mumbai, Adani stayed in Ahmedabad, becoming the state's most recognisable businessman. The duo were said to get on well. Adani was loyal too, defending Modi in the aftermath of the bloody Hindu–Muslim riots that hit Gujarat in 2002, a time when Modi faced fierce public criticism.[5]

Symbols of Adani's wealth were hard to escape around the state. Adverts for his office blocks and residential property projects dotted roadsides in Ahmedabad. At the airport our plane passed a handful of other Adani private jets idling on the runway, all bearing the tycoon's distinctive purple livery. This fleet of aircraft attracted political controversy the following year, when it emerged they had ferried Modi around India to speak at rallies during his campaign to become prime minister.[6] Both sides denied anything untoward, claiming the jets were part of a long-term leasing arrangement. But this did little to stop critics attacking a perceived cosiness between the politician who so often railed against crony capitalism and the tycoon whose businesses had blossomed on his watch.

There was controversy too about the large expanse of land onto which our plane touched down an hour later, at an airfield built by Adani's company. A sign in purple letters above the terminal read: 'Welcome to Adani Ports and SEZ'. India had begun developing special economic zones – or SEZs for short – during the 2000s, inspired by the trade-friendly enclave set up in Shenzhen by Communist Party leader Deng Xiaoping in 1980, whose exporting industries helped to kick off China's own economic transformation. Most of the Indian zones flopped, although Adani's did better, a fact its owner put down to canny management.[7] Critics, including Congress leader Rahul Gandhi – Sonia Gandhi's son, and the latest in the Nehru–Gandhi dynasty to lead his party – pointed to different factors. Specifically, Gandhi accused the tycoon of benefiting from favourable deals, arguing that he had acquired land from Gujarat's government at advantageous rates.[8]

Back at the port, the facility's amiable chief executive, Captain Unmesh Abhyankar, talked excitedly about the mechanics of the place: a world of berth occupancy, throughput rates and turnaround times. Mundra had an unusually deep harbour, allowing it to attract some of the world's biggest cargo ships, he explained, giving it an edge over rivals elsewhere along India's western coast. 'We focus on the three Cs: coal, containers and crude,' he said of the cargoes the ships brought in. Exports were more of a mish-mash, including everything from bauxite and cars to iron ore and wood. India's dilapidated road network made it hard to move this in and out, so Adani built a 60-kilometre private freight line to the main rail network. Most Indian ports were state owned and inefficient, taking a couple of days or more to unload a ship.[9] At Mundra, however, cargo was mostly whisked in and out over a morning. Abhyankar expected his facility to become the country's largest port later that year, handling 100 million tonnes of goods, the first in India ever to do so.

Even at dusk the giant container cranes were easy to spot from the window, as our plane took off that evening and flew us back to Ahmedabad, ready to meet Adani the next day. The day's last light glinted on the grey of the Gulf of Kutch in the distance. A few years earlier a team of oceanographers had found an ancient stone anchor lying 50 metres below the waves, of a type used by merchants more than a millennium before.[10] For centuries, those same waters had been India's trading artery, bringing wooden dhows and then steamships across from Africa and the Middle East. Through such trade and commerce, India had been an early pioneer of globalisation, at least until Nehru launched his new age of self-enclosure in the aftermath of Independence in 1947.

Now the ships docking at Mundra harked back to those earlier eras, from the ninth-century Chola dynasty, which forged ties from Babylon to China, to the Emperor Babur in the early sixteenth century, whose Mughal dynasty traded on favourable terms with the Portuguese, Dutch and British. India's record in colonial times was less impressive, as centuries of exploitation left its economy barely larger in the mid-twentieth century than it had been when the East India Company first seized territory in the 1600s.[11] Yet even then India remained closely tied to the world economy and played a sizeable role in global events. The Indian army supplied millions of men for Allied efforts in both world wars, fighting across Africa and Europe. Holding only a blue British-Indian passport, Indians were free to travel throughout the empire, as Gandhi did when he studied in London then practised law in South Africa. Chants from Gujarati temples still spill out onto the streets of Nairobi and Dar es Salaam in eastern Africa, while the strains of the Gujarati language can be overheard in the school yards of Leicester and Edison, New Jersey. In America, roughly a third of all motels are owned by families of Gujarati descent.[12] Drawn outwards by commerce, 'Gujjus' became India's consummate globalists. In novels and Bollywood movies, they are portrayed as traders and wheeler-dealers, a reputation that extended most obviously to Adani himself.

So rapid had Adani's rise been, and so large did his holdings become, that he eventually attracted the attention of Paranjoy Guha Thakurta, a veteran journalist who made it his business to pore over the dealings of India's more controversial business empires. Guha Thakurta made his name taking on the Ambani brothers in a controversial 2014 book called *Gas Wars: Crony Capitalism and the Ambanis*, which detailed the fierce disputes between the two men's respective energy businesses following their 2005 fallout. In the book he laid out various allegations of cronyism, which both Ambani brothers denied, and which Mukesh Ambani's Reliance Industries countered with an unsuccessful defamation suit. Undeterred, Guha Thakurta turned next to Adani, a man who was viewed by many in India as the purest inheritor of the industrial spirt of the Ambani family. For all Adani's undoubted talents in business, Guha Thakurta questioned whether it was in part his political connections, rather than just his entrepreneurial abilities, that explained the secret behind the tycoon's rapid entry into the upper echelons of the super-rich.

'His is a truly remarkable story,' Guha Thakurta told me a few years after my visit to Mundra. We were sitting drinking tea in his higgledy-piggledy office on the upper floor of a colonial-era home in one of the nicer neighbourhoods in central New Delhi. Guha Thakurta himself looked every inch the agitator, with wild curly hair and the well-worn clothes of an elderly academic. At the time he was editor of the *Economic and Political Weekly*, a storied but generally little-read journal of the Indian left, whose weekly editions were printed on cheap paper and filled with dense argumentation. But while his publication's prose could be heavy going, Guha Thakurta in person talked with great animation, galloping through sentences as he explained the scale of Adani's achievements and the various ways in which he had pushed his way towards to the top of India's billionaire class.

After building Mundra, Guha Thakurta explained, Adani went on to buy or build half a dozen other ports around India, making him the country's largest port owner. He was the largest private electricity producer too, even though he had opened his first coal-fired power station less than ten years before. He was also getting big in solar, having unveiled the world's largest plant in Tamil Nadu in southern India. Even further south, in Australia, close to the Great Barrier Reef, Adani was midway through building a controversial mining and shipping complex, whose vast scale attracted the ire of global environmental groups. Adani's dozens of other corporate entities variously built office parks, traded diamonds and imported oils made from soybeans, sunflowers, mustard and rice. 'He even dominates in fruit!' Guha Thakurta said with a final flourish, noting that one Adani company was India's largest supplier of apples. 'More than almost any billionaire in India, his has been a meteoric rise,' Guha Thakurta told me. 'The question is: just how did he do all this?' And behind that question lay a deeper issue: just how had India's billionaire boom come about in the first place?

A NEW BILLIONAIRES' CLUB

Jayant Sinha first began pondering India's new super-rich during his time at McKinsey, the management consultancy. Sinha joined the firm in the 1990s, eventually rising to become a partner, opening its first office in Mumbai and winning its first Indian clients. He was an adviser who inspired confidence: precise in his language and elegant in his dress, with rimless glasses and neat thinning hair. Although born in India, his accent retained an American twang, the legacy of studying at Harvard Business School and working on the US east coast. Business often took him back to India during the mid-2000s, when the economy and stock market were booming. Back then, as Sinha moved around the upper reaches of his country's business elite, it was not just the quantity of new wealth that struck him, but the way it was being made. 'The more I looked, the more worried I became,' he told me when we met at his home in New Delhi in 2017, but recalling India's business scene more than a decade earlier. 'It was very clear that there was a rigged game going on.'

There were no Indians on *Forbes*'s annual billionaire rankings until the early 1990s. The four Indian-born Hinduja brothers – today the richest family in the UK, with a combined fortune of $15 billion – did make the list, but their businesses were mostly registered in Switzerland or London, so they counted as British.[13] A smattering of names then began to appear, starting with Kumar Mangalam Birla, head of the venerable Birla conglomerate. Dhirubhai Ambani inched his way on next, along with Lakshmi Mittal, a pugnacious steel maker, and Sunil Mittal, a telecoms tycoon, and one of the few men able to challenge Gautam Adani for the title of India's most successful first-generation entrepreneur. Dozens more then joined their ranks after the turn of the millennium, as each year's list came in fatter than the last. Some new arrivals, like Adani, made their own money. Others like Vijay Mallya expanded what they inherited. In 2010 *Forbes* ranked two Indians – Mukesh Ambani and Lakshmi Mittal – among the five richest men in the world.[14] Four years later India's billionaire total crossed the one hundred mark, with Adani's fortune jumping most of all, up $4 billion in that year alone.[15]

But how rich were India's billionaires compared to those in other countries? Nobody seemed to know. In 2008, Sinha tried to find out. Ploughing through old editions of *Forbes*, he typed each tycoon's worth into an Excel sheet, including the size of the economy of their home countries. The results were stunning. Measured relative to gross domestic product, India came second only to Russia for the proportion of national wealth held by its very richest people. 'One tends to think of India as a poor country, and to find that India has a concentration of wealth which is almost literally at the top of the charts was quite astonishing,' Sinha told me of his early research.

Russia boasted eighty-seven billionaires, at a time when the country's economy was worth roughly $1.3 trillion. But Sinha's spreadsheet showed that India came in not far behind, with fifty-five in an economy that at the time was only a fraction smaller. India's ratio was also well ahead of countries like America and Brazil, both of which were known for their stark extremes of wealth.[16] 'We had been running a socialist economy for so long,' Sinha said. 'And in only fifteen or sixteen years we had created this incredible wealth concentration, perhaps more quickly than any country in history.'

Rather than just its quantity, Sinha also wanted to find out how all this new money was being made. The son of Yashwant Sinha, a veteran BJP leader and former Indian finance minister, he grew up well acquainted with politics. At Harvard, he studied under management guru Michael Porter, writing papers examining how Indian businesses used political connections to bend the rules of the Licence Raj. Now he became convinced that something similar was going on once again, as the super-rich reaped excessive profits in ways that reminded him of earlier eras in the United States. Long before he co-authored his 2011 *Financial Times* article on crony capitalism – the one that began my own thinking on the subject of inequality and corruption – Sinha wrote an essay in the weekly Indian magazine *Outlook*, comparing explicitly the 'Barons of America's Gilded Age' and the new Indian elite they resembled.[17] 'Too many businesses were accumulating wealth because of their ability to manage the government rather than manage innovation,' he told me. 'I felt angry. The economy was being manipulated for very few people. This was a collusive system.'

Political risk analyst Ian Bremmer defines emerging economies as those in which 'politics matters at least as much as economic fundamentals for market outcomes'.[18] Businesses in developing nations often struggle to operate in the face of laws and regulations that are neither transparent nor well enforced. Instead they learn to rely on connections and patronage to expand. Before liberalisation India was unusually susceptible to these problems, with its convoluted 'crony socialism' regime of rules and licences. Free market intellectuals hoped this system would wither once these controls were torn down. For a while, heightened competition did indeed push older business houses into relative decline. In their place, initially at least, there rose a new generation of entrepreneurs who seemed better able to grasp the opportunities of India's global era.[19]

Technology outsourcing was one celebrated example, as blue-chip companies in countries like America and Britain began to hire inexpensive software experts in distant Indian cities to fix their IT systems. The story of software group Infosys became the stuff of particular corporate legend, as a group of middle-class engineers, supposedly with just a few hundred dollars in start-up capital, managed to build a world-beating company based in Bangalore, the southern city that became India's technology hub. Founded in the early 1980s, Infosys came of age after liberalisation. Alongside a handful of other big IT businesses, it helped to craft a new image of India as a land of pioneering start-ups and vast call centres. Narayana Murthy and Nandan Nilekani, the company's best-known co-founders, were admired as models of social mobility and ethical practice, as well as being among India's first tech billionaires. It was a throwaway phrase by Nilekani – 'Tom, the playing field is being levelled' – that inspired American journalist Thomas Friedman to write *The World Is Flat*, his breathless 2005 opus hailing a new era of global capitalism.[20] Infosys successes encouraged a new generation too. 'To be successful in commerce here, when I was growing up, you really had to be born into an industrial family,' Meera Sanyal, the former India head of Royal Bank of Scotland, once told me. But billionaires like Infosys's Murthy 'represented a middle-class aspiration to win in business, but do it in a clean way. He became like a beacon of hope.'[21]

Yet it was not long before such hopes began to ebb in the face of darker trends brewing elsewhere in the economy. At the time India was still lauded abroad: a 2006 editorial in *Foreign Affairs* described it as 'a roaring capitalist success story'.[22] But back at home this roaring growth created ideal conditions for corruption. 'Until roughly the year 2000 becoming a billionaire was something that everybody saw as a good thing in India. They saw it as a coming of age,' I was once told by Rajeev Chandrasekhar, a tech entrepreneur turned parliamentarian (and a Lamborghini-driving billionaire himself).[23] The generation who rose in the 1990s mostly amassed their new fortunes in businesses like IT, pharmaceuticals and automotive manufacturing. Those that followed more often operated in sectors with closer ties to the state. 'In the last decade, almost all of the billionaires created in India have been created because of the proximity to politics,' Chandrasekhar said. 'They have been created in specific areas where government policy determines whether you make a billion or you don't.'

Not long after finishing his Excel sheet, Sinha sent it to Raghuram Rajan, the future governor of India's central bank. The two men were both undergraduates at the Indian Institute of Technology, the country's most prestigious engineering college, and had stayed friends in the years since. At the time, Rajan was still teaching economics in Chicago, although he had also just taken a job as an informal adviser to the then prime minister, Manmohan Singh. He was struck by Sinha's research and mentioned it in a speech he gave in Mumbai later in 2008. In that speech, Rajan posed a simple question: 'Is there a threat of oligarchy in India?'[24]

Citing Sinha's data, Rajan argued that there was. Public resources were being gifted to industrialists in increasingly vast quantities, he argued, allowing them to rake in outsized and undeserved profits. 'Three factors – land, natural resources, and government contracts or licences – are the predominant sources of the wealth of our billionaires,' he argued. 'The numbers are alarming – too many people have gotten too rich based on their proximity to the government.' These ideas anticipated almost exactly the corruption scandals that washed over Singh's government a few years later, in which assets like land and coal were found to have been doled out to favoured businesses, creating losses of tens of billions of dollars from the public purse. So deep rooted did these problems become that Rajan eventually coined a new term to describe them: the 'Resource Raj', rather than the Licence Raj, meaning a Russian-style system in which politicians, bureaucrats and industrialists colluded to carve up access to valuable natural resources and shared the proceeds among themselves.[25]

Around the time those scandals were emerging, Michael Walton, an academic at Harvard, decided to tease out more precisely the link between cronyism and the super-rich. British by birth and a political scientist by training, Walton moved to New Delhi in 2007, where his wife worked for the World Bank. Both lived in Mexico beforehand, a country known for the momentous wealth of its plutocrats and the cronyism of its political leaders, many of whom made fortunes during the privatisation of formerly state-owned industries in areas like telecoms and banking. Walton fretted that India was now falling into the same trap. 'I got interested in the striking fact that India had such high levels of billionaire wealth,' he told me. 'The worry that India was going to turn out like Mexico seemed clear.'

Having seen Sinha's spreadsheet and read Rajan's speech, Walton began digging into the *Forbes* data himself. In the mid-1990s, India's billionaires owned assets equivalent to just one per cent of GDP, he found. A decade later that had soared to ten per cent.[26] Walton wanted to know what explained this huge increase. To find out he split the billionaires list into two. The first included companies in sectors that were mostly untouched by government, in which business success was assumed to come mostly from efficiency and innovation. The second featured businesses in what Walton called 'rent-thick' sectors, meaning those where firms made money – or 'rents' – via access to favours. Economists worry about what they call 'rent seeking', meaning the way some businesses earn profits beyond what they could make in a competitive market, for instance by owning the rights to land or resources or intellectual property. Some companies earned rents by lobbying or bribing, others from operating in cartels or as monopolies. The term 'rentier' was sometimes used by left-wing thinkers to describe the same thing, meaning those who grabbed valuable resources, such as licences to drill oil fields or develop real estate. Digging into the data, Walton found a clear pattern. In the early years after its 1991 reforms India's new billionaires operated mostly in areas like IT services, which had little in the way of rent-seeking opportunities. But as the economy took off and globalisation jacked up demand for things like commodities and land, so the wealth of billionaires shot up most of all in rent-thick sectors, from mining and property to cement, infrastructure and telecoms.

Over the years since, the various billionaires' fortunes had ebbed and flowed. Sometimes Walton's data showed them rising to astonishing levels, as in the stock market boom of 2008, when net billionaire wealth ballooned to a stunning twenty-two per cent of GDP. At other times they dipped back, as when India's economy hit a rough patch in 2013 and 2014, a period when many industrialists in rent-thick sectors faced particular struggles. But overall billionaire wealth stayed high and stable, holding steady at roughly a tenth of GDP between 2010 and 2016 – one of the highest levels of any large economy.[27] 'For a very poor country, India is a clear outlier for the wealth owned by billionaires relative to its economy, and one that isn't far behind Russia,' he told me. 'And it's this, more than anything, I think, that has led to all of these comparisons between India today, and the nineteenth-century robber barons of America's Gilded Age'.

Dividing India's billionaires in two was a crude but illuminating exercise. Ruchir Sharma, an author and investor at investment bank Morgan Stanley, did much the same thing when he drew a distinction between what he called 'good and bad billionaires', meaning those who made money through innovation and those who relied on graft and favouritism.[28] In real life these distinctions were often blurry. Men like Mukesh Ambani, Vijay Mallya and Gautam Adani were controversial, but all three were also self-evidently talented managers and deal makers. By contrast, even India's supposedly honest IT tycoons sometimes faced awkward questions about just how they had acquired the land for their software campuses or whether their governance standards were as good as they at first appeared. In 2009, for instance, India suffered one of its worst ever corporate scandals when the software group Satyam Computer went bust in a $1 billion accounting scam that drew comparisons with the collapse of Enron, the disgraced American energy group.

That said, the Bollygarchs tended to be easy to spot. They operated mostly in rent-thick industrial sectors, running tightly controlled family-owned businesses. Their affairs were almost always organised as sprawling conglomerates, rather than narrowly focused enterprises with the kind of distributed shareholding structures common in Western companies. A handful made money in ways that echoed the oligarchs of Russia, snapping up state-owned assets using capital provided by state-owned banks. But most merely operated in sectors that were tied closely to the government, where they could put their connections to good use. There was even a special local word for the tycoons themselves: 'promoters', a term that referred to the individual or family who owned most of the equity in the business and who in turn tightly controlled its operations.

The business of rent-seeking in India led many tycoons to build up sophisticated influence machines. Some, like Vijay Mallya, became politicians themselves. Others created modern versions of the old Reliance Industries 'intelligence agency' in New Delhi, the sophisticated lobbying operation built up over the decades by Mukesh Ambani's father. There were more indirect techniques of influence too, as prominent tycoons expanded their business operations to open hospitals, schools, hotels and newspapers. 'The reason is simple,' as Sharma put it. 'Most people understand it is wrong to take cash bribes, but few in India see much of a problem in accepting gifts in kind, even one as valuable as free medical treatment for a family member, free schooling for a child, free hotel banquet facilities for a niece's wedding, or favourable coverage for one's business or political ambitions in the local rag.'[29]

The picture painted by Sinha and Walton's research was at once exciting and troubling. It showed a new kind of capitalism being built in
India after 1991, and especially in the aftermath of booming growth
and global reintegration of the 2000s. This was far from entirely dominated by cronyism. Large chunks of India's economy remained in the
informal sector, where most Indians still worked as farmers or smallholders. Other areas were dominated by globally competitive firms, in
sectors from e-commerce and IT to media and financial services. Then
there were the 'public sector undertakings', the state-backed giants
which still accounted for perhaps a fifth of national output. But there
was clearly a sizeable portion of the Indian economy in rent-thick
sectors operating 'a unique Indian business model', as one academic
study put it, 'in which cultivating political connections in Delhi became
the core competence and the most important survival imperative for
businesses.'[30]

Sinha, who later went on to win election as a member of parliament
for the BJP and serve as a junior minister under Narendra Modi, blamed
many of India's difficulties at that time on the ruling left-of-centre
Congress Party and its weakness for corruption. But at a deeper level, he
also pointed to a three-way split at the heart of Indian business. First,
there was state capitalism, meaning those many companies that were
still run by the government in areas like steel and mining. Second was
liberal capitalism, meaning those sectors that tended to be most
connected to the global economy, and which were also the most
competitive and least corrupt. Finally, and most troublingly, there was
crony capitalism: the sectors dominated by the Bollygarchs, most of
whom enjoyed deep connections with the state. A fierce battle was
under way between them, Sinha said, one whose outcome would define
the kind of country India would become.

AN UNEQUAL FORTUNE

The rise of India's billionaires mirrored changes that had swept through
the world economy over recent decades, bringing with them new anxieties about inequality. Data compiled by Thomas Piketty showed the
share of national wealth held by the richest Americans hitting levels not
seen since the 1930s.[31] A similar story was true in many advanced

European economies. Yet while hedge fund magnates and Silicon Valley entrepreneurs came to represent the excesses of Western capitalism, it was in countries like India, with its newly powerful Bollygarch class, that the super-rich were expanding quickest of all.

In the mid-2000s, developing countries accounted for around a fifth of the world's 587 dollar billionaires. A decade later that figure had jumped to more than two fifths, while the overall total of billionaires had shot up to 1,645.[32] China made up the largest part of this increase, but India, with its hundred or more billionaires, made a sizeable contribution. India was unusual too for the proportion of national wealth held by its super-rich and the speed at which its fortunes were growing. In 2016 research from Credit Suisse showed that India had 178,000 dollar millionaires, just a fraction of America's total and only a tenth as many as China.[33] But over the coming decades the investment bank predicted the millionaire population would expand more quickly in India than in any other country bar China.[34]

At one level India's billionaire fortunes tracked the overall economy, meaning the wealthiest prospered when India itself was doing well. This was especially true when the stock market rose, inflating the shareholdings of India's 'promoter' tycoons. Some saw this as an example of 'trickle-down' economics – the flip side of an economic package that lifted hundreds of millions of people from poverty in the decades since 1991. A more sophisticated case for optimism, however, came via Caroline Freund, an American economist and former executive at the World Bank. Against those who saw billionaire wealth as a symbol of social dislocation, Freund claimed it was better understood as part of a natural process of economic advancement.

'All countries that have developed rapidly over the past 200 years have experienced some version of this process of "tycoonomics",' she wrote in her 2016 book *Rich People Poor Countries*.[35] The amount of money being made by industrialists like Mukesh Ambani or Gautam Adani might look extraordinary at first. But much the same thing happened in America and Germany during the second half of the nineteenth century, an early era of globalisation in which many entrepreneurs prospered by building up 'mega-firms' closely tied to world markets. Then, as now, their owners were amply rewarded for the risks they took: 'The smartest, pushiest, and luckiest of the founders of this group of firms become the super-rich.'[36]

Freund's argument drew in turn on the changing way economists understand trade. Textbooks tend to describe this as a process between nations: country X makes butter; country Y makes wine; the two exchange for mutual benefit. But more recent research has focused instead on ties between firms, given that more than half of all globally traded goods and services flow through a relatively small number of huge multinational corporations.[37] Most of the goods arriving at Adani's Mundra Port, for instance, would have been sent in and out by large global companies, like car maker Maruti Suzuki, or indeed Adani's businesses themselves.

This insight sounds unremarkable at first, but it had radical implications. In markets like India, foreign multinationals did not just dominate trade. They also provided overwhelmingly the most important source of foreign direct investment. Rather than viewing innovative start-ups and fast-growing small businesses as the most important source of economic growth, this kind of thinking suggested that it was big corporations, and the international supply chains flowing within them, that acted as the true engines of globalisation. Domestically, Indian companies that earned income abroad grew more rapidly than those with purely domestic operations. They created more jobs too, and tended to be more productive. Often their activities helped to restructure the sectors in which they operated – as, for instance, Mukesh Ambani's Reliance did in petrochemicals – forcing local companies to up their game and making entire industries more efficient. Because of this, Freund argued, it was predictable that owners of such companies would make giant fortunes. This fact should be welcomed as an indication of successful economic change.

This more relaxed attitude about the rise of the super-wealthy in turn echoed a wider intellectual tussle between two of India's greatest living intellectuals, the economists Jagdish Bhagwati and Amartya Sen, which in its own way came to define the contours of the country's debates about its own economic progress.

A professor at Columbia University in New York, Bhagwati is a gregarious if sometimes cantankerous free-marketeer, with a waspish sense of humour and a talent for argument. Although most famous for his academic work on trade policy, he began agitating for an end to the Licence Raj from the 1970s, providing the intellectual ballast for many of the market reforms that eventually followed decades later. Now in his eighties, he has long been dogged in the defence of economic liberalisation, pointing out that India's prosperity post-1991 led to sharp reductions in poverty, while poorer Indians also enjoy much higher consumption of basic goods like food and clothing.[38]

Bhagwati tended to downplay worries about inequality, or at least to argue that policies designed to ensure fast economic growth should precede any tilt towards redistribution.[39] More controversially, he also became a vocal enthusiast for Narendra Modi, arguing that the politician's economic successes in Gujarat – with his emphasis on large-scale infrastructure investment and export-focused manufacturing – should provide a template for the rest of the country to follow.[40] His vision of India's future has emphasised a path similar to that taken by China and most other successful east Asian nations, with their focus on industrialisation and trade, an area where India's economy has been notoriously weak.

Sen, perhaps India's most celebrated public intellectual, gave the contrary view: that economic reopening had indeed created a more vibrant economy, but one that was less equal and fair. A kindly Bengali, also in his mid-eighties, he studied first at Cambridge, where he was a contemporary of both Bhagwati and Manmohan Singh. His subsequent career ranged widely across economics and philosophy, from social choice theory to research on famines and sex-selective abortions, all of which contributed to his winning the Nobel Prize in Economics in 1998.

Sen's more recent work, written largely with Belgian economist Jean Drèze, has been sharply critical of India's post-liberalisation record, which for all of its growth has slipped behind that of neighbours like Bangladesh on measures of human development, from child nutrition to the advancement of women.[41] The duo argued that this was mostly the fault of an under-funded and under-developed welfare state, which has in turn contributed to a growing imbalance between rich and poor. In his own way, Sen also looked to the successful 'tiger' economies of east Asia, but mostly because of the way that they grew rich by investing heavily in basic health and education, which in turn helped to provide social support to poorer workers as they moved from farms to factories and onwards into the middle class. Modern India, by contrast, more often looked like an economy in Latin America, with a weak social safety net and yawning inequality.

This argument between Bhagwati and Sen has continued for the best part of a decade, making it hard to adjudicate a victor. Since Modi's arrival as prime minister, Bhagwati's side has been more influential and his arguments have been used by reform advocates within the BJP. Sen, by contrast, has been sharply critical of India's prime minister, both for his economics and for his Hindu nationalist politics, and he has often found himself attacked by Modi's supporters in return. Yet for all of their ferocity, the debates have hidden a peculiar intellectual consensus. On the right, Bhagwati has claimed that growth matters more than its distribution. On the left, Sen has focused on conditions at the bottom. For both, the gap between rich and poor has been secondary. 'Some critics of the huge social inequalities in India find something callous and uncouth in the self-centred lives and inward-looking preoccupations of a relatively prosperous minority,' as Sen wrote in the *New York Review of Books* in 2011. 'My primary concern, however, is that the illusions generated by those distorted perceptions of prosperity may prevent India from bringing social deprivations into political focus.'[42]

Long before it reopened its economy, India was riven by profound divisions between its different religions and castes. There were also stark differences between villages and cities, and between regions, with the more industrialised south and west growing prosperous more quickly than the relatively backward north and east. Anyone visiting for the first time would have concluded that India suffered wide inequalities. Yet the idea persisted that India was actually a relatively egalitarian nation. This was partly a hangover from its decades of socialism, when even its elite earned low incomes by global standards. Indian government data also often focused on consumption, a measure that gave the country a middling position in global rankings of inequality, rather than income or wealth.

More recent research has proved beyond doubt the depths of India's social divide. Churning through new data in 2016, Branko Milanovic, an economist at the World Bank, found India had higher income inequality levels than America, Brazil and Russia, leaving it 'more egalitarian than only South Africa', a country famous for its jarring stratification.[43] Other surveys found similar results.[44] An IMF working paper from the same year showed that India had one the highest and fastest-growing inequality rates in Asia.[45] Its score on the Gini index – a measure of inequality where 0 means total equality and 100 total inequality

– rose from 45 in 1990 to 51 in 2013. China's increased even more quickly, from 33 to 53. But 51 is still unusually high: a level common in Latin America, but far above Asian economies like Japan and South Korea.

The threshold for entry into the wealthiest 'one per cent' differed wildly across countries, according to research from Credit Suisse in 2016. In North America it required $4.5 million in assets; in an average European country $1.4 million. In India the same figure was just $32,892. Yet within that group, the richest one per cent owned fifty-eight per cent of wealth, one of the world's starkest gaps, up from thirty-nine per cent at the start of the decade.[46] Meanwhile the bottom half of the country owned a paltry four per cent.

The reasons for this rising inequality are complicated and economists still disagree about which factors matter most. Some of it stems from positive factors linked to liberalisation, as entrepreneurs built larger companies with links to global markets, making fortunes for themselves and paying higher wages to their workers. Rapid urbanisation and the way in which new technologies rewarded the highly skilled played a role too, boosting incomes among the educated, urban upper middle classes. 'It looks as if a lot of this inequality is coming within urban areas, where the already rich are getting even richer,' I was told by Johanna Schauer, one of the IMF paper's co-authors. Then there were other trends, for instance a growing gap between richer parts of India, such as Kerala in the south, and poorer areas like the heartland state of Bihar.[47] Tens of millions more people could have been lifted from poverty, according to the Asian Development Bank, had these various kinds of inequality not increased so sharply.[48]

Most striking of all was a 2017 paper published by Thomas Piketty, whose opus *Capital in the Twenty-First Century* first raised worries about an era of renewed inequality across the industrialised world. Along with co-author Lucas Chancel, Piketty compiled data from tax records to show that the share of national income taken by India's top one per cent was at its highest level since records began to be collected under the British Raj in 1922. In the West, the relative wealth of the ultra-rich dipped in the mid-twentieth century before bouncing back over the last two decades. India showed the same trend, albeit mostly for different reasons. Most inequality studies had little to say about the super-rich, who are tiny in number and thus hard to capture in research surveys. But Piketty's data also showed the share held by the very richest – the '0.001%', as he called them – shooting up even more quickly.

Echoing Bhagwati, not everyone viewed this widening gap as a problem. One theory – known as the Kuznets curve, after economist Simon Kuznets – suggests that rising inequality is transitory, as most countries become more unequal in their early stages of development and then less so as they grow rich. As a result mainstream economists have often argued that inequality acted as a spur to effort and that in any case it would decline in time. But more recent research, much of it again from the IMF, has begun to overturn this consensus, showing that unequal nations tend to grow more slowly, and are also more prone to financial instability.[49] Countries with sharp economic divisions – for instance between business owners and their workers – also find it harder to create the kind of broad social agreements that can buttress support for structural economic reforms, a point made by Harvard economist Dani Rodrik and others. Countries that become unequal in their early stages of development, such as Brazil, also seem to face greater struggles reversing that trend later.

Back in 2015, I watched Piketty speak at a packed book festival one morning in Mumbai. The economist was given a rock-star reception, even as his thick French accent baffled many in the audience. The rich world had from time to time managed to curb the inexorable rise of inequality, Piketty argued, although this mostly happened only after the violence of world wars and revolutions. The tragedy of these events pushed national elites to accept that the rich should pay more tax and that the poor should receive greater social support. India now had inequality levels that were among the highest in the world, he argued, with no sign of remedial action. Piketty was highly critical of India's political and business class, who he claimed had done little to invest in basic things like healthcare and education, or to ensure that the super-rich paid their fair share in taxes. 'I hope the [Indian] elites understand this,' he said at one point during his talk. 'Because otherwise capitalism is not sustainable.'

A QUIET TYCOON

Gautam Adani's office was unexpectedly modest, housed in a squat glass and steel building set back from a noisy main road in the centre of

Ahmedabad. When I met him in 2013, Adani was not quite what I'd expected either. We met upstairs, in a reception room with light yellow drapes and golden sofas. He was unimposing: not terribly tall, with rounded features and a bulbous nose. His moustache quivered slightly as he spoke, and for a man with such a forceful reputation, he seemed almost withdrawn.

To break the ice, I asked about his background and what it had taught him about business. 'I don't have formal education, but I'm a good listener,' he said quietly. 'I analyse in my own way, in very simple, no-jargon terms.' Later he talked about his dislike of public events. 'Either you are extrovert or introvert, so I am an introvert. I only meet the people that I need to.'[50]

Adani's reticence came through most clearly when I asked about two moments of drama in his life. The first happened in 1997, when he was kidnapped on the outskirts of Ahmedabad by a gang of underworld criminals. The case turned out to be a simple but traumatic case of extortion, as the young industrialist was held hostage for a day, until a ransom was said to have been paid.[51] The second came in November 2008, when terrorist gunmen assaulted the Taj Mahal Palace hotel in Mumbai, where Adani happened to be having dinner. 'I got out only when the commandos entered. My mobile was working so I was trying to contact friends,' was all he would say of a night spent sheltering in a business club on the hotel's first floor, as militants roamed the halls, killing bystanders and setting the building alight. In general, Adani said, he preferred to avoid the limelight. Unlike his fellow Bollygarchs, he avoided flaunting his wealth, living a relatively reclusive life. Until his mother died in 2010, he told me, he had never gone on holiday without her.

Yet while Adani was no Vijay Mallya, he did splash out from time to time, as I discovered a year or so after moving to Mumbai. A delivery man turned up at my apartment one day, and handed over a pink, jewel-encrusted box, about the size of a small briefcase. It contained an invite to the wedding of Adani's eldest son, Karan, and the daughter of Cyril and Vandana Shroff, a husband-and-wife team who headed one of India's largest law firms. Inside there were various sweets and nuts, along with a series of curious charcoal etchings of the happy couple, drawn by the father of the bride. A stiff card provided details of an all-expenses-paid ceremony at a plush resort in Goa, one of a series of celebrations dotted around the country to mark what India's business newspapers had already heralded as the high-society wedding of the year.

My wife and I declined the invitation. We had met neither the bride nor the groom, nor indeed anyone from their respective families. No one had explained that it was quite normal to accept an invitation to a fancy Indian wedding, even if you did not know anyone involved. It was a decision we came quickly to regret, as reports of the ceremony filtered out the next year, including what one newspaper described as its 'Who's the Real Who of India Inc' guest list.[52] The celebrations included a series of lavish parties in venues around the country. The Goa leg was said to have clogged up the state's tiny airport for days, as private jets ferried in a glittering array of corporate big names, including both Ambani brothers, Vijay Mallya and Narendra Modi himself.

Adani shrugged when I mentioned the invite, saying with a smile that all Indians loved big weddings. He talked about his business growth in similarly circumspect terms, describing an expansion that, in his own telling, seemed almost mundane. His first trading business was born of the frustrations of running a factory under the Licence Raj. 'When I required 10 metric tons of raw material, I could hardly get 1 or 1.5 metric tons,' he explained. 'So for four, five, six days I can't run my business, and basically it was closed.' In the mid-1980s he began importing to fill those gaps. After 1991 he went into exports, and as liberalisation opened more sectors to competition he ventured into infrastructure, beginning with ports. He credits that decision to a childhood visit to a government-run facility not far along the coast from Mundra. 'I saw what actually at the time was a small ship, but to me it was like looking at a big, big ship,' he recalled, explaining how the sheer scale of the place had inspired a desire to build one of his own. Gujarat first permitted private sector port operators in the 1990s, allowing Adani to begin his plans for Mundra. He then moved into energy in 2009, growing to become India's largest private sector producer in barely five years.

Some observers found this kind of rapid expansion suspicious. Adani credited it instead to his willingness to take risks, as well as a relaxed attitude to debt. He took cash earned from trading, he explained, and funnelled it into infrastructure projects. When those were finished he used them as collateral to load up more debt to build more projects and so on. This approach left him with a debt pile worth about $14 billion at the time, one of the largest ever built by any Indian company. 'I'm not worried about the debt part,' he said. 'Once you are not investing further, then in five years, the debt will come down.'

Questions about Adani's success focused in particular on Mundra, and the treatment it received during Modi's time as chief minister of Gujarat. Over the years Adani leased thousands of hectares of land from the state government, both for the port and for its neighbouring SEZ. That land came on long leases at low prices, some of which Adani then re-leased at higher rates.[53] Adani denied anything untoward and complained that he was being judged unfairly. 'You can say very well that land has been given to Adani,' he once told a reporter. 'So what? Has Adani taken away land and not developed anything?'[54] Still, scrutiny of the two men's friendship only increased as India's worries about crony capitalism grew. Shares in Adani's own companies rose especially rapidly in the year prior to Modi's election as prime minister, with some more than doubling in value, seemingly on expectations of eventual benevolent treatment.[55]

Accusations of favouritism continued after Modi's victory. About six months into his premiership, Adani joined the prime minister on a trip to a G20 summit in Brisbane. In Australia, the tycoon announced a $1 billion loan agreement with State Bank of India, the country's largest lender, to help finance his coal mine complex near the Great Barrier Reef. That agreement eventually unravelled, but not before it had sparked suspicions that the SBI gave the loan under duress from the government – a charge the administration, the bank and Adani all denied. It was not the first time Adani had faced charges of favouritism. India's government auditor wrote a report in 2012 accusing Modi, as chief minister, of providing cheap fuel from a state-run gas company to Adani and various other businesses.[56] Adani also endured a long court battle over accusations by local residents that he had originally been allowed to build his SEZ at Mundra without proper environmental clearances, charges which the tycoon denied. (His zone secured its various clearances in 2014.)[57]

A further set of allegations were then made by Paranjoy Guha Thakurta, during his time as editor of the *Economic and Political Weekly*. In 2017 Guha Thakurta published a number of articles claiming that Adani's companies had received special treatment on Modi's watch.

One argued the government 'tweaked' rules covering special economic zones, allowing Adani to enjoy a tax windfall.[58] Another said the government failed to follow through on a tax department investigation into Adani's trading of gold and diamonds.[59] Adani's company denied wrongdoing and sent a notice claiming defamation to the magazine over the first article, which the magazine subsequently removed from its website. Guha Thakurta stood by his stories, but resigned as editor following a row with the publication's owners over its response to Adani's complaints. Whatever the truth of his claims, his decision to step down prompted sharp criticism, both of the magazine, for not standing behind their editor, and of Adani, for his legal tactics, which did not result in further court action. Led by Amartya Sen, a group of more than a hundred academics wrote an open letter in protest at the magazine's decision. 'Legal notices have unfortunately become the standard means used to intimidate and suppress investigative journalism,' the letter said.[60]

Both Adani and Modi have consistently rebuffed suggestions of anything improper in their dealings. Still, many experts remained sceptical about their state's corruption-free image. 'Gujarat wasn't as bad as other places, but there is this image that Gujarat was like a kind of Singapore, which is rubbish,' I was once told by Aditya Mukherjee, a left-leaning historian who studied the relationship between business and politics at New Delhi's Jawaharlal Nehru University. 'The state still had a model of business in which you could grow hugely with the help of government favours and in return businesses would pour money into the political system.' Here Adani and Modi enjoyed at least a marriage of convenience: the mega-project-obsessed politician and the ambitious young industrialist, both gradually becoming indispensable to one another.

When we spoke, Adani bristled at any suggestion that his expansion had been helped along by preferential treatment. 'Modi is not directly helping any individual, that I can tell you. Modi is helping industries through policy,' he told me, pointing out that his original plans for Mundra had pre-dated Modi's arrival in office. He was critical too of those who complained about India's government. 'Our philosophy as a group is we never go and cry to the government that "you have promised this and you have not done this". We never do that. We always go along with the government . . . Irrespective of whatever we say about corruption and other things, at end of the day, they [the government] also want to see development.' Throughout our conversation, Adani's admiration for his friend the politician was clear. 'We like Modi not because he's helping on x, y and z, but because we like his kind of character,' he said. 'Once he's convinced himself that this is good for his state he will stand by you.'

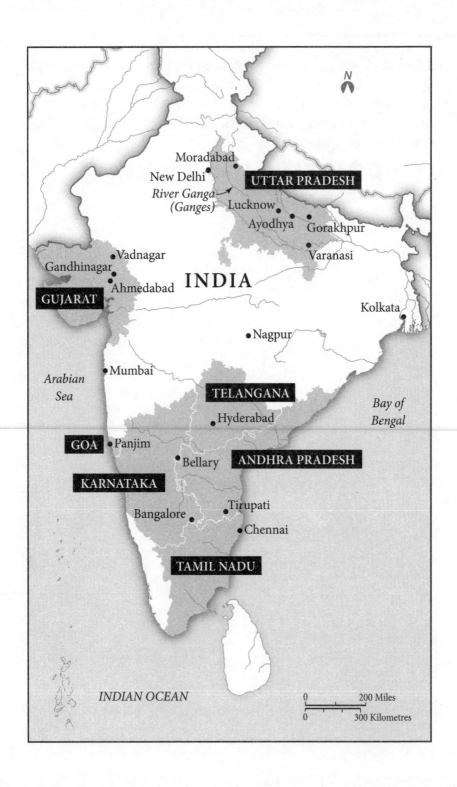

PART 2

POLITICAL MACHINES

More than one thousand died when mobs of extremist Hindus attacked Muslims during communal rioting in Gujarat in 2002, leaving a lasting stain on then chief minister Modi's reputation.

CHAPTER 4

INDIA MODIFIED

THE TSUNAMO

Ringed by armed guards, Narendra Modi pushed through the throng and ducked into a silver-coloured jeep. It was the afternoon of 16 May 2014 – election results day – and already the scale of his triumph was becoming clear. Hundreds of supporters began gathering that morning at the BJP's Gujarat headquarters, their numbers swelling with each passing hour. Men in orange shirts danced in the outer courtyard as victory reports filtered in. Confetti floated through the air. Modi's image was everywhere, gazing down from posters and staring out of cardboard face masks. A bearded lookalike stood at the back, posing politely for selfies. The crowd surged as the real Modi emerged later that afternoon, lifting me off my feet as we pushed nearer to the car. Hands holding smartphones reached out as the jeep inched towards the exit, eager for a photograph of the leader within. Dressed in a waistcoat and smart blue and white shirt, Modi looked impassive in the passenger seat, as if contemplating the magnitude of his win. A perfunctory wave brought one final cheer from the crowd, the gates opened and the man who was soon to be India's fourteenth prime minister sped away.

I had taken the hour-long flight from Mumbai early that morning, on what was already a painfully hot day in one of the warmest months of the year. Traffic moved easily up the neat six-lane highway north from the airport towards Gandhinagar, the state capital and Modi's long-time seat of power. Small scenes of his achievements as chief minister zipped by the window, from technology parks and glass office buildings to the

Mahatma Mandir, a giant convention centre named after Mahatma Gandhi, who was born in the state and for much of his life lived in a modest ashram nearby. The scene was prosperous and orderly; a model for the country Modi aspired to lead. Over the previous year he had criss-crossed India delivering rousing speeches attacking corruption and economic mismanagement. It was the most expensive election campaign the country had ever seen, and Modi's message was simple: the ruling Congress, once the party of the poor, now stood firmly on the side of the super-rich. At its conclusion, more than half a billion people lined up at nearly one million polling stations, in a voting process that stretched out over a month.[1] And as the largest democratic exercise in human history wrapped up that afternoon in May, even fervent BJP supporters struggled to come to terms with the scale of their win and what it would mean for the man the newspapers now referred to simply as 'NaMo'.

The BJP headquarters was a modern three-storey building not far from the Sabarmati River. Party flags with lotus flower logos hung limply around the perimeter walls, as if wilting in the heat. Television vans idled outside when we arrived earlier that morning, their crews sheltering in the shade of a few nearby trees. A mural on the floor inside the compound featured a map of India made of multicoloured sand, alongside an image of Modi's face ringed with flowers. Supporters in the crowd outside lavished praise on their leader. 'India needs Modi,' Vivek Jain, a teller in a local bank, told me when I walked back outside. A fervent admirer, he had taken the day off, and rode up on his motorbike to join the celebrations. He wore faded blue jeans and a rumpled white shirt, over which he had slipped a cardboard singlet with the slogan 'NaMo: Education for everyone'. Others quickly chimed in. Modi understood ordinary people, having been born into a poor family. He was honest and would bring an end to corruption in New Delhi. He brought development to Gujarat and would do the same for India. He had neither children nor close family – barring his elderly mother, to whom he was devoted, and at whose house he had spent much of that morning – so there was no risk that his rule would degenerate into dynasty, as the Congress had done. 'All the people of India want this same development he had brought here to us [in Gujarat],' Jain said, finally. 'He will make India work again and stop all this crony stuff that has been going on.'

Gujarat held a special place in India's political imagination long before Modi became chief minister. His muscular brand of Hindu nationalism shared little with the secular pacifism of earlier nationalist leaders like Gandhi and Nehru. But the BJP leader still often mentioned Gandhi in his speeches, along with the special role their state played in the fight against imperialism, notably during the salt march of 1930, a celebrated act of civil disobedience in which the Mahatma led a procession in protest against a salt tax levied by the British. Under Modi's leadership the state then acquired a new image, this time as a beacon of economic development. Elsewhere in India businesses struggled to find land, suffered power cuts and saw their expansion plans frustrated by corruption. In Gujarat the lights stayed on, land was easier to come by and the bureaucrats were mostly honest, for fear that their stern chief minister would find out if they were not.

On Modi's watch the state built irrigation canals, laid highways and fixed a bankrupt electricity system. He had a knack for drawing in investment from abroad, presiding over Chinese-style double-digit growth rates. Economists hailed his 'Gujarat model' for combining export-focused manufacturing with efficient agriculture and modern services.[2] Foreign investors were equally enamoured. 'We've had the usual small issues with water and power,' one executive from Ford told me back in 2013, as the car group readied to open a $1 billion factory in the state. 'But when that happens we all go and see the principal secretary of industry and mines, and he says: "Hey, you guys, go and get this fixed!"' With its dirty air and traffic-clogged streets, Ahmedabad was far from perfect. But the city still looked different from the typical chaos of urban India, with its orderly system of bus lanes and plans to turn the banks of the Sabarmati into a series of supposedly Parisian-style riverside paths.

To supporters like Jain, Modi seemed a natural choice as prime minister, but even the day before the result his victory remained in doubt. The BJP christened his campaign 'Mission 272', the number of seats needed for a majority in the lower house of parliament, the Lok Sabha. Many analysts thought this target improbable; the BJP had only managed at most 182 seats in earlier elections. But on that afternoon it won a stunning 282, the first time any party other than the Congress had managed to win more than half of the seats on offer.[3] The Congress itself was humiliated, reduced to a rump of just forty. In India, this was what a landslide looked like – or a 'TsuNaMo' as one headline put it.[4]

'Narendra Modi has scripted one of the most gloriously spectacular political triumphs,' wrote Pratap Bhanu Mehta, a respected political commentator, the following day. 'He was an outsider, demonised by the intelligentsia, with a central government arrayed against him. But he has broken through and will now produce the biggest churning that India's power structure has seen since Independence.'[5] Modi tapped into a powerful dissatisfaction brewing within India, as its people grew angry at the greed of the political class and the industrialists with whom they conspired. Back in Gujarat, having seen their leader leave, Modi's supporters dispersed, joining thousands of others around the city, waving flags from the back seats of motorcycles and dancing happily on street corners. Around the rest of the country many felt less jubilant, however, and reflected upon a simple question: how did the most controversial leader in modern Indian history, a man even many of his own supporters thought too divisive to win, get to the position of becoming prime minister in the first place?

BAL NARENDRA

A little more than a year later a friend and I drove the three hours north from Ahmedabad to Vadnagar, the town of Modi's birth, on a damp monsoon morning. The trappings of modernity thinned out as we left the city. Neat pots of rose-coloured flowers disappeared from the road-side as the highway narrowed from four lanes to two, and eventually just one. Camels pulling blue trailers piled high with wood trudged down the verge, alongside occasional groups of women, balancing pails of water on their heads. Little more than a village in Modi's youth, Vadnagar was now a bustling small town, filled with half-finished build-ings propped up by bamboo scaffolding. Hole-in-the-wall shops selling mobile phone cards dotted the town centre, while its road junctions were festooned with adverts for cement. The tops of ruined temples poked out between the construction, hinting at an older settlement, now mostly forgotten: a minor centre of Buddhism in the seventh century and then later a medieval trading hamlet around which the modern town had spilled out.[6]

Modi's father Damodardas was born around 1915 into an unremark-able lower caste, the Ghanchi. By tradition they earned a living extracting and pressing cooking oils. Today they are officially designated as 'backward' under the government system that ranks India's castes, placing Modi firmly in the lower half of India's social scale. Modi has talked rarely about his earliest village days, although a few fables have emerged nonetheless, notably via *Bal Narendra*, a comic book of uncertain authorship recounting tall tales from his childhood. Its colourful cartoon panels showed the young Narendra saving a friend from drowning in the town's crocodile-infested lake, and then later bringing a baby crocodile back to his home, to the consternation of his mother. At one point he is congratulated for a staging a play to raise funds to repair a school wall; at another he helps a teacher to identify a bully by secretly marking his shirt with blue ink. At home he is dutiful and helpful with chores, but also resourceful. 'I should keep this washed shirt under my pillow, so that all the creases are gone,' a thought bubble shows the young Modi thinking, lying at night beneath a kerosene lamp on a neat single bed.

The bully story drew a blank look from one of his actual teachers, Hiraben Modi, a former primary school instructor, who was by then well into her eighties. The name Modi was common in the area, but she said she wasn't a relation. Sitting in her modest three-room home, a few streets from the one in which Narendra Modi grew up, she recalled a confident, if not exceptional, young student. 'He used to do homework properly, he was disciplined,' she told me. In a dingy homeware shop not far away, Jasood Pathan, a childhood friend, described a happy and harmonious upbringing in which young Muslim boys like him played happily with Hindus like Modi. Surrounded in his store by racks of Chinese-made torches and boxes of brass locks, he recalled youthful days of kite-flying, swimming in the lake and impish attempts to distract the musicians who played during wedding celebrations. 'We were quite naughty, and did a lot of mischief together,' he said, smiling.

The reality was almost certainly less idyllic. When Modi was born in September 1950, Vadnagar was small and poor, without power or running water. Schooling was basic and medical care limited. There was little contact with the rest of the country, beyond the occasional Bollywood movie and the town's railway line, which brought trains up and down from Ahmedabad. Back then the average Indian would die not long after thirty. Fewer than one in five could read or write.[7] 'I had a lot of pain because I grew up in a village where there was no electricity and in my childhood we used to face a lot of hardships,' Modi once told his biographer in a rare candid comment.[8] The tiny home he shared with his six siblings still stands in a narrow muddy street close to the heart of the old town, although his family no longer owns it. It was sold on after their father passed away, Modi's younger brother Prahlad told me later: 'When we were there it was not a cement house and on the rooftop there were still iron sheets.' The new owners added brick walls, an extra floor and a proper roof.

Before Modi's election in 2014, all but one of India's prime ministers had been drawn from the upper ranks of the caste system. Rather than play down his modest heritage, however, Modi fashioned from it perhaps the defining image of his campaign: the place he took as a child helping his father to sell tea from their family's wooden stall, next to Vadnagar railway station. This image was a relatively recent invention. People in Ahmedabad who followed Modi's career told me the tea story began featuring in his speeches only around 2012, when he was first positioning himself as a national political figure. Before then he almost never discussed his family background. 'No one really knows the real Narendra Modi,' the *Times of India* said of him in 2007, during his second term as chief minister. 'He even dines alone.'[9] By 2014, however, Modi referred proudly and often to his humble beginnings: the lower-caste birth; the boy who swam bravely in the crocodile-infested lake; the sacrifices he made leaving his family for a life in politics; and especially the story of the humble son of a *chai-wallah* who now yearned to lead a nation.

The town's lake was still there, although the crocodiles had long since disappeared. Damodardas's tea stall was gone too, but half a dozen much like it stood on a muddy roundabout just outside the train station, with a large tree at its centre. A handful of auto-rickshaws idled hopefully nearby. Modi's basic high school was a few streets away. Inside the station, little had changed, with just one platform and a narrow single track. A few travellers sheltered from the drizzle beneath a corrugated iron awning, painted in yellow and with the town's name spelled out in black script. 'The school was just opposite the railway station, so during the recess, sometimes we brothers would go to the tea stall, but most of the time it was just Narendra,' Modi's brother told me. Just a handful of trains would come each day. 'He would go to the stall, take the kettle and the cups, and walk down the carriage asking if anyone wants to take tea.' In *Bal Narendra*, the scene is recreated with added pathos. Kettle in hand, Modi pours tea for two men in uniform sitting inside a carriage. The caption reads: 'A patriotic Narendra ensured to the best of his ability that no *jawan* [soldier] was left unreplenished.'

Rather than the station platform, it was the old village parade ground nearby that had the most profound influence on Modi's youth. From the age of eight he returned home each day, threw down his satchel and headed out to attend the *shakha* (branch) meetings of the Rashtriya Swayamsevak Sangh (RSS) – the Hindu religious organisation that in time gave birth to the BJP. Anyone watching would have seen a group of stick-carrying uniformed men and boys, dressed in khaki shorts, engaging in communal calisthenics and singing patriotic songs. Founded in 1925, the RSS began its existence with a seemingly innocuous focus on charitable works and religious brotherhood. Its name translates simply as 'National Volunteer Organisation'. Today it describes itself as the world's largest non-governmental body, with perhaps five million members, and more than fifty thousand groups nationwide.[10] Although it does not field candidates, the RSS wields enormous political influence, not least because its members act as field organisers for the BJP. Many prominent BJP politicians, like Modi, have deep backgrounds in the movement. Yet few institutions evoke more distrust among Indian liberals, many of whom view the RSS, with its forceful religious views and paramilitary aesthetic supposedly modelled on the imperial British army, as proto-fascist in nature.[11]

As it developed the RSS pushed a vision of Hinduism that stood in implicit opposition to the secular multiculturalism of moderates like Gandhi and Nehru.[12] Its followers, known as *swayamsevaks*, were inspired instead by the theory of *Hindutva*, or Hindu-ness, which argued that Indian identity and the Hindu faith were inextricably intertwined. Rejecting the divisions of caste, it formally claimed as Hindus all those whose religions viewed India as their spiritual homeland: a typology that included Sikhs and Jains, but pointedly excluded Muslims and Christians, who today make up about fourteen per cent and two per cent of the population respectively.[13] It was an idea that had its most tragic consequence when Nathuram Godse, a *Hindutva* ideologue and former RSS activist, assassinated Gandhi in 1948, shooting him in the chest as he made his way to an evening prayer meeting. Nehru outlawed the organisation, claiming 'these people had the blood of Mahatma Gandhi on their hands', one of three occasions on which the group has been banned since Independence.[14] But a year later it was allowed to re-form. In the years that followed it went on to spawn a wider family of Hindu nationalist organisations, known as the Sangh Parivar, covering everything from trade unions and farmers' organisations to youth and student groups, and eventually the BJP itself.

Jasood Pathan, Modi's childhood companion, played down the idea that his young friend had been a young Hindu fanatic, telling me that many young boys in Vadnagar attended RSS meetings, mostly to stave off boredom. Still, Modi clearly warmed to the sense of brotherhood and purpose the organisation provided. Pathan recalled his young friend taking inspiration from his parade ground meetings to give impromptu talks in school about the need to respect India's military. 'It would last ten to fifteen minutes, and he talked about the duties of the soldier,' he said. 'It was well received.' *Hindutva* also instilled in Modi a sense of his place in a great civilisation led astray, as the RSS taught him that India had been traduced first by Muslim invaders under the Mughal Empire, then by British colonialists, and finally by the modern, English-speaking elites of New Delhi, with their exotic notions of secularism and socialism. The RSS's martial nationalism introduced him to broader influences too: first the nineteenth-century monk Swami Vivekananda, whose visits to America helped Hinduism gain recognition as a world religion; and then Vinayak Savarkar, whose 1923 book *Hindutva: Who Is a Hindu?* made him the movement's theologian and one of Modi's intellectual heroes.[15] Many of the core tenets of the RSS – the importance of family, duty to the nation, social order, cleanliness and personal honesty – were plain to see in Modi's speeches, as was the unbending line he would later take on corruption.

The confidence Modi took from the RSS almost certainly contributed to the most singular episode of his young life, when he left home in his late teens after a family row. As a toddler he was designated to marry a girl called Jashodaben from a nearby village, part of a local tradition of child marriage. As adulthood approached the time came to formalise and consummate the union. The couple undertook a ceremony when Modi was eighteen and she one year younger, apparently against his wishes.[16] One day not long afterwards he abandoned his young wife, beginning a two-year pilgrimage. 'I loitered a lot in the Himalayas,' he told his biographer. 'I had some influences of spiritualism at that time along with the sentiment of patriotism – it was all mixed. It is not possible to delineate the two ideas – I was also unclear at that stage about what I wanted to do.'[17] Eventually he returned home carrying just a small bag of clothes. The joy of his mother at her son's return was short lived: he stayed for a single night, before packing up his bag again and leaving for good.[18] Of his marriage he said nothing for decades, declining to disclose it even to the RSS and admitting to his wife's existence only in 2014, just before he ran for national office.[19]

Back in Ahmedabad I met Modi's younger brother Prahlad, now a successful businessman, who lived in a leafy suburb on the edge of the city. Garlanded images of Hindu deities decorated the walls of his living room, as he and his wife sipped coffee sitting on plush cream-coloured sofas. Prahlad wore a light brown *kurta*, with gold-rimmed spectacles perched on his nose. He looked strikingly like his brother, with the same slightly puffy lips and closely trimmed salt-and-pepper beard, although he was both welcoming and avuncular, where his elder sibling was said to be withdrawn and distant. Having left home, Prahlad explained that his brother moved to Ahmedabad, where he worked briefly at a second tea stall, owned by one of their uncles. 'Narendra did not like it, which is why he quit,' he told me. Instead, Modi joined the RSS as a full-time volunteer. 'He went very deep into the RSS and its works on nation building and patriotism . . . And then he decided to dedicate his life to that.'

Modi lived in the group's Ahmedabad headquarters, sleeping on a mattress on the floor, running errands for senior members and leading a modest life as a teetotal, vegetarian, celibate bachelor. He rose quickly, becoming a *pracharak*, or propagandist, and falling deeper into the group's lifestyle of discipline and abstinence. Visits from women were strictly forbidden. His three brothers saw him rarely. He returned to Vadnagar 'for a few hours' when his father died in 1999, but beyond that almost never went back to his childhood home.[20] Prahlad referred respectfully to his elder sibling as *bhai*, meaning 'brother', even as he explained that Modi had cut off ties with almost all relatives, except their mother. At one point as we talked Prahlad's gangly teenage son walked in to say hello, dressed in relaxed Western-style sports clothes. His son had barely met his famous uncle, Prahlad explained. No family member attended Modi's swearing-in as prime minister in New Delhi. 'The last time we saw him was back in 2007,' he said. 'Narendra *bhai* had won re-election, and was being sworn in as chief minister, and we came to watch.'

As a *pracharak*, Modi travelled from town to town, sometimes on foot and sometimes by scooter, spreading the RSS message and developing the mesmerising speaking style that would in time become his trademark. Yamal Vyas, an accountant and now a BJP spokesman, recalled Modi visiting his family's home in the 1980s, to seek a meal and proselytise on the issues of the day. 'He was a canvasser . . . A kind of marketing man,' he told me, sitting in a cramped office in Ahmedabad. Modi and other organisers were forced into hiding when the RSS was banned once again during the Emergency, Indira Gandhi's authoritarian period of rule by decree between 1975 and 1977, in which liberties were suspended and opponents jailed. Sometimes he was forced to travel incognito from city to city; a rare black and white photograph from the period shows the young Modi disguised as a Sikh, complete with a dark black beard, sunglasses and a white turban.[21] Throughout this period he managed the printing and distribution of anti-Emergency pamphlets, becoming an important cog in the RSS's political resistance, and in the process fomenting a lifelong hatred of Indira Gandhi's Congress party.

With democracy restored in the spring of 1977, Modi's profile within the RSS began to rise further. He authored a pamphlet about the Emergency, and spent time both at RSS headquarters in Nagpur in central India and then in New Delhi, at the heart of its political operation. Even back then those who knew Modi say he stood out for his confidence: a man who could be at once argumentative and charming, belligerent and persuasive. He dressed sharply too, wearing a neatly trimmed beard in contravention of strict RSS rules on personal dress. 'Other people used to come, but I don't remember their names,' Vyas said, recalling the times Modi would turn up to talk at his parents' house. 'He used to be a little different, even then, in the way he carried himself.'

Modi's growing profile saw him drafted into the BJP in the mid-1980s, not long after it had been founded. Established as a broadly centre-right alternative to the Congress, the party drew support from conservative upper-caste groups and small business owners, as well as Hindu ideologues. Modi proved adept at organising, with a particular talent for elections, where he kept tabs on party candidates dotted around his home state. 'Between 5 a.m. and 8 a.m. he used to sit at the BJP office and tell four or five young boys to sit on different telephone

lines,' Vyas told me, describing Modi's role in the early 1990s. 'Most of
the candidates would be sleeping when they called, so it would take
four or five minutes to get on the line. So when they were waking
them up, he would talk to one or two others.' Such efforts helped Modi
build ties with other national leaders. The most significant of these
came in 1990, when Modi helped to organise the *Ram Rath Yatra*, a
rabble-rousing procession led by L. K. Advani, a prominent BJP politician.[22] Advani travelled across India in a Toyota truck redecorated to
resemble the chariots described in Hindu myths and legends, agitating for the construction of a temple to the Hindu god Ram on the site
of the ancient Babri Masjid mosque in the holy city of Ayodhya in
Uttar Pradesh. The journey would have profound and violent consequences, culminating two years later when rampaging Hindu activists
destroyed the mosque, throwing India into one of its bloodiest periods of communal strife.[23]

By that time Modi had already developed a firebrand reputation of his
own, as an enforcer and hardliner; a man capable of whipping up a crowd.
He prospered as the BJP itself grew stronger, taking power first in the state
of Gujarat, then briefly at the national level in 1996, and again two years
later under Prime Minister Atal Bihari Vajpayee. Gujarat itself became a
kind of laboratory for the spread of Hindu nationalism, a place where
Modi could find other *Hindutva* ideologues, fearful about the weakening
of Hindu civilisation and the risks of being overrun by Christians and
Muslims. Ashis Nandy, a left-wing social theorist, interviewed him
around this time during his years as a *pracharak*. In an essay published in
2002, Nandy claimed to have identified an unbending 'authoritarian
personality', driven by hardline convictions. 'I still remember the cool,
measured tone in which he elaborated a theory of cosmic conspiracy
against India that painted every Muslim as a suspected traitor and a
potential terrorist. I came out of the interview shaken.'[24]

NO APOLOGIES

Just before 8 a.m. on 27 February 2002, a packed train pulled into the
town of Godhra in the east of Gujarat, about 120 kilometres from
Ahmedabad. On board were hundreds of Hindu pilgrims returning
from Ayodhya, the holy city whose Babri Masjid mosque had been

destroyed ten years earlier. Other trains packed with worshippers and activists had gone along the same line in the days beforehand, returning from demonstrations in favour of building a new Ram temple on the mosque's ruined site. This procession caused tension with local Muslims, who lived and worked near the station. On that morning those tensions boiled over as the train was set alight, either deliberately or accidentally, depending on which account you believe.[25] Hours later, rescuers removed fifty-nine charred bodies from the carriages.[26]

News of the deaths reached Modi in the chief minister's office later that day. In the evening he agreed to an official 24-hour period of mourning, a decision critics would later paint as an invitation to street protests.[27] Community tensions in India were already heightened, as Hindus worried about the rise of a newly militant breed of global Islam in the aftermath of America's September 11th attacks. Angry mobs took to the streets of Ahmedabad, convinced that Godhra had been a bloody act of mass murder against pious Hindu pilgrims, beginning a three-day orgy of violence. Around the city, Muslim homes were looted, shops burned and mosques destroyed. Armed men roamed Muslim neighbourhoods performing acts of medieval brutality: mass killings, mutilations of corpses, and the rape of women and girls. The riots were the first in India to play out live on television, horrifying viewers with their savagery. Twenty thousand Muslim homes and businesses were destroyed, along with 360 places of worship. Some 150,000 people were displaced as violence spread around the state. An official report later said that 1,044 died in the carnage, although estimates from human rights groups and others suggested a death toll more than twice as high.[28]

What many referred to as a pogrom – an orchestrated massacre with official support, rather than simply disorganised rioting – left a lasting stain on Modi's reputation. His supporters gave excuses: he was inexperienced, having been appointed as chief minister only a few months before; he brought the killing under control within three days, where previous Indian riots raged for far longer; he himself bore no direct responsibility. Yet critics still blamed him for doing too little to stop the bloodshed, much of which was orchestrated by members of his own Hindu nationalist movement,[29] accusing the chief minister of negligence at best and even complicity at worst. Two months after the violence the charity Human Rights Watch produced 'We Have No Orders to Save You', a detailed report laying out how extreme Hindu groups helped to organise the killing.[30] The rioters 'came armed with swords, *trishuls* (three-pronged spears associated with Hindu mythology), sophisticated explosives, and gas cylinders,' it said. 'They were guided by computer printouts listing the addresses of Muslim families and their properties, information obtained from the Ahmedabad municipal corporation among other sources, and embarked on a murderous rampage confident that the police was with them.'

Many find it hard to credit that Modi, a leader renowned for his exacting organisation, had no idea who was behind the violence and could not have done more to bring it quickly under control. Instead, Modi's accusers say his actions permitted the killing to proceed in order to placate furious Hindus and also to teach the state's restive Muslims a lesson. A decade later, Sanjiv Bhatt, a senior police officer who served during the riots, told a court that Modi instructed security chiefs to let Hindus 'vent their anger', although Modi very strongly denied this and Bhatt himself was later fired.[31] Human Rights Watch suggested that Modi only intervened directly once the killing had escalated out of control. 'The most disturbing feature was the complicity of officers of the law at all levels,' Harvard University's Martha Nussbaum, a fierce Modi critic, went so far as to claim a year after the riots.[32]

There has never been a full independent investigation into the events of 2002, so Modi's personal role has never been conclusively determined. It probably never will be. For his critics his guilt is unquestioned. That view had been shared until relatively recently by many foreign governments. Modi's presumed actions during the violence led him to be banned from visiting America in 2005. He was also discouraged from visiting Britain and other countries, restrictions that were lifted only around the time he became prime minister.[33] For his supporters, Modi's innocence is also beyond doubt. In 2011, the Supreme Court found no evidence of his direct involvement, as part of a case brought by the widow of a Congress politician who had been brutally murdered during the mayhem. Two years later Modi was cleared by a second court. 'God is great,' he tweeted after the verdict, before organising a three-day public fast, an event supposedly in support of communal harmony that looked suspiciously like a victory celebration.

Modi has never truly escaped the controversies of 2002, although he worked diligently to rehabilitate his image. Inspired by the examples of Singapore and South Korea, he began to downplay the fervent views of his youth and converted instead to the cause of economic development. Bringing a taste of autocratic east Asia to India, he dedicated himself to the cause of manufacturing facilities, highways and power stations. He launched a glitzy new 'Vibrant Gujarat' investor jamboree, in which India's tycoons trooped into the Mahatma Mandir convention centre, paying homage to Modi and unveiling billions of dollars in pledges for his state. He improved his faltering English too, the better to strike deals with visiting foreign chief executives. His was a no-nonsense, no-dissent style of rule. 'His lovers and haters share an essentially identical impression of the man,' as essayist Vinod Jose once observed. 'Both believe Modi possesses an almost absolute authority and a willingness to defy institutions and rules, as a strong and charismatic leader who "gets things done" without concern for protocol or established hierarchies.'[34]

Modi's record as chief minister was not a simple one, however. For all its pristine highways and new fibre-optic cables, his state ranked less impressively when judged by its numbers of malnourished or under-educated children, a point often made by critics like Amartya Sen.[35] Modi was known for his personal probity, but his record was still tainted by scandals involving the abuse of state power, from deploying security services to harass opponents to police involvement in waves of extrajudicial killings. Modi also did precious little to promote reconciliation with Muslims in the aftermath of 2002, as he built one of India's most economically powerful but socially segregated states, its cities dotted with fearful Muslim-only enclaves. Modi's own tailor was struck by the fact that the chief minister, who so often gave speeches dressed in brightly coloured outfits, would never wear green, a colour deeply associated with Islam.[36]

The Modi who ran for national office in 2014 was nonetheless a changed man from the forceful religious figure of old. Having won re-election as Gujarat's chief minister for a third time in 2012, he moved quickly to consolidate power within his own party. Many of the elderly politicians who traditionally dominated the BJP were sceptical about Modi, viewing him as too divisive to win a national election in which he would have to gain support far outside the party's traditional base. Yet these grandees proved surprisingly easy to dismiss, as Modi drew on his image as a hero to the party's Hindu nationalist base to push his opponents aside. Modi then drew on his record as an honest technocrat in Gujarat to present himself as the solution to India's problems of corruption and economic under-performance. His election manifesto barely mentioned the tropes of Hindu nationalism, from the construction of Ram temples to the protection of cows, which many Hindus consider sacred. Instead the document was packed with populist slogans about development. As political scientist Ashutosh Varshney noted, this was a conscious attempt to create 'Modi the moderate', a leader whose earlier divisive rhetoric was now absent.[37]

That moderate turn never did extend to 2002, however, a topic about which Modi remained firmly defensive. As he positioned himself for national office, many predicted he would be forced to make some kind of a symbolic statement of apology, if only to soften his image and prevent his opponents using the riots to attack him. Occasionally he did express a mild form of regret. 'I was shaken to the core,' he wrote in 2013. 'Grief, sadness, misery, pain, anguish, agony, mere words could not capture the absolute emptiness one felt on witnessing such inhumanity.'[38] Previously he had compared his feelings during the riots to those of a passenger in a car that accidentally runs down a dog, an analogy many in India found offensive. 'If someone else is driving a car and we're sitting behind, even then if a puppy comes under the wheel, will it be painful or not? Of course it is,' he told an interviewer.[39] But on no occasion did he take personal responsibility or offer a broader show of contrition. The BJP appeared to calculate that any apology would lose as much support as it gained. Such was Modi's confidence in his own appeal that he guessed India would vote for him anyway. He did not want to say sorry. In the end, he did not have to.

THE LAST MAN

Modi was sworn in as prime minister at a grand ceremony in New Delhi a few weeks after his election victory. It was a baking afternoon in late May and half a century to the day after the death of Jawaharlal Nehru. This was an irony not lost on the more liberal quarters of India's political establishment, many of whom feared their latest prime minister would soon begin to demolish the secular edifice built by its first. Yet while the magnitude of Modi's victory settled definitively the question of his electability, it introduced a new mystery about the kind of national leader he would become: a reform-minded Indian variant of Singapore's Lee Kuan Yew, focused solely on economic development and committed to communal harmony, or a more extreme figure whose earlier antipathy toward minorities would re-emerge once he opened the door to the nation's highest office?

Before his victory, India's newspapers had salivated over the prospect of a 'Modi versus Rahul' battle, as the BJP leader went head-to-head with Rahul Gandhi, Nehru's grandson. The battle quickly disappointed, however, as Modi painted Gandhi, the handsome but inexperienced Congress figurehead, as an incompetent dynast unfit for high office. The two campaigns were poorly matched too, as an exhausted Congress struggled to counter Modi's sophisticated campaign apparatus. 'People don't get that in India there are three different campaigns,' Praveen Chakravarty, a political analyst with ties to the Congress, told me during the 2014 election. 'You have the nineteenth-century India of the villages, the twentieth century of the urban middle classes, and now the youth of twenty-first-century India, who use smartphones and want to communicate online.' Modi targeted all three, using mass rallies to reach the first and spending heavily on television adverts for the second. A blanket social media campaign then sought out younger voters via Facebook pages, WhatsApp messages and a new 'NaMo' YouTube channel. Christophe Jaffrelot, a political scientist, dubbed the result a 'Modi-centric' campaign, with an unprecedented presidential air. 'Modi was projected as the sole leader of the BJP,' he wrote. 'The party minimised its collegial character . . . to promote one man only.'[40]

Modi's mass appeal stemmed from his understanding of middle-class aspirations: a job with a salary, a reasonable school for your children, and the chance to buy a motorcycle, or perhaps even a car. He flew by helicopter and private jet, but he visited parts of India long ignored by the BJP, from the very south to the smaller states of the north-east. Polling showed ordinary Indians were worried about finding jobs and rising prices of basic goods, problems Modi pledged to solve with an unrelenting focus on *vikas* (development). His central theme was corruption, and the epidemic of scams over which the Congress had presided. The rewards of India's prosperity had grown unbalanced, with rules that favoured the super-wealthy and their friends in politics. There were contradictions in Modi's promises to reverse this trend, not least the fact that he pledged to bring India's Bollygarchs to heel in a campaign lavishly funded by their donations. Yet in pledging an end to graft, Modi had still found an issue that tied together his own image for probity and the greatest weakness of his scandal-plagued opponents. At the start of 2014, he gave a speech in Amethi in Uttar Pradesh, the Gandhis' traditional stronghold. 'My mantra is I will not eat, and I will not allow others to eat,' he said, bringing roars from the crowd, who knew only too well what 'eating' meant.[41]

Just as America's Republican Party draws support from a mixture of evangelical Christians, small business owners and Wall Street financiers, so Modi used this anti-corruption message to build an unusual political coalition of his own, bringing together Hindu religious hardliners and middle-class moderates. His strength was not that he was a pure-bred technocrat or a recovering hardliner. Rather he represented both of these things, and did so in a way that offered India the hope of prosperity and a stronger sense of self. 'What the BJP promises is not so much the restoration of a Hindu Golden Age as a strong, modern Hindu state with Ayodhya as its Vatican,' as author Ian Buruma once wrote.[42] Although Modi's campaign in 2014 spoke mostly of development, there were still signals for his political base, such as his decision to take a parliamentary seat in Varanasi, one of Hinduism's holiest cities. An election billboard on Mumbai's Marine Drive during the election featured a giant image of Modi and the slogan 'I am a Hindu Nationalist'. For all of the problems presented by the bloody events of 2002, the riots also explained a measure of his popularity among his own party, who viewed their leader's stubborn refusal to apologise to his liberal critics as a signal of strength.

As India's decades of growth dismantled old hierarchies – as lower-caste politicians won political power, and wives and daughters entered the job market – so Modi's pitch also appealed to the Hindu majority, who wanted to feel pride in their heritage while at the same time enjoying the material prosperity of a modern market economy. His election triumph overturned years of conventional wisdom about the fragmentation of political power. In the three decades since Rajiv Gandhi last won a victory on a similar scale, both the Congress and the BJP had been weakened by regional and caste-based political rivals, and fragile governing coalitions had become the norm in New Delhi. But now

Modi had crafted a new and popular nationalism, which drew strength from the decline of the older identity the Congress represented.

Modi's career had barely begun in 1989, the year when Francis Fukuyama wrote 'The End of History', his essay in the *National Interest* predicting the triumph of Western-style free market democracy. 'It is not necessary that all societies become successful liberal societies, merely that they end their ideological pretensions of representing different and higher forms of human society', Fukuyama argued.[43] Already a democracy, post-socialist India should have provided a neat test case for this brand of free-market democratic shift. Indeed, Modi was just the kind of technocratic leader who might have been expected to bring it about.

Yet as India tore down the vestiges of socialism it became rapidly more capitalist but barely, if at all, more liberal. Instead, its citizens turned to a politician who offered the prospect of material prosperity, but also the comfort of a strong sense of Hindu identity and protection against external forces, be they the threat of radical Islamism or the equally unsettling forces of global economic disruption. As American author Robert Kaplan once wrote: 'The spirit of India has undergone an uneasy shift in this new era of rampant capitalism and of deadly ethnic and religious tensions, which arise partly as violent reactions against exactly the social homogenisation that globalisation engenders.'[44] Modi was part of a wider pattern, taking his place alongside a wave of conservative, nationalist leaders from Vladimir Putin in Russia and Shinzo Abe in Japan to Recep Tayyip Erdoğan in Turkey, and ultimately, in America, Donald Trump. 'I always say that to me secularism means "India first"', Modi said in 2012.[45]

Yet for all of his popularity, Modi's vision still left many in India deeply uneasy. I headed back to Ahmedabad just before the sun set on election results day in May 2014. On the road south, young men on motorcycle weaved through the traffic, their pillion passengers brandishing BJP flags. Modi had won a clean sweep of all twenty-six seats in his home state that day. But not every part of Gujarat was celebrating, as I discovered when I drove into Juhapura, Ahmedabad's main all-Muslim ghetto.

Flat-bed trucks carrying BJP supporters moved slowly through the streets outside, their speakers booming celebratory dance music. But as the light began to dim, and as the call for Friday prayers echoed out on the first evening of India's new political era, the narrow streets inside were mostly empty. A teeming city-within-a-city around seven kilometres south of downtown, Juhapura had roughly 400,000 residents, although its quiet lanes gave it the feel of a village. The area's population swelled after the 2002 riots, as thousands of Muslims displaced from elsewhere around the state sought safety in numbers, in an area physically walled off from the Hindu majority neighbourhoods nearby.

'Muslims living here know all about Modi and the riots but they view him as the cause of many other problems,' explained Waqar Kazi, a local political activist, sipping tea quietly inside his sparsely decorated home.[46] 'The Modi model of development never came here . . . [and] because my name is Waqar, I cannot stay outside this area . . . Ahmedabad is totally divided along religious lines,' he said. As we talked, Kazi seemed anxious about the evening ahead and the risk of violence that the celebrating BJP supporters might bring. Would we mind checking back later that night, he asked, to see if everything was OK?

Modi won his election triumph by promising to bring Gujarat's successes to India. It was a message that even proved popular with many Muslims, who in 2014 ended up voting for the BJP in larger numbers than usual. For its adherents, Modi's Gujarat embodied the best of what India was becoming: a churning entrepôt marked by industrialisation and urbanisation, a birthplace of billionaires and home to a developing middle-class, consumerist society. Modi himself was fond of quoting India's most famous national founder, claiming that his own model of business-friendly development would ultimately benefit the least privileged as well. 'Mahatma Gandhi used to say: "What is there for the last man?"' Modi once told an interviewer. 'So my development parameter is very simple. It is about how the poorest of the poor can benefit.'[47] Yet after a decade of his rule little such development had reached Juhapura, whose residents complained of unpaved roads, unreliable water supplies and inadequate schooling. Kazi remained sceptical even of Modi's signature promises to combat cronyism, noting the BJP politician's friendliness with tycoons like Gautam Adani. Muslims in Gujarat, he said, still had to pay bribes most days.

With neat streets and tidy houses, Juhapura itself was not a slum. Rather it was a place that provided sanctuary for Muslims of all backgrounds, from struggling refugees to middle-class professionals and prosperous business owners. In 2002, even Gujarat's wealthiest Muslims were given a brutal reminder of the perils of living in Hindu neighbourhoods. 'This isn't a ghetto in the American sense, with only poor people. It is a ghetto like Jewish areas in nineteenth-century Europe, where all classes were forced to live,' Zahir Janmohamed, an Indian-American author and human rights campaigner who lived in the area, told me. Across the country that night, Modi's record in Gujarat provided many with a source of hope that India's path to economic development would now be smoother and that victories would soon be won in its battles against corruption. But in this small corner of his home city, that sentiment was almost exactly reversed, as those who knew it best poured doubts on Modi's polished image for honesty and good governance, and questioned what he might achieve as he moved to New Delhi. 'You hear people here say that the only good thing about this election is that Modi won't be our chief minister anymore, so things will get better for us,' Janmohamed said. 'But will they? For Juhapura, I doubt it.'

Demonstrators in the southern state of Kerala form a human chain to protest against Modi's sudden 'demonetisation' anti-corruption drive, which caused chaos by replacing all the country's 500 and 1,000 rupee notes overnight.

CHAPTER 5

THE SEASON OF SCAMS

THE ROAD TO PURIFICATION

There was an autumn chill in the air as India's cabinet shuffled into their wood-panelled meeting room in the heart of New Delhi. Dressed in a white shirt and sleeveless jacket, Narendra Modi called proceedings to order, and prepared to make the most dramatic announcement of his first two years as prime minister. Earlier in the day his office had sent out two unusual messages. First, ministerial attendance at that night's meeting was mandatory. Second, no mobile phones were to be allowed.[1] But even as they settled into their seats, with a bland agenda paper dated 8 November 2016 in front of them, almost no one round the table knew what was coming. 'I had no idea that such a big move was going to be announced,' Piyush Goyal, the government's talkative energy minister, said later. '[Then] the finance minister looked at me and smirked. That's when I realised something was on.'[2]

Modi's plan was conceived in strict secrecy. A small team worked for the best part of a year from his residential bungalow, only belatedly bringing a few ministers and central bank officials into the loop.[3] 'There comes a time in the history of a country's development when a need is felt for a strong and decisive step,' Modi said in a television address later that night.[4] 'To break the grip of corruption . . . we have decided that the 500-rupee and 1,000-rupee currency notes presently in use will no longer be legal tender from midnight.' In a country where almost all transactions were made in cash, this was not just unexpected: it was an earthquake.

Banks would close the next day, Modi explained in his address to the nation. After that, anyone in possession of the two highest-denomination notes – worth $7 and $14 at the time, and collectively accounting for $220 billion – had to exchange them for new ones. The move caught the media by surprise, distracted by events in that day's US presidential election. Few experts saw it coming either. 'I was absolutely shocked, it was the last thing I expected,' admitted economist Ila Patnaik, who until that year had been one of Modi's most senior advisers.[5]

The idea behind what became known as *notebandi* (demonetisation) was simple. India suffered a huge problem of 'black money', meaning cash or wealth on which no tax had been paid. The term covered everything from the proceeds of criminality to the earnings of the respectable middle classes, who merely forgot to declare them to the revenue authorities. That absentmindedness was something of a national habit: only 37 million Indians out of more than 1.2 billion were paying income tax, one of the world's lowest rates.[6] But speaking that evening Modi focused instead on corruption and crime, arguing that his bank note ban would target illicit wealth held by terrorists and gangsters, as well as bribe-taking government employees, who kept 'currency notes stashed under [their] beds'. Anyone with large quantities of illicit cash would be forced to turn it in at the bank and explain where it had come from. 'There may be temporary hardships,' he added. '[But] in this movement for purifying our country, will our people not put up with difficulties for a few days?'[7]

Those difficulties became clear just two days later, when banks reopened and were quickly overwhelmed. Replacement currency had barely begun to be printed, leading to severe shortages. Long lines formed at ATMs, which swiftly emptied. Confusion grew about the rules under which old cash could be deposited and replaced. Economists criticised the move's implementation and questioned its effectiveness. An almost daily stream of clarifications and rule changes confirmed that Modi and his team had not thought through the details of their experiment. For weeks, newspaper front pages pictured snaking queues, as hundreds of millions endured one of the most disruptive policy changes in modern economic history. And as those queues showed no signs of shortening, a decision that many hailed at first as a master-stroke began to look ever more like a debacle.

Conspiracy theories spread that demonetisation was actually a political scam. All political parties relied on under-the-table cash for their election campaigns, the theory went, but the well-funded BJP would cope relatively better than its rivals during the cash crunch, giving it an advantage in forthcoming state elections. But in truth there was a simpler calculation in Modi's mind: the desire not to be outflanked on corruption. Since taking power in 2014 his government had proved reasonably effective. There had been few genuinely bold economic reforms, but Modi had nonetheless presided over reasonable growth rates, falling inflation and high poll ratings. On corruption, though, his record was patchier. On the plus side the mega-scams of the previous Congress government had mostly ceased. Modi's decision to auction off public assets like coal and spectrum, rather than handing them out to friendly businesses, helped put an end to scandals in allocating natural resources too. Business leaders in general praised Modi's intolerance of influence-peddling. 'The days when I would wake up to read in the papers about some regulation that mysteriously benefited one of my rivals . . . those have thankfully stopped,' one billionaire industrialist told me in mid-2015.

For ordinary Indians, however, the tawdry reality of routine bribe-paying seemed little changed. Two years prior to Modi's election, one poll showed that more than nine in ten still thought their country corrupt.[8] In 2016, the country ranked seventy-ninth in the annual Transparency International corruption perceptions index, a score that had barely changed in five years.[9] One year later, a second survey from the same organisation found that 69 per cent of Indians had paid a bribe to access state services during the previous twelve months, the highest rate in Asia.[10] Kickbacks and payoffs still dominated large swathes of national life, from land acquisition to public contracts. New anti-graft measures, including an earlier amnesty on black money, proved low profile and ineffective. Corruption in state and local governments remained unchecked, while probes into older scams dragged on without results. Half of those who dealt with the government each year ended up paying bribes, according to another study.[11] A place at a school, a bed in a hospital, a water connection, a birth registration, a marriage licence, a death certificate; in India, the very rudiments of life seemed to require illegal payments. Meanwhile almost none of the industrialists who had grown rich by exploiting their ties with the state had been punished. Modi risked being attacked as the leader of a '*suit-boot ki sarkar*', a rare memorable phrase from opposition leader Rahul

Gandhi, meaning a government of, for and by the suited, crony-capital-ist rich.[12] *Notebandi* proved the lengths to which the prime minister was willing to go to avoid this charge, regardless of the costs it imposed on the small businesses normally thought of as part of the BJP's political base.

A few weeks later I went into a tailor's in our neighbourhood in Mumbai, on a back street filled with crumbling colonial-era houses. A dozen people were lined up at a cash machine on the far side of the road, one of the few in the area that still had money. Sitting behind his front desk, surrounded by piles of neatly folded shirts ready for collec-tion, the shop's elderly owner, Mukesh Pahuja, complained that his business had all but collapsed. Sales were down by as much as seventy per cent, as customers stopped spending, in an industry dominated by cash. 'Everything is black money,' he told me. 'In the business of clothes . . . if you take one good outfit, and embroider it, it will cost one and a half lakh rupees [150,000 rupees or $2,200]. So who pays with a card? Nobody.'

Rather than Mukesh, Pahuja went by 'Michele', pronounced the Italian way, so the final syllable rhymed with 'hay'. He was given the nickname as a younger man by a visiting Alitalia air steward, who stayed at the nearby Taj Mahal Palace hotel and came to his store to buy cheap made-to-measure clothes. Black money had been part of the industry since before his own shop opened in 1994, he told me. Most 'black' transactions involved nothing criminal, beyond the fact that the tax man was not to know. But the larger a purchase – a wedding dress, a gold watch, even a house – the more likely it would be made under the table. Buying an apartment was an extreme example, which often involved an official 'cheque' price and then a side-payment of half as much again. 'In a big jeweller's store, even a solitaire that costs two million rupees [$30,000], it is all exchanged in black,' Pahuja said. 'Nothing is official.' Still, he seemed conflicted. His business paid its taxes, or so he claimed, but now even 'white' customers were spooked by the cash crunch. 'How can you do this?' he asked. 'You are squeezing people who are honest taxpayers. But Modi, he has to do something, to stop all this corruption. Maybe this will help.'

India's black money problem dated back at least as far as the heights of Prime Minister Indira Gandhi's tryst with socialism during the 1970s. For a time, wealthy Indians faced punitive top rates of tax as high as

97.75 per cent, teaching the prosperous to hide their assets and entrepreneurs to disguise profits.[13] 'In theory, this should have ushered in a
socialist paradise,' as economist Swaminathan Aiyar once put it. 'In
practice, it converted India into a massive black economy.'[14] Any family
with means learned to buy and sell off the books. 'My dad had to sell his
car,' a friend who worked in finance in Mumbai once recalled of his
upbringing in the 1980s. 'We went down the road to the local store,
where we used to buy eggs, bread and milk. Dad told the shopkeeper
what he wanted to do and the shopkeeper said he'd sort it out. So next
day some guy came to our house with a suitcase full of money, and we
gave him the keys, and that was how we and everyone else would have
sold a car.'

This same ingenuity in evading the authorities became clear as
demonetisation took hold. Those stuck with hoards of illicit cash quickly
found clever ways to launder it. One technique involved using middlemen, who bought up old notes at a discount and distributed them in
small amounts to poor villagers in rural areas. In exchange for a fee,
these villagers then deposited the money into their bank accounts, as if
it was their own, before returning it to its original owner at a later date
in new, clean bills. Modi's evocative image of cash-filled suitcases hidden
beneath beds turned out to be largely illusory, because anyone who
earned black money typically invested their cash quickly in hard assets
like gold or real estate. Vast quantities of illicit wealth were stored in
so-called *benami* properties, meaning those registered in someone else's
name, or transferred around India through '*hawala*' networks of informal money traders. No one knew for sure the size of this shadow economy, beyond the fact that it was huge. A World Bank study put it at a
little over a fifth of GDP in 2007, while another academic estimate
suggested it could be as high as two thirds.[15]

For all the hardship it inflicted on others, Modi described his new
corruption battle in self-sacrificial terms. 'My dear countrymen, I have
left my home, my family, everything for the nation,' he said in an
emotional press conference a few weeks after his first announcement, at
times seeming to struggle to hold back tears. 'Didn't you vote me into
power to fight corruption? Didn't you choose me to curb black money?'[16]
In his own mind, this meant taking on powerful vested interests, albeit
ones he could never quite name. 'I will not stop doing these things, even
if you burn me alive,' he said in the same speech. 'They may not let me

live, they may ruin me because their loot of seventy years is in trouble.'[17] Rather than the rational explanation of a technocrat, this language of purification and cleansing lent demonetisation an almost ritualistic feel, and one delivered in moral terms reminiscent of the Rashtriya Swayamsevak Sangh ideologies of his youth. To those who questioned his capacity for boldness, he had delivered a sharp rebuke, and one presented as part of a painful process of national rebirth.

Demonetisation was a flawed weapon with which to battle corruption, not least because it caused such needless collateral economic damage. But it also smacked of an alarming kind of arbitrary populism, as Modi courted public opinion by whipping up anger against the wealthy. In the weeks after demonetisation began, television reporters searched fruitlessly for irate customers in bank queues, or farmers unable to sell their produce. Instead they found that Indians mostly seemed to support the ban. Modi cleverly targeted a cast of villains in the public mind – the bribe-taking policeman, the dishonest bureaucrat and the inexplicably wealthy politician – all of whom demonetisation appeared to punish. 'Psychologically, this is seen as a slap in the face of the all the cronies and the corrupt, which pleases the middle class so much,' I was told by Rajiv Kumar, an economist in New Delhi. 'Those who got rich by all the wrong means have gotten their comeuppance and people are delighted.'[18]

SCAM-A-LOT

Corruption has appeared in one way or another throughout modern Indian history. Graft allegations dogged generations of British imperial administrators, from the fortunes pillaged by Robert Clive, the buccaneer who seized Bengal for the East India Company, to the trial in 1788 of Warren Hastings, the first governor general, on charges of profiteering. These graft problems became so severe that 'loot', an old Hindi word for plunder, soon took its place in the English language, as historian William Dalrymple is fond of pointing out.[19] Matters had barely improved by the twentieth century, as the clamour for Independence grew ever louder. 'We seem to have weakened from within,' Mahatma Gandhi raged in 1939, dismayed over financial misbehaviour within his own party. 'I would go to the length of giving the whole Congress a decent burial rather than put up with the corruption that is rampant.'[20] Optimistic Indian nationalists expected that freedom from British rule would bring clean governance. These hopes had largely died out by the time Indira Gandhi took power in the 1960s. So common was corruption under the Licence Raj that it even became a mainstay of newspaper horoscopes. 'All round improvements but not without strings,' the *Hindustan Times* warned Virgos in 1985, before adding: 'If paying a bribe to anyone, see that the job is done.'[21]

Advocates for economic liberalisation then predicted that the demise of the socialist state would bring an end to corruption. In some ways they were right. After 1991, no one any longer had to pay bribes to buy of a bag of cement or a scooter, or to get a new telephone connection. But rather than putting a stop to bribery entirely, the process of reform merely ended up creating new and far grander avenues for the unscrupulous. Previously unimportant parts of the economy, such as telecoms or airlines, began to grow rapidly as state controls were relaxed. The value of assets like land and commodities shot up too, especially in sectors that were closely connected to the global economy. 'These price increases have multiplied the scope for government officials (and colluding businessmen) to make vast sums of illegal money,' as Jagdish Bhagwati put it.[22] Small-scale retail corruption did not disappear, but a new species of grand wholesale corruption grew up alongside it. As a result, the scandals that washed over India in the 2000s were of an entirely different order from those that had come before, both in terms of their focus and the sheer scale of the looting.

The term 'corruption' – often defined to mean the abuse of public office for private gain – is vague, covering everything from bribery and vote-buying to racketeering and nepotism. But in India, as in other emerging markets, what mattered was the rise of a new crony capitalism – defined by political scientist Minxin Pei as 'collusion among elites' – and the big-ticket graft that went with it.[23] The sight of politicians, bureaucrats and businesses plotting to seize valuable public resources occurred across developing nations. In Russia, entire industries were ransacked after 1989 and subsequently passed into the hands of pliant oligarchs. There was no full-scale privatisation programme as part of China's economic reform process, but Communist Party officials still worked with businesses to take control of, or extract resources from, giant state companies. India's story was similar, as liberalisation took an economy long under state control and moved large parts of it back towards the private sector.

As this happened, political leaders and civil servants found themselves in control of suddenly valuable state assets. The kinds of rent-seeking that followed came in many shades, as Milan Vaishnav pointed out in *When Crime Pays*, his study on Indian corruption and criminality. Some flowed from the ability to change rules to suit one business interest or another. Others involved doling out scarce natural resources, from mineral rights to land. A third variety involved politics, and in particular the need to provide illegal funding to political parties.[24] Economic growth itself was not to blame for this: some countries, such as Poland, managed to introduce market reforms without an accompanying wave of cronyism. Rather, corruption turned out to be a political problem, in which liberalisation required changes to the way the state managed and regulated India's economy. When this did not happen, it was all too easy for those with power and connections to build what was often described as a 'nexus', linking together tycoons, politicians and bureaucrats to their own ends. The word 'corruption' implied rottenness in something previously healthy, but in India corruption was in fact a dynamic and highly entrepreneurial process, marked out by crafty backroom deals and daring attempts at regulatory capture. Indeed, for a time during the 2000s, it looked as if the cronyism that India's reform process had unleashed would simply be unstoppable.

CRONYISM, PURE AND SIMPLE

Yet this was never an entirely one-sided fight, and if any figure could be credited with bringing the country's new spate of corruption under control, it was Vinod Rai, a quiet, bespectacled former civil servant, whom I met one humid morning in Singapore in 2016. At that time Rai had taken up a part-time post at a local university. He looked relaxed, wearing brown trousers and a blue and red checked shirt, with swept-back silver hair and black eyebrows that shot up as he talked. His office looked out over a leafy campus, a view that seemed worlds away from the hubbub of New Delhi, where in 2008 he signed on to become India's eleventh comptroller and auditor general.

The chief auditor's role was traditionally as dull as it sounds: a post for cautious, elderly men, who churned out dry reports that almost nobody read. But Rai arrived in a city swirling with intrigue. New Delhi was being turned into a construction site as preparations raced ahead for the Commonwealth Games in 2010, an event designed to showcase India's economic rise which soon turned into a corruption-ridden fiasco. At the time, Manmohan Singh's government was also busily handing out telecoms and mining licences to large industrial houses in circumstances that reeked of favouritism. Dozens of bribery and graft scandals soon erupted in what became known as the 'season of scams'. And just as India seemed to be losing its moral bearings, so Rai became an unlikely public hero, publishing sparsely written reports that exposed the true scale of his country's corruption problems, while showing a mixture of quiet decency and thinly veiled anger at the venality of its political class.

Rai took up his role in January 2008. 'Of course, lots of people in Delhi circles knew bad things were going on,' he told me. 'There was talk and gossip. But you needed proof.' That arrived two years later with his first blockbuster report, which dealt with the misallocation of the second-generation (or 2G) telecoms spectrum. Until then, telecoms had been one of India's post-liberalisation successes. Shashi Tharoor, the author and Congress politician, once described his memories of making intercity phone calls back in the 1980s. This meant booking a line many hours in advance, unless he was willing to pay extra for a special 'lightning' connection, which required a wait of merely thirty minutes. 'This being India, even lightning took a long time to strike,' he said. Prior to 1991 home landlines were a luxury available only to the rich. Just two decades later more than half a billion Indians had mobile phones, making it the world's second largest market after China.[25] 'The mobile phone is to my mind the instrument that is most emblematic of India's transformation over the last twenty years,' Tharoor said. It was about to become the greatest symbol of its corruption.

The '2G scam' kicked off just a few days after Rai took up his new position. Singh's government planned to hand out valuable telecoms spectrum licences using a murky 'first come, first served' system, rather than an open auction. On 10 January 2008 the telecoms department summoned bidders to its office in New Delhi, at just a few hours' notice. 'Fifteen applicants assembled at the appointed time, armed with

bankers' cheques, bank guarantees and the relevant papers – preparations that would normally have taken days,' as one account put it. 'It was
clear that the favoured few had been tipped off.'[26] Chaotic scenes ensued,
as executives rushed to fill forms and dashed from room to room. By
day's end, more than one hundred licences had been handed to eight
companies in a deal that would besmirch India's reputation for years to
come. Details began to dribble out bit by bit, revealing a story that
seemed to have everything, from shell companies fronting for major
industrial houses to leaked salacious calls between lobbyists and
tycoons. Behind it all stood telecoms minister Andimuthu Raja, a
colourful politician from the southern state of Tamil Nadu.

It was only when Rai published his 2010 report that the scale of the
alleged telecoms scandal became clear, costing the state Rs 1.8 trillion
($26 billion) in lost revenues, the auditor claimed, at least when
compared to what might have been raised had the licence been
auctioned.[27] A criminal investigation put Raja behind bars pending trial
in 2011, while the Supreme Court cancelled all 122 licences one year
later.[28] Various telecoms executives were imprisoned for a time too. The
resulting media storm turned Rai into a controversial figure, at once
hailed as a crusader and attacked as a zealot bent on sullying corporate
India's good name. Unbowed, the auditor began churning out more
reports, examining everything from irregularities in the run-in to the
Commonwealth Games to corruption in natural gas contracts. These in
turn covered only a portion of the many scandals that erupted in the
later 2000s, in which 'hundreds of billions of dollars' were siphoned
away, according to one estimate.[29] In the 1980s, economist Robert
Klitgaard defined corruption as a process involving 'monopoly plus
discretion minus accountability'.[30] Until Rai came along, India's scandals followed this formula almost exactly.

Perhaps the most significant scandal was the last to come to light: the
'coal scam', which the auditor revealed in a 2012 report.[31] For the best
part of a decade India handed out free coal-mining licences to industrial companies, on the proviso that the fuel was used only in nearby
industrial projects, such as steel mills and power plants. At first almost
no one applied, because coal was available cheaply on international
markets, or via Coal India, the state-owned mining giant. But as global
prices rose in the 2000s, driven by breakneck Chinese growth, the value
of domestic mining rights skyrocketed. More than two hundred licences

were awarded between 2004 and 2009. Many were handed out to well-known industrialists. Others went to companies that, until then, had shown little interest in mining. 'Let's say I'm a newspaper magnate in a particular state with good connections with the minister of coal,' Rai told me, explaining the process. 'And I say: "I am contemplating setting up a power project, so why don't you give me a mine?" And so they get given a mine, in exchange for who knows what.' Taken together, his team calculated that the mining policy handed the various tycoons windfall gains in the region of $30 billion.[32]

India's scams followed a pattern, although each had its own *modus operandi*. The Commonwealth Games was a cash-for-contracts affair, presided over by the head of the national Olympic committee. Wrongdoing first came to light with stories of inflated costs, including the purchase of toilet rolls for the athletes' village at Rs 4,000 ($62) each.[33] Other allegations involved handing out contracts to companies with ties to the organisers in exchange for kickbacks. The 2G scandal, by contrast, appeared to involve the payment of bribes to acquire licences, as well as smaller firms acting as fronts for larger conglomerates. However, those caught up in the scandal consistently denied they had done anything wrong and claimed vindication in late 2017 when a special court set up to bring prosecutions in the case cleared Raja and a host of others, including representatives from various companies involved. The judge's ruling followed a seven-year investigation, and harshly criticised prosecutors for failing to provide enough evidence to justify a conviction.[34]

Coal was perhaps the most complicated of the scams, only brought to a close when in 2014 the Supreme Court suddenly cancelled all of the various licences handed out during the Congress years, describing their original allocation as 'arbitrary and illegal'.[35] It was also the only scandal that indirectly affected Manmohan Singh, who served as a stand-in coal minister for a period during the early portion of his two terms as prime minister. Although badly weakened by the various scandals, the embattled Congress leader staggered on. At various points he tried to stop the coal giveaways, but such were the limitations of his authority that he failed to get his way.[36] Instead the scam pressed on, as an array of politicians, bureaucrats, industrialists and sundry middlemen carved up the mining rights between them. Perhaps more than any other scandal, it was collusion of this type that came to represent the rot at India's heart.

'It was cronyism,' Rai said, summing up the whole affair with a sigh. 'Absolute cronyism. Pure and simple.'

MARCH OF THE MIDDLEMEN

In his Man Booker Prize-winning novel *The White Tiger*, Aravind Adiga imagines corruption happening with thrilling directness, with a suit-case filled with money delivered to the heart of power. His book tells the story of Balram, an impoverished rural villager, who finds work as a driver for a wealthy family in New Delhi. Eventually Balram murders his employer and rises to become a small-time (and thoroughly corrupt) businessman himself. In one scene midway through the story, he drives his boss and a friend into Lutyens's Delhi, the administrative district designed as a new imperial capital in the early 1900s by British architect Edwin Lutyens. 'I drove towards Raisina Hill, and then all the way up the hill, stopping each time a guard put his hand out and checked inside the car, and then stopping right in front of one of the big domed build-ings around the President's house,' Balram recounts.[37] His employer disappears inside, and returns hours later feeling angry and guilt-ridden, having just handed over his suitcase in exchange for vague promises of help with a future investment project. As they drive away, the employer suddenly spots a statue of India's famously virtuous national founder. 'We're driving past Gandhi having just given a bribe to a minister. It's a fucking joke, isn't it?' he says. 'Things are compli-cated in India,' his friend replies.

Real-life bribery rarely happened this dramatically, although it normally did involve a calculated risk, hence the presence of intermedi-aries who could provide a measure of trust between the parties. Rai told me it was widely known in New Delhi that associates of particular poli-ticians could be approached to act as middlemen, able to broker deals or favours. Some were party functionaries or trusted associates of veteran political leaders. Others were family members of senior politi-cians or trusted confidants drawn from their home town or caste. Often they were simply political entrepreneurs, who sprang up to help busi-nesses navigate red tape and make introductions to those in power. In the decades after liberalisation India became 'a society beholden to gatekeepers', in the words of academic Sunil Khilnani. 'The changes of

recent decades have merely enhanced the stakes, potential and neces-
sity for corruption,' he wrote not long after the publication of Rai's telecoms report in 2010.[38] 'At the top of the new caste order are those who
can fix "access" to the durbars of politicians, the file-bestrewn offices of
bureaucrats, the Vitra-fitted boardrooms and salons of CEOs.'

Rather than an entirely new phenomenon, these gatekeepers were
descendants of an earlier class of fixers who hovered around the edges
of the socialist state. 'In old India, people would say "I came to Delhi to
buy this or that, but I met the wrong people",' I was once told by Anuvab
Pal, one of the country's best stand-up comedians. As a teenager, Pal
came to realise that bribery and intermediaries were needed to buy
even basic consumer products. 'Being a child of that economy, I still feel
more comfortable buying something from a person who says "I'll get it
done", even now when you have more transparent options online, and
even though that person is almost certainly lying.' After 1991 brokers
were no longer needed to buy televisions or fridge-freezers, but they
grew ever more essential in businesses. For those officials or politicians
taking the bribes, meanwhile, fixers helped to save face by removing the
risk and embarrassment of demanding money in person. 'Middlemen
reduce transaction costs for citizens and officials alike,' as one study put
it. 'They know whom to approach, and how to do so, and which officials
will "stay bought".'[39]

Middlemen proved invaluable in even mundane situations, as I
discovered when my own time in India began to wind to a close, and my
wife and I began to grapple with the problem of how to export our
cats.[40] We had arrived with two Maine Coons, a breed with thick furry
coats quite unsuited for hot Indian summers. Bringing them into the
country had been hard enough, but getting them out proved to be an
administrative nightmare of form-filling and veterinary visits. On the
advice of friends, I hired a pet export agent, in exchange for a sizeable
fee. Towards the end of the process I found myself driving out of
Mumbai one morning, with the agent's assistant and both cats, heading
to a government office in the suburbs. We sat in a car park for an hour,
awaiting an inspector from the agriculture department. Eventually he
turned up, gave a perfunctory glance at both animals and handed over
a crucial certificate, the need for which no one could quite explain. It
was never clear how much of our fee the agent had passed on in 'speed
money'. And in the end this element of deniability was the point: I was

happy to have the agent's help getting the forms filled in correctly, but happier still not to know if any bribes had been paid.

Although a hassle for the prosperous middle classes, gatekeepers were especially pernicious for the poor. Around half of Indians survived on less than Rs 38 ($0.50) a day, according to one academic estimate, a group for whom even the smallest 'harassment' bribe could be crippling.[41] I once visited the southern city of Hyderabad, where I met Jayamma Dumpa in Nandanavanam, a slum with dirt paths and roofs of corrugated iron, whose name translated as 'celestial garden'.[42] Dressed in a faded red and green sari, Dumpa stood outside her one-room home and showed me how she cooked for her family of seven, fabricating a makeshift stove from a metal bucket. Mostly she used brushwood, although other potential fuels lay on the ground nearby, including an old punctured football. In theory the authorities were meant to provide cooking stoves for free, but getting them meant paying bribes to go-betweens, which Dumpa said she could not afford. Instead she spent hours each week buying wood at a local market and carrying it back on her head. One day she hoped to get her stove, but she wasn't expecting it any time soon. 'It is meant to be free,' she told me. 'But nothing here is free.'

As India's economy grew, agents appeared to help fix almost any task, from getting goods through customs to passing a driving test, as one ingenious academic study discovered.[43] The researchers followed various test candidates in New Delhi, finding that nearly three quarters hired agents, and almost all of them passed. Those who tried to navigate the test process on their own were far more likely to fail, even if they were more skilled drivers. The agents passed some portion of their fee to the instructors in bribes, the study's authors concluded, while testers often arbitrarily failed those who did not use agents, to teach them to hire one next time. Driving test complaints were unsurprisingly common on ipaidabribe.com, an anti-corruption project launched in 2011, and filled with anonymous reports of shakedowns. The site gave a real-time breakdown of the 'going rate' for any particular activity, from Rs 200 ($3) to issue a state identity card to Rs 10,000 ($157) to forgo an electricity inspection. More complex processes, such as registering land, required payments many times larger. Sometimes a well-placed bribe could help to avoid a task altogether. One post in 2017 boasted of winning a driving licence even without having to take the test. 'There was no direct bribe paid by me,' the author wrote. '[But] the fact that I went through an RTO [Regional Transport Office] agent should mean that some palms were greased.'[44]

Fixers proliferated in business above all, often facilitating corruption on a grand scale. Global companies were a particular target. In 1991, India attracted just $100 million in foreign direct investment. By 2017 that had ballooned to $60 billion.[45] As capital flooded in, so a new class that were once described to me as bureaucratic 'escort services' began to emerge, designed to help hapless foreigners navigate local rules and win the good graces of politicians. India is one of the world's largest weapons importers, with fixers readily available to help seal lucrative arms deals. Middlemen are particularly important for those from countries like America and Britain, where anti-corruption laws forbid paying bribes abroad, but where agents could provide an element of deniability. Foreign businesses also often teamed up with domestic firms and allowed local partners to manage dealings with the local bureaucracy. When we met, Vinod Rai recounted a story from around the time he left his job as auditor in 2013. He had gone for lunch with the head of a foreign telecoms group who had struck a joint venture with an Indian company and eventually become embroiled in the 2G scandal. 'He was very frank,' Rai said of the foreign executive. 'He said: "We were told this is the only way to do business in India." And if anything went wrong, he clearly thought he could take the plea that this was the fault of my Indian partner. So he turned a blind eye, and he got caught out.'

THE STATE WE'RE IN

Whichever way you looked at it, corruption in India was complicated. The middle classes fumed at sleazy politicians and shady tycoons, even though they themselves were typically expert bribe payers and tax avoiders. Bribery had become so socially entrenched that Kaushik Basu, the government's chief economic adviser, called in 2011 for it to be made legal.[46] His idea caused a furore, although its logic was clear, namely that people were more likely to admit to having made illegal payments if they faced no penalty, which in turn could help police identify those who had demanded money in the first place.

Not everyone even agreed that corruption was a social ill. Sociologist Ashis Nandy, a grand old man of the left, caused a similar ruckus a few years later when he described bribery as 'an equalising force' that could help the poor, particularly those from lower castes.[47] A similar story was told by American author Katherine Boo in *Behind the Beautiful Forevers*, her depiction of life in a slum close to Mumbai's airport. Boo painted a sympathetic portrait of Asha Waghekar, a destitute woman who gained a measure of power by becoming a local political fixer. 'Among some in the Indian elite, this word, corruption, had purely negative connotations, it was seen as blocking India's modern, global ambitions,' Boo wrote. 'But for the poor . . . corruption was one of the genuine opportunities that remained.'[48]

The link between corruption and growth turned out to be equally confusing. Intuitively it seemed the relationship should be negative. All of the world's most corrupt countries were poor. Corruption also distorted economic activity, reducing trust in business and government while diverting capital away from productive uses and towards areas from which it could easily be stolen. India's economic record seemed to reflect this account too, as the economy took a hit in the years after the season of scams hit its peak around 2013.

Yet there was another side to this argument, one made most famously by Samuel Huntington, the American political scientist. Huntington claimed corruption was not simply an unfortunate side effect of economic development, but often a desirable one: 'a welcome lubricant easing the path to modernisation'.[49] Plenty of countries managed to combine high growth and high levels of graft, most obviously China. The same was true for the 'tiger' economies of east Asia: 'Clientelism and other forms of rent-seeking were widespread during Asia's high growth period,' according to one academic study.[50] In these cases, side payments on business deals encouraged bureaucrats and politicians to act in ways that in turn encouraged investment. This bringing together of cronyism and growth became a deliberate economic strategy, as author Joe Studwell explained in his 2013 book *How Asia Works*. In countries like South Korea and Malaysia, businesses were tacitly allowed to skim off the top, so long as they did so while investing in the kind of exporting industries and infrastructure developments their governments wanted. 'Rents are the bait with which the successful developing state captures and controls its entrepreneurs,' as Studwell put it.[51]

Huntington's argument suggested a rather different problem, namely that India had allowed graft to flourish without using it strategically to promote development. Even so, India's old system had still helped to grease the wheels of investment, a fact that became clear in the years after the season of scams. Modi's anti-corruption efforts – in combination with heightened scrutiny from public auditors, judges and the media – began to put a stop to the worst of that cronyism. But while the old corrupt system stopped working, no new and more honest system replaced it. The result was paralysing inaction in New Delhi, as bureaucrats declined to make decisions for fear of being accused of malfeasance, and businesses stopped investing in new projects. Industrial investment plunged.

Behind these corruption issues lay the longer-term problem of the weakness of India's state. The country's rapidly growing economy placed new demands on its government, as it tried to keep pace with a more dynamic business environment. Yet the machinery of the state was often woefully equipped for this task. Manish Sabharwal, the chairman of Bangalore-based outsourcing group TeamLease and a thoughtful observer of the interplay between business and government, once put it to me this way: 'We have this state heritage where everything is forbidden unless it is expressly permitted, which dates right back to Raj,' he said. For decades India had defined its 'reforms' in economic terms, while doing little to fix basic issues like public procurement. China managed to combine high growth and high corruption partly because its government machine was impressively efficient. By contrast, India's was intrusive in some areas and incompetent in others. It suffered, in short, from what Sabharwal described as 'bureaucratic cholesterol', meaning an inefficient, corruption-riddled system that was clogged up from the inside.

Each year the World Bank's 'ease of doing business' survey gave a stark reminder of how badly the state was performing. In 2016, the year in which Modi introduced demonetisation, India came in a dismal 130th out of 190 countries.[52] Many problems were enshrined in legislation. The much-feared Factories Act of 1948, for instance, included rules setting out when a factory owner had to whitewash staircases or varnish window frames.[53] Fifty-seven permits were needed to open an industrial plant, according to one estimate, or ninety for a hotel.[54] United Spirits, the liquor group formerly owned by Vijay Mallya, once claimed it needed a staggering 200,000 licences to operate.[55] There was then a fearsome array of enforcement officials – the chief inspector of factories, the vigilance inspector, the boiler and pressure vessel inspector – who could bring production stuttering to a halt.[56] An administrative headache, this also provided ideal conditions for corruption, as inspectors threatened delay until the right palms had been greased.

Harvard academic Lant Pritchett once described the Indian state as 'flailing', rather than failing. By this he meant that the state was competent in parts, mostly at its upper levels, but overwhelmed the further down you went. 'In police, tax collection, education, health, power, water supply – in nearly every routine service – there is rampant absenteeism, indifference, incompetence, and corruption,' he wrote.[57] Acquiring land was one notorious problem, where complex rules made it hard for businesses to buy plots directly from farmers, forcing them to rely on government-held 'land banks' instead. Bureaucrats also controlled reclassification for industrial use, allowing them to vastly increase land values. All of this was an invitation to collusion, giving birth to what was often described as a 'land mafia', meaning a loose coalition of entrepreneurs and officials who plotted to buy up land, reclassify it and sell it on for huge profits. Many other state assets were carved up in this way, from the 'water mafia', who controlled the trucks delivering water to buildings in cities like Mumbai and Bangalore, to the 'sand mafia', who mined river beds illegally across the country to feed the insatiable demands of the construction sector.

State inefficiency created corruption in other ways. In Jharkhand, a poorer eastern state with abundant mineral resources, one study suggested that investment projects needed 240 layers of government clearance before beginning operation.[58] This serpentine exercise in box-ticking began in lowly clerical antechambers, then moved upwards through the offices of engineering inspectors and authorising committees, before arriving finally at the desk of the chief minister himself. The problem was not just the process; big industrial schemes in other countries also have to go through many layers of government clearances. Rather it was that, in India, each step brought the possibility of costly delay. Businesses attempting to set up industrial projects would talk despairingly about their 'file' getting stuck, meaning the physical file of papers concerning any particular project, which was passed slowly from department to department. This risk of delay then created a strong incentive for a businessman to strike a deal towards the top of the decision-making chain, and preferably with a senior bureaucrat or politician, who could ensure their file was hurried along.

While in this way India's state could appear fearsome, it was more often an oddly feeble beast and one that appeared increasingly overwhelmed by the task of governing so complex a nation. The Indian civil service employed roughly three times as many as China as a proportion of its population.[59] Meanwhile, the Indian Administrative Service (IAS), the elite cadre of officials that hold the most senior central and state government positions, numbered fewer than five thousand. Most of them worked outside New Delhi, holding positions with titles like 'district collector', a kind of local governor with sweeping powers to run regions the size of many small countries.

For all the power it wielded, the structure of the IAS itself had changed little since the days of the old India Civil Service, the colonial system through which fewer than one thousand British officials managed the lives of hundreds of millions of Indians. Known affectionately as *babus*, IAS officers were often portrayed as out of touch, incompetent and prone to corruption. In the popular imagination they dressed in white uniforms, and spent their days being chauffeured around New Delhi in curvy old Hindustan Ambassador cars, with curtains on the rear windows and flashing blue lights on the roof. Even so, civil service jobs remained hugely prestigious and were available only through one of the world's most competitive entry examinations, with some half a million applicants each year for about a thousand places.[60] IAS officers were often intellectually formidable and viewed with great trepidation by business leaders, given the sweeping powers they wielded to change or enforce regulations. In private, however, many in the service bemoaned its relative decline, fretting that private sector competition had sucked away the best talent, and that too many of their number working outside New Delhi ended up throwing their lot in with powerful local politicians, helping to create more corruption themselves.

Corruption damaged the fabric of the state in other ways, most obviously through job appointments. In a country with a bulging youth population even lowly civil service jobs were fiercely fought over. In 2015, an advert for a delivery boy in Uttar Pradesh, with a monthly salary of Rs 16,000 ($240), attracted over two million applicants.[61] Senior positions were valued less for their prestige and more for their ability to extract kickbacks. British political economist Robert Wade wrote a celebrated paper in 1982 revealing the intricate system of payments that controlled the appointment of irrigation engineers in southern India.[62] These employees, he discovered, could raise hefty sums in bribes, for instance by directing water to one town rather than another. But instead of passing a cut of each bribe upwards to more senior bureaucrats and politicians, Wade uncovered a simpler and more ingenious system, in which each engineer would pay an unofficial fee to take their job in the first place, commensurate to the value of the cash that could be extracted from it. At that time an engineer would pay Rs 100,000 ($1,570) for a basic 'operation and maintenance' job. Having secured the post, the engineer could then earn nearly three times as much in bribes: 'a most pleasing profit', as Wade put it.

Corruption of this type spread throughout India, creating a well-entrenched black market for public sector jobs. The system was riddled with perverse incentives. One study found that policemen in Mumbai would pay more to be transferred into jobs in high-crime areas, given these provided the best opportunities to take money from both criminals and victims alike.[63] In the same way excise officials paid for transfers to larger ports, and tax officials angled for jobs where they inspected larger and more profitable businesses. The more money that flowed through a position, the more that could be extracted from it. IAS officers faced an unpleasant choice of turning a blind eye to this corruption or sharing in its largesse. Honest candidates were unlikely to even apply for positions that required payments. Those who kicked up a fuss were quickly transferred to more mundane and less lucrative postings.

India's go-go years threw up many examples of the way limited state capacity acted to worsen corruption, although few were as clear as those that swept through the seaside state of Goa. Known for its palm-fringed beaches, the former Portuguese colony began attracting less welcome attention in the late 2000s, as reports of rampant illegal mining began to emerge. For decades, tourism and mining had been the twin mainstays of its economy. Goa's beaches were glamorous, while its iron ore mines provided a stable kind of prosperity. The sector was dominated by local family businesses, who dug up the state's red soil and sold its contents onwards to local steel producers. All that started to change as global commodity prices began to shoot up, however. 'It was around 2005 that China came into the picture,' the state's BJP chief minister, Manohar

Parrikar, told me one afternoon, sitting in his plush residence overlooking Panjim, the state capital. An able administrator by reputation, Parrikar had swept to power on an anti-corruption platform in 2012. A year later, he recalled how China's frantic building spree in the build-up to the 2008 Beijing Olympics had sharply pushed up global iron ore prices. In Goa, a mining boom began, as local producers madly increased production to meet Chinese demand. 'The rush started,' as he put it. 'People who had no experience in mining wanted to make money while the sun shines, including some with political contacts.'

That boom was long since over by the time I visited in 2013, but its after-effects were still clear to see. I drove inland one morning with Ambar Timblo, the head of one of the state's largest mining groups.[64] We passed first through small towns with Catholic churches painted in brilliant white, then smaller villages of neat single-storey houses, many with large, colourfully painted dump trucks sitting in their driveways. As the boom took off and global ore prices spiked, Timblo explained, a kind of mania descended upon Goa. Normally it took years to open a mine but suddenly new licences were being handed out willy-nilly. An array of speculators and conmen arrived to supply everything from mining equipment to black market financing. Millions of tonnes of ore were dug up illegally. Timblo seemed almost embarrassed as he recounted the delirium. 'Mining leases were given to politicians and friends of politicians . . . Everywhere there was cowboyism, with new faces, traders, truck contractors, bad things going on.' Many villagers bought dump trucks on credit and set themselves up as transport-for-hire with local miners. When China's economy began to slow and global commodities prices collapsed, their services were no longer needed, leaving hundreds of trucks idle by the roadside in villages across the state.

An even crazier boom hit the state of Karnataka, Goa's larger neighbour to the south, led by the powerful Reddy brothers, a trio of entrepreneurs who worked in cahoots with the local government.[65] Gali Janardhana Reddy, the most prominent of the three, won his first mining licence in 2004, just as global ore prices began to rise. Reddy went on to transform the mining town of Bellary; it filled with heavily guarded compounds and luxury foreign cars, becoming somewhat reminiscent of the hideout of a Colombian drug cartel rather than a mid-size Indian town. Hundreds of mining companies sprang up, extracting enough ore to fill thousands of trucks each day, which then thundered off to nearby coastal ports ready to be shipped out to China. Political interference was minimal, especially once Reddy became a minister in the state government. An official investigation later blamed a 'collapse of administration and governance' for the scandal, and cited gross misconduct by more than seven hundred public officials.[66] Reddy himself denied wrongdoing, but was arrested in 2011 on charges of illegal mining, and spent more than three years in jail, before being released on bail.

These scandals underlined the new demands that globalisation placed on India's creaking state. One of the country's richer and better administered regions, Goa and its civil service were still rapidly overwhelmed. The phrase 'illegal mining' became a catch-all to cover anything from miners who dug up more ore than their licences allowed, to those who started new mines with no licences at all. Officially, production doubled during the boom. Unofficially, everyone seemed to know that far more had been dug up on the sly and exported without being registered. Environmental activists catalogued dozens of infractions, including mining in wildlife sanctuaries and forbidden forested areas. The relevant authorities – the local Forest Department, the Directorate of Mines & Geology – lacked even basic tools to enforce the law. Goa became an example of what economists call regulatory capture, as those meant to curb improper mining instead profited from its rise. Claude Alvares of the Goa Foundation, an environmental group, told me many officials ended up in the pay of the mining lobby and the politicians that ultimately controlled it. 'Everyone was making money,' he said.

In the end, it took outside intervention to bring the scams to a stop. Beginning in 2011, the Supreme Court brought in a series of blanket iron ore bans, first in Karnataka and then in Goa.[67] In the same vein as their later decisions to cancel telecoms and coal-mining licences, these were a kind of shock therapy from a judiciary that had grown impatient with corruption. 'Mining stands for all that is wrong with unreformed India,' as author Gurcharan Das put it. 'The nexus among politicians, officials, police and big business, a powerful labour mafia, disenfranchisement of local residents, [and] damage to the environment.'[68] Yet the sector's problems provided a wider lesson too, namely that corruption was not just the result of greed, but also the far more complex problem of state incapacity.

Behind this there was the vexed question of politics. China and India both suffered severe corruption, but only India was a democracy. Behind almost every corruption scandal there lay the deeper problem of political party funding and the way in which political parties relied on under-the-table donations from businesses. As we finished our own conversation in Singapore, I pushed Vinod Rai for specifics. During the season of scams, what sort of collusion were we talking about? Were these deals as crude as handing over envelopes stuffed with cash, or was there a more sophisticated quid pro quo? Most importantly, how much was taken by the politicians, and how much was left over for their party? Rai sighed, and admitted that even he had never been able to figure out the going rate for a coal or telecoms licence, or indeed the exact circumstances under which cash was handed over. 'There was jockeying, there was lobbying, and obviously people were willing to pay a price to get these [coal] blocks under the table . . . For every 100 rupees the [politician] might give 70 to his party and keep 30 for himself. Or he might have kept 70 and given the party 30, who can tell? But the sums involved were clearly very large.'

Modi arrives by helicopter to address a mass rally in the eastern state of Jharkhand in 2014. Indian election campaigns are increasingly marred by rising costs and worries about corruption.

CHAPTER 6

MONEY POWER POLITICS

EVERYBODY USES BLACK MONEY

Settling back in his spacious office after a long day, Akhilesh Yadav allowed a moment of candour. It was election time in Uttar Pradesh, India's most populous and politically significant state. Yadav had addressed seven mass rallies that day, zipping by helicopter from one to the other, before flying back to his residence in Lucknow, the capital. Tomorrow, there would be half a dozen more. It was February 2017 and I had come to meet him with a group of academics and journalists to discuss the state of the polls. He bustled in with the air of a man with better things to do, dressed in the same plain white *kurta* and black waist-coat he wore out campaigning. In his early forties with swept-back black hair, Yadav's boyish face seemed incongruent with the angle of a crooked nose, the victim of a youthful football accident. There was a poster montage on the far wall, featuring a picture of Yadav's face made up of dozens of other tiny images of himself. Outside it was dark; a clock on his desk in the shape of a bicycle, his party's logo, read 7:55 p.m.

Uttar Pradesh – or 'UP' for short – went to the polls every five years, in what was always the world's largest local election. Home to some 220 million people, the state stretched from the borders of New Delhi in the west to the holy capital of Varanasi nearly 800 kilometres to the east, lying at the centre of what was sometimes referred to as the 'cow belt'.[1] Criss-crossed by the sacred Ganges and dotted with innumerable spiritual sites, this was India's heartland; a region that acted as the bosom of its identity both as an independent nation and under the British and

Mughal empires beforehand. Sheer weight of population ensured elections in UP were India's most politically important, but 2017's was especially fierce: Yadav's Samajwadi ('Socialist') Party had taken power five years earlier, but now they faced an emboldened BJP, who had swept the state in Narendra Modi's 'wave' election in 2014.

Out on the campaign trail the various party leaders traded barbs about corruption, accusing one another of siphoning cash from state projects and trafficking in black money. But sitting in Lucknow, Yadav admitted that India's problems of money in politics now affected all parties, including his own. 'It's not money that is black or white, it's how we do business,' he said of attempts to curb corruption in New Delhi, and in particular Modi's demonetisation experiment, which he, not entirely surprisingly, judged to have been a failure. 'In the villages, people buy houses and cars; they don't know they have to pay taxes. They feel "This is our money", they have earned it,' he went on, explaining why so few people admitted their earnings. 'But how can you take tax from the poor? They don't have any money . . . How will corruption decrease, you tell me? Everybody is using black money in elections!'

Political scientist Ashutosh Varshney suggests three 'master narratives' have come to define India over the last century.[2] First came secular nationalism, the ideology of Nehru and Gandhi, and still the official state creed. Second was Hindu nationalism, a reaction to the first, led by the BJP and the RSS. Finally came 'caste-based social justice', in which political parties representing lower caste groups began to win political power. Yet to these three, if you were only a little cynical, you might add a fourth: cash.

Before liberalisation Indian democracy was a cheap, low-tech affair. But money began flooding into politics after 1991, particularly as its economy began to expand rapidly from the middle 2000s. Officially, political parties spent modestly, constrained by strict spending limits. But unofficially everyone knew the bill for India's perpetual jamboree of elections now ran into billions of dollars: $5 billion for the 2014 poll alone, according to one academic estimate.[3] This placed India not far behind the United States as the world's most expensive democracy, except that in India's case most of the money was unaccounted for. It was widely agreed that India's problems of corruption and cronyism would be impossible to fix without first lancing the boil of the issue of illicit cash in politics. Yet this was also a topic very few politicians liked to discuss, making Yadav's candour – 'Everybody is using black money in elections!' – all the more intriguing.

Founded in the early 1990s by his father, Mulayam Singh Yadav, the Samajwadi Party was a prominent example of the revival of caste in Indian politics. Broadly speaking, the millennium-old caste system divided Hindus into four groups, with the priestly Brahmins at the top and labouring Shudras at the bottom. There were then myriad other sub-castes, while below them all came the Dalits, once called 'untouchables', who stood outside the system altogether. In some ways caste became a less important feature of India's social fabric after 1991, as the country urbanised and the fluidity of city life began to break down old rural hierarchies. It was a change long predicted by B. R. Ambedkar, the Dalit social reformer and architect of India's constitution, whose caustic view of rural life – 'What is the village but a sink of localism, a den of ignorance, narrow-mindedness and communalism?' – stood in clear contrast to Gandhi's more romanticised idylls.[4] Yet in the aftermath of economic reopening, caste also became a more important political force in many parts of India. This was especially so when the government established a new set of official caste categories during the early 1990s – forward castes; other backward castes; scheduled castes and tribes – and began to use them as a basis for the distribution of scarce public sector jobs. Although its name suggested a left-wing ideology, the Samajwadi Party was firmly caste-ist in its orientation, drawing support in particular from Yadavs, a caste group traditionally comprising mostly peasant farmers and making up about a tenth of UP's population.[5] With the party as their vehicle, the Yadavs soon became UP's dominant caste force.

Folksy and blunt, Mulayam Singh Yadav was by all accounts a masterful politician: the type who cultivated contacts in distant villages, and rarely forgot a birthday or wedding. He won the post of chief minister three times before his son took the job in 2012. Once known as the United Provinces, the state he ran had previously been the jewel of colonial India, blessed by lush farmland and dotted with cosmopolitan cities. But after Independence, India's old regional balance gradually began to reverse. Once undeveloped parts of the south and west grew quickly, while UP and other northern heartland states slid gradually backwards, hobbled by feudalism, administrative incompetence and grinding poverty. Later, a new phrase hung over the place: '*Goonda Raj*', taking the Hindi word for thug as shorthand for lawlessness and graft.

UP also won a reputation for brutal patronage politics, in which support came through caste favouritism, backed by ruthless violence. Large swathes of the state, especially in its wilder eastern fringe, were said to be controlled by criminals, many of whom were co-opted into political parties. As chief minister, Akhilesh Yadav had tried to shed this dark side of his state's image. Educated in Australia, he came across as an Indian everyman in his early forties with few airs and graces. His young wife Dimple, who had the looks of a Bollywood heroine, added a smidgen of glamour to their regime.

Speaking in his office, the younger Yadav rattled off his achievements: investments in mills and factories, a free phone number for police and ambulance services, and a new toll road connecting Lucknow to New Delhi. Much like Narendra Modi, he favoured grand infrastructure projects and technological gimmicks, including a scheme that gave away one million laptops to children. Electricity had improved on his watch, he said, with no blackouts in major cities and power 'for sixteen to eighteen hours in villages'. He identified with the state's burgeoning youthful popu-lation, talking lyrically about those who came to his campaign events. 'I observe the crowd, they come in blue jeans, they all have mobiles clicking photographs,' he said of a rally earlier that day in a town in a far corner of the state. 'I can say we are living in very transparent times.'

Yadav's attempts to clean up his party's image had proved only partially successful. UP still languished towards the bottom of state league tables for economic development, and towards the top for crime. Its newspapers remained filled with tales of murder, kidnap-ping and arson. In the months before I met him, Yadav had feuded publicly with his father, wresting control of the party apparatus, but in the process damaging his own clean image. More than one million young people spilled into the state's labour market each year, only to find few jobs waiting for them in a state that enjoyed little of the indus-trial development seen in India's most prosperous west and south. Social indicators remained woeful, especially for women, with sexual assault a particular problem. In 2014, Mulayam Singh Yadav was pilloried for appearing to excuse a widespread culture of rape, after being reported to have remarked somewhat blithely that 'boys commit mistakes'.[6]

Other poor northern Indian states – Madhya Pradesh on UP's southern border, for instance, or Bihar to the east – fared little better on these measures. But UP's size and symbolic importance attracted special attention. Here was the state that had produced eight of India's fifteen prime ministers, and stood centre stage during all three of Varshney's 'master narratives': first a Congress bastion and bedrock of secular nationalism; then the backdrop for the BJP's Hindu reawakening in the 1990s; and finally the cradle of a new lower-caste politics too, as both Yadav's father and Mayawati, a charismatic Dalit leader, took power as chief minister. Yet through all this the state made little economic progress, in part because it was also in the vanguard of the fourth change that reshaped India's democratic landscape – what Shahabuddin Quraishi, a former head of the Election Commission, dubbed the rise of 'money power'.

A TAINTED DEMOCRACY

If for no other reason, the recent influx of money into Indian politics matters because it has tainted one of history's most remarkable constitutional experiments. Beginning in 1947, India began to assemble a full parliamentary democracy. The early omens did not look promising. Modern academic models suggest that democracies rarely succeed in poor countries. In one study, the Polish-American political scientist Adam Przeworski found that countries below a certain level of GDP – $6,055 per head, to be precise – almost never manage to sustain democratic government.[7] At the time of its independence India was nowhere close. It was also deeply hierarchical, almost entirely rural, and with four fifths of its population unable to read. Textbook models strongly suggested it would slide quickly into autocracy, as happened in Pakistan, its post-Partition neighbour. 'Most wealthy countries are democratic, and most democratic countries – India is the most dramatic exception – are wealthy,' as political scientist Samuel Huntington once argued.[8]

Barring a brief hiccough during Indira Gandhi's 'Emergency' in the mid-1970s, this precarious constitutional experiment more or less worked. 'The old certitudes of Indian politics had crumbled,' as academic Sunil Khilnani put it in his book *The Idea of India* in the late 1990s, referring to the declining power of secular nationalism in Indian politics. 'Yet one powerful continuity stretched across this half-century of spectacular and often turbulent events: the presence of a democratic state.' Liberals like Khilnani often regretted this decline in India's secular identity, and its eclipse by powerful religious, caste-based and linguistic political movements. Others blamed the complexities of democratic rule for India's slow economic progress, and in particular its inability to build Chinese-style infrastructure. Yet India's democracy also proved successful, binding together a subcontinent that was far more linguistically and ethnically diverse than China, and which could easily have ended up divided into as many nations as Europe.

All the money that gushed into Indian politics has not corrupted the polls themselves. Despite extensive evidence of voter bribery, the country's elections tend to be both free and fair, with little evidence of ballot-tampering. Armed with its 'model code of conduct', the Election Commission of India acts as a fierce policeman. Boisterous street campaigning is banned, while balloting is run remarkably cheaply. The real problem is exorbitant and rapidly rising election costs for political parties, which has pushed them to raise huge quantities of illicit funds, mostly from larger businesses. In turn, political leaders have built political machines whose wealth and power comfortably exceed the likes of Tammany Hall in nineteenth-century New York.

The pernicious influence of money on politics was clear enough to Vineet Victor, a man I met on a roadside in eastern UP, a few days after sitting down with Akhilesh Yadav. It was a warm Saturday morning in late February, with blue skies overhead, when I stopped in a small village close to a curve in the river Ganges, a two-hour drive west from the holy city of Varanasi, over bumpy roads that often degenerated into little more than dirt tracks. The town's voters would head to the polls in a few days to elect a member to the state assembly in Lucknow. Two-wheelers buzzed by as we talked, standing on the roadside next to a shack selling snacks and tobacco, with two sticks holding up a tarpaulin awning for shade. Four green and white minarets rose up above the trees from a nearby mosque.

Victor worked as a local school teacher, but dressed in jeans and a lime green polo shirt, set off with sharp rimless spectacles, he looked as if he could have been an accountant or IT consultant. Akhilesh Yadav seemed like a decent man, he told me, but his party, a powerful presence in the local area, was full of *dacoits* (bandits). Their rule had delivered little for his town, but the local council was led by a Samajwadi politician elected a few years before, who had enjoyed a rapid transformation in her own fortunes. Victor simply called her *begum*, a word that means 'powerful woman'. 'It all goes in their pocket,' he said of the politician and her family. 'They had nothing, no proper house to live in, no proper vehicle to ride on. Now they have all sorts of facilities.'

A crowd gathered around us, chipping in examples of other local politicians who spent generously to win power and used it to benefit themselves. Money from state schemes designed to help the poor was diverted for their personal use, they explained, while bribes were solicited to win construction contracts or government jobs. The police were dominated by Yadavs and paid little attention to complaints from other caste groups, let alone Muslims or Christians. There was a particular scam, one person told me, that involved stealing money from a new initiative – designed to fund new indoor toilets for those in the village who did not have one – in which conspiring politicians and builders used fake pictures of latrines to claim a generous government subsidy.

'People like us, normal people, we try to work for our whole lives, and we are not able to get those kind of treasures,' Victor said ruefully. Still, he thought himself fortunate: he had a job as a school teacher; he owned a small home with running water, where he lived with his wife and two children. He wore a chunky watch, bearing an approximation of the Calvin Klein logo. Few of his neighbours were so fortunate, he said. Employment was scarce, forcing men to labour in farming or construction. At least half of the young people in the area would leave, seeking work in Lucknow or New Delhi, or Dubai if they were lucky. Ten years back he had also tried to leave to find a job in Europe, only to scrap his plans at the last minute, in order to care for his elderly parents.

Victor lived in the heart of the UP's crime belt, in an area often called the 'wild east' which featured as a locale for Bollywood movies featuring *dacoits* and mafia dons. But when travelling through the area it was lethargy rather than lawlessness that stood out. Brick kilns were the only industry to speak of, their conical smoking towers dotting a picturesque landscape filled with mustard and wheat fields, but almost entirely empty of factories. The larger towns showed some signs of development: mobile phone masts rose up along the roadside and satellite dishes peeked out from walls. Most of these walls were at least made of brick, but it took only the slightest village detour, along roads that turned quickly to dirt, to see wonky old *kutcha* houses, fashioned uneasily from straw and mud.

The region's larger cities were generally teeming and squalid, with garbage piled on the sides of the street and smog thick in the air. Yet even here roadside advertising hoardings hinted at a burning sense of aspiration, offering bags of cement, or branded Ayurvedic goods from a company run by a famous yoga guru. By far the most numerous were billboards for education – 'DPS World School', 'St Margaret's College', 'Divine Public School' – dozens upon dozens of which whizzed by in every town. Each product in its own way held out the promise of escape from a part of the country which had failed to find even modest economic success: a new home, a modest consumer lifestyle or the chance to educate your children, so they could leave and find work somewhere else.

Back in Kachhawan, Vineet Victor blamed a mixture of caste politics and corruption for UP's weak progress. Vote-buying would be common in the upcoming election, he said. The various parties went door to door in the village on the evenings before polling day, passing out alcohol and money. Thinking back to Akhilesh Yadav's boast when we met in his office, I asked about the local power supply. Victor gestured up at the black wires that snaked through concrete pylons up above. Unlike some nearby villages Kachhawan had been connected to the electricity grid not long back, he explained. Some roads, including the one on which we were standing, even had street lights. 'We have got good wires now, and these days we get a good supply,' he said, explaining that power had improved mysteriously in the months prior to the election. But once the polls were over he predicted the supply would worsen, returning to just six or eight hours a day during the scorching summer in a few months' time. 'Before elections we have good power, but after the parties win we will get nothing.'

A NICE DAY FOR A FAKE WEDDING

Indian democracy did not come cheap. Over a generation the number of political parties contesting elections had shot up, from slightly more than a dozen in the years after Independence to nearly 500 in 2014.[9] Only a tiny fraction of these were major national players, but their proliferation still meant that local contests were now much more likely to be fought out between three or four parties, making races both more competitive and more expensive. The number of registered voters had also shot up, reaching 814 million in 2014.[10] Meanwhile India's rapidly expanding economy had also increased the value of political power, in terms of what could be extracted from it, bumping up further the sums parties were willing to spend to hold onto it. In the absence of regulations to keep spending in check, and with plenty of businesses ready give funds off the books, the question became: how much could you raise?

Mass political rallies were the iceberg tip of election spending. One morning in UP I pushed through the throng to watch Narendra Modi enthral a packed field of supporters on the outskirts of Deoria, a dusty down-on-its-luck kind of town in the state's eastern corner. Tens of thousands of mostly male, saffron-clad enthusiasts waved flags and chanted BJP slogans. Local villagers stood in small clusters on nearby rooftops, waiting for the entertainment to begin. Indian politicians often arrived at rural rallies by helicopter, mostly to avoid long journeys and road delays, but also partly for the theatre of it all. Anticipation of their arrival – the speck on the horizon, the gradually rising thud of the rotors, the swirl of dust upon landing – added drama to proceedings, and it was common to see attendees streaming towards the exit having watched nothing but the touchdown. The helicopter was generally parked next to the stage, as a visible symbol of the speaker's power. And as if to make his own pre-eminence completely clear, Modi arrived that morning in one military chopper escorted by two decoys to foil possible assailants.

The trio of vehicles idled to the left of the stage as Modi began, dressed in a bright yellow tunic, and with an orange and green scarf slung over one shoulder. Speaking in Hindi, his rhetoric held the crowd spellbound for the best part of an hour, as he castigated Akhilesh Yadav's record and defended his own recent *notebandi* experiment. At one point, without naming them, he mocked 'intellectuals from Harvard and Oxford', a reference to Amartya Sen and former prime minister Manmohan Singh, both of whom had been vocally critical of demonetisation. 'On the one hand these are intellectuals from Harvard,' he said, his voice dripping with mockery, 'and on the other, there is this son of a poor mother, trying to change the economy through hard work.'[11] Modi worked the crowd with emphatic two-handed gestures and long theatrical pauses, often leaning in and resting on one elbow, as if beckoning the audience in to share a secret. To make a point he gripped both sides of his lectern, before slowing his delivery and looking across the audience from left to right. Only then did the pace quicken, as one arm swept around and the other thrust into the air, a finger wagged for emphasis. 'I was born to serve the poor. So now they [the wealthy] are all attacking me. So when they come to attack me, who will protect me?' he asked towards the end. 'We will!' the crowd roared back.

As he spoke I glanced around and tried to tot up the cost. As well as the helicopters, there was staging, sound equipment, seating and awnings for local bigwigs. Hundreds of guards armed with metre-long wooden sticks held back the crowd. Orange flags, caps and bibs had been handed out to supporters, many of whom were bussed in from nearby towns, and perhaps paid a few hundred rupees to attend. Some estimates have suggested that large public rallies of this type, especially in big cities, could cost well over $1 million apiece.[12] Then there were all the other elements of a modern campaign: pollsters, political consultants, roadside posters, television adverts and Facebook posts. The result fused electoral techniques from the nineteenth and twenty-first centuries, and incurred the expense of both.

Even these legitimate outlays made up just a small portion of what the political parties actually spent, as Shahabuddin Quraishi, the former election commissioner, explained to me about a week after Modi's speech. A former IAS officer, Quraishi took the job as India's election regulator in 2010. With pure white hair and outspoken views, he quickly became one of the post's more recognisable holders. 'From my first press conference, we said we'd go after all this money power, with a kind of new shock treatment,' he told me.

Over the next few years Quraishi kept a list of the artful ways parties tried to buy votes. 'They were all very crafty,' he said. 'Some would hand out money, others held fake weddings to entertain villagers with food and liquor, or handed out mobile phones, or SUVs, or saris, or jobs, or almost anything you can think of.' His autobiography included a compendium of forty or so methods, from cash funnelled through village headmen, to gifts of solar lamps, narcotics, cows or manure. It was hard to tell, he said, which were effective. His sense was that the parties knew what they were doing, and handed out their goodies carefully, either to win over wavering voters or to ensure a good turnout among the already committed. Voters were free to take inducements and vote for whoever they liked. But at the very least, in contests where rivals were offering freebies, refusing to offer any of your own was a sure path to defeat.

Election Commission rules say that parties can spend whatever they like in elections, so long as they submit accounts. The BJP admitted to spending Rs 7.1 billion ($111 million) in 2014, although this was a fraction of what most experts think they actually spent.[13] Local politicians had stringent limits, however: $43,000 per candidate during the 2017 state assembly poll in UP, or a little over $100,000 for an aspirant MP in the last national campaign.[14] In private almost everyone admitted that these limits were widely flouted. In 2013, Gopinath Munde, a senior BJP politician, caused a furore by briefly admitting in public that he spent around Rs 80 million ($1.2 million) to win his seat in the western state of Maharashtra.[15] Munde rapidly retracted his remarks, but Quraishi told me similar spending figures were common elsewhere around India, with many politicians rumoured to spend millions of dollars. 'With all these business guys from mining or liquor or property, there is no dearth of money,' he said. 'The attitude was that we have such a lot of money to give away. It might work, it might not work. But why not try?'

Keeping track of this was all but impossible. The Election Commission sent officials to poke around at campaign events, trying to intercept physical cash as it moved around India, by road or private jet, in the run-up to poll time. It claimed to have seized $18 million in cash during the first few weeks of campaigning in UP alone, along with two million barrels of alcohol and 2,725 kilograms of drugs, all supposedly destined to win over wavering voters.[16] But just as fast as Quraishi put a stop to one vote-buying method, the parties dreamed up another. Many of the problems that plagued the early days of India's democracy, from logistical snarl-ups to violence at the polls, had been fixed, he argued. But the rising tide of illegal funding showed no signs of receding. 'We haven't been able to control this problem of money power,' he said at the end of our conversation. 'Every party, every individual is violating these rules. It is just a question of who gets caught.'

HE HAS THE CAPACITY

These glimpses of India's illegal election spending only invited a further question: where did the money come from? Officially, large businesses could donate whatever they liked to political parties via special electoral 'trusts', although only a small number of big conglomerates actually set them up.[17] Much larger quantities were donated by individuals, whose names had to be declared only if they gave more than Rs 20,000 ($300).[18] Below that level donors could stay safely anonymous, while there were no rules stopping them giving multiple bundles of Rs 19,999 to skirt the system. Even then, most election funding experts thought these official funding routes made up just a fraction of the total that the parties took in under the table. Of the $5 billion estimated to have been spent during 2014's poll, around four fifths could have been raised and spent illegally, according to one report.[19]

Very few politicians were willing to speak openly about 'black' political funding. Rajeev Gowda, a gregarious economist turned Congress MP, whom I had met about six months before my trip to UP, was an exception. In 2014, Gowda took a seat in the Rajya Sabha, India's upper house of parliament, representing the southern state of Karnataka. Educated at Wharton and Berkeley, he spent much of his career in the US, churning out academic papers on behavioural economics and financial risk. I came across him via a more recent article on the malign influence of money on politics, written after he returned home to Bangalore. His interest in campaign finance flowed from frustration, he told me over email, as he initially tried and failed to stand for parliament himself.

We agreed to meet one evening in August 2016, during New Delhi's periodic monsoon. That night the rains held off, and I took an auto-rickshaw to his MP's bungalow on the edge of Lodi Gardens, a lush public park dotted with fifteenth-century tombs. Gowda met me outside the front gate, dressed informally in a plain Nehru jacket and crisp white shirt. In his early fifties, he spoke rapidly and often ended his sentences with questions, like an academic fearful of losing his students' attention. Sitting in a sparsely decorated living room, and sipping a glass of wine, he explained that his father and grandfather had both been politicians, and that he had moved back home to India hoping to follow them.

Armed with a famous family name and an impressive CV, at first Gowda was optimistic. He nosed around, sounding out party officials about becoming a candidate for various seats in the Lok Sabha, the lower house of parliament. The knock-backs began to mount up. 'As soon as they discovered I didn't have much money to bring to the table, they suddenly weren't interested, if you understand what I mean?' he told me. He tried seat after seat, failing in each. 'The people they consider to be viable candidates are people who they consider to have huge amounts of black money, OK?' He went on: 'You don't hear people saying "This guy is a complete crook, we don't want to be seen with him". They say "This is the right guy, he has made a lot of money. He has the capacity."'

Capacity meant the ability to provide cash for party workers, food for volunteers, and cars and buses to ferry them around. It meant stumping up for campaign rallies and public meetings and advertising and entertainment. Demands for funds began with basic 'booth' expenses, meaning the thousand or more polling booths into which each local constituency is divided. 'Party involvement itself is expensive,' Gowda said with a smile. 'They will say "OK, we will come and do a rally in your constituency, we will bring some star campaigner." But who has to pay for that rally? You have to make that happen.' As election day approached, and cash began to be distributed, capacity mattered more than ever. Money alone wasn't always enough to ensure victory, but without it the odds of even being selected were slim.

In the end, Gowda gave up trying to win a seat, and managed to win a berth in the upper house, an appointed post that avoided the need to win an election entirely. But other candidates of limited means were forced to cultivate rich backers, to provide the capacity they lacked. Some approached local business figures. Others cultivated lower-level politicians, and asked them to fundraise on their behalf. 'In fact, why do you think I was foolish enough to think I could contest the Lok Sabha?' Gowda asked me. 'Because I have enough networks that I would think I could have figured it out, even without having the money in my own pocket.'

I heard similar stories from another well-known national politician. Any candidate in a close national parliamentary race needed to spend at least 'six or seven crore' (roughly $1 million), he told me. If you were lucky, some portion of this might be given to you by your party. But most of it had to be raised solo. 'If you are very lucky, you can go to a single smooth operator in your local political scene,' the politician explained. 'Ideally, this would be someone who will tell you they believed in you, and who won't immediately ask for any quid pro quo.' If an amenable businessman could not be found, lower-level political operatives were often the best choice. 'There are people raising money in your name who you might not even know about,' he explained. In this way, even personally honest politicians were drawn unavoidably into a system of corruption. 'It's a sad business, but that is how it works. There isn't another way around it.'

These relationships between politicians and supporters were typically based on trust, given neither party wanted details of their arrangement in the open. Some who provided cash were public-spirited and asked for little in return. Another politician, this time one who ran a party machine in southern India, gave me an example involving one of his operatives, a newspaper seller who won a seat on the local municipal corporation. The man was well liked but poor, travelling around the city by bicycle. The politician wanted him to run for the state assembly. 'I said: "You are going to contest an election." He started crying,' the politician told me. 'He said: "Sir, I don't have a car, so how can I do this?" But I knew he was popular, and would win the election. So what happened? Well, I went to this business guy, and I said: "You have an extra car, please give it to him." And I went to this other guy, and I said: "This man needs some new clothes, get it done please." And everyone did it.'

Most funders do demand something for their support, however. Having invested heavily in winning, the politicians also try to recoup their costs, extracting what they can from the office they hold. These local problems are then magnified many times over in New Delhi, as national party leaders, facing rocketing election costs, come to rely ever more on the generosity of the larger tycoons. At base, India's money power system makes it all but impossible to win elections honestly. 'Think of a politician today,' Rajeev Gowda told me. 'You don't think: "My God, I want to be like him." You say: "My God, why doesn't the bastard give some of his wealth to me?" . . . This is actually out of control, and it will continue to be out of control. There is no limit, it is an arms race.'

THE SOPRANOS OF MORADABAD

UP's election results were released on a Saturday morning in early March, a few days after the final round of voting was wrapped up. They left Akhilesh Yadav's hopes in tatters. The young chief minister had campaigned doggedly for a second term in office, but despite his efforts the BJP won a landslide victory, providing a thumping reminder of Narendra Modi's heartland appeal. Modi's promises to tackle corruption and create jobs, alongside his subtler appeals to Hindu pride, had broadened his party's support far beyond its traditional base, enabling it to take around four fifths of the state's assembly seats. As well as being an endorsement of the prime minister, the vote was a rejection too: of the crime-ridden, black-money-infused style of government for which UP had become notorious.

UP's politicians were more blatant than most, but all major political parties played India's black money game. Some were notably inventive in the ways they raised cash. Mamata Banerjee, the diminutive chief minister of West Bengal, turned to art to fund her Trinamool Congress, which ruled the eastern state for much of the last decade. An amateur painter, she claimed to have persuaded various friendly business leaders to donate as much as Rs 2 million (about $31,000) to buy each of her works, creating an artful means of legally raising large sums.[20] For most leaders money-raising options were more limited. Either you inducted rich people into your party and tapped them for funds, or you befriended rich people outside it and asked them to bankroll you anyway. Given the large sums involved, I was often struck by how wearying this fundraising process must have been, given the ceaseless pressure to bring in money on the one hand, and all of the clandestine inferences and understandings and debts to be paid back on the other.

The dramatic rise of so-called *crorepati* politicians – meaning those worth more than a crore, or ten million, rupees – provided one of the clearest signs of India's recent political dash for cash. More than three quarters of those elected to UP's assembly on that Saturday in March crossed this threshold, meaning they had assets of roughly $150,000 or more. At the national level, the average MP was worth at least $2 million.[21] Then there were the truly wealthy: the businesspeople whom parties tempted into the fold with offers of safe seats or cosy berths in the upper chamber. In the mid-2000s, the Samajwadi Party recruited

Anil Ambani to the Rajya Sabha, at a time when the billionaire tycoon happened to be investing in the state. Mayawati, the Dalit leader of UP's Bahujan Samaj Party (BSP), enjoyed a reputation for especially inventive fundraising schemes during her own periods in power. One involved the alleged sale of 'tickets', meaning the right to represent her party in parliament. Although this is something Mayawati has denied, a leaked US diplomatic cable released by WikiLeaks suggested that the going rate for a BSP ticket during the 2009 national elections came to 'roughly 250,000 dollars'.[22] The same cable, poetically entitled 'Mayawati: Portrait of a Lady', made further allegations concerning the excesses of her various spells as UP's chief minister. 'When she needed new sandals, her private jet flew empty to Mumbai to retrieve her preferred brand,' the author claimed. Such stories had often attracted the attentions of India's police, who unsuccessfully investigated various corruption allegations against her over the years, all of which she firmly denied.[23]

The need to raise money had another unfortunate side effect: the relentless rise of criminal politicians. Voters in most countries would shun candidates whose background came with hints of criminality. But in India, parties like the BJP and the Congress actively recruit such candidates. Roughly one fifth of MPs elected in 2014 had 'serious' criminal records, ranging from kidnapping and racketeering to murder, nearly double the rate ten years earlier.[24] Rather than turn against them, voters often took violence and extortion as perverse signs of strength; a signal that a criminal politician could offer protection or extract resources from the state. 'Many voters vote for politicians because, rather than in spite, of their criminal reputations,' Milan Vaishnav wrote in *When Crime Pays*. Such was the attraction of a criminal background that candidates facing criminal charges were three times more likely to win a seat than those with a clean record.

This complex intermingling of politics, wealth and crime was explained to me one afternoon by Gilles Verniers, a genial young Belgian academic, who had settled in New Delhi and become a respected analyst of UP politics. 'It is very similar to *The Sopranos*. In fact, it is amazing how that series has opened my eyes,' he told me once over a cup of sugary tea, sitting in his home in a southern suburb of the city, dressed in a flowing white *kurta*. Just as Tony Soprano officially made his money as a waste management consultant, so UP's colourful tycoons typically had a legitimate base in a single industry like liquor or construction. Expanding their operations, however, meant taking on other rivals with criminal tendencies. 'If you reach a certain scale, it is a dangerous business, so you need protection,' Verniers told me. 'One way is to become a politician, or to get protection from politicians. And of course the politicians are happy, because you come with money.' The rise of crime-tainted politicians diminished public respect for the political system overall. Yet when elected, these criminal figures often turned out to be Robin Hood figures with a populist common touch. 'It doesn't matter that these people are gangsters,' Verniers said. 'It is that they are generous. Criminal politicians who were perceived to be too greedy get wiped out.'

Few people embodied UP's occasional nexus of crime, business and politics more precisely than Gurdeep 'Ponty' Chadha, an infamous alcohol magnate and money man. In November 2012, aged just fifty-two, Chadha was killed in a gunfight at his home in a leafy enclave of southern New Delhi. 'Chadha had gained a surpassing reputation for the kind of entrepreneurial success that is born of great intimacy with power,' as journalist Mehboob Jeelani wrote in *Caravan* magazine.[25] Shot following a feud with his younger brother, his demise only heightened his image as modern India's greatest gangster tycoon.

Chadha was a tall man with a sizeable paunch and a taste for rich men's clothing. But he was born poor, in a small home in the industrial city of Moradabad, about a three-hour drive east of New Delhi. His father and uncles owned a wholesale booze business, where Chadha began working as a teenager, going on to fashion a liquor empire that came to dominate much of northern India in only a few decades. At first he expanded his business using hired goons and plentiful bribes. But he also learned the value of political patronage, delivering bags of cash on behalf of his father to help Mulayam Singh Yadav fight an election in 1989. He grew close to Yadav's party, and prospered during the politician's first spell as chief minister in the 1990s. As well as liquor, Chadha moved first into sand-mining and real estate, then eventually everything from sugar-refining and food-processing to Bollywood financing. He cultivated connections, hosting what Jeelani described as 'Gatsby-style farmhouse parties' – 'farmhouse' being a euphemistic New Delhi term for 'mansion'. Out-of-town guests were often flown in on chartered jets for these gatherings, while media reports talked of his habit of handing out 'thousands' of Rolex and Omega watches as gifts during the annual Diwali festival. 'Everyone would be wearing the same model,' an acquaintance recounted.[26] 'They'd see the watch and everyone would know.'

The kind of political patronage Chadha enjoyed could be fleeting. Businessmen who acted as 'bag carriers' for politicians – meaning those who donated, stored and laundered money – often suffered rapid reversals if their patrons lost power. But Chadha proved unusually deft, starting out as an intimate of the Yadavs before switching sides and growing even more successful under Mayawati, their great rival. For UP's leaders a relationship with Chadha was both lucrative and uncomplicated; he gave freely and kept his requests reasonable. Yet over time he earned the kind of bounty that only political goodwill could provide: liquor licences, cheap land, favourable tax status, police protection and lenient treatment from the judiciary. Not long before his death, Chadha even made a dash for respectability, consolidating his businesses into Wave, a conglomerate focused on property and shopping malls, with a subsidiary that won lucrative government contracts to provide free lunches to schoolchildren.[27]

If Chadha was UP's most notorious businessman, his fame was still eclipsed by that of a second local tycoon, who also forged a rags-to-riches story at the intersection of money and power. Subrata Roy, chairman of Sahara India, a conglomerate based in Lucknow, also began his career modestly, delivering snacks on a Lambretta scooter in Gorakhpur, an impoverished city in the east of the state. In the late 1970s he set up a small 'parallel banking' business, offering generous rates of interest to poorer people without access to formal banking services, from farmers and taxi drivers to household servants. Roy's offers attracted millions of customers. As more signed up, so their deposits provided the capital with which he built a business empire of more than a hundred companies, with interests stretching from finance and housing to infrastructure and consumer goods. At his peak, Roy launched an airline, owned a Formula 1 team, sponsored the shirts of India's cricket team, and snapped up a clutch of foreign hotels, including New York's Plaza and London's Grosvenor House.

As his wealth grew, the cult of Roy's personality expanded with it. Sahara's more than one million employees addressed him as their 'managing worker', and were told to wear black-and-white uniforms once a week, including white socks, to mimic the black waistcoat and white shirts Roy typically wore himself. Tall and slim with boot-polish-black hair and a neatly trimmed moustache, Roy was famous for presiding over lengthy company-wide meetings, beginning with a rousing rendition of the Sahara corporate anthem. Those attending would greet one another using the Sahara salute, placing their right hand over their hearts with an open palm, before listening as the managing worker held forth on the importance of patriotism, or his near-mystical personal philosophy, which he dubbed 'collective materialism'.[28] Yet Sahara's business prospered despite its many oddities, amassing assets worth $10 billion or more, including an array of flashy airport hotels and high-end residential 'townships' dotted around India.

Roy also used his money to build Sahara Shaher, a sprawling estate in eastern Lucknow filled with lush lawns and glistening white marble, and featuring its own auditorium, cinema, golf course and cricket field. More akin to a Mughal fort than a mere mansion, Roy lived there as a recluse, emerging occasionally to host glittering parties filled with Bollywood celebrities and government powerbrokers. He courted politicians of all parties, although his links with the Yadavs were especially close. On the night Akhilesh Yadav became chief minister in 2012, Roy hosted a giant victory party, ferrying guests around the grounds of his mansion in a fleet of white Mercedes saloons.[29] As with 'Ponty' Chadha, Roy's alliance with the Yadavs did his businesses no harm. As he diversified into property during the 2000s, Sahara managed to acquire large tracts of land around the state, part of a drive that eventually left him holding 34,000 acres around India, an area about three quarters the size of Washington, DC.[30] In his pomp, Roy had holdings larger than any publicly listed Indian company, a feat that would have been virtually impossible without help from friends in politics.

Some questioned whether Roy's political bonds went deeper, asking if the millions of deposits he took from impoverished customers included money from politicians seeking to conceal its origins. 'Does Sahara keep politicians' money?' journalist Tamal Bandyopadhyay, who wrote a book on Sahara, asked Roy outright in 2014, around the time that his businesses began to come under serious official scrutiny.[31] 'Is Sahara a vehicle for turning black money white?' Roy firmly denied both accusations, just as Sahara consistently rejected the charge that its investment schemes were structured like a Ponzi scheme. Still, the question of where exactly Sahara raised its money remained unanswered. Back in 2012, regulators demanded that Roy refund more than $3 billion to his investors.[32] Three years later, then aged sixty-five, he was sent to New Delhi's Tihar jail on charges of contempt of court, having failed to appear at a hearing investigating another of his financial products. He remained in prison, off and on, for much of the next few years, trying to rescue his tottering business, finishing a trilogy of florid autobiographical management books, and vigorously denying any wrongdoing.

Men like Chadha and Roy, trusted allies willing to donate sizeable sums, provided a pleasing solution for cash-starved politicians. The circle of cronyism was self-reinforcing: the stronger the friendship, the richer the tycoons became, and the more they could donate in turn. 'The cost of elections skyrockets,' Gilles Verniers explained. 'It is not just the money you spend in each campaign. It is the money you spend to build the patronage networks, to become a candidate in the first place.' Political leaders needed not just to win power, but also to hold it over the long term. They also needed spare resources to rebuild, if voters kicked them out, as Akhilesh Yadav found to his cost in 2017. 'So the circle is complete,' as Raghuram Rajan argued during his time at the Reserve Bank of India. 'The crooked politician needs the businessman to provide the funds that allow him to supply patronage to the poor and fight elections. The corrupt businessman needs the crooked politician to get public resources and contracts cheaply. And the politician needs the votes of the poor and the under-privileged. Every constituency is tied to the other in a cycle of dependence.'[33]

As my trip to UP drew to a close, I put this point about the relationship between rising election costs and the need for ever-greater quantities of black money to a high-ranking civil servant, whom I met one evening at a party. We were standing in the garden of a large home belonging to another government official in Gorakhpur, the eastern city in which Sahara's Subrata Roy began his career. A squalid, beat-up place, roughly 270 kilometres east of Lucknow, Gorakhpur was notorious even in UP for its toxic mixture of poverty, criminality and violence. Yet all that seemed far off as we stood on a warm, pleasant evening, gossiping in the garden about the ongoing elections, and swatting away mosquitoes.

Modi's *notebandi* experiment had actually cut the quantity of black money sloshing around during that year's poll, the civil servant told me.

But he recognised the wider problem: spending on elections had risen sharply over the last decade, and without action it was likely to keep rising in the future. Still, he frowned when I asked if money power was an especially pronounced issue in his state. 'We have our problems here, but you have to remember UP is a poor place, and Gorakhpur is very poor,' he replied, looking vaguely offended. Corruption scandals in northern India tended to involve criminals stealing money from state welfare programmes designed to help the poor, he explained. But because the state itself had relatively very large, wealthy businesses able to donate large sums, election spending was actually quite restrained compared to other parts of the country. 'If you want to see really clever cronyism,' he said with a smile, 'you have to go to the south.'

Waves of grief swept through the southern state of Tamil Nadu in 2016 after the death of chief minister Jayalalithaa, widely known as 'Amma', or Mother, by her supporters.

CHAPTER 7

CRONYISM GOES SOUTH

THE CULT OF AMMA

I walked up a quiet tree-lined avenue in Chennai one spring morning in 2014, to visit a personality cult. Ahead stood an elegant white three-storey building, its entrance draped with flags. The place had a colonial feel, with Greek-style columns and a balcony on the first floor. Curvy script announced it as the headquarters of the All India Anna Dravida Munnetra Kazhagam, or AIADMK, one of two parties that had dominated politics in the southern state of Tamil Nadu for a generation or more. A small gold statue in the forecourt showed its male founder, wearing a hat and thick glasses and holding his arm aloft in a victory sign. But his image was dwarfed by the party's modern icon: Jayaram Jayalalithaa, a diminutive but powerful woman, whose unsmiling face stared down from four giant billboards, one of which stood almost as tall as the building itself.

The commercial capital of the south, Chennai had a different vibe to the rest of urban India. It was still a megacity, with seven million people and steamy, fetid weather, but the pace was slower than in Mumbai or New Delhi, with a downtown of hushed streets and low-rise buildings, rather than half-finished glass towers. The local elite viewed themselves differently too: a people who rose early, spent frugally and venerated pursuits of the mind, from calculus to 'Carnatic' classical music. Many still referred wistfully to Madras, as the city had been christened by the British. (The name changed to Chennai in the mid-1990s to honour Damal Chennappa Nayagar, a local ruler from the time before the East India Company arrived in 1639.) Yet these restrained habits only made Jayalalithaa's cult-like status seem odder, as if they somehow left the place more vulnerable to demagoguery, and the peculiar southern variant of crony capitalism that went along with it.

Both autocrat and recluse, Jayalalithaa by then almost never appeared in public. But in Chennai she was inescapable, staring out from thousands of brightly coloured posters that decorated road junctions, bus stops and highway flyovers. Dozens more were pasted to the walls of her party headquarters. Street stalls outside hawked memorabilia to party loyalists: gilt-framed Jayalalithaa pictures, Jayalalithaa postcards, even garish Jayalalithaa rugs and throws. A former Tamil-language movie star, she had been strikingly beautiful in her youth, and some images showed her from that period, gazing coquettishly at the camera. There were a few more contemporary pictures of her smiling too, looking off into the middle distance and resting her hand on her chin. But mostly she appeared in the same austere depiction, showing an older woman dressed in a conservative sari, her face jowly and pale, with a red bindi on her forehead and her long dark hair drawn back modestly in a bun.

To her acolytes Jayalalithaa was known only as 'Amma' – 'mother' in Tamil – a moniker that now adorned a bewildering array of public institutions and commercial ventures. Many dozens of Amma cafes dotted the streets of Chennai, where workers could buy a heavily subsidised breakfast of *idli*, a savoury rice cake, or *pongal*, a kind of porridge made of rice and yellow lentils, for just a single rupee. Elsewhere Amma stalls sold cut-price vegetables, while the chief minister's face stared out from bottles of Amma drinking water and bags of Amma cement. A madcap exercise in political brand extension, her image eventually adorned everything from cut-price pharmacies and cinemas to salt and tea. Out in the villages, where her party drew much of its support, her face was if anything even more prominent. From the brazenness of her populism to the ubiquity of her face, Jayalalithaa would have made many a Middle Eastern dictator blush.

This intense focus on image was born partly of Tamil Nadu's passion for movies. Bookish and clever as a child, Jayalalithaa was persuaded to try filmmaking by her widowed mother, herself a former actor. Jayalalithaa's first break came in her teens when she met Marudur

Gopalan Ramachandran, or 'MGR', the most celebrated Tamil actor of the age and the man depicted in gold outside the party's headquarters in Chennai. The duo became co-stars, then friends, and then powerbrokers, as she followed him into politics during a moment of fierce conflict over caste identity.

Beginning in the 1950s, a local party called the Dravida Munnetra Kazhagam – meaning Dravidian Progress Federation, or DMK for short – launched a movement to improve the treatment of Tamils from lower castes, while at the same time attacking the disproportionate power held by upper-caste Brahmins. When it first took power in 1967 the DMK began expunging Brahmins from the state's political life. Once a loyal party member, MGR launched the AIADMK as a rebel off-shoot twenty years later, eventually becoming chief minister in 1977. As his companion and political lieutenant, Jayalalithaa inherited the party after his death in 1987, although only after a fierce, public battle with his widow. Over the next three decades Jayalalithaa then waged a further back-and-forth struggle with the DMK, a party whose leader also happened to have a background in the movie business.[1] 'Tamil Nadu has the unique distinction of having been ruled for nearly fifty years by a screenwriter and two actors, all masters of their craft',[2] as one biography put it.

During her five spells as chief minister Jayalalithaa pioneered an imaginative new kind of populism. Assuming that voters cared little for ideology, many Indian politicians learned to win voters' affections through handouts and freebies, in a process sometimes known as 'competitive populism'.[3] Come election time this often meant pledges to cancel farmers' bank loans or provide eye-catching sops to the poor. But Jayalalithaa was more inventive. In 2011, she pledged to give nearly seven million laptops to schoolchildren across Tamil Nadu at a cost of $2 billion or more, handing them out in rucksacks decorated with images of her own face.[4] Other giveaways focused on female voters, giving away Amma-branded electric mixers and food grinders, or targeted farmers with free seeds, sheep and goats.

These bonanzas were mocked for their brazenness, as was Jayalalithaa's periodic habit of taking out full-page national newspaper advertisements to boast about her own largesse. But as a political strategy it was undeniably successful. Jayalalithaa took power first in 1991;

by 2014 she was midway through her fourth spell as chief minister and unquestionably Tamil Nadu's dominant political force. She grew more imperious as her time in office lengthened, almost never talking to journalists or giving speeches. Her supporters also acquired a reputation for vindictiveness, as even minor critics were harangued in court or assaulted in the streets. A former civil servant turned potential political rival had acid thrown on her face.[5] Jayalalithaa became especially notorious for filling her party with an all-male cast of toadies and supplicants. Some showed loyalty to their leader by prostrating themselves in her presence; others had tattoos of her face inked into their forearms.

All important decisions in the state were said to be taken by Jayalalithaa herself, along with many that were much more trivial. No one could speak for her, but given that she herself rarely spoke in public, the state often seemed stuck in perpetual confusion about her intentions. One of her few confidants was Cho Ramaswamy, an elderly cultural impresario with a background as an actor and screenwriter. At the time we met in 2014, he ran a low-budget satirical newspaper akin to a Tamil version of *Private Eye* or *The Onion.* 'She is a determined leader, someone not afraid,' he told me one afternoon, sitting in the paper's chaotic downtown office, where the smell of incense hung in the air. 'Sadly, it has become a habit with her party men,' he added with a hint of embarrassment. 'They are very submissive, very obsequious.'

Trying to learn more, I went to see a man named Pandiarajan, a business leader and state legislator, who was said to maintain a modicum of independent judgement. He had defected from the DMK not long ago and thrown his lot in with Jayalalithaa, although most people seemed to think that his previous loyalty to her rivals meant she would never truly trust him. Still, if anyone could provide some insight into the intrigues of Amma's inner court, various friends told me, it would be him. We met in his office, where he kept a large picture of Jayalalithaa on his desk and another on the wall.

Pandiarajan was the founder of a successful recruitment consultancy, and at first we chatted amiably enough about business. But his tone changed when I broached the topic of his leader, and he began to treat me to a loyal discourse on Jayalalithaa's many fine characteristics: her unbending focus on development; her surprisingly detailed knowledge of world affairs; her facility with languages, of which she was said to speak as many as eight; even her eminent suitability as a future national prime minister. As this wound tediously on I found myself staring at his clothes. Pandiarajan, like all politicians in Amma's party, wore a white shirt with a translucent front pocket. Tucked inside was a clearly visible picture of Amma, worn in the most public possible demonstration of loyalty, her face turned outwards to watch over us sternly as we talked.

If servility was one side of Jayalalithaa's rule, corruption was the other. Uniquely among serving Indian chief ministers, she was jailed in 2014, having been found guilty of acquiring 'disproportionate' assets while in office. During her first period in power in the early 1990s, her personal holdings rose from virtually nothing to around Rs 530 million ($8 million), despite having a notional salary of just R1 a month.[6] Subsequent court proceedings revealed lurid details of her wealth, including the findings of a police raid at one of her homes, which unearthed a collection of more than seven hundred pairs of shoes and ten thousand saris, along with substantial holdings of gold jewellery.[7] The case dragged on for the better part of two decades; its latter portion moved to the neighbouring state of Karnataka, for fear that a fair trial would be impossible within Tamil Nadu. The eventual guilty verdict created a sensation: Indian chief ministers were often accused of corruption, but until then none had actually been convicted. Local media reported more than a dozen suicides in response, while many more supporters were said to have died of shock.[8] Her temporary replacement as the state's leader, a steadfast party man, refused even to sit at the chief minister's desk, while he waited loyally for her to resume her duties.

Jayalalithaa's incarceration did little to dent her popularity. Although sentenced to four years, she served less than a month before being acquitted on a technicality, allowing her to return as chief minister for a fifth time. At the next state poll in 2016, Tamil Nadu's seventy million people handed her another thumping victory, in the process making her the first chief minister in a generation to win re-election in the state's topsy-turvy political system. Her campaign showed all of the usual touches. 'Voters were already speculating whether Amma will give away refrigerators or motorcycles this time,' as an essay in *Outlook* magazine noted just before the poll. 'She didn't disappoint.'[9] Among the various treats on offer were free mobile phones, subsidised scooters, yet more laptops for students, and a free 8-gram gold coin for women who were soon to marry.[10]

Her supporters' fanaticism continued despite her conviction. In 2015, to mark the chief minister's sixty-seventh birthday, Shihan Hussaini, a karate instructor and ardent Jayalalithaa loyalist, crucified himself in her honour. Wearing a white T-shirt with the word 'Amma' across its front in large red letters, he stood arms stretched out as students from his karate school nailed him to a plywood cross for six agonising minutes. An audience of invited party workers looked on, along with a handful of television cameras, who broadcast proceedings live.[11] Two years earlier, Hussaini had honoured her sixty-fifth by fashioning a bust of her face from 11 litres of his own blood, which he had drawn carefully over a period of years. Such acts were undoubtedly extreme but more modest forms of self-mutilation in the chief minister's honour remained fairly common.

More sceptically minded Tamils questioned whether this personality cult – the fawning party men, fervent acts of affection and periodic bouts of self-harm – disguised a regime that had lost touch with its people, as if those involved were simply reading from a script that had lost all real meaning. Yet as far as I could tell the affection and respect for Jayalalithaa was real. Despite her reputation for corruption, many wealthy professionals in Chennai rated her a competent administrator and showed a sneaking admiration for her authoritarian style. Local villagers, many of whom had received unexpected gifts bearing the chief minister's name, saw her as a caring benefactor, something akin to the 'mother' of the Tamil people that her own propaganda suggested.

Certainly the outpouring of emotion that greeted her death in late 2016 seemed genuine. Rumours of Jayalalithaa's failing health had swirled around Chennai for years, providing an explanation for her ever-more reclusive behaviour. Public discussion of the topic was largely forbidden, however: loyalists did not mention that she was a long-time diabetic, while journalists were wary of writing about it, for fear of facing legal action. Perhaps this was why her death, when it finally came after an extended hospital stay, caused such shock. More than one hundred supporters were said to have taken then own lives, as the state was overwhelmed with extravagant demonstrations of grief, including a spate of further unsuccessful suicides, and one supporter who respect-fully cut off his own finger.[12] 'This anxiety surrounding her health, or rather her mortality, acquired an absurd resonance,' as Tamil historian V. Geetha wrote in an obituary, published shortly after her death.[13] 'The injunction to even imagine that her health could be deteriorating, showed her in a new and vulnerable light: she was literally being placed outside the pale of what we consider human.' Her death brought with it a sense of closure, as if the state Jayalalithaa had dominated as a kind of indestructible demigod could now finally begin to contemplate the inevitability of her absence.

SOUTHERN SATRAPS

Jayalalithaa fitted almost too easily the image of comedy autocrat, with her record of personal enrichment and periodic brutality. But she was also a complex and in many ways admirable figure, as well as one whose ruling style illustrated the rich variety of crony capital-ism found across India. Her story resonated with the public for its cinematic quality, from the glamour of her film stardom to the determination of her political rise, with its many pitfalls and fight-backs. She rose to power not just as a woman in a patriarchal society, but also as a Brahmin in a state where upper-caste status remained toxic. At times she drew on her femininity: early in her career she won sympathy by storming out of the state assembly having been manhandled by a male politician, in an episode that drew compari-sons with Draupadi, a character in the *Mahābhārata* who suffered the humiliation of being disrobed in public.[14] Yet she later tran-scended this same feminine image too, abandoning the starlet of her youth and fashioning in its place a public persona that was at once matronly and menacing.

Jayalalithaa's personal life was complicated, not least her long-time friendship with a female aide, who lived for decades in her plush Chennai bungalow. The arrangement was the subject of much intrigue, but through force of will, Jayalalithaa had it accepted. Unlike many Indian political leaders she made little effort to establish a dynasty, a fact that became obvious when her party collapsed into infighting after her death. Newspapers revelled in lurid details of her wealth, notably her shoe collection, which drew comparisons with former Philippine first lady Imelda Marcos. Yet her later popularity sprang more from the supposed modesty of her lifestyle and the conservatism of her demeanour. Those who knew her described an intelligent and thoughtful leader, who spoke in flawless convent-school English and preferred literature to politics. 'She read widely, and used to ask me for book recommendations,' an experienced diplomat in New Delhi who worked closely with her once told me. As her health worsened, even her reclusive habits invited sympathy. 'The past, which shapes her present, is marked by her loneliness,' the Tamil writer Vaasanthi, her unofficial biographer, wrote a few years before she died.[15]

Yet besides these personal intrigues Jayalalithaa represented a deeper conundrum, namely the unlikely success of Tamil Nadu itself. In northern states like Uttar Pradesh, cronyism tended to go hand in hand with poor economic development. For all of its corruption, Tamil Nadu by contrast made great progress under her rule. She took power just as liberalisation began in 1991, and grew dominant over the 2000s at the height of India's wider re-embrace of globalisation. Her state became one of the country's most internationally connected regions, propelled by its large diaspora, busy ports and location close to the shipping lanes that connected east Asia to the West. Already one of the most industrialised states, it built up an enviable record of attracting foreign investment. In 1996 Jayalalithaa persuaded Ford to set up its first Indian factory in Chennai, tempting the US auto giant with free land and tax breaks.[16] Hyundai, Renault, BMW and others followed, turning the city into a self-styled 'Detroit of India'.

Chennai became a technology hub too, as business parks and software centres sprang up along the main highway south of the city, towards the old French colonial trading post at Pondicherry. The state made quick social progress, helped along by innovative public programmes, including a pioneering 'mid-day meals' initiative giving free lunches to schoolchildren and a child adoption programme, designed to stop female infanticide. Under her rule Tamil Nadu grew safer, richer and better educated.[17] In 2016, a survey judged it one of the country's two best-governed states,[18] despite being led for the best part of two decades by a leader who mixed prodigious corruption, autocratic whims and a fondness for politically expedient handouts. 'Jayalalithaa has become, for better or worse, the template that all India's successful chief ministers seek to follow,' as commentator Mihir Sharma put it just after her death.[19]

Even at the time of her death few bothered denying that Jayalalithaa had run a state built on graft. Court records showed her personal wealth to be a little under $10 million, a significant sum, but hardly enormous. Her indignant supporters often pointed to the far bigger sums extracted by supposedly respectable politicians in New Delhi. These holdings in turn were trivial next to the vastly larger amounts she and her fellow Tamil politicians needed to bankroll their election spending and patronage networks. Yet Jayalalithaa and her rivals managed to raise these funds without greatly damaging their state's economic record, or indeed causing the kind of blockbuster scandals that in time brought New Delhi grinding to a halt.

This style of crony capitalism distinguished India's five prosperous southern states – Kerala, Tamil Nadu, Karnataka, Telangana and Andhra Pradesh – from the laggards of the north. Of these, all except Kerala were stunningly corrupt. Karnataka was India's most graft-ridden state, one survey suggested, while Andhra Pradesh and Tamil Nadu came in second and third.[20] But all were also economic success stories, with development levels that stood closer to south-east Asia than sub-Saharan Africa. The south had long enjoyed a distinct political identity, based in part on the common set of Dravidian languages most of its people spoke, and the way their leaders tended to resist creeping political and cultural influences from the Hindi-speaking north. But the region developed its distinct model of cronyism too, and one that acted as an endorsement for Samuel Huntington's theories that corruption and growth could go hand in hand. 'In the south, you can say that politicians learned to steal, but to do it while expanding the cake at the same time,' as Devesh Kapur, a professor of political science at the University of Pennsylvania, once put it to me. 'In north India they just went about taking as much of the cake for themselves as they could, and soon there wasn't any cake left for anyone else.'

Perhaps more than anyone Jayalalithaa embodied this southern model. She was one of a series of powerful regional politicians who won power in the decades before Narendra Modi's victory in 2014.

Often known as 'satraps', the grouping included other leaders with power bases far outside the south, from Mamata Banerjee in West Bengal to both Mulayam Singh Yadav and Mayawati in Uttar Pradesh. Manish Sabharwal, the head of recruitment group TeamLease, once drew a distinction between their various records, contrasting their 'roving bandit' and 'stationary thief' models of political power. 'The roving bandit is a politician like Kublai Khan in ancient China, who says "Give me everything you've got",' Sabharwal told me. 'The stationary thief says "Give me ten per cent of the value of this project, and now tell me how you are going to grow it".'

This distinction echoed Mancur Olson, the American economist, who argued in his book *Power and Prosperity* that the decline in antiquity of roving-bandit-style political leaders, and their replacement by more geographically rooted rulers, marked an important stage in human development. Sabharwal's point was that modern north Indian politicians were more likely to show bandit-like traits, helping themselves to whatever loot they could find. Because their regions lacked business investment this typically meant plundering the state, for instance taking money from welfare programmes for the poor. By contrast, southern politicians developed efficient cronyism more akin to that in China or Malaysia, countries whose recent mixture of rapid growth and rampant corruption has sometimes been dubbed the 'East Asian Paradox'.[21] Southern India 'had the fortune of having more stationary thieves,' Sabharwal told me. 'It is a more Chinese form of profit-sharing, where the incentives of the politician and the interest of their people are more closely aligned, and so the corruption is less rampant and embarrassing.'

Jayalalithaa gained an early reputation for greed and excess. Public anger focused in particular on a gigantic wedding reception she hosted in 1995 for her adopted son, inviting more than a hundred thousand guests at an estimated cost of $23 million.[22] The ceremony still holds two Guinness World Records, one for largest wedding banquet, the other for most attendees.[23] 'The three-mile drive from the temple to the grounds of her mansion was adorned with illuminated Grecian columns and statues of Indian princes in erotic poses,' as one report put it.[24] The celebrations were a social triumph but a political disaster, and the main reason she suffered a heavy defeat in the next year's election.

When she returned as chief minister in 2001 Jayalalithaa ruled more modestly. One of her most senior civil servants talked me through the changes in an Indian politician's behaviour, sitting one afternoon in an anonymous office building close to Chennai's city centre. The more brazen style of her first period in power, he explained, fitted a pattern common to Indian politicians who lacked money early in their careers. 'They believe in building a substantial corpus of wealth: a personal nest egg for themselves, their children, their children's children,' he said. But this kind of personal enrichment was less important and involved smaller amounts than the far larger sums politicians were forced to raise to meet their party's needs for election spending. 'They operate what you might call a "portfolio selection approach", in which they want to make some money in some areas, but they also want to deliver certain services in others,' the civil servant said. Money could be taken from government contracts or extracted from investment projects, or misdirected from state spending programmes. Choosing between these options involved weighing up the risk of being caught. But it also meant keeping in mind the need to deliver growth, or at least to build the kind of high-profile infrastructure and public spending projects that voters seemed to like.

This was the conundrum of Jayalalithaa: a leader who was a believer in a certain kind of good governance, albeit one that left plenty of room for personal enrichment and the necessities of political fundraising. Her instinct for populist giveaways was genuine, and if anything it deepened as she grew older. This was especially true when she lost another election in 2006: she found herself in the unusual position of being been out-promised – her DMK rivals offered free televisions to voters – a mistake she was careful not to repeat. Despite the ferocity of their rivalry, there was little ideological difference between the two main Tamil political parties. Both believed in holding power and viewed a mix of methodical corruption and election-time generosity as the best means of achieving it. But Jayalalithaa at least also believed in economic development, and managed to push policies that delivered it.

'They have found out that corruption doesn't matter,' the civil servant told me. Tamil Nadu's electorate did not seem to mind if their leaders were on the take, so long as they were not looting extravagantly and they delivered progress in other ways. Business leaders were similarly phlegmatic, viewing this kind of corruption as akin to a tax: a cost of doing business, but a predictable and manageable one. 'They prefer Jayalalithaa because her AIADMK is more efficient at delivering,' one American government official wrote in a diplomatic cable, leaked by WikiLeaks.[25]

THE ANDHRAPRENEURS

From a distance India's parliament building looks serene: a squat amphitheatre ringed with columns, its outline visible through the thickest New Delhi smog. Upon completion in 1927 its outer walls hid three chambers: the House of the People, the Council of States and the Chamber of Princes, the last acting as a gathering place for monarchs from the various 'princely states', which notionally still ruled much of the country under the British Raj. Designed by Sir Herbert Baker, the building was a temple to power and imperial order, fusing classical Greek and Indian styles. Not everyone liked it: 'It resembles a Spanish bull-ring,' one critic wrote in 1931, 'lying like a mill-wheel dropped accidentally on its side.'[26]

The elegant Central Hall went on to host many of independent India's formative moments, from the transfer of power in 1947 to the high-minded debates over the drafting of a new constitution which followed over the next few years. More recently the building's discussions turned rowdy, notably in the lower house, where Lok Sabha debates grew notorious for slanging matches and staged walk-outs. Yet even in the annals of India's bad-tempered democracy, a special place will surely be kept for the extraordinary scenes of 13 February 2014, and the man who caused them: Lagadapati Rajagopal.

That day's argument involved a bill proposing the creation of a new southern Indian state, known as Telangana. The latest in a series of 'bifurcations', the legislation aimed to carve the existing state of Andhra Pradesh into two, unpicking the single entity created as a home for all Telugu language speakers in the 1950s, part of a national movement at the time to reorganise India's states along broadly linguistic lines.

Almost ever since that time campaigners from the poorer Andhra Pradesh interior had been agitating for a state of their own, arguing that the people of the richer, fertile coastal belt had come to dominate the state's politics, creaming off its resources in their own interest. Decades of separatist agitation finally produced results in 2013, when India's ruling Congress government relented, and promised to table legislation to split the old state into two.

News of the Telangana decision proved divisive, prompting a mixture of celebration and angry protests across the region. On that day in 2014 the violence spilled into parliament. In the heat of debate, various angry anti-statehood MPs rushed into the centre of the Lok Sabha chamber and began to trade blows. One ripped a microphone from his seat, wielding it with such vigour that press reports later mistook it for a knife. Another held up a sign reading 'WE WANT UNITED ANDHRA PRADESH' and parked himself in front of the Speaker's chair. Rajagopal, a Congress parliamentarian, but also a staunch Telangana opponent, rushed to join the melee. He tangled briefly with another MP, before suddenly pulling a can of pepper spray from his pocket, brandishing it aloft, and firing its contents into the air.

Shocked MPs held handkerchiefs to their faces as they rushed out of the chamber, tears streaming down their cheeks. One suffered a heart attack during the ruckus, and was hurriedly bundled into a waiting ambulance.[27] Others emerged ready to denounce a new low for India's tainted democracy: 'the most shameful day in our parliamentary history,' as one MP told a throng of waiting cameras; 'disgraceful, unprecedented and unforgivable,' fumed another.[28]

From that day forward Rajagopal become known as the 'pepper spray MP', but he was intriguing for a different reason too. 'The man credited with the worst conduct ever in the history of our Parliament (and it would take some doing to get that distinction) was not your usual politician, but a fabled and much-favoured star of corporate India,' wrote Shekhar Gupta, a newspaper editor and intellectual, a few days after the fracas.[29] With declared assets of Rs 3 billion ($47 million), Rajagopal was one of the country's wealthiest MPs. But he was also part of a growing band of Indian industrialists turned parliamentarians, who, like Vijay Mallya, had perfectly lawfully used their personal resources to fashion political careers, which were then often helpful to their business interests.

These politician-business leaders were common across southern India, including in Jayalalithaa's Tamil Nadu. But it was the tycoons just over the border in Andhra Pradesh who developed a particular reputation for amassing wealth at the intersection of commerce and politics. They even came to earn their own nickname: the 'Andhrapreneurs'.

Rajagopal was cheerfully unrepentant about the pepper spray farrago, as I discovered when I visited his home a few years later. By then he was no longer an MP: the state he disgraced himself to save was ultimately split in two in mid-2014, a decision that prompted him to resign from parliament in protest. He still worked in politics, acting as what in America would be known as a lobbyist for his family's conglomerate, which was now officially run by his brother. When parliament was in session he lived in a modern three-storey house nestled inside an upscale New Delhi enclave, tucked in next to the Danish embassy, with a grey gate and armed guards outside. He arrived more than an hour late, entering the sitting room full of apologies for having been delayed in a meeting with a government minister. There was a gold band on his wrist inscribed with the words 'Om Shanti', a mantra and salutation often used in meditation. As we talked he was gentle and solicitous, offering tea and chatting about his young son, all of which was hard to square with his public image, which was part political hooligan, part adept crony capitalist.

In his own telling, Rajagopal's behaviour that day in 2014 was more gallant than deplorable. 'What I did was self-defence, not for myself, but safeguarding one of my colleague MPs,' he told me, explaining that he had intervened to defend an elderly parliamentarian caught up in the scrum. His criticism of the Telangana movement had made him a target for political violence: 'Many times people tried to attack me, so I always used to keep this spray, because I don't want to use a gun or a knife,' he said. He neither regretted his actions nor had he suffered any real censure for them. In fact, back home in coastal Andhra Pradesh, he had become something of an unlikely hero, winning respect for his extraordinary efforts to halt the state's division.

A member of the business-minded Kamma caste, Rajagopal had as a younger man joined Lanco – or Lagadapati Amarappa Naidu and Company Infratech, the company founded by his father. Their business grew gradually during the 1980s and early 1990s, moving first into pig iron, then cement. After liberalisation it expanded rapidly, developing a particular speciality in infrastructure, building everything from fancy Hyderabad residential estates to new coal-fired power stations. Fuelled by giant quantities of debt, the business took off during the mid-2000s, and became expert in the public–private partnership (PPP) model that India began using to fund big infrastructure projects. In China, bridges and roads were typically built by government-owned companies. But in India, just as happened in America during the railway boom of the 1870s, it was private sector conglomerates that took the lead.

For a while these PPP programmes seemed almost magical, bringing billions of dollars of new investment while officially adding barely a rupee in debt to the public finances.[30] Inspired by similar models in the West, early supporters of the deals hoped that their strict delivery contracts would also act as an anti-corruption panacea, ending the kind of discretionary deal-making that had dominated India's infrastructure sector up to that point. In fact the opposite happened, as PPPs created an entirely new mechanism for astronomical rent extraction. So pervasive did the model become, and so powerful were the companies delivering it, that commentator Pratap Bhanu Mehta claimed in 2013 that India itself had grown as a 'contractor state' – a 'government of contractors, by contractors, for contractors'.[31]

The PPP model proved especially popular in Andhra Pradesh, whose conglomerates emerged as masters of the new form, bidding for everything from highways and ports to airports and public housing schemes. Travelling around India I often found that different parts of the country took a perverse kind of pride in the ingenious and questionable practices of their own local business elite. Bankers in Mumbai held a sneaking appreciation for financial shenanigans, for instance, while in Uttar Pradesh the finesse with which politicians ripped off welfare projects was often deplored and quietly admired in equal measure. But it was Andhra Pradesh, with its sophisticated patronage-based politics and billionaire Andhrapreneur tycoons, that represented perhaps India's most refined form of crony capitalism, and one whose sheer artistry acted as a model that others would soon go on to follow.

HOW TO BE A CRONY CAPITALIST

Hyderabad, capital of the newly independent Telangana and home to most of the Andhrapreneurs, has long been associated with wealth. It was the largest city in India's grandest princely state, led until 1948 by a monarch known as the Nizam, the head of an Islamic dynasty dating back to the early eighteenth century, and a successor state to the Mughal Empire. Osman Ali Khan, the title's final holder, was not just the world's richest man but also said to be one of the wealthiest who had ever lived, the recipient of a fortune drawn both from vast land holdings and from ownership of the state's lucrative Golconda diamond mines.

Even as his rule crumbled the Nizam's eccentricities were legion: the fleet of Rolls-Royces he employed to collect rubbish from Hyderabad's streets; the eunuchs that guarded his mighty jewellery collection; and above all the intricate complexities of his love life, with its dozens of concubines and countless illegitimate children. 'The last Nizam had a total of 14,718 employees when he died,' according to one account. 'In his main palace alone, there were about 3,000 Arab bodyguards, 28 people paid to fetch drinking water, 38 to dust chandeliers, [and] several specifically to grind walnuts.'[32] His rule ended in 1948, when his state was forcibly folded into a newly independent India. But the excess of his rule left behind a city known as much for the splendour of its palaces and the sophistication of its culture as for the stunning rocky terrain of the surrounding Deccan Plateau.

More recently Hyderabad has grown into one of southern India's most important business hubs, and one known for wealth of a different sort. Visitors land at a shiny new airport, developed by GMR, one of the more prominent Andhrapreneur conglomerates, and then whizz into the city along an elevated expressway built by another local contractor, which offers impressive views over the glass and steel buildings downtown. During the 1990s parts of Hyderabad were officially rebranded as 'Cyberabad', as its enterprising chief minister, Chandrababu Naidu, began to transform the city from a sleepy provincial capital into a major IT hub, attracting investment from Microsoft and Oracle. India's tech sector is often thought to be largely free of corruption, but here Hyderabad was also an exception: Satyam Computer, the city's most prominent outsourcing group, collapsed spectacularly in 2009 when its chairman admitted to inventing more than $1 billion of revenue, in one of Asia's largest cases of corporate fraud. Yet the city's modern wealth, as well as its reputation for financial chicanery, have come from traditional sectors like land and construction dominated by the Andhrapreneurs, the new class of 'carpetbagging but hugely risk-taking Telugu infrastructure entrepreneurs' whom Shekhar Gupta dubbed the 'Andhra oligarchs'.[33]

'You are now in a part of the country where the situation is arguably the worst,' anti-corruption campaigner Jayaprakash Narayan told me, sitting in his office in the city one afternoon in mid-2016. The room was sparsely decorated, with a single map of India on the wall and a small bust of Gandhi in the corner. A slim, elegant man, Narayan had once founded his own political party, campaigning for clean government and even at one point winning a seat for himself in the Andhra Pradesh state assembly. But over time he grew disenchanted with the rough-and-tumble of India's elections, and set up instead the Foundation for Democratic Reforms, a think tank headquartered on the eighth floor of a shabby residential building, next to one of the city's larger hotels.

Narayan ushered three of the think tank's interns into his room as he began to talk, before painting a grimly detailed picture of the state of local corruption. Both Andhra Pradesh and Telangana, he claimed, had some of the nation's most expensive elections, and thus almost certainly its highest levels of illegal campaign financing as well. These rising election costs then pushed the region's political leaders to dream up ever-more devious schemes to bring in black money from their allies in business, funds they then deployed for the mass acquisition of votes. 'We are probably the innovators,' he went on, describing the growth over recent decades of a highly refined local model of cronyism, in which the interests of politicians and developers grew so closely intertwined that they became virtually indistinguishable. 'This is a land where this process has been institutionalised and professionalised – although much of the rest of the country is quickly following suit.'

Narayan explained the genesis of this system by way of the rivalry between two men who came to dominate politics in Andhra Pradesh in the decades after liberalisation. First came Naidu, the architect of Hyderabad's renaissance, who ran the state for the best part of a decade from the mid-1990s as the head of the Telugu Desam Party. A business-friendly technocrat, he focused on infrastructure and had a knack for luring in foreign tech companies. His record won plaudits: in 1999, *Time* dubbed him 'the subcontinent's most visionary politician'; a year later President Bill Clinton came to visit the new HI-TEC City technology park, and heaped praise on his investment-friendly policies.[34] Yet for all his economic nous, Naidu was roundly defeated in elections in 2004 by his great antagonist Y. S. Rajasekhara Reddy, or just 'YSR', a more pugilistic and overtly populist Congress leader, who governed until his death in a helicopter accident in 2009.

'These were two exceptional politicians, who were unscrupulous, ambitious, hard-working, and bitter political rivals,' Narayan said. 'They were both identical in their totally amoral approach to power.' Both men were masters of political machine-building, wielding influence through powerful patronage networks. Naidu's reputation was cleaner, although even he began his life in modest circumstances and ended up a wealthy man. But of the two it was YSR who cemented Andhra's reputation as a hotbed of cronyism, with an ability to bring together economic development and incorrigible corruption that perhaps only Tamil Nadu could rival.

As chief minister, YSR launched a slew of new state spending programmes in areas like healthcare and housing, which also provided rich pickings for graft. Andhra Pradesh's economic vitality pushed up the price of land, which the chief minister doled out happily to favoured business contacts. There were economic reforms too – YSR streamlined the state's bureaucracy, cut its deficit and made it easier for businesses to invest – but these were obscured by populist largesse and shady development schemes. Among the most prominent was a huge irrigation plan known as Jalayagnam, later dubbed 'the mother of all frauds' by the *Times of India*.[35] Auditors found many billions of dollars had gone missing from contracts handed out to half a dozen politically connected local companies. An American diplomatic cable, released by WikiLeaks, noted dryly how 'corruption beyond the pale (even for India)' had become a hallmark of YSR's rule.[36] 'We thought Naidu was bad,' the same document quotes a local newspaper editor as saying, 'but that was child's play compared what is happening now.'

At one level this reputation for adventurous cronyism did Andhra Pradesh little harm. Much like Tamil Nadu, it enjoyed strong growth and enviable levels of social development in the decades after 1991, all seemingly unencumbered by the greed and collusion of its elites. The efforts of its two duelling leaders left behind some of India's best infrastructure, almost all of it built by half a dozen local contracting groups. Companies such as Lanco, GMR and their rival GVK grew into powerful national conglomerates. But while others also presided over a system in which corruption and development co-existed, the genius of Andhra Pradesh was to fashion the nexus between politics and business so tightly that it became virtually impossible to judge where the line between the two was drawn.[37]

'The links between the politicians and the contracting class became very deep,' Narayan told me. The benches of the state assembly were filled with politicians who also happened to be businesspeople, or at least who were drawn from the same families and caste groups as prominent industrialists. Some industrialists, like Lagadapati Rajagopal, became national politicians too. As chief minister, Naidu used the slogan 'Bye-bye Bangalore, hello Hyderabad' to boast that his city would soon surpass its more famous rival as India's premier technology hub. But one venture capitalist from Andhra Pradesh made a different distinction. 'The difference between Bangalore and Hyderabad is that the guys in Bangalore who are making money are separate from the guys who run the city,' he told me. 'In Hyderabad the businessmen and the politicians are intertwined. It is people who are from there, the entrepreneurs and their families, who have ties with people who are in politics.' It was this overlap, and the bonds of trust that came with it, that provided uniquely fertile grounds for corruption.

At one level the deals struck in Andhra Pradesh worked in the same way as elsewhere in India, as valuable infrastructure contracts and government land were doled out to friendly companies in exchange for kickbacks. There were plenty of entrepreneurs eager to receive such bounty. But the politicians still had to be cautious, according to Harish Damodaran, author of *India's New Capitalists*, a book about the often-complex interplay between caste and business. For figures like YSR the risk was that one party to a deal would run off with the cash, or not deliver what they promised, or let details slip to the media. In Andhra

Pradesh, caste bonds often provided a sense of reassurance; nearly all those involved in big infrastructure schemes were drawn from either the Kammas or the Reddys, the two mercantile communities who dominated commerce in the state. 'They wanted someone they could really trust,' Damodaran told me. 'That meant someone from the same caste, or ideally the same family.'

In a perfect world, this meant having kin on both sides of a deal, and often the easiest way of achieving this was for one member of a business family to enter politics directly. As legislators they could then cut deals from the inside, lobbying for rule changes and providing useful intelligence. 'Blatantly, what some of them said was "Damn it, why don't we influence them, why the hell don't we become politicians?"' I was told by Konda Vishweshwar Reddy, another wealthy businessman turned national MP, who represented a constituency which included Hyderabad's airport. 'Andhra Pradesh took the leadership in that,' he added, with a thinly disguised sense of pride, pointing to the success of the state's infrastructure companies. 'Those guys are the big guys. They got plum power projects, they got plum land, they got plum infrastructure contracts.'

It also went the other way round, as politicians set themselves up in business and gifted contracts and favours to their own operations. Sometimes this happened openly. More often the process was clandestine, with a politician's ultimate control disguised via *benami* chains of relatives or associates. Common in southern India, these arrangements soon spread to New Delhi, as politicians realised that corruption's grandest profits were often to be made by owning businesses and then fiddling the rules to help them grow. 'We have a completely unique phenomenon in India, which I call political entrepreneurship, that has taken root in the last five to six years,' I was told in 2012 by Rajeev Chandrasekhar, the former telecoms entrepreneur and then-member of India's upper house of parliament. 'They [the politicians] are saying: "We don't want briefcases full of cash and Swiss bank accounts and all that any more. We want to own businesses ourselves. We want equity stakes."'[38]

Profiting from this required operators adept at 'managing the environment', an often-used Indian euphemism for influence-peddling. Companies seeking public contracts in competitive tenders often entered unrealistically low bids, for instance, in the expectation that their connections would allow the contract to be renegotiated later for a much higher fee. On other occasions contracts would be gifted without bidding, or through a process so clearly fixed in advance that other serious bidders were discouraged from entering the fray. Then over-bidding was the preferred method: a company would make an unusually large offer and siphon away the difference between that figure and what the work actually cost.

Yet even here there was a balance to be struck, as one civil servant who worked with various governments in southern India explained. Rather than going for the very lowest bidder, or the one who was likely to extort the most money, wise politicians tended to avoided outright cowboy contractors. Instead, they favoured those companies who were both willing to play the game and competent in delivering projects, meaning that they would make a decent fist of building the irrigation schemes and airport terminals in question, while also being generous with their profits. 'They [the better contractors] will charge you 140 rupees for work which should have cost 100 rupees, but they will actually spend 100 rupees and do a good job,' the civil servant said. 'You have others who will quote 105, and will spend 80 of it, and do a substandard job, which will fall apart three years from now, so them you want to avoid.'

Other techniques were craftier still. Under YSR, the most infamous were pioneered by his son, Jagan Mohan Reddy, who set himself up as an entrepreneur during his father's time as chief minister. Handsome and charming, the younger Reddy founded a slew of companies in sectors from cement to real estate, in addition to a media group whose newspaper acted as a mouthpiece for his father. Reddy had little back-ground in business but proved a curiously successful fundraiser. This in itself was not unusual: India's family-run enterprises were adept at rais-ing capital, including from naive global private equity funds, many of which sank significant sums into Hyderabad-based contracting compa-nies. But Reddy's strategy was more ingenious, police investigations later claimed, as investors were said to have bought stock at hugely inflated rates in exchange for favours from his father's government.[39] Government auditors later claimed that YSR had handed out thousands of hectares of land to friendly contacts, a good portion of which went to companies controlled by his son.[40]

The scheme eventually caught up with Jagan Reddy: he was

arrested on corruption charges in 2012, and spent the best part of two years in jail awaiting trial before being released on bail. (Reddy's case remained pending at the time of writing.) The year prior to his arrest he had been elected to parliament in New Delhi and declared his personal worth to be $57 million, making him India's richest MP. Prison time did not dent his ambitions: he split from the Congress following his father's unexpected death and set up a new party – the YSR Congress – to capitalise on his legacy. His popularity was partly explained by a local population thoroughly inured to the corruption of their leaders, according to essayist Praveen Donthi, as well as the fact that Reddy's schemes tended to involve private sector transactions, rather than the ransacking of government spending programmes.[41]

Of all the techniques pioneered in Andhra Pradesh, shady land deals were perhaps the most infamous. Many of Hyderabad's bustling main roads snaked alongside tall, white concrete pillars, ready to support rail lines for a long-promised urban metro. The project was unusual both for its longevity – it had been conceived in the early 2000s, but there were still no signs of trains when I visited in 2017, more than a decade later – and for the inventiveness of its financing. 'Unlike the vast majority of the world's rail transit systems, this metro would not be wholly funded by public money,' journalist Mark Bergen wrote of the scheme. Instead, Hyderabad's government gifted plots of land to developers near planned rail stations, on the theory that they would recoup the costs of developing the project from increases in value of the land itself.[42]

The resulting plan was widely questioned. '[The] Metro is only a mask,' as one protestor put it; 'the real agenda is real estate.' It was accepted wisdom in Hyderabad that the various planned metro lines would in time be extended to connect with plots of land owned by powerful political families, vastly increasing their value. This kind of brazen deal-making still seemed somewhat unlikely, but in a state whose infamous 'land mafia' often snapped up cheap plots from farmers after tip-offs about development plans, and where real estate itself acted as a kind of informal currency between the political and business elite, it was always hard to tell for sure.

It was land that also often provided the final piece in the state's elegant system of cronyism, providing the link between infrastructure kickbacks and illicit election funding. Here political leaders faced a problem of timing, namely that having raised cash through some misdeed or other, they then needed to store it until they next went to the polls. 'Politicians will park their money with people involved in real estate,' political scientist Devesh Kapur once told me. 'They are confident the real estate guys aren't going to run away with it, because they still need the politicians to get more land in the future.' Such deals worked well for both sides. Real estate developers got cheap capital from their friends in politics, which they could then deploy as they liked, at least until polling time came around and the politicians asked for it back. There were various ways businesses could realise these funds quickly, one senior politician told me, 'but mostly they [the tycoons] sell land, because if you sell land, you get seventy or eighty per cent of the value in cash'.

Kapur and co-author Milan Vaishnav once tested this theory via an ingenious academic study. Construction magnates suddenly asked to take capital out of their businesses to re-fund their political allies would then be short of cash for other activities, they hypothesised, most notably starting new buildings.[43] 'Cement is an indispensable ingredient for construction,' Kapur told me. 'So we looked for data to see if cement demand would fall around election time. And it did. In fact, the link shows up beautifully.' Such relationships need not even have a precise quid pro quo, just an understanding that over time each party would help one another as needed. 'It was all goodwill, what you give in elections,' one industrialist from the state told me. 'In India, business still depends on the government. So you need the goodwill of the rulers, to make friends with them.'

For a time this system worked beautifully for the Andhrapreneurs, underpinning years of breakneck expansion, the results of which are clear to see at almost every major Indian airport. As recently as 2008, Meghnad Desai, an economist at the London School of Economics, wrote: 'When you go to China you see new airports and empty highways and the Shanghai maglev. In India, the airports are slums.'[44] Yet later that same year GMR opened Hyderabad's new terminal, delivered under a PPP contract, before unveiling an even grander international terminal in New Delhi in 2010. Equally shiny facilities followed for passengers in Bangalore and Mumbai, this time built by GVK. In a little under a decade India went from having some of the world's most embarrassing airports to some of its best. Over roughly the same period Hyderabad's infrastructure companies grew from little-known local builders to national champions.

Back in his sitting room in New Delhi, Lagadapati Rajagopal reflected on the vaulting ambitions he and his fellow tycoons showed during that period, and the hubris which ultimately undid them. 'The problem was that India was growing at nine per cent in those days, and everyone was expecting it to grow at double digit rates, like China,' he told me. Lanco was especially ambitious: having done well early in the boom, the group took on ever more debt, on the assumption that the cycle of economic growth and infrastructure investment would keep going indefinitely. Rajagopal raced to build power stations, dig mines and lay highways. Many of his local rivals did the same, turning to state-backed banks to raise funds and ploughing them back into even more ambitious projects. At the time the theory was that India suffered an enduring structural gap between its rising demand and limited supply, and especially so in the infrastructure sector. Aiming to close that gap, the five largest Andhra Pradesh infrastructure companies built up a staggering $22 billion worth of debt. 'All the major infrastructure players have two interesting things in common: they are either [run by] politicians or close relatives and most owe enormous sums to public sector banks,' as one study put it.[45]

But gradually at first and then all at once, things began to go wrong. Rajagopal rattled off the list: the global financial crisis in 2008; a subsequent slowdown in India's growth; the 'season of scams'; and finally the new 'administrative paralysis' that took hold in New Delhi, as a wave of anti-corruption investigations shocked the political and business class. 'A lot of economic activity came to a standstill,' he said. 'The demand–supply gap vanished. All of us as entrepreneurs, we took pains to set up all of these projects, looking at this growth potential, which never happened.'

Suddenly, the same tycoons who for years seemed uniquely equipped to prosper within India's complex business climate found that even they were undone by it. Problems affected industrialists all across India, although the once-mighty infrastructure giants of Andhra Pradesh were especially badly hit. And few represented their plight more clearly than Rajagopal himself, the man who won infamy with a can of pepper spray, as he spent his days trundling around New Delhi, trying to fix investment projects that had gone sour and figure out how to repay the giant sums that his struggling company now owed. 'Naturally, if you can't service the debt,' he said ruefully at one point, 'the business goes down into the toilet.'

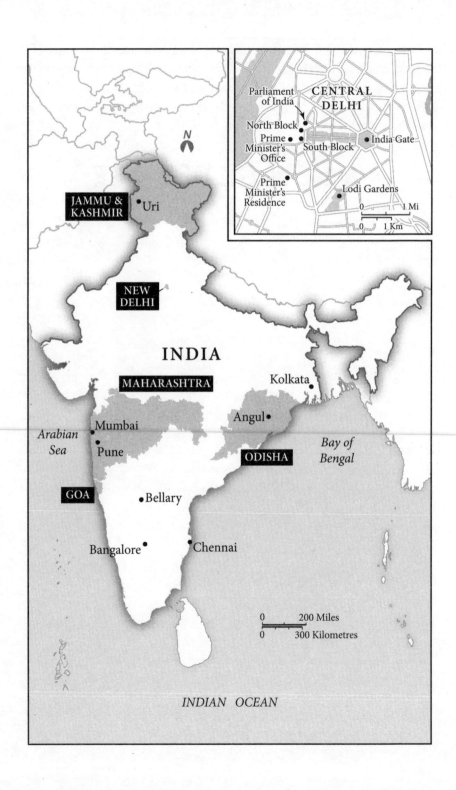

PART 3

A NEW GILDED AGE

Billionaire steel magnate and polo enthusiast Naveen Jindal was one of India's highest-flying young tycoons – until his businesses became engulfed in the scandals often known as the 'season of scams'.

CHAPTER 8

HOUSE OF DEBT

THE BIG BULL

Five hours in, and I was beginning to understand the warnings: an evening out on the town with Rakesh Jhunjhunwala was not to be taken lightly. Beginning on the terrace of his Mumbai office with a $450 bottle of Johnnie Walker Blue, the night had wound on, first to a local watering hole, then a favoured Chinese restaurant. I was much the worse for wear. My companion was just warming up.

A colourful financier with outspoken views and a taste for ribald jokes, the legend went that Jhunjhunwala began investing with just $100 in his pocket, turning it into $1.25 billion, according to *Forbes* in 2012, the year we met.[1] He cut an outsize figure: a big man with a rotund face and a protruding stomach, which gave his white shirt a tent-like look. The waiters greeted him with familiar reverence and fussed as he wedged himself in at the table. 'I only manage my own money, not for anyone else,' he told me at one point, once we'd been sat for a while, a generous glass of whisky clasped in one meaty hand. 'I like my freedom, boss. I don't want to be answerable to anyone. Fuck 'em. That is why I can say what I want.'

More even than his plain speaking, Jhunjhunwala was known for his relentlessly upbeat views. On India's frenetic business news channels he was known as the 'Big Bull', a glancing reference to both his physique and the unswerving confidence of his investments. The first financier to join the country's swelling band of billionaires, he had a special knack for spotting under-valued companies: Titan, for instance, a little-fancied watchmaker, whose stock went on a tear for much of the 2000s. He also held a messianic belief in India's own prospects. 'The factors that drive India's growth are irreversible,' he told me. 'The democracy. The demographics. The entrepreneurship. Much more is going to come.'

I came to meet Jhunjhunwala on a sweaty October evening in 2012, just after the end of the monsoon, and found him parked behind a desk watching data whizz by on no fewer than five terminals. He mumbled a greeting as an assistant ushered me in, but remained transfixed by the screens. I stood in one corner for a few minutes as he watched the numbers float down, like something out of the *Matrix* movies. Occasionally he grabbed the phone and barked 'buy' or 'sell' instructions down the line in Hindi, in amounts that appeared to involve trades in the millions of dollars. He was dressed plainly except for a huge diamond ring on one finger, which distracted the eye from the many cigarettes he smoked, leaving a deep, musty smell in the air. In one corner there was a garlanded shrine to Ganesha, the jovial Hindu elephant god, a deity thought to bring good fortune to commercial ventures, and whose generous pot belly somewhat resembled Jhunjhunwala's own.

The day's trading done, we moved to the outside terrace, which boasted a well-stocked bar on top of a fake grass lawn and fine views over the rickety skyscrapers of Nariman Point, southern Mumbai's clapped-out financial district. From fifteen floors up, gazing between the buildings, I could see the distant outline of Malabar Hill, the fancy neighbourhood across the bay where Jhunjhunwala lived, with his wife and three young children. The cantilevered silhouette of Antilia loomed off to the north, its lights glinting as dusk fell.

I asked Jhunjhunwala about his beginnings, which he said were modest. 'The Ambanis and all these big industrial houses, they are empire builders. They have inherited legacies. I inherited no legacy,' he told me. His interest in stocks came from his father, a tax official, who talked about markets with friends over a drink. 'I was a very, very curious child,' he said. These teenage interests pushed him to become a full-time trader. The Bombay Stock Exchange opened as Asia's first bourse back in 1875, but even a century later India's markets remained small-time. Finance was considered disreputable – 'My mother said: "Who will marry you?" But I went anyway,' he told me – while trading was dominated by cartels of brokers, and was prone to manipulation.

'It was not a very transparent market, it was the Wild West,' Jhunjhunwala recalled fondly of the old Dalal Street, Mumbai's equivalent of Wall Street. 'But I always thought India would shed its socialism, and if there were new temples in India, they would be its stock markets.'

When we moved to the restaurant I asked about his approach to investing. He replied with bawdy humour. 'Markets are like women,' he said: 'always commanding, always mysterious, always uncertain, always volatile, always exciting!' Later on he asked me to turn off my recorder, and launched into a second lewd soliloquy about why markets were also like sex, which I promised not to repeat. I did not let on that I had heard him make a similar comparison – albeit in less filthy terms – during a bravura, finger-jabbing performance at a conference the week before, when he had conducted a screaming argument with a fellow panellist, and won laughs by claiming that Mumbai would never succeed as a global financial centre until it had better nightclubs and strip bars.

During our dinner Jhunjhunwala talked rapidly in slightly broken English, a reminder of his modest upbringings, pausing only to smoke more cigarettes, an addiction that came with a hacking cough. He ate with gusto. 'I'm a foodie. I *love* food,' he said at one point, allowing the fact to sink in via the occasional uninhibited belch, delivered at a volume sufficient to alarm nearby diners.

All this played to his flamboyant side: the Bentley-owning financier who said he planned to buy a private jet and had thrown an extravagant fiftieth birthday party a few years before, flying two hundred guests to Mauritius. Yet there was a charming kind of modesty to him too. The Mauritius jaunt was unusual, he said, because he disliked going abroad; he had never been to America, and did not really care to go. His almost millenarian faith in India was touching too. 'I became extremely optimistic about India around 2001,' he explained, in reference to the terror attacks in New York. 'I thought the death of three thousand Americans wasn't going to change the course of history.'

In 2002, he wrote an article arguing that India was 'at the threshold of a secular and structural bull market', as reforms introduced by the then BJP government began to bear fruit. 'I am shouting at the top of my voice in 2003,' he recalled. 'Buy, buy, buy! Sell your bloody wife's jewellery, and buy!' It proved prescient. India's financial markets went on a glorious five-year run, hitting a series of all-time highs. Some of his better investments, including Titan, jumped in value many times over. India flourished too: the list of dollar billionaires grew ever more crowded, Jhunjhunwala now among them.

As a pure financier, Jhunjhunwala's place among India's super-wealthy was unusual. There were a handful of money men on the *Forbes* list, including Uday Kotak, the self-made founder of Kotak Mahindra, a private sector bank, who lived a few streets away from Jhunjhunwala's office. Hedge fund managers and bankers personified the West's new moneyed super-elite, but in India it was still industrialists who dominated. But if the source of Jhunjhunwala's wealth was a rarity, his buoyant views were more conventional, given the sense of optimism that at the time coursed through the upper echelons of India's corporate scene.

In the later 2000s the idea took hold that India was about to enter a Chinese-style growth spurt, delivering a decade of growth at eight per cent or more. Even as the global financial crisis hit in 2008, India seemed resilient. Business leaders pointed to those same underlying factors that Jhunjhunwala had mentioned. A youthful population; the self-evident need for more infrastructure investment; the benefits of a rules-based democratic system (no matter how imperfect); the palpable sense of aspiration among its people; all were core beliefs held by the Indian bulls.

The problem was that these bullish views were about to come abruptly into conflict with reality, as the season of scams began to erupt and anxiety about corruption started shooting up the political agenda. We discussed all this as the alcohol sank in, and Jhunjhunwala turned reflective. At one point he mentioned a variant of a phrase used by Andrew Carnegie, the Gilded Age steel baron, who once said that 'the man who dies rich dies disgraced'. Jhunjhunwala had announced plans the year before to give away a quarter of his fortune. The move was partly inspired by the man to whom, in India at least, he was often compared: Warren Buffett, the celebrated US investor, who had cajoled the world's wealthiest to give away more of their fortunes. There was a cartoon on the wall outside his office quoting a Buffett aphorism: 'If past history were all there was to the game, the richest people would be librarians.' But I sensed that his decision had been prompted by a deeper worry, namely his desire not to be sullied by the recently declining reputation of his fellow billionaires. I asked him whether he planned to give away even more of his wealth. He seemed uncertain. 'Maybe I'll make it half, who knows?' he said finally, as if unable to escape the investor's urge to double down.

As our evening wound drunkenly to an end, Jhunjhunwala offered me a lift home in his Mercedes, and I flopped unsteadily into the back seat. His own ambition remained the same, he told me as we were driven off, with India's recent corruption problems still obviously on his mind. 'I want to earn the greatest wealth in the world, but with the greatest practical integrity.' The business empires and inherited dynasties would all decline in time, he said, citing a Hindu proverb that wealth petered out by the seventh generation. I asked if he worried about the country's growing reputation for corruption. 'I have no dealings with the government. I haven't taken any licences, I don't own any coal mines, I have no politicians as friends, I never go to a government office,' he said. 'I don't like boasting, but I have an impeccable reputation. All banks are ready to finance me.'

HOUSE OF DEBT

Ceejay House in midtown Mumbai was an unlikely venue for the shaming of corporate India to begin. A square, squat twelve-storey office block perched on the Arabian Sea, it stood next to the main road that connected the airport to Nariman Point, where Rakesh Jhunjhunwala had his office. The location was ideal, not far from the residences of Altamount Road, and only a short hop from the Four Seasons hotel, where local financiers gathered to gossip and plot. On the building's left there stood a showroom full of gleaming Jaguars and Land Rovers; on the right stood a slum by a fetid canal, with sewage flowing into the ocean. The landlord was a wealthy former Congress minister – one of the richest politicians of them all, it was rumoured – who lived up in the penthouse. But elsewhere inside it was almost all bankers: Barclays, Rothschild, Nomura, even Lehman Brothers, before it went bust. For a time, the newspapers dubbed it 'India's most expensive office'.[2] Few locations seemed more likely to be friendly to the nation's big companies and the tycoons who led them. But it was here, in a spartan office on the ninth floor, that the rot at the heart of Indian capitalism first began to come to light.

Ashish Gupta had worked in Ceejay House since the late 2000s, when he joined Credit Suisse, the Swiss investment bank, which kept an office in the building. A stock analyst in his late forties, he spent his career working for financial institutions, developing a particular expertise in the banking sector. A slim man with black side-parted hair and an aquiline nose, he wore wire-framed glasses and talked with lawyerly precision. As head of research, his job involved churning out research notes packed with bullet points and charts. These were sent to clients on the 'buy side', meaning investment groups and hedge funds, who then paid the bank to trade stocks on their behalf. As well as poring over financial statements, this research required Gupta to attend rounds of meetings with the businesses and banks he covered. The reports tended to be dry and carefully worded. But in private conversations he could speak more freely, digging into business problems, gossiping about personalities, and picking up intelligence in return. It was through meetings like these, not long after the global financial crisis, that Gupta started hearing alarming stories about the health of some of India's biggest business names.

'What I began to find, anecdotally, was that a lot of these big guys were struggling,' he told me in 2017, as he cast his mind back to the start of the decade, when the aftershocks of the crisis were still reverberating around the world. Around 2010 most local analysts were upbeat. Like China, India appeared to have ridden out the worst of the global turbulence, which at the time many in Asia were still dubbing the 'Western' financial crisis. The re-election of Manmohan Singh in 2009 had further buoyed optimists like Rakesh Jhunjhunwala, who predicted that the prime minister would now push forward with radical economic reforms, further boosting growth. India's industrial conglomerates were on a roll too: snapping up trophy assets abroad and pushing onwards with ambitious new investment projects at home. When he became finance minister in 1991, Singh had talked of his hopes that economic reforms could restore India's 'animal spirits'.[3] As his second term as prime minister began, he seemed to have succeeded.

As he moved from meeting to meeting, Gupta picked up quite different signals. At first it was just titbits of gossip: this big industrial project was in trouble, or that tycoon had taken on debts he could never hope to repay, fiddling his books in the process. The stories came in gradually at first, but soon enough Gupta began to hear the same rumours repeated in different places. Then executives at the companies began to admit that all was not well, readying their excuses as to why. 'When I was meeting these big corporates, I found few of them were very confident,' he recalled. 'I decided I needed to do a deeper dive.'

The result of that research was emailed to clients in August 2012, and quickly caused ripples. Bank reports typically had dull, mechanical titles, but this time Gupta opted for something a touch more poetic: 'House of Debt'.[4] The crisp 35-page document laid bare the huge financial mess that India's decade-long investment boom had left behind. Beginning in the early 2000s, many of the country's major tycoons had gone on a serious borrowing binge, vacuuming up bank loans, layering on leverage and using the resulting funds to fire up bold new projects, from power stations and toll roads to ports and bauxite mines. Most of these projects did well, delivering handsome returns. Then, roughly around the time of the financial crisis, another round of big investments began, funded by yet more bank loans. The tycoons' notorious love of debt even began turning up in fiction. 'Leverage is flight. Leverage is a way for small to be big and big to be huge . . . To leverage is to be immortal,' as Mohsin Hamid wrote in his 2013 novel *How to Get Filthy Rich in Rising Asia*.[5]

It was these second-round investment projects, conceived of as sure things, that then began to run into trouble. Not all the big names were affected: the two largest, Tata and Mukesh Ambani's Reliance, had balance sheets that remained in reasonable shape. Instead, Gupta's report dug into the performance of the country's ten most heavily indebted industrial companies. The three largest from Andhra Pradesh – GMR, GVK and Lagadapati Rajagopal's Lanco – were all included. So was Gautam Adani's group, and Anil Ambani's half of Reliance. Then there were a handful of others, including Essar, a power and infrastructure business headquartered in a skyscraper just down the road from Ceejay House.

Gupta's commentary on all this was brief and sober, but the situation it described was clearly grim. 'The total debt level of these ten [companies] has jumped 5× in the past five years,' he wrote. There were plenty of other big names with huge outstanding bank loans who had not been included, from Vijay Mallya's Kingfisher to its clapped-out state rival, Air India. But the borrowings of just these ten 'House of Debt' companies were on an entirely different scale. Together they then owed

$84 billion, or more than an eighth of the amount lent out by the entire banking system.

The report's implications for India's banking system were dire. Indian lenders, Gupta explained, were now among the most vulnerable in Asia in terms of their exposure to the debt levels of these kinds of large firms. More to the point, the closer you looked at the balance sheets of these big companies, the clearer it became that they were not just struggling to repay what they owed, but that they were probably never going to be able to repay.[6] Around that time, some investors had begun to worry that the dangerously high levels of debt in China's economy might cause some kind of economic crisis. Now it looked as if India's situation could be even worse. 'The [financial] world read the contents of that innocuously titled "House of Debt" report gobsmacked,' wrote the *Economic Times*, India's biggest business paper.

At first glance it might seem odd that all this came as such a surprise, but 'House of Debt' attracted attention precisely because in India this kind of detailed financial information was unusually hard to dig out. The country's industrial conglomerates were normally structured to be deliberately opaque, with holding companies that sat on top of multiple layers of subsidiaries, and money flowing back and forth between them all in ways that were fiendishly difficult for outsiders to track. Some parts of these groups were listed on the stock market, and therefore published at least some financial information for their investors. But others were held privately, and were obliged to release almost no data at all.

To make things more complicated, as globalisation had accelerated, many of these same Indian companies had rushed to go global, snapping up mining assets in Africa or building industrial projects in Britain. This created an additional problem for those trying to scrutinise their finances, because it meant that some portion of their cash, as well as potentially quite a large chunk of their loans, was stored somewhere far off shore and often funnelled through tax havens. All of this meant that analysts like Gupta could find out fairly easily how funds had been raised for any single new investment project, such as a steel mill or power plant. At the level of the conglomerate itself, however, no one except the 'promoter' – as India's tycoons were often known – knew the real extent of their borrowing, or from whom it had been borrowed. For Gupta and his team, finding out the true

picture at each of their ten companies meant many months of painstaking research, poring over financial documents and talking quietly
to sources at banks. But bit by bit, their data began to show glimpses.
'The answers which started popping out were very, very surprising,' he
told me.

Part of the shock came from realising just how large some of these
companies had grown during the boom of the 2000s. 'What amazed
me was when I looked at the power sector,' Gupta explained. At the
time, billions of dollars were being invested through public–private
partnerships to build dozens of new coal-fired stations, including a
new generation of especially large 'ultra-mega' plants, such as those
which rose up next to Gautam Adani's Mundra Port on the coast of
Gujarat. Gupta found that around three quarters of all this investment was being undertaken by just the ten companies in 'House of
Debt'. 'It was extraordinary,' he said. 'Many of them were unknown a
decade ago. Now they are doing [investments worth] $10 billion or
$12 billion.'

Even more extraordinary were the industrialists' financial miscalcu-
lations. These were India's most illustrious tycoons, admired both for
their proficiency in judging risk and for navigating the country's labyrinthine politics. In particular, they were known for 'managing the
environment', as the ability to win sweetheart deals was known. Yet
now, just when they needed it, the Bollygarchs' touch deserted them:
the constraints that made India such a perilous place to do business for
everyone else suddenly began to apply to them as well. New Delhi stood
transfixed in the aftermath of the season of scams, as once-pliant
bureaucrats declined to hand over the dozens of official permissions
any major industrial project needed to move forward. With their plans
stuck in limbo, the tycoons' hopes of paying back their debts began to
look perilous too.

Gupta began fielding angry calls the day the 'House of Debt' report
was emailed out. Bankers protested that the loans they issued would
come good in time, and accused Gupta and his team of spooking the
market by needlessly exaggerating the scale of their problems. The ten
companies were furious, claiming special circumstances and arguing
that their stalled projects would soon be back on track. 'There were guys
who called and blasted me,' Gupta recalled. 'Then there were guys who
called my global CEO.'

Yet over the next year India's bad-debt problem only worsened. A second version of 'House of Debt', released in August 2013, showed debts at the ten companies soaring to over $100 billion.[7] In public, the tycoons blamed a wider economic downturn. In private, they raged at the government, claiming that political inaction was sabotaging otherwise viable investments. The phrase 'policy paralysis' began to be bandied about in New Delhi, to describe the way accusations of cronyism had led government decision-making to judder to a halt.

The government saw things differently, claiming any delays were the tycoons' fault. 'These guys didn't bother getting the clearances they needed at first, and said "I'll manage it when I come to it", I was told later by Jairam Ramesh, a combative economist turned Congress politician. Back in 2013 Ramesh had been India's environment minister and a particular *bête noire* of the tycoons. He often blocked investments, including a number of major mining and power projects in forested areas. The tycoons pushed their luck, he argued, starting work without proper permission, with the aim of creating 'facts on the ground' and assuming that their political connections would smooth over problems later. 'You also had the prime minister, a man of great integrity, who kept talking about unleashing animal spirits,' he told me. 'This just reinforced the sentiment among industrialists that they could do whatever they wanted.'

While some of these political snarl-ups were indeed outside the tycoons' control, 'House of Debt' revealed a further issue that was squarely their own fault: the tricks they used to raise debt. 'Let us say a power plant costs $100, so you borrow $70 and you put in $30 worth of equity,' Gupta explained. This was the kind of sensible balance between debt and shareholders' equity found in finance text books. The equity component was important, because it ensured the entrepreneur had 'skin in the game', acting as a cushion if a project went wrong. Bankers typically wanted tycoons to put in some their own funds, not only to provide an incentive to ensure the project went well, but also because it would be used to absorb losses if things went wrong. But Gupta discovered that this equity component was often a mirage. The tycoons deployed a clever deception, telling Bank A they were putting equity into a particular project, when the money had in fact been raised as debt from Bank B, as part of the financing of an entirely different project, and then quietly transferred over. Both Banks A and B were kept in the dark, while the tycoon had to put in no money of their own.

To try and get a sense of the scale of this problem, 'House of Debt' included a complex spider web of diagrams for each conglomerate, with arrows flowing back and forth between their various different sub-companies. When deciding whether or not to provide a loan, Gupta discovered that the banks looked only at the health of the individual companies who wanted to borrow, rather than the total debt levels of the wider conglomerate. Many of the banks simply failed to notice that the tycoons had been quietly shuffling money around, building up far larger levels of overall debt than had previously been realised.

Arundhati Bhattacharya, the head of State Bank of India, the biggest bank of all, later admitted to me that she and her fellow bank chiefs had missed a trick. 'We really weren't monitoring the overall group gearing,' she told me in 2013, just a few months after the second 'House of Debt' was released.[8] Projects that looked properly capitalised were revealed to be funded almost entirely by debt, with little or no equity. If such projects went wrong, there was no money to soak up losses, meaning the banks were immediately on the hook. Meanwhile the total debt of each tycoon, much of it taken on by creatively shifting funds around, had reached alarming levels. 'We called this the layering of debt,' Gupta said. 'And that was why it was called "House of Debt", because you had these industrial houses with debt everywhere, and no equity, ready to fall down.'

The more charitable explanation was what economists Daniel Kahneman and Amos Tversky call the 'planning fallacy', a psychological bias in which those setting up projects use 'forecasts that are unrealistically close to best-case scenarios'.[9] In India, this meant that new steel mills were built on the assumption that steel demand would rise forever. In the same vein, power stations were planned on the basis that coal imports would always be cheaply available, hence why so many were built on India's western coast, thousands of kilometres away from the country's main coal supplies in the east. More generally, it was assumed that Indian growth would keep purring along, while any bureaucratic problems could be managed away. The tycoons grew giddy. 'At the promoter level, there was just this sense of exuberance,' Gupta told me. 'If the guy in the next bungalow to you on Altamount Road is building two new power plants, then you want to do it too.'

At its worst the tycoons' creative accounting could stray into outright corruption. Indian promoters were known as masters of extracting cash from projects, even those that ended up losing money. The most common ruse was 'gold-plating'. Here a business approached a bank with a proposal to build a project, say a steel mill, costing $2 billion. Of this a portion – $1.5 billion, for instance – would be funded through bank loans, while the remaining $500 million would come as equity put in by the owners. The trick was that the entrepreneur knew the steel mill could actually be built for $1 billion. The difference between the amount raised from the banks and the true cost – in this case $500 million – could be pocketed as profit and used to fund investments elsewhere.

Further deception would be managed via understandings with suppliers, involving a technique called 'over-invoicing'. Here project bills – from the builders who constructed a steel mill, for example – would be inflated, with the difference shared between the supplier and the company. Bankers would be kept in the dark. Similar methods could also be used to over-value imports, like coal or iron ore, or to rig the terms of public–private partnership contracts.[10]

'All of this was the worst form of crony capitalism,' as Jayant Sinha, by then a junior minister in India's Ministry of Finance under Narendra Modi's government, put it to me in 2015, describing the previous Congress government. 'They [the banks] were taking depositor money and giving it to all of these crony capitalists in Mumbai and Hyderabad, who then went off and built all of these projects, some of which they must have known had no chance of being viable. But they were making so much money they didn't care.' Debt problems did not affect every industrial company. Businesses in sectors like consumer goods tended to borrow more sensibly. But many projects still ended up under-capitalised. 'Gold-plating of project costs was widely used by developers to take out their equity through means other than project cash flows,' Rajiv Lall, an economist and banker, wrote in 2015.[11] The tycoons had grown out of control. 'The atmosphere was one in which the prime minister talked about unleashing the animal spirits,' as Jairam Ramesh put it to me. 'But the animals became man eaters.'

At its most fundamental level 'House of Debt' revealed that a crucial cog in India's economy had broken. The conglomerates, the backbone of the industrial sector, found their biggest projects stuck. Hit with what economists call a debt overhang they grew either unable or unwilling to invest again, plunging the wider infrastructure sector into recession. For all their vaunted aggression, the tycoons stumbled because they did not adapt to a significant change in India's political economy. Many had come of age before liberalisation, a time when capital was scarce but political problems were easy to negotiate. These two foundational assumptions then changed. First, capital became cheaper, as globalisation extended its reach during the 2000s and long-starved tycoons helped themselves to as much funding as they could find. But then, against a backdrop of corruption scandals, the promoters found their old political tricks no longer worked. Saddled with debt, their powers to work the system suddenly vanished.

THE BAD BANKS

As India's central bank head, Raghuram Rajan was the man most directly responsible for helping India's banks to clear up the mess on their balance sheets. But to do this, he first needed the banks themselves to recognise they had a problem. 'I remember one public sector banker saying to me that he had made a loan to this tycoon, who shall remain nameless,' he told me, about a year after his term as central bank chief had ended in 2016, and he had left Mumbai to return to the classroom in Chicago. 'The banker found out that he [the tycoon] had been diverting cash away from one of his investment projects. And he [the banker] told me, when he found out, he said: "I was so angry with him, I cut his credit line by ten per cent!" And when I heard this I almost started laughing. That is what you did to him? You cut his credit line by ten per cent?! It was ridiculous.'

The timidity of the banker's response, in which a major breach of the rules had been met merely with a slap on the wrist, drove home to Rajan the deeper imbalance at the heart of India's financial system – between its risk-taking, plutocratic 'promoters' on the one hand and its cautious, poorly paid state bankers on the other. 'I don't want to suggest the bankers were afraid. But you have to understand that they knew these guys [the tycoons] had so much more power relative to them, and more influence in the corridors of power,' he went on. 'For all of their lives, they had seen these tycoons on the TV, or in the newspapers, or in the gossip columns, and so suddenly having to stand up to them was difficult.'

Rajan's academic background was especially well suited to fixing this imbalance. Many economists who study banking prefer to stick with the neatness of theory and avoid the messy everyday realities of the financial system. Rajan was the opposite. His PhD thesis at MIT, entitled 'Essays on Banking',[12] featured a trio of papers casting doubt on the idea of perfectly efficient financial markets, the last of which looked directly at the ties between corporations, lenders and debt. In his early academic career he went on to explore a range of other unfashionable corners of the financial sector, from bond pricing and bank credit to capital structures.

Rajan had an interest in corruption too. After the late 1990s Asian financial crisis, he published a paper explaining why countries with 'relationship-based systems' of investment like Malaysia and Thailand – meaning those that suffered from rampant crony capitalism – were especially prone to financial collapse.[13] Then, at the International Monetary Fund, where he was made the youngest ever head of the research department, there was his 2005 speech highlighting the dangers posed by risk-taking financiers and predicting much of the coming global financial crisis.[14] Yet for all this, Rajan told me he still had no real sense of the scale of India's debt crisis when he arrived at the Reserve Bank of India. It took him the best part of two years to find out.

At first he had other problems, beginning with inflation, a scourge that India had never properly managed to bring under control. Then, a few months before he took over, India was hit by a serious financial crisis, as US Federal Reserve chair Ben Bernanke hinted that he would begin to throttle back America's quantitative easing effort, the multi-trillion-dollar cash-printing machine that had helped to stave off the worst of the global crisis. Investors around the world panicked, pulling capital out of emerging markets and from India in particular, with its historically weak public finances and ominous current account deficit. India was suddenly plunged into its worst financial crisis since 1991: the rupee crashed, financial markets went haywire, and the government flailed, trying to come up with a coherent response.

Rajan walked into the RBI's press room on a Wednesday afternoon in September 2013 to make his first speech as governor. Not a man given to exaggeration, he put the situation as calmly as he could: 'These are not easy times, and the economy faces challenges.' Yet even then he gave a clear hint of the wider battle he would soon begin to fight against India's more delinquent tycoons. 'Promoters do not have a divine right to stay in charge regardless of how badly they mismanage an enterprise,' he said, towards the end of his speech. 'Nor do they have the right to use the banking system to recapitalise their failed ventures.'[15] Coming from an Indian central banker, these were fighting words. 'I wanted to be clear that it wouldn't just be the bankers taking the hit,' he told me later. 'The industrialists taking the upside when it was good, and shoving the downside down the throats of the banks when it was bad. That had to stop.'

At the time, official data showed around a tenth of India's bank loans had gone bad, one of the worst records in Asia. The figures were weaker still at the public sector lenders, which controlled about three quarters of India's banking market, and also dominated lending to larger industrial companies. That many of these banks were in a state of some financial disrepair was no secret. Rajan had moved into the RBI governor's mansion, just down the street from Mukesh Ambani's Antilia on Altamount Road, only a few weeks after the release of the second 'House of Debt' report, which made clear enough the parlous state of many of the banks' balance sheets. But for years Mumbai insiders gossiped that the true extent of the banks' problem was actually much worse: the result, it was said, of a system in which industrialists often simply bribed their lenders to provide them with new loans, while barely worrying about whether they could actually be repaid. If things went awry, the tycoons could always use their connections in New Delhi, applying political muscle to pressure their lenders to go easy on repayments, or to begin generous restructuring of existing loans, or to swap debt for equity on favourable terms. At its worst this was known as 'ever-greening', a ruse by which companies struggling to repay one loan from a bank would simply be given another, and quietly use the money from the second to repay the first, delaying their financial day of reckoning until some far-off future date.

In his earliest days at the RBI, Rajan asked P. J. Nayak, a soft-spoken former India head of Morgan Stanley, the US investment bank, to lead a commission examining why the state banks were so badly run. Nayak's report, published in mid-2014, painted a grim picture of uncompetitive, capital-starved institutions, led by cautious bureaucrats and hobbled by political interference.[16] India's bad-loan problems were likely to get worse, Nayak argued, requiring yet more emergency capital to be pumped in by the government to keep them afloat. Yet without drastic changes to the way the banks were run, even this recapitalisation would simply mean throwing more good money after bad.

Inside the RBI, Rajan's main weapon to monitor the banks was a small army of inspectors: assiduous bureaucrats who kept tabs on financial institutions, making sure they weren't getting into trouble. After Nayak's report, he told his inspectors to look more carefully at the banks. The inspectors began to dig, pressing executives for answers about the state of their books. Their findings revealed a distressing picture. Many big loans, officially in good shape, had actually gone bad and were never likely to be repaid. Meanwhile major industrial projects that were officially said to be in good shape were in fact stuck in some political logjam or other, while bleeding money for their bankers and owners alike. 'I got a sense that the numbers were hiding a darker problem,' Rajan admitted. 'And that was when we said we really needed to uncover the size of the hole.'

By this time a sense of hope had returned to India's economy, as the market panic of 2013 petered out and business newspapers hailed a 'Rajan rally' in honour of the country's sure-footed central bank chief.[17] More important was Narendra Modi's election in mid-2014, and the hopes for reform he brought with him. Optimists predicted a shake-up of the banking system, with its public sector laggards put under new management, or perhaps even placed into private hands. But despite this, the underlying bad-loans problems only grew worse. Hopes that Modi would restart moribund power and steel projects – two major sources of bad loans – proved illusory. With each passing quarter these loan problems ticked up. To get a grip on the issue, Rajan launched an innocuous internal project the following year, known as the asset quality review. A special team scoured the bank's loan books, forcing them to reveal their problems, and building for the first time a complete picture of the bad loans on their books. Yet even having steeled himself, Rajan was stunned. 'It was at least two or three times what I expected, it was quite shocking,' he told me. 'Then we had the issue of how to get them [the banks] to 'fess up that this was there.'

Part of what Rajan's team discovered was problems of outright corruption. From time to time a scandal would erupt in which police caught a financier accepting cash. The chairman of Syndicate Bank, an undistinguished mid-sized lender, was arrested in 2014, on charges of accepting a bribe in exchange for giving a loan to a struggling steel tycoon, before being released on bail.[18] (The case remained pending at the time of writing.) These public cases were rare, but the wider system was thought to be riddled with similar smaller examples, from managers accepting fancy watches to executives finding clever ways to restructure old loans or offer new ones in exchange for cash.

'Typically a corrupt [bank] boss uses senior executives . . . for sanctioning loans to undeserving borrowers and pockets a small portion of the loan amount,' Tamal Bandyopadhyay, a finance expert, wrote after another bank chairman was charged with accepting bribes in 2016.[19] I was often told that the country's cleverest industrialists found ways to parachute pliant bankers into positions where they could help them get loans approved. This was hard to verify, but given the generous terms on which many loans were given to otherwise hopeless businesses, it didn't seem entirely far-fetched. 'I met with a number of retired chairmen of banks, and the kind of stories they told me about dishonesty in the banks were really extraordinary,' P. J. Nayak told me later, talking about the research process for his report. 'There is corruption in the system, and there is no point pretending otherwise.'

Yet, as Rajan explained, graft was not the real problem facing India's financial system. Instead, it was the subtler but more significant power imbalance between creditors and the tycoons to whom they lent. It was not just that the banks were run badly. Rather, it was that they lacked the tools that financial institutions in most other countries deployed to keep their borrowers in line. One problem was information, given that lenders were unable or unwilling to dig into the overall condition of the conglomerates themselves, or to find out whether their owners were shifting debts around between companies. India also had no functioning bankruptcy rules, which made it all but impossible to kick out owners at a failing company and sell off its assets. Capital was expensive in India largely because it was so hard to get it back if things went wrong.

In most countries, entrepreneurs who hit a rough patch were forced to plead with their bankers to keep their companies, and would therefore take whatever deal their lenders offered. But in India the deals worked the other way round. 'The essential game was that if you were an industrialist, and you got into trouble, then you don't have to pay back unless you want to,' Rajan told me. 'And the only reason you want to pay up on one loan, is if you want to get more loans in return.'

BATTLES HALF WON

Rather than poring over their balance sheets, just walking into a branch gives a clear sense of the weaknesses of most Indian public sector banks. Syndicate, the lender whose chairman was arrested in 2014, had a ramshackle outlet just next to my office in southern Mumbai, with an ATM I used to use from time to time. The bank's orange logo featured an Alsatian dog and the slogan 'faithful and friendly'. Inside it was all shabby furniture, piles of yellowing paper and slow-moving clerks. The single cash machine normally did not work. Barely half of Indians had bank accounts, but those that did mostly used branches like this, attracted by their safe and sober reputations.

Institutions like Syndicate were not run directly by the government: they tended to be listed on stock exchanges, but with the state holding most of the shares. But the government still exerted control via thickets of rules put in place after Indira Gandhi's bank nationalisation in 1969. Although they were inefficient, savers thought these public banks reliable, with implicit public backing if things ever went wrong. Entry-level positions were much sought after, offering lifetime job security and reasonable benefits. Senior managers were paid poorly compared to the private sector: Arundhati Bhattacharya at State Bank of India, the largest lender, earned roughly $45,000 a year.[20] But these jobs were prestigious, and came with other perks, like free fancy bungalows. The system overall rewarded safe pairs of hands. It even had its own name: 'lazy banking', a term used to mock bankers who fled from risk and happily placed most of their capital in ultra-safe government bonds.[21]

This ultra-cautious reputation made the reckless lending spree that India's bankers had begun all the more surprising. 'I remember talking to one of the well-known construction promoters, and he told me that he had these guys [the bankers] running after him with cheque books,' Rajan recalled. 'They were begging to lend.' The banks had found it easy to raise money, with global interest rates during the 2000s at unusually low levels. But times looked good domestically too. Most of the big projects built in the early 2000s had done well, and their loans had been easily repaid. The assumption had been that this could now be repeated on a far larger scale.

The industrialists were exuberant about India's future, showing an enthusiasm that soon infected supposedly risk-averse bankers too. Vijay Mallya's Kingfisher was one obvious example. When things began to go wrong, the banks restructured the tycoon's loans and gave him more time to fix his finances, while also swapping debt for equity at generous rates.[22] When it became clear that Mallya was not going to be able to repay, they were stuck. They had no legal means to take control of Kingfisher, or even to force Mallya to repay what he could. The power imbalance between lender and debtor was too great.

Despite this, Rajan's efforts did begin to have an effect. There were a few high-profile examples, notably Mallya himself, where banks gradually moved to seize assets, including his villas and planes. The sight of a tycoon of Mallya's stature being pressed for repayments had a chilling effect on others with heavy debts. In private, the industrialists complained of a witch-hunt. 'The promoters ran to Delhi . . . and started complaining, and to Delhi's credit, they said "You have to deal with it yourself"', Rajan recalled. Prime Minister Modi showed little enthusiasm for a radical banking shake-up, and ruled out privatisation, but he did promise a new era of 'no interference' by politicians in bank lending.[23] In New Delhi, Jayant Sinha, Rajan's former classmate, had been given a portfolio that included pushing for banking reform. He helped Modi's government develop a new package of banking reforms, which included a new bankruptcy bill, injections of extra capital for struggling state lenders, and the promise of new management. The idea was to solve three issues at once: force the banks to admit their problems, give them more money to get through them, and help them grapple with their debtors; 'recognition, recapitalisation and resolution', as Sinha put it.

Yet to put the system right Indian bankers needed to act more like lenders in other countries: writing down debts, forcing companies to sell assets and getting tough and kicking out their management. Every step of this chain proved difficult, however. Banks that wrote down debts risked being accused of cronyism, for in effect letting an indebted tycoon off the hook. Attempts to remove a promoter by force would end up in court. 'The legal challenges could just tie you up in knots,' Arundhati Bhattacharya told me in 2014.

Potential purchasers of distressed assets, from power projects to toll roads, were wary too, fearing that they would run into bureaucratic hurdles, or end up in disputes with the previous owners. Even lenders who did want to act forcefully had their hands tied, because Indian banks tended to lend in groups. Vijay Mallya's debts, for instance, were spread over a consortium of no fewer than seventeen lenders, all of whom had to agree on how to chase the tycoon down. In theory this spread risk, but mostly it provided an excuse for inaction. 'They [the banks] have been a little bit like deer in the headlights, paralysed by the risk,' Rajan told me. 'They have this powerful incentive to think, why should you upset the apple cart when maybe you are three months away from retirement, and this will get everyone so upset?'

During 2016, Ashish Gupta flew to New Delhi to give a private presentation to officials in the Finance Ministry. In it he hinted that the bad-debt problem would end up closer to twenty per cent of all loans, a staggeringly high number. Even then, many troubled projects still had not been recognised as 'non-performing', meaning that their debts were never likely to be repaid. Many of these projects were delayed, or had simply run out of money, meaning that the tycoon had also lost interest, given that such equity as they had put in was now worthless. Much of the Rs 390 billion ($6 billion) in debts built by Lagadapati Rajagopal at Lanco was yet to be classified as bad, for instance. Even in cases like these, banks and borrowers still tended to claim that things would come good. Yet this was normally an illusion used to justify giving the debtor more time to repay – an approach known as 'extend and pretend'.

This slow progress reflected deeper political problems, as Arvind Subramanian, the government's chief economic adviser, later explained to me. Almost everyone involved knew that some kind of deal was needed to fix India's broken industrial economy. Pain had to be shared: banks needed to write down debt; companies needed to sell assets and raise new funds; and the government needed to help companies with stuck projects and give extra capital to state banks. The problem was that any action seen to be doing favours for tycoons was politically toxic. Once big investment deals went off the rails, there was no easy way to recover the money and no legal means to kill off debt-laden zombie companies. This predicament, Subramanian argued, marked a shift in India's economic development. Under the old socialist system companies were unable to enter new markets, either because private players were banned or because complex licences protected incumbents. Liberalisation changed that. But now in a host of sectors – power, steel, construction, aviation and even banking itself – capital was stuck inside struggling enterprises. India had moved from 'socialism with restricted entry to capitalism without any hope of exit', as Subramanian put it. Creative destruction was not being allowed to work. The system was stuck.

Mild-mannered by temperament, Rajan was an odd figure to try and break all this open. His was an establishment background: although he did not know it as a child, his father was one of India's most senior spies, and a founding member of the equivalent of America's Central Intelligence Agency or Britain's MI6. Before leaving for America, he had studied at the Indian Institute of Technology in Delhi, then the Indian Institute of Management in Ahmedabad, the twin training grounds of the country's corporate elite. Although inventive, his economic views were fairly orthodox, with a faith in markets and a suspicion of government. Yet his distaste for cronyism also had a clear moral edge. 'Some people in India were very rich not because they were good businessmen but because they knew how to work the system,' he told me. 'I wanted to bring capitalism back, which is a system where you get the rewards if you take the risks, but not more than that.' Before moving back to India he co-authored a book that summed up his intellectual views: *Saving Capitalism from the Capitalists*.

The problem in the end was not that Rajan lacked the temperament for the fight, but that he lacked the time. India's central bank governors typically serve two terms of three years each. But one Saturday afternoon in June 2016, Rajan issued an unexpected statement saying that after 'due reflection' he would quit after only one.[24]

The news sent India's hyperactive rumour mill spinning. Rajan offered no explanation, beyond saying it was time to return to academia. Friends hinted at the special interests that had been stacked against him. 'Though it was the right thing, this policy has produced collateral damage,' wrote Luigi Zingales, a co-author and colleague at Chicago, suggesting that Rajan's battle against crony capitalism had been in some way responsible for his departure and blaming 'those Indian oligarchs who had enjoyed easy credit'.[25] Rajan's habit of giving politically tinged speeches had also caused disquiet in New Delhi, irking some hardline Modi allies. But media reports pondered whether anxious industrialists had also pressed for his sacking. Whether they did or not, the bankers and tycoons were surely glad to see him go. Worse, less than a month after Rajan's exit, Jayant Sinha was shifted too, shunted aside to a different junior ministerial post in a cabinet reshuffle.[26] Together, the duo had tried to reform India's broken banking system and bring the worst excesses of its cronyism back under control. Their departures left that job at best half done.

Sinha put a gloss on what had been achieved. 'India is on a journey to a new system of capitalism, in which the cronyism of old is being swept away,' he told me, after he had switched jobs. 'The prime minister [Modi] is fully committed to this, and while that journey is not completed yet, there is no going back.' By the time he and Rajan departed, the banks' problems were at least out in the open, even if the debt problems were far from fixed. The basic structure of the old state-dominated banking system also remained in place. Most state banks remained in financial trouble; indeed, having finally confessed to the true extent of their bad loans, many were actually in worse shape than when Rajan arrived. Most of the fixes suggested by P. J. Nayak's commission were ignored. 'In my report, we said "If you don't act quickly and radically the problem will get much worse", and it has got much worse,' Nayak told me in 2017. The culture of inaction among India's public banks remained. Even today, it still seems unlikely that the cautious banker Rajan gently mocked in his story – the man who punished an errant tycoon by timidly cutting his credit line – would have acted more boldly.

Still, if the battle was only half finished, it was also half won. Long-time observers of Indian corporate life saw a change. The tycoons' 'divine rights' that Rajan attacked in his first speech as governor – to stay in charge no matter what, and to misuse bank funds to do so – were no longer quite so sacrosanct. Attempts to bring debtors to book caught a few big fish, with Vijay Mallya in exile. Other tycoons were feeling pressured as banks pushed for asset sales and debt recovery deals. The billionaires featured in 'House of Debt' might not have paid back their loans, but they were also unlikely to get new ones on anything like the same favourable terms. The security of the old world – the sense that connections and guile would allow them to keep their empires intact – was at least in doubt. Where once India's tycoons were brim full of optimism, now they looked ever more anxious.

Mining tycoon Gali Janardhana Reddy, only recently released from jail following allegations of corruption, hosts a lavish wedding ceremony for his daughter in 2016, estimated to have cost Rs 5.5 billion ($85 million).

CHAPTER 9

THE ANXIOUS TYCOONS

THE INDIA OF OUR DREAMS

Standing on a platform high up on a steel tower, Naveen Jindal pointed off towards a distant hill, blanketed in trees. A giant industrial facility sprawled out far below: the three red and white striped chimneys of a power plant; a steel mill; and a sponge iron facility, topped off with a lofty viewing area made of rust-coloured metal, reached via a slow, rickety lift. Jindal wore a hard hat, along with an expensive-looking powder blue shirt. It ought to have been a moment of triumph: the young billionaire, gazing down at his nearly completed mega-facility. But then he looked the other way instead, where there was nothing but forest. 'It is out there, the coal block, maybe a few miles that way,' he said, as a frown crossed his face. 'Because of the coal, that is the reason we are here.' He turned back around and gestured towards the plant below, the hot morning sun glinting off his sunglasses. 'That is the only reason all of this is here. And then they cancelled it, and we were stuck.' He paused, and then flashed a cheerful grin, as if suddenly conscious that he was being too downbeat: 'So this happens, and then you have to say "Oh! What to do?"'

Jindal's plant at Angul, in the mineral-rich eastern state of Odisha, was to be one of the largest in India: an integrated complex churning out millions of tonnes of steel and thousands of megawatts of power each year.[1] At its launch it seemed a fittingly ambitious project for a glamorous tycoon. The youngest son of Om Prakash Jindal, a steel maven in the decades before liberalisation, Naveen Jindal inherited a portion of the family business when his father died in a helicopter crash in 2005, and when he himself was only in his mid-thirties. Jindal quickly acquired an image that was part young Turk entrepreneur, part playboy: a snappy dresser, polo player, champion marksman and, for a time, the country's best-paid businessman, awarding himself an annual salary as high as Rs 730 million ($11 million).[2] He followed his father into politics too: at the time of his death the elder man was a minister in the government of Haryana, a state to the west of New Delhi; the younger became a Congress MP in 2004, representing Kurukshetra, a seat in the same region, which his father had held roughly a decade before.

Critics accused Jindal of conflicts of interest, given that his company relied on land and minerals that only the government could provide. He denied it. Unlike fellow elected tycoon Vijay Mallya, he also carefully avoided raising issues related to his businesses in parliament. Even so, when coal rights were handed out during the 2000s, Jindal Steel and Power Limited (JSPL) won more than any other company.[3] The flip side of that good fortune only became clear in 2014, when the Supreme Court cancelled all of those licences during the 'Coalgate' scandal, along with dozens of others belonging to other industrial groups. The decision hammered Jindal's share price and saddled him with a half-built facility at Angul with no coal to fuel it.

Three years later I went to have coffee at Jindal's headquarters in New Delhi, to find out how his attempts to rescue the business were going. As I was about to leave, as if on a whim, he asked me fly down with him to see the plant the following day, telling me to turn up at the VIP terminal of New Delhi's airport. Having arrived a little after 6 a.m., I was ushered into a sparse private lounge, with marble flooring, cream leather couches and garish floral art. A plastic model of a private jet stood beneath a Pyrex dome in the middle of the room, in case a passing dignitary wanted to buy it. There was a second secluded area in one corner, hidden behind frosted partitions and presumably reserved for especially important persons.

After about half an hour I walked through a private security line, along with various JSPL executives and half a dozen other men in ill-fitting suits, who turned out to be from a large bank. We all emerged into the early dawn light, where a fleet of white cars with orange flashing lights picked us up and drove across the tarmac at thrilling speed, weaving between stationary commercial airliners to bring us to our own waiting plane. It was only then that Jindal himself arrived, bounding out of an SUV to shake hands with his staff, before walking over a short length of red carpet and leaping up the steps.

The cabin inside was comfortable, with twenty leather executive-style seats, polished walnut panelling and a cupboard by the door, where you left your shoes. A single stewardess busied herself handing out juice as we taxied down the runway. Jindal huddled in a separate cabin towards the rear with the bankers, who I later discovered were employed by one of JSPL's big lenders, and were visiting the plant to discuss the loans Jindal needed to tide the troubled project over. It was no great secret that he needed money – Jindal claimed the coal cancellation had cost him $1 billion or more – although in this he was hardly alone.[4] Many industrialists hoped that Narendra Modi would help them to revive their moribund projects. But by the time Jindal and I met, more than two years after Modi's 2014 election triumph, disappointingly little had changed. Laden down with debt and facing intractable political obstacles with existing investments, many once buccaneering tycoons had in effect gone on strike, and simply stopped deploying new capital at all.

Our plane landed around two hours later at Savitri Jindal airport, an isolated airstrip and terminal building named after Jindal's elderly mother, a few kilometres away from the Angul plant. Two dozen company salesmen were waiting to greet him outside the terminal, having flown down from Rajasthan, where they sold rebars, the thin steel sticks that provide the reinforcement in reinforced concrete. Jindal's face visibly brightened: although no longer an MP – he lost his seat three years earlier, swept aside by Modi's wave – he still enjoyed the backslapping of retail politics, and posed happily for selfie after selfie. Jindal looked almost boyish, a small, lean figure, surrounded by heavy-set moustachioed men. As if settling into an old routine, he gave a brief speech, complimenting the salesman on their efforts. 'I believe if we keep working that India can become the country of our dreams,' he said towards the end. 'And you are all part of that.'

Settling into the back of a bulky white Toyota jeep, Jindal used the ride to the plant to tell me about its many misfortunes. He had decided to build the place only after having secured rights to the 'Utkal B1' coal block, the same one he would later point to from the tower. He visited the area at first by helicopter – there were no roads – and found only isolated villages, scrubland and forest. But he pushed on, attracted by coal deposits large enough to supply his facility for a quarter of a century or more, and began construction in 2008. By the time the coal licences were cancelled six years later, the facility was already well behind schedule, having sucked up the best part of $3 billion.[5] Industrial projects elsewhere in Odisha often had problems with Maoist Naxalite rebels. But in Angul, before the coal cancellations at least, the headaches had been more humdrum: project delays, environmental protests, regulatory wrangles and the odd local villager, unhappy with the money they had been paid to leave their land. As we pulled up at the plant office, I got out of the car, and struggled to shut the door. 'It's armour plated, so there is a reason they are hard to close,' Jindal said, before adding with a smile: 'You can't be too careful.'

For the next few hours Jindal led the various bankers on a tour of the plant, driving from one huge industrial building to the next in a fleet of cars. The coal cancellations had forced him to mothball part of the planned facility, he explained, but he decided to spend more money and build a new steel blast furnace instead. Then he had to buy expensive coal on the open market, in order to get both his steel and power plants up and running. Even this was no panacea: global steel prices were depressed at the time, and he complained often about cut-price Chinese steel imports, to supportive nods from the group. Jindal's image was everywhere around the plant, peering down from placards and staring into the middle distance from safety posters. One billboard showed his smiling face with the slogan 'Our leader: he knows the way, shows the way and goes the way'.

Near the entrance we passed a roundabout with a giant Indian tricolour raised on a giant flagpole, allowing Jindal to stop and discuss one of his favourite political achievements. Having studied in Texas, he returned home to India impressed by America's habit of flying grand ceremonial flags. At the time, India's constitution allowed its citizens to hoist up their own only on a handful of national holidays. Jindal campaigned successfully to overturn the rule.[6] The flag became a kind of personal symbol, as well as a useful political vehicle, given that it positioned him as the head of a patriotic movement with whose aims almost no Indians would disagree. Jindal always wore a flag lapel pin, as did all of his staff. His foundation paid for the construction of dozens of monumental poles around the country, topped with flags the size of swimming pools. '207 feet high,' he said, looking up with pride. 'India has the most number of monumental flags of any country now. Thanks to us.'

Well before he died, Om Prakash Jindal split his businesses between his four sons.[7] Jindal's portion was small, just a steel mill and a few mines. But he expanded quickly, showing an adventurous appetite for risk, and raising turnover from almost nothing in 1998, when he took over, to well over $3 billion in 2012, the year his troubles really began.[8] He proved inventive too, making a minor fortune setting up India's first private sector merchant power plant.[9] Acquiring scarce resources, notably coal and iron ore, was a particular skill. He expanded abroad, developing mines in Australia, Botswana and South Africa, and signing a $1 billion deal to explore a vast Bolivian iron ore deposit.[10] That deal collapsed in 2012, although by then Jindal had bigger problems, after four of his coal blocks were mentioned in a report from auditor Vinod Rai.[11] The licences for all four were then cancelled by the Supreme Court two years later. In the years that followed, police began to probe the tycoon's various coal deals, raiding JSPL's offices and launching official corruption cases.[12] Jindal consistently denied wrongdoing, but the episode proved chastening, turning an unusually image-conscious tycoon into one of the most prominent faces in India's long battle against cronyism.

Later that day I watched as Jindal sat at the head of a boardroom table, with his various executives on one side, and the half-dozen bankers on the other, going back and forth over project milestones and delays. The discussions were cordial but tense. Jindal already had outstanding debts of nearly $7 billion.[13] The bankers pressed to understand why yet more was needed. At times the talks reached an impasse, and all eyes turned deferentially to the head of the table, waiting for Jindal to find a way forward. Watching him, I was struck by the stress of his position: the billions in loans, the half-finished projects and the thousands of workers who saw his face on posters and expected him to find a way to fix them. 'The bankers all want your personal guarantee, the government wants you to do this and that,' he told me later, sitting in his sparsely decorated plant office. 'For the good things that happen, the credit goes to the owner, and anything which goes wrong, all the burden as well, whether he deserves it or not.'

In person Jindal was courteous and pleasant, showing no signs of a rumoured other side of his character, one involving a short fuse and a habit of bawling out employees. Even so, it was clear that an impetuous streak lurked beneath the charm. In the midst of Coalgate, he once picked a public fight with Subhash Chandra, a fellow tycoon and owner of television station Zee News, which had run numerous critical items about JSPL. Seeking revenge, Jindal launched a sting operation, in which he sent executives from his company to meet two of the channel's journalists, and recorded them soliciting bribes.[14] The fall-out was messy and did little to help the reputation of either man. It wasn't hard to paint Jindal as a patrician figure, with his polo-playing, stables filled with horses, and a taste for immaculate black Nehru jackets, which made him look ever so slightly like a Bond villain. But it was an image that sat at odds with the everyman patriot persona of his political days. 'In Kurukshetra, he sheds his well-tailored suits and aviator sunglasses,' essayist Mehboob Jeelani wrote in a profile in 2013.[15] 'He prides himself on his refusal to attack the opposition, and he shies away from the sort of hot-button topics that fuel shouting matches on prime-time television.'

Jindal was equally careful not to criticise Modi's government for his troubles. His prominent Congress ties made it unlikely he would get much help from the BJP in any case, although eventually he did hope to get back the Utkal B1 block, he said. There was a legal case winding through the courts about it, although he did not seem confident that it would produce a quick result. Where once he had denied that a conflict of interest existed between his roles as politician and industrialist, now he admitted that his choice created problems. 'If people ask me, I would tell them "Do not get into politics and business",' he said, 'although I couldn't follow that advice myself.' From time to time as we spoke, again as if sensing that he might be coming across as too pessimistic, he would turn unexpectedly cheerful. 'I believe we have to change to be the country of our dreams, otherwise it's empty talk,' he said at one point, the third time he had used a variant of that phrase during the day. I asked if he wanted to return to parliament, which I sensed that he did. (He still kept a political website, with a similar slogan – 'committed to building the nation of our dreams' – plastered on its front page.) He smiled, and dodged the question, saying he didn't think it likely.

In the public eye, Jindal and his fellow industrialists were viewed as consummate insiders with many helpful friends in New Delhi. It was striking how differently Jindal saw things, painting his own role as one of ceaseless struggle against official and technical obstacles. He was clearly still irked by the various corruption cases against him, hinting that they were politically motivated. 'In a lot of places people expect you to pay them,' he told me. 'We actually never did, and then they hold that against you, and they say "OK, you are like this", and they find fault with you.' Most observers agreed that the original process by which coal blocks were handed out had been deeply flawed, and the new auction system introduced to replace it was both fairer and more efficient. But Jindal still showed especial annoyance with the idea that he had been gifted blocks for free. He pointed out more than once that he had won his coal under the rules that applied at the time, and that the right to mine itself was just the start of a decade-long process, and one marked by huge expense and uncertainty as you tried to dig the stuff out of the ground. 'Our name has been so much sullied. Coal scam? We are committing a scam here?' he said at one point, pointing to the vast facility around him. 'It's like the Golden Gate Bridge in San Francisco, the scale of this, 30,000 people have been working here. And they say we are doing a scam?'

LALA LAND

I pondered Jindal's troubles, and those of India's industrialists more generally, as I settled back into my seat for the return flight that evening. The stewardess served sparkling wine, and in the cabin at the back the tycoon and his bankers clinked glasses, suggesting their discussions had gone well. It was hard to feel too sorry for a billionaire returning home on his private jet, but Jindal cut a chastened and somewhat sympathetic figure even so.

Few people had encapsulated more clearly the adventurous spirit of India's boom times. Yet here he was, parlaying with bankers and trying to keep the plates spinning, for fear he might now lose one of his most ambitious investments. His critics accused him of influence-peddling and moving ahead illegally with projects without proper permission. Whatever the truth of those allegations – he firmly denied them all – they also embodied a different dilemma, and one faced by almost anyone trying to build big industrial projects in India, namely that if you followed every rule and waited for each official green light, you could be reasonably certain that nothing would ever be built. Yet even behind that issue, there lay a different set of questions, about the future of the kind of sprawling business that Jindal had built, and indeed the country's industrial conglomerates themselves.

For all his self-confidence, Jindal clearly felt under-appreciated, as if his sizeable fortune was not reward enough for the technical achievements of his projects, or for the acts of sheer will needed to transform patches of rural scrubland into forests of concrete and steel. Earlier I'd asked him what he had learned from the various difficulties faced by his business empire. 'That you have to be really, really careful about everything,' he replied, after a few seconds' thought.

When he began building projects like Angul, banks were eager to lend and foreign investors were plentiful. There were few limits to what might be built: the country of our dreams seemed within reach. Jindal did not say this exactly, but I guessed it was also an intoxicating time to be a promoter, sitting amid a web of fundraising and deal-making, expanding his operations into new areas, and enjoying a period of industrial possibilities at a scale almost unimaginable to men of his father's generation. Against the backdrop of two decades of hyper-globalisation, when money was easy to come by and the political system flexible to their needs, he and other industrial titans had bet their businesses on India's bright future. But then corruption worries flared up, bureaucrats got cold feet, and swings in global commodity prices left many of their power stations and steel mills unable to operate. Cash flows shrank and debts mounted. The heads of business houses who would once have expected to win handsome rewards for their boldness suddenly found themselves struggling to stay afloat.

Jindal's predicament was just one extreme example of the stormy recent history of India's conglomerates more generally. Sprawling organisations like JSPL had long fallen out of fashion in the West. Business schools there taught the virtues of core competencies, drawing on the work of Indian-born management thinker C. K. Prahalad among others. Financial investors also marked down diversified companies with a hefty 'conglomerate discount', believing them to be bloated, unfocused and, in the case of family-owned businesses, unduly prone to the whims of their founders.

Yet family enterprises had dominated commercial life for so long in India, as they had in the rest of Asia, that they seemed almost part of a natural order. Secure in their own ownership, their Indian heads were meant to be able make bold, long-term investments, ignoring the short-term demands of shareholders. Their admirers claimed they exhibited a sense of stewardship, showing loyalty to workers and communities that went far beyond what might be expected from a typical Western PLC. They also often had long-established political relationships, a clear competitive advantage in a country like India, where the good graces of government often meant the difference between commercial triumph and disaster. Most importantly of all, men like Jindal were meant to be adroit judges of risk, not least because they were so often using their own capital to invest, and thus were said to have 'skin in the game'. Over the years there had been were plenty of Western experts who thought the Indian conglomerates would gradually fade away, to be replaced by a more orthodox Anglo-Saxon model, with diffuse corporate owner-ship and clear splits between managers and shareholders. But for all their frequency, these predictions never actually seemed to come to pass.

There were plenty of cultural and historical theories to explain the conglomerates' successes, but mostly it came down to what Swedish economist Gunnar Myrdal once called India's 'soft state'.[16] Western companies could raise capital through financial markets, and rely on the state to build good quality infrastructure. They also hired graduates from good universities and used the courts to settle disputes. In India all of this was different: capital was expensive, infrastructure dilapi-dated, talent scarce, and the judicial system typically creaky and unreli-able.[17] Many businesses decided they needed to do these things themselves.

There was then a wider 'institutional void' where the state should have been, in the words of Tarun Khanna, the author of a widely quoted *Harvard Business Review* article back in 1997, which explained the success of diversified businesses in emerging markets.[18] Financing was a particular challenge. Because raising capital was so expensive, Indian tycoons became masters at shuffling money between their various busi-nesses, often doing so covertly, as Raghuram Rajan discovered during his tenure as the head of India's central bank. Raising more money from within their own company also allowed India's promoters to keep complete family control, rather than diluting their ownership by selling any more than a small quantity of shares to outside investors. At their

worst, these kinds of enterprises were mockingly dubbed '*lala*' companies, using a Hindi word implying a business operation where the family
owners were basically in sole charge, while signs of professional management and good governance were basically absent.

If conglomerates prospered because India's state was weak, they also
came to thrive because it was mighty. Back in the days when Jindal's
father ran their family's businesses, the government controlled production using industrial licences. They were handed out sparingly, encouraging entrepreneurs to snap up any they could get their hands on. This
created odd-looking companies, with operations stretching across
entirely unrelated industries, such as the one built by Vijay Mallya in his
earlier days, which stretched from whisky and beer to pizza retail and
industrial electronics.

Incoherent though this licensing system was, it often proved oddly
popular with business owners, who viewed their licences as a means to
protect themselves from potential competitors. More often than not the
system also encouraged influence-peddling. Business houses built up
lobbying operations in New Delhi to win new licences and tweak regulations. As prime ministers, both Jawaharlal Nehru and Indira Gandhi
wanted to use the state for good socialist purposes by curbing the power
of big business. Perversely their policies had the opposite effect, as
politically connected major industrialists proved skilled at navigating
the bureaucracy in ways that smaller businesses simply could not match.
Meanwhile the shape of the state the two leaders created – intrusive in
many areas, but barely present in others – provided the ideal conditions
for conglomerates to flourish.

Rising competition after 1991 did then push some older Indian business houses into decline, but to others liberalisation proved a bonanza,
allowing real estate businesses to launch mobile phone arms and newspaper magnates to build power stations. Anand Mahindra, one of India's
more cerebral tycoons, told me once that his Mahindra conglomerate,
which he insisted on describing as a 'business federation', had gone on
to thrive. 'C. K. Prahalad used to come here and berate a lot of Indian
companies for their lack of focus,' he said. 'And I used to go for this
voluntary flogging every year. He used to say "Why don't you stick to
your knitting?"' But with the old licences gone, Mahindra said wide-
ranging businesses like his own – which now dabbled in everything
from cars and solar power to aerospace and holiday resorts – could

actually provide the best means of launching new and innovative ventures, which he claimed could be incubated within other older business lines.

There was something to this argument, but even after 1991 most of India's conglomerates seemed to prosper rather more for the same old reasons they always had. The state still did a poor job providing basic infrastructure, pushing industrialists like Jindal or Gautam Adani to build their own railways and roads, just as America's nineteenth-century tycoons did before them. Lobbying for industrial licences was no longer needed, but as the economy boomed there were plenty of other regulations and rules that could be gamed, keeping the industrial embassies in New Delhi busy. 'Elements like environment rules became the new playground for whimsical government conduct, a new kind of license-permit-Raj,' as author T. N. Ninan put it.[19] Rather than fulfilling predictions of decline, the conglomerates actually became more dominant, making up 'a whopping 90 per cent' of the country's fifty largest companies by revenue in 2013, according to a study by management consultants McKinsey.[20] Credit Suisse, the investment bank, calculated that two thirds of the country's larger listed companies were family-run too, the most of any major world market.[21] For all the travails faced by Naveen Jindal and his fellow tycoons, their sprawling conglomerates still dominated India's new Gilded Age, just as their equivalents had in America more than a century before.

BIG FAT TYCOONS

Naveen Jindal's red-brick headquarters in New Delhi, like those of many conglomerates, had the appearance of a family shrine, with pictures of his father dotted throughout the building. Mukesh Ambani's office in southern Mumbai had a similar feel, which was something more like a medieval court than a modern multinational corporation. The Tata group might no longer have been controlled directly by the Tata family, but its own offices, just up the road from where my wife and I lived, were still filled with their statues and portraits, demonstrating the way family ties in India continue to act as a powerful commercial glue.

Caste often plays a similar role, especially in the north of the country, where major business families are mostly drawn from just a handful of castes and communities. Some are Brahmins like Vijay Mallya, a proud member of a sub-caste known as Goud Saraswat Brahmins, or GSBs. But more numerous are the Banias and Marwaris, the two trading groups which dominate the upper reaches of each year's *Forbes* billionaire list, and which include among their number the Ambanis, Gautam Adani and the Ruia brothers of Essar. Indian business is controlled by a 'Brahmin–Bania hegemony', as one account put it.[22] These bonds have built trust, making it easier to do deals or raise money, while creating business cultures that prize loyalty, history and community as much as profits and revenues. Yet these same bonds of caste and kin have often provided an ideal backdrop for back-scratching and cronyism too, which is why even the word *bania* has highly negative, unscrupulous connotations.

'They bred not employees but cult members, whose motivation was not just money but glory,' as novelist Rana Dasgupta once wrote, describing what he called the 'martial' enterprise culture that came to dominate many of the country's larger commercial clans. 'North Indian business families have always considered themselves to be at war, and the sight of calamity and destruction revives their spirits. The early twenty-first century shake-up allowed the more forward thinking of these families to greatly increase their economic reach.'[23] The changes this shake-up brought were partly a function of scale, as small-time *lala* business owners suddenly found themselves transformed into full-blown tycoons, with global ambitions and vastly expanded fortunes. But they also followed shifts in attitude and style among the traditional business elite, a sentiment I once heard from Subhash Chandra, the charismatic media tycoon who founded Zee TV, and also the man with whom Naveen Jindal had conducted a brief feud. 'Our country has come through four or five hundred years of slavery, right from the Mughals to the Portuguese, then to the British,' he told me once, as we sat in his office in midtown Mumbai. 'Our people were suppressed for more than maybe eight hundred years . . . That is changing.'

That change of style manifested itself most clearly in a new culture of bling, as India's once-dowdy business families began investing in a familiar panoply of luxury cars, private jets and mega-yachts. Few things then demonstrated their success more clearly than an outlandish new family home, an area where Mukesh Ambani once again proved to be the pioneer: the first Bollygarch to display his wealth via a building no one could reasonably ignore. Not every Bollygarch built themselves a defining new pad: Jindal, for instance, lived in a spacious old bungalow in the heart of New Delhi, while also keeping a giant ranch-style home on the edge of town, with stables for his dozens of thoroughbred horses. Others bought older homes and did them up, for example elderly pharmaceutical mogul and horse-racing enthusiast Cyrus Poonawalla, who spent Rs 7.5 billion ($113 million) to buy an old seaside palace in Mumbai's Breach Candy neighbourhood in 2015. Originally known as Wankaner House, the building had belonged to the Maharaja of Wankaner, a minor aristocrat. It was in a state of some disrepair when the Poonawallas bought it, with plans to turn it into a palace once again, in what was reckoned to be the most expensive residential property purchase in Indian history.[24]

Even so, it is the newer buildings that are most striking, a further example of which stands just down the road from Poonawalla's planned mansion. A thirty-six-storey residential skyscraper, it dwarfs the nearby neighbourhood, casting a long shadow over Windsor Villa, the ornate house nearby where the young Salman Rushdie had once lived. In *Midnight's Children*, the novelist recalled gazing from his bedroom as a child and watching pale European swimmers 'cavorting in the map-shaped pool of the Breach Candy Club' just over the road.[25] Now the newer building, dubbed JK House, looms over the club, having risen to become India's tallest family home, even outstripping Antilia once it reached its full height of 145 metres. Its owner is Gautam Hari Singhania, the fifty-something heir to the Raymond Group, which among many other things owns India's best-known chain of men's suit and fashion retailers.

Rather than their size, it was the likeness between Antilia and JK House that stood out. Just like its more famous doppelgänger, Singhania's building featured a cantilevered design, with numerous slab-like balconies that jutted out from its main body. A newcomer to Mumbai might well have been forgiven for thinking that Ambani had in fact built himself two houses, rather than just one. Inside, Singhania's interiors were said to be correspondingly lavish, with two swimming pools and a private museum to house memorabilia from his family's textile dynasty. Purely coincidentally, Singhania had begun to develop plans for his home around the time Antilia was nearing completion. His building process was not smooth: in 2012 Mumbai's city council halted construction at JK House, citing planning violations.[26] Years of legal wrangling followed, leaving the building's half-completed skeleton covered in dark green wrapping.

I watched JK House in its various stages of construction, not least when I went swimming in the pool at the Breach Candy Club, from where the building works, or the lack of them, were clearly on view. Eventually I became curious about its owner, and in particular the odd psychology that led Singhania to design a vastly expensive home that was little more than a pastiche. The changes sweeping over India were so profound that it almost no longer seemed remarkable that a wealthy man would build himself a huge residential skyscraper. Even so, Singhania fitted almost too perfectly the image of the playboy tycoon: a party animal, nightclub owner and lover of every kind of fast, expensive vehicle. He raced Ferraris, flew jets and owned a quartet of speedboats, named variously after the James Bond movies *GoldenEye*, *Goldfinger*, *Octopussy* and *Thunderball*. The patriarch of a Mumbai club for supercar enthusiasts, he was said to have included many floors of garages in JK House to house his own vast collection.

Singhania dressed flashily too, as one might have expected from a textiles tycoon. He agreed to meet me at his office, not long after construction of his home had finally been completed in 2016, and arrived wearing white and black slip-on loafers, and a striped purple and orange shirt. To my disappointment he politely declined to discuss his house, or indeed its curiously familiar design, although he chatted amiably enough about his love of motor racing, and plans for his Raymond conglomerate. The company made fibres and fabrics, but was best known for its suit shops, including a flagship store which occupied the bottom two floors of JK House. Much like Anand Mahindra he said he didn't like describing his business as a family-run conglomerate. He favoured 'family-managed professional organisation', he explained, meaning one in which skilled outsiders were hired in to run most businesses, but where the family held most of the equity and made the most important strategic decisions. Much as with Naveen Jindal, I sensed his slight irritation with the playboy image that he had spent so much money creating, as if he felt that his passion for expensive hobbies drained credibility unfairly from his more serious commercial plans.

Drawn from the Marwari community, the Singhanias had once been one of India's oldest and most important business families, with textile operations dating back to the 1920s. But while their name remained storied, their businesses had more recently been eclipsed by newer, more aggressive rivals. I wondered if the sheer visibility of Singhania's home was part of a simpler ploy to maintain his family's place among Mumbai's A-list. Although Singhania himself said he welcomed economic liberalisation, at times he almost seemed nostalgic. 'It used to be that when I went on a Mumbai to Delhi flight, I'd know pretty much everyone on board, and today I often know no one,' he told me. 'There are many more opportunities but it is much more difficult to make money,' he added. 'It is a different environment. There is no more licensing. Your skill set was managing the government in those days. Today it is managing a free economy.'

If modern-day palaces like JK House or Antilia act as physical displays of a tycoon's achievement, their displays of wealth also often come in a more social setting: the big fat Indian wedding. Famous for their length and opulence, marriage ceremonies carry particular significance in a country long conscious of hierarchy and caste, but also increasingly stratified by symbols of wealth and taste. The pre-eminent responsibility of any Indian parent towards their children, even modest Indian wedding celebrations last for many days, and often involve guest lists stretching into the thousands. There is intense competition for desirable venues on auspicious days during the wedding season, which runs through the cooler winter months. Even middle-class parents will borrow heavily to ensure the perfect ceremony, which could involve half a dozen bridal costume changes, and a white horse for the arrival of the groom. But among the business elite, where money is basically no limitation, the only question became: how big and fat could a wedding grow?

My first taste of this came when I was sent the fancy boxed invitation for the wedding of Gautam Adani's son, not long after arriving in Mumbai. But even this seemed positively orthodox compared to the tens of thousands of luxurious blue boxes sent out in 2016 by mining tycoon Gali Janardhana Reddy, the most prominent of the Reddy brothers caught up in the iron ore scandals that hit the southern state of Karnataka. Reddy's box opened to reveal a small television screen built into the lid. A video began in which the tycoon, alongside his daughter and her husband-to-be, performed a Bollywood-style song, set against a backdrop filled with CGI-generated bulls garlanded with flowers and dancing white horses.[27]

Even in a country famed for extravagant marriages, the wedding that followed was remarkable. Spread over thirty-six acres in central Bangalore, the venue included a mock-up of the mining baron's home-town fiefdom of Bellary, in the east of Karnataka, complete with actors in costume, along with buildings designed to recreate the ruins of Hampi, a nearby UNESCO World Heritage Site. Some fifty thousand guests attended many days of celebrations, in which the bride's saris and jewels alone were reported to have cost millions of dollars.[28] The wedding's total expense became the subject of escalating speculation, not least because it took place in the midst of the cash crunch caused by Narendra Modi's 'demonetisation' drive – an experiment that itself played havoc with the old wedding tradition of using plenty of black money to pay for festivities. Reddy claimed a modest outlay of Rs 300 million ($4.6 million); India's newspapers suggested the entire affair came in at a rather grander Rs 5.5 billion ($85 million).

For Reddy himself, the ceremony offered a kind of social redemp-tion: he had only recently emerged from jail, after he and his brothers had been accused of orchestrating a mining scandal, in cahoots with the state's BJP-led government. Even the venue, the Palace Grounds at the heart of Karnataka's capital, appeared designed to announce his return to the state his activities were claimed to have disgraced, and to chide those in the city's legal and political establishment who had once courted his friendship and then turned against him. Reddy's celebration was just one particularly stark example of the way that elite weddings have become a focus for 'competition, conservatism, and assertion of power', according to Parul Bhandari, a sociologist who studies matrimonial culture.[29] More often than not it also seems no accident that the most over-the-top ceremonies tend to go together with the most insalubrious hosts, from the record-breaking wedding jamboree hosted by Jayalalithaa in Tamil Nadu, to the opulent party hosted for the 2004 marriage of the son of Subrata Roy, the head of Sahara group, in his palatial Lucknow mansion.

At one level these weddings are designed to showcase their host's elevated taste and social sophistication. The best of them involve fancy destinations, from Goa to the historic cities of Rajasthan, where actress Liz Hurley married textile tycoon Arun Nayar in Jodhpur in 2007. Locations outside India are even more prized: Singapore, Mauritius, the Maldives, or even Paris for steel magnate Lakshmi Mittal, whose daughter's wedding began with an engagement ceremony at Versailles, kicking off a week of celebrations estimated by one newspaper to have cost $39 million.[30] Yet for the tycoons, these extravagant events play a further role, bringing the worlds of family and business together. Often enough the unions involve members of the same business caste, as happened with the Reddy wedding, where the groom was the son of a fellow industrialist from the same caste, and thus also called Reddy. The celebrations also often take on a corporate air: Gautam Adani's wedding included a reception in Ahmedabad, to which thousands of Adani group employees were invited, and then another in Mundra, the township next to his port. And behind it all are displays of raw political power, as tycoons attend celebrations for the scions of political dynasties, and politicians grace gatherings for the children of business titans. From time to time Mukesh Ambani uses Antilia's ground-floor ballroom to throw wedding receptions for favoured relatives, drawing in hundreds of high-powered guests. 'The main show of strength of any elite weddings is in its guest list,' as Bhandari put it. 'Attendees reflect the power and position of the host.'

COPING WITH DOWNFALL

All these glitzy weddings and extravagant new homes signalled the growing self-confidence of India's business elite. 'Those days of socialist values, where display of wealth put people off, seem to have become redundant,' as one writer put it, a few days after the ceremony for Reddy's daughter.[31] This was by no means unique: a new culture of bling stretched across major emerging markets, from the oligarchs of Russia to the new rich in China. Yet the need to demonstrate prosperity proved especially acute in India, a country where the gap between those who had it and those who did not remained so striking.

These displays also fitted into a wider culture, which Raghuram Rajan had once described as 'relationship-based capitalism', in which generosity and influence fused together: where employees and friends were looked after, and where those who were helpful to a company were rewarded in return. These traits could be admirable, as with venerable business houses like Tata and Birla, which enjoyed distinguished charitable records, running hospitals and funding civic institutions. But in less scrupulous hands this relationship-based system showed a darker side: a school scholarship offered to the child of an employee could also be handed as a reward to a helpful government official; a family chari-table foundation, in addition to funding good causes, could also be used to funnel money to friends or business contacts. In India, this line between hospitality and influence was often ambiguous at best.

This was also often a matter of temperament, given that India's tycoons were a generally charming and gregarious bunch. I was once invited for a drink at a mansion in Goa belonging to billionaire Ravi Ruia, one of the two brothers who founded Essar, another heavily indebted industrial group. His company had an aggressive reputation, but Ruia was solicitous and easy to like, with a jocular energy that belied a man well past his sixtieth birthday. Perched on a hilltop overlooking the sea, his home stood just a few kilometres from Vijay Mallya's Kingfisher Villa, and Ruia said the two families used to spend enjoyable days messing around on one another's boats. Inside, the house was vast and ornamental, with a bar in black marble, and a music area just off the lounge, with a drum kit and keyboard, and expensive-looking art hung nonchalantly on the walls. The same habit of hospitality extended to the parties the family hosted in their main residence in Mumbai, a far larger mansion, with lawns overlooking the Arabian Sea and rooms sufficient to house the entire extended Ruia clan: the two founding brothers and their sons, along with their respective wives and children. Prashant Ruia, one of the sons, once told me the family made most of its business decisions around the dining room table, meeting regularly for lunch and dinner to hash out plans and deals.[32]

The elder Ruia's conviviality seemed perfectly genuine, as if part of a culture in which showing kindness to friends and their associates, even those you didn't know well, would turn out to be good for business. Much like other Indian industrial titans, the Ruias were proud of the projects they built, which included an ultra-modern oil refinery in Gujarat, just next door to Mukesh Ambani's giant complex, as well as various other power stations and steel mills. Few businesses had grown more rapidly: Essar's revenues rocketed from roughly $2 billion in 2005 to around $27 billion a decade later. The company snapped up steel mills from North America to Zimbabwe, as well as an oil refinery in Cheshire in north-west England, and for a time had a subsidiary listed on the London Stock Exchange.[33] But that growth was also fuelled by gargantuan quantities of debt – a cool \$15 billion according to the second 'House of Debt' report in 2013 – which Essar struggled to pay back once it found itself hit by a mix of regulatory snarl-ups, project delays and fluctuating commodity prices.[34] The company had a history of precarious finances too. Debt defaults were virtually unknown in India, where banks tended to step in to provide yet more loans. But somehow Essar managed it, when its steel division defaulted on a foreign debt repayment back in 1999.[35]

More to the point, it was hard not to conclude that the family's instinct for hospitality extended far into its business affairs too. During the season of scams Essar found itself entangled in the 2G scandal, although they, like others involved in the case, were formally acquitted of wrongdoing in 2017 when a special court reported there was insufficient evidence to bring prosecutions. In 2015, the *Indian Express* published a trove of leaked internal emails revealing that Essar had hosted Nitin Gadkari, a senior BJP politician, along with his family, aboard the Ruias' yacht off the French Riviera.[36] The same emails provided details of efforts to lobby officials, win favour from journalists and give jobs to friendly contacts. None of this was illegal, and Essar denied it had done anything wrong. But it at least suggested that, as conglomerates like Essar had grown, so their lobbying operations in New Delhi had become more sophisticated. A year after the leaks, the magazine *The Caravan* published an essay about the company's operations, which claimed Essar was 'better at managing the government than managing its finances'.[37] Essar again denied wrongdoing and sued the magazine for damages, albeit unsuccessfully.

This same culture of influence was reflected in the kind of companies that Indian tycoons built. I lost count of the times business owners like Gautam Singhania told me their operations were family-owned but 'professionally managed'. But more often than not their senior executives were drawn from the same caste or region as the owners, and acted entirely as loyal family retainers. The company's corporate boards tended to be stacked with well-paid, elderly yes-men, again often drawn from the same business community. Foreign private equity groups that invested in Indian family-held companies often emerged shocked by their secrecy and opaque decision-making. Yet these habits made sense, making it hard for outsiders to exert influence, be they minority shareholders or anxious bankers, trying to recover money they now feared might never be seen again. The strategy worked too: with only a very few exceptions even India's most heavily indebted tycoons managed to keep control of their companies when they ran into trouble.

All that said, in the aftermath of the season of scams, a major change still came over India's business houses, from which few emerged unscathed. To an important extent, the old relationship-based way of doing business stopped working. Attempts to win political favours in New Delhi were suddenly rebuffed. Politicians and bureaucrats became wary they might be accused of cronyism. The same was true with banks, where executives and managers felt less able to give out generous loans to friendly businesses, making it more difficult for those businesses in turn to raise new debt. Many tycoons found themselves in the unhappy position of being forced to dispose of assets, Essar included, which eventually sold off its prized refinery in Gujarat to a Russian oil company.[38]

It goes without saying that the tycoons did not recognise their image as peddlers of influence. Rather they saw themselves as entrepreneurs and nation builders, overcomers of obstacles that might hold back those of lesser abilities; men who could build projects and create wealth in situations where others would fail. Most denied they offered bribes. 'I don't think that payments per se work,' Mukesh Ambani once told the *New York Times*, when pressed on Reliance's historic reputation for influence-peddling. 'I personally think that money can do very little . . . We believe in relationships.'

As I learned more about the inner workings of India's conglomerates, I continued to be struck by the unique stresses they placed on their owners. Most obvious were the worries about money, especially for those with a record of imaginative financing. The most artful companies were said to keep two sets of books – one for public consumption and another entirely private document, to be kept within the family, which showed where the money had actually gone. Then there were concerns about the government, given the way politicians and bureaucrats could make life miserable for any business. The weaker a company's finances became, the more its owners felt vulnerable to the whims of politicians, and they therefore behaved with even greater deference towards them. 'They expect the industrialists to be there with folded hands and a suitcase, and to keep giving them money,' as one tycoon put it to me. This was never more obvious than at each annual government budget, when captains of industry would line up to praise measures unveiled by the finance minister. The next day's newspapers would carry reports in which other business leaders would rate his efforts with fawning marks out of ten. Anything less than an eight was vanishingly rare.

Then there were the usual stresses of family control: the disagreements between fathers and brothers and sons, and indeed the intricacies of succession itself, as children jockeyed for control or, even worse, proved uninterested in it. Given the strains of running a family enterprise, perhaps it was no surprise that so many tycoons proved to be religious or superstitious.

The importance of faith was clear for Vijay Mallya, with his annual pilgrimages and temple donations. Narayanaswami Srinivasan, the southern Indian cement tycoon who presided over the body that governed Indian cricket, was also noted for his pious Hindu beliefs. Yet few could match Jaiprakash Gaur, the elderly founder of Jaypee Group, another over-leveraged conglomerate and member of the 'House of Debt' group, which built India's first Formula 1 track, as well as one of its best highways, running between Delhi and Agra, home to the Taj Mahal. In meetings, Gaur often commented while simultaneously seeking blessings from one of the Hindu deities whose portraits adorned his office walls.[39]

This sense of anxiety among the tycoons was remarkable, especially given that it came from the class that Rana Dasgupta had described as war-like. Rather than relishing the battle, in the years after Modi's victory, India's business dynasties became uneasy, worried places. Their ups and downs were in one sense just part of doing business. The point of being a tycoon was to take risks. Big industrialists perennially took on excessive debts during America's railroad frenzy in the 1870s, and then afterwards crashed spectacularly back to earth. But the psychological impact of these booms and busts on the tycoons themselves remained real. Many in India who had once invested fearlessly now lacked not just the funds to spend, but the animal spirits too. The India bulls were not feeling quite so bullish.

Back in Angul, Naveen Jindal told me of how his own ambitions had changed. Once, he said, he had aspired to build a collection of steel mills and power stations as large as any his country had seen. Now his aims had to be more modest: to pay back what he owed, finish the projects he had started, and only then to begin to think of the future. At one point he told me he was even cutting back on his polo habit, for fear that his beloved sport would distract him from repairing his business affairs.

'We used to go all out, now we will be very conservative,' he said of the new attitude he shared with his fellow industrialists. Over the previous few years allegations of corruption had swept through to every corner of the Indian economy, hitting not only the big industrial tycoons but almost every other important institution, from the media to cricket, that most venerated of national pastimes. Set against this tempestuous backdrop, the sense of possibility and ambition that had characterised the 2000s had grown weaker too. 'Right now I feel that is gone, although it might come back,' Jindal said. 'People will learn how to be more prudent. I, for one, am going to be extremely conservative,' he added, before holding up his hands: 'In India we have this idea that we come empty handed, we go away empty handed. These are challenging times.'

Cricket fans protest in the streets after a high-profile match-fixing
and betting scandal blew up in 2013.

CHAPTER 10

MORE THAN A GAME

OPERATION U-TURN

Operation Marine Drive U-Turn began late on a humid evening in the middle of May 2013, just yards away from the Arabian Sea. Shanthakumaran Sreesanth pulled out of the main gate of Mumbai's Wankhede cricket stadium a little before midnight. His team, the Rajasthan Royals, had lost that evening's match in the Indian Premier League (IPL). But no matter: drinks were in order, and the star bowler sped off to join friends in a nightclub in Bandra, a fashionable northern suburb. He had no idea the police were following him. Or that they had been doing so for weeks.

Operation U-Turn took its name from the quiet cul-de-sac at the end of the city's Marine Drive where a team of police officers waited as the game wound on, close enough to hear cheers floating over from the ground. When it finished, three squads fanned out across the city. One trailed Sreesanth as he drove north. A few hours later the squad moved in, pulling the disorientated fast bowler from his car. Two more Rajasthan Royals players were arrested that same evening, while eleven bookmakers were taken in night-time raids across the country. The most serious scandal in the history of India's treasured national game had begun.

News of the arrests leaked out quickly, sending India's cricket-crazed media into a mania by the time police commissioner Neeraj Kumar sat down at a press conference in New Delhi the next afternoon. A portly, balding man in a dull khaki uniform, Kumar seemed weary as he laid out the allegations. The many silver badges on his uniform glinted as the cameras flashed. 'There was an agreement between the bookies and the players that in a certain over they would give away a minimum amount of runs,' he said; a scam known as a 'spot fix', in which a small part of a cricket match was rigged, allowing gamblers to bet on the outcome of that particular passage of play, but in which the result of the match as a whole was not necessarily affected.

Prearranged signals showed the fix was on, Kumar explained: a hand gesture here, a rotated watch there or, in Sreesanth's case, a towel tucked into his trousers as he sprinted in to bowl. The police released clips of the suspicious incidents, and suggested that bags filled with as much as $70,000 in cash had been the players' reward. And somewhere, far beyond the stadiums, these seemingly innocuous incidents had apparently been the source of huge profits, by way of illegal bets laid by groups unnamed – high-rolling punters, shady betting syndicates and international underworld criminals. 'The mastermind is sitting abroad,' was all Kumar would say.

Right from the time of its launch in 2008, the IPL had been plagued by scandals. A self-consciously brash reboot, the two-month tournament rapidly transformed the image of cricket: from a game played by men in white over five long days, often ending in a draw, to a pulsating three-hour jamboree, where the players dressed in brightly coloured kits and draws were impossible. Where matches were once watched politely by elderly men in half-empty grounds, now India's cricket stadiums were filled with delirium for eight weeks each spring. Enthusiastic young supporters packed in to see the world's biggest stars play alongside beloved Indian internationals, egged on by pitch-side cheerleaders and entertained by enough blaring music to drown out the gentle thwack of leather on willow.

Most important of all was the money, as the IPL tapped into a seemingly limitless demand to watch cricket among the country's rising consumer classes, while providing a format perfectly designed for an evening's television viewing. From time to time, India would play its neighbour and arch-rival Pakistan, pushing the television audience as high as half a billion people.[1] But prior to the IPL, the country lacked a high-profile, consumer-friendly league to meet that demand. In 2007, just before the first IPL tournament began, the organisers auctioned off eight city-based franchises for $723 million, selling mostly to big-name tycoons like Mukesh Ambani and Vijay Mallya, alongside a smattering of Bollywood stars. Billions more came from broadcast and sponsorship deals. Cricketers used to earning a pittance were offered minor fortunes for just two months' work. But rather than just satisfying pent-up consumer demand, all that money created new temptations, as players, administrators and hangers-on alike realised what cricket was really worth.

In India, cricket mattered for reasons that stretched beyond the passion of its supporters. India itself was often described as a superpower in the making. But there were few areas where the country's global supremacy was already unquestioned. In fact, there was only one: cricket. Even before the IPL's launch India loomed over the dozen or so other countries that played the game seriously, gradually eclipsing England and Australia, traditionally cricket's pre-eminent nations. India had more fans than the rest combined. Cricket also enjoyed total domestic dominance: the streets emptied for big matches, while analysts lumped other, lesser pastimes like football and basketball together as mere 'non-cricket sports'.

The weight of that public support had been present for generations but it was only after economic reopening in 1991 that it translated into a more lucrative form of power: television rights. Barely one million Indian homes had a television at the time of liberalisation, with sets that showed only Doordarshan, a deadening government-controlled channel.[2] But by the mid-2000s, as India's economy raced ahead, the media landscape was transformed into a jumble of hundreds of cable and satellite channels, in which the rights to broadcast cricket were prized above all. With the launch of the IPL, and the multi-billion-dollar deals that went with it, the financial power of the sport became clear.

There were few clearer emblems of the country India was becoming. A game once administered by amateurs was suddenly professionalised by a mixture of international management companies and experts, drafted in from other sports. Multinationals rushed in to sponsor IPL teams, and paid players like Sreesanth eye-catching fees as brand ambassadors. Consumer companies found in cricket the only reliable way to reach hundreds of millions of increasingly affluent shoppers. Capital was pumped in by global media giants, including both Rupert Murdoch's Star Sports and Sony, with the latter stumping up an unheard-of $1 billion for ten years' worth of IPL television rights. As the event grew, estimates of its worth grew too. A figure of around $4 billion was often mentioned, an estimate of its 'brand value' calculated by a marketing company.[3] 'It is no longer correct to speak of the "globalisation" of cricket,' the Australian writer Gideon Haigh once said. 'We face the "Indianisation" of cricket, where nothing India resists will occur, and everything it approves of will prevail.'[4]

For all its glitz, the IPL was troubled. Orthodox supporters bemoaned its television-friendly format, known as 'Twenty20', and the relentless commercialism that came along with it. India did not invent Twenty20, which had been launched in England a few years before. But it took the idea and supercharged it, to the dismay of those who worried that the 'spirit of the game' was being ruined by grubby commercialism. The IPL's star players turned up routinely in India's tabloids for drinking, brawling or worse. There were management bust-ups and questionable finances. As the financial stakes increased, so the rows over control became fiercer too, in a country where cricket administration was already uniquely politicised. In its second year of operation, the entire IPL jamboree moved to South Africa, amid worries over terrorism in the aftermath of the 2008 Mumbai attacks. In its third, the league returned home, only to see its charismatic architect, Lalit Modi, begin an epic battle for control of the event against Narayanaswami Srinivasan, the powerful tycoon who led the Board of Control for Cricket in India (BCCI), the game's governing body.

Yet for all the furores that dogged the event, the events revealed by Operation U-Turn were of an entirely different order. Sreesanth was an international cricketer, and this was the first time one of the nation's beloved, elite cadre had been accused of cheating in this way. Images of the bleary-eyed player being hauled out of police vans were played on repeat across every news channel, leaving one of India's most charismatic and cocksure cricketers looking shocked and defeated. The allegations prompted Srinivasan, as head of the BCCI, to promise an immediate investigation. But barely a week later, and just days before that year's IPL finale, Srinivasan's son-in-law, Gurunath Meiyappan, was also taken into custody.

The police said that Meiyappan had been gossiping with bookmakers, handing over information about another IPL team, the Chennai Super Kings, which the son-in-law ran, but which Srinivasan himself ultimately controlled. The revelations sent India's already indignant news channels into a round-the-clock frenzy of allegations and resignation demands. A cement mogul turned cricket baron, Srinivasan's role at the BCCI, which owns the IPL, often saw him described as the sport's most powerful man: a brooding figure whose influence, while hard to pin down, stretched into every corner of the game. Now these latest allegations appeared to drag him into the scandal directly. He denied personal wrongdoing, but the arrest of Meiyappan made it look increasingly as if the IPL's growing crisis would no longer be restricted to just a few bad-apple players. Rather, the rot appeared to go close to the top. And while beleaguered fans debated why a star like Sreesanth would risk his international career for a small bag of money, the scandal raised more urgent questions – about the scourge of corruption, and whether Srinivasan, and the IPL itself, could survive.

Rather than the simple passions of sport, the IPL scandal brought to mind a different side of India, one of shabby governance and financial chicanery that seemed unerringly similar to the problems in industries like telecoms and mining. The small-time institutions that had run cricket before liberalisation were overwhelmed by the sudden rush of money that followed it. The IPL's finances were opaque, but conflicts of interest between administrators, sponsors and team owners were obvious, and especially so in Srinivasan's case. And behind all this stood the spectre of the world's $750-billion illegal betting industry, and the shady syndicates that were said to control it, all of whom thrived in a country with a fierce love of gambling, but where sports wagers were officially prohibited. It was only on that muggy night in May 2013, as the police tailed Sreesanth north, that these various forces came together, creating a furore that rocked not just cricket but the country as well. And behind it all were the stories of the rise and fall of two men of contrasting styles, who in their own ways embodied the newfound power of the game: Lalit Modi, the brash architect who brought the IPL to life, and Srinivasan himself, the brooding powerbroker, who shepherded India to global cricketing dominance, and then gradually began to see his empire fall apart.

LAND OF THE MODI CAM

The change the IPL brought to cricket was clear from its very first match, fought out on a humid Thursday afternoon in April 2008, at Bangalore's M. Chinnaswamy Stadium. On one side were Royal Challengers

Bangalore, owned by Vijay Mallya, the city's pre-eminent local tycoon, who had shamelessly named the team after his own brand of Royal Challenge whisky. On the other were the Kolkata Knight Riders, fronted by Bollywood icon Shah Rukh Khan and named, for reasons no one could exactly explain, after the 1980s American television series.

The opening ceremony was glitzy enough: stilt walkers and acrobats cavorted around the ground; daredevils in team colours rappelled from the roof; and a team of cheerleaders, borrowed from the Washington Redskins, danced against a backdrop of fireworks and laser lights. But it was on the pitch that the fireworks really began, as New Zealand international Brendon McCullum battered 158 runs from 73 deliveries, the highest-ever score in a Twenty20 match. Cricket had never seen the like. And presiding over it all, from inception to opening night, was one man: Lalit Modi.

Some sports administrators preferred to operate from the seclusion of the backroom, but Modi lapped up any and all public attention. He attended matches when the IPL was in season, flying from city to city by private jet and holing up in fine hotels close to the ground. Before play he kept a sleepless schedule: meeting players, sponsors and franchise owners; chain-smoking and firing off instructions into his BlackBerry. At the games he was conspicuously visible, wearing sharp Armani suits and rimless glasses, and sweating slightly in the heat. During play a special 'Modi Cam' would zoom into his face, in the process revealing the movie star, politician or local tycoon with whom he happened to be seated. At the end, often close to midnight, he would lead a procession to the post-match party, at which players would carouse with off-duty cheerleaders, as elderly grandees looked on bemused and tried to grasp what exactly their once modest sport had become.

Modi was known officially as the IPL's chairman and commissioner. Today his website describes him as the tournament's 'founder and architect'. But in truth he was less administrator than impresario: a showman, organiser and instigator; an ideas man; a creator of theatre. Like the 'owners' who sometimes appeared ringside during the circus of America's televised wrestling contests, Modi soon became a lead character in a show of his own creation, one in which he also wrote the script and controlled the outcome down to the smallest detail.

Among the many oddities of Modi's character, one stood out in particular: it was never exactly clear that he liked cricket. Born into an old business dynasty, he grew up with money and went to fancy schools, where he showed no talent for batting.[5] In his teens he left to study in the United States, attending Duke University. It was there, so legend has it, that he became entranced by the professionalism of basketball and baseball, and began pondering whether similar techniques could transform cricket in India.[6] It was there also that the destructive tendencies that marked his later career first emerged, when he was arrested, along with three fellow students, having cobbled together $10,000 to buy half a kilo of cocaine from a drug dealer.[7] 'The seller, in fact, had no cocaine; he did have a shotgun, which he used to coax the students out of their $10,000,' writer Samanth Subramanian later recounted.[8] 'The next day, the quartet fell upon a fellow student whom they accused of setting them up for the robbery.' The episode left Modi facing accusations of drug-trafficking, kidnapping and assault. He pleaded guilty to the charges, but returned home not long afterwards to serve a period of community service, having persuaded an American judge that he was suffering from ill health.

Back in India, Modi declined a position in his family's conglomerate, which dealt mostly in tobacco. Instead he fashioned himself as a media magnate, setting up a company called Modi Entertainment Network. These were the years after liberalisation, in which dozens of channels began sprouting up. Modi struck deals with foreign companies seeking a slice of the market, many of which flopped. An early foray into cricket in the mid-1990s failed too: he tried to convince the BCCI to let him set up a new tournament, but was rebuffed. Yet those setbacks only seemed to drive him onwards, fuelling a desire for recognition, and honing a business style that was at once abrasive and dynamic.

Convinced of his vision for cricket, he began ingratiating himself within its establishment, building alliances with politicians and winning a senior position at the head of one of the country's influential state-level boards. Even then, Modi's character was an oddity: an animated and persuasive man, but one with a patrician capacity for rudeness and a gossipy disdain for those he was ostensibly meant to be cultivating.[9] Yet while he made enemies easily, those who had worked for him also spoke glowingly of his energy, his head for figures and his instinctive grasp of how to structure a business deal. 'He was entertaining to work with,' I was told by one executive at IMG, the global sports management group that helped Modi craft the IPL. 'He took decisions, he would talk to people, he was transparent. He was power-hungry, I suppose, but he loved being the centre of attention.' Above all he seemed driven to fashion for himself a new category of business figure – the cricket tycoon – fit to preside over the money-spinning enterprise he planned to build.

The tournament Modi created was a raucous, seat-of-the-pants affair, and one that became quickly notorious. 'It was pretty wild, the parties, the girls,' a former IPL franchise manager told me. He recounted a story about one of the world's best-known cricketers, who played in the early seasons. 'I remember this player coming to me once, and saying: "Some people have alcohol addictions but I have a sex addiction, and I need women. I play better if I've had sex the night before a match,"' he said. 'And so what do you say? I called up someone, and told them this and they said they'd take care of it.'

The cheerleaders, mostly shipped in from eastern Europe or North America, created particular temptations. A few years later a blonde 22-year-old South African called Gabriella Pasqualotto began publishing a then-anonymous blog, 'The Secret Diary of an IPL Cheerleader', filled with hints of misbehaving married sportsmen. 'We are practically like walking porn,' one post read, before its author was eventually discovered and sent home in disgrace. 'Eventually they started putting them in different hotels,' the team manager recalled. 'We learnt pretty quickly that that was the safer option, to put the cheerleaders a couple of miles away from the players.' More generally, however, the administrators at first took a hands-off attitude to the stars and those who hung around them. 'The management became more relaxed; the owners became very magnanimous,' he told me. 'They said: "Oh, we've just won a match, let the boys drink, why do you need to be such a pain?" And at some point people end up saying: "Why should I bother? Why do I want to be the bad guy and enforce discipline?"'

For all of its carnival image, Modi's IPL was also a serious operation, and one that aimed to make serious money. He launched the event at a press conference in September 2007, with start-up funding from the BCCI but no teams, stadiums or sponsors, and just a handful of star players. Six months of frenzied deal-making later, the competition opened in Bangalore, with eight franchises signed up, a clutch of big-name corporate backers on board, and a roster of the world's biggest stars ready to bat and bowl. Modi's deal with the cricket board gave him complete control for five years, a remit he used to micro-manage every aspect of the contest. He showed a particular gift for marketing, convincing wary companies that his untried venture would succeed.

Almost every element of the IPL was carefully branded, with logos on jerseys, bats and corporate boxes. There were even sponsors for the after-match parties. In its early years, the event was known as the 'DLF-IPL', after the infrastructure company that paid Rs 2 billion ($31 million) for overall 'title' sponsor rights. Modi managed to squeeze seventy or more television advertising slots into a single game. Each team was also allowed a series of 'strategic' time-outs, ostensibly a chance for a mid-match stocktake, although in reality simply a helpful gap to pack in one more commercial break. To draw in viewers, he struck upon the simple but brilliant idea of combining India's two defining passions – cricket and Bollywood – by persuading prominent film stars to take stakes in IPL franchises, and then to cheer on the teams enthusiastically from the stands.

Belying his caustic reputation, Modi built the tournament through charm and guile. Top players were tempted with salaries of $1 million or more, and sold in hyped-up televised auctions, in which Modi appeared as commentator. His dynastic background gave easy entry into the upper echelons of corporate India, where he convinced billionaires to buy franchises at $100 million or more. One IPL team official recounted how Modi played on his bidders' anxieties, suggesting to one prominent tycoon that a major rival was interested in taking the Mumbai team, or telling another that he risked losing a franchise to another city entirely. The historian Ramachandra Guha, a noted cricket lover, was not alone in noting a pattern: 'Indian companies known for their professionalism, entrepreneurial innovation, and technical excellence have stayed away from the IPL,' he wrote in 2013. But the sight of A-list Bollygarchs getting involved still added to the tournament's credibility, as Andhra Pradesh infrastructure group GMR took the Delhi franchise, and India Cements, the company owned by Narayanaswami Srinivasan's family, did the same for Chennai. Alongside Shah Rukh Khan, Bollywood actresses Preity Zinta and Shilpa Shetty were drafted in as owners for franchises in Punjab and Rajasthan. Global television deals soon followed. 'Foreign capital was supporting the cable companies who were booking this,' one senior cricket administrator told me later. 'You had lots more money to throw around.'

The IPL's gathering momentum only confirmed the worst fears of the game's anxious traditionalists. Yet viewed through Modi's eyes the league actually had a noble purpose: not simply to revolutionise a tired game, which he felt had grown out of touch with India's rising generation, but also to clean up its murky governance. 'All cricketers playing in the inaugural IPL are role models for an entire generation,' he said in an emotional speech at the opening ceremony in 2008. 'It is crucial for youngsters all over the world to learn straightaway the values of this great game, and the spirit in which it should be played.' This anti-corruption rhetoric partly involved the settling of old scores. He nursed a grudge from his earlier failed tournament, which he claimed collapsed after he had declined to pay a bribe to a BCCI official. 'We were burnt very badly,' he said later. 'It became an ambition of mine to go out and clean it up.'[10] Surprising though it seemed to his critics, Modi's talk of cleansing the sport appeared genuine. Inspired by the spirit of a newly liberalised India, he planned the IPL as a libertarian paradise, in which the backroom stitch-ups of old would be replaced by open rules and a system of transparent auctions for players, teams and media rights. 'My job is to break cartels,' he told one interviewer in 2006. 'I believe in free markets deciding everything. If there is no value, there is no value. Let people decide.'[11]

As the IPL's debut season drew to a close in a thrilling finale, the people's verdict was easy to judge. Stadiums were packed. Tens of millions tuned into watch each match. After the first season, the value of a franchise rocketed, as Modi auctioned off two more for more than $300 million each. But even amid the delirious popularity there were also signs of discord, as Srinivasan and other BCCI grandees grew unhappy about the many controversies dogging the event, and in particular the imperious style of its new commissioner. There were rows with conservative Hindu groups about scantily clad cheerleaders, and streams of headlines about player misbehaviour. Modi managed to shift the second tournament to South Africa, but not without irking powerful politicians in New Delhi. More to the point, while everyone agreed the IPL was making money, few seemed sure exactly how much, or where it was being spent. Grumbling grew about Modi's lavish operation, which he ran from a suite high up in Mumbai's Four Seasons hotel.[12] Anxious that the IPL's financial pull would see star players transfer their loyalty from national teams to the league, cricket administrators in England and Australia began openly to agitate for Modi's removal. Many in India agreed.

For a man well versed in the sport's politics, Modi also had a knack for making enemies. One immediate cause was the second franchise auction. Press reports at the time said the front-runners for the new teams were Gautam Adani's conglomerate and Videocon, a media and electronics group – until the BCCI suddenly cancelled the process and demanded that it should be rerun. The second auction was then won by two other bidders, one in the western city of Pune, led by Sahara, the property empire owned by flamboyant billionaire Subrata Roy, and a second in the coastal Keralan city of Kochi, which went to a consortium of investors under the name Rendezvous.

Modi was furious at the board's interference, and began openly agitating against the decision. In particular, he cast aspersions on the ownership of the Kochi franchise, launching an incendiary assault on Twitter shortly after the results were announced. This hinted at irregularities in the victor's shareholding patterns and linked them to Shashi Tharoor, an urbane Keralan politician and minister in the ruling Congress government. The allegations prompted a new media frenzy. Tharoor denied doing anything wrong, but he was forced to resign his post, damaging a government that at the time was already reeling from the fall-out from the season of scams. In an Indian political environment in which businessmen were expected to stay studiously subservient to their masters in New Delhi, Modi's impetuous attack brought rapid and severe consequences. A few days later, revenue inspectors raided the IPL's premises and those of its teams, while leaked reports from tax inspectors investigating irregularities in Modi's business empire became front-page news.

This escalating drumbeat of dissatisfaction with Modi came dramatically to a head following the IPL's third-season finale. In the hours after the match, the BCCI suspended Modi from his post, accusing him of various infractions. Some were relatively minor, such as the claim that he had failed to inform the board that three of the team IPL franchises were controlled by his own relatives. But others were more serious. A thirty-four-page letter from Srinivasan listed more than twenty charges of impropriety, including allegations of kickbacks – described as 'facilitation fees' – on broadcast deals, to permitting the use of shell companies in Mauritius to hold stakes in teams. The most serious referred to the auction farrago itself, which the BCCI hinted that Modi had arranged in order to ensure that Adani and Videocon won franchises. Modi vehemently denied wrongdoing in all cases, and dug in to fight a court battle. For months the two sides traded lawyers' documents, before the BCCI finally sacked Modi outright six months later. Fearing for his safety, Modi moved to London, where he talked darkly about earlier assassination attempts for refusing to fix matches in India and fought legal disputes with his one-time employers, leaving behind an air of rancour and melodrama from which the IPL never really recovered.

WICKET WAGERS

The recriminations over Modi's ousting remained the IPL's defining scandal, until the evening that Operation U-Turn began. The events of that night plunged the tournament into fresh crisis, although their aftermath suggested an even darker possibility: not just that the IPL's management was opaque and quarrelsome, but that a handful of players and senior executives might actually have fixed matches in cahoots with murky global betting syndicates.

The idea that world cricket had a gambling problem burst into the open more than a decade earlier, when Indian police released a taped call between a local bookie and Hansie Cronje, the South African captain, during a series between the two countries. Cronje was banned for life, in the process ending cricket's reputation as gentlemanly game unsullied by the kind of illegal betting problems that afflicted so many other sports. More scandals then followed, notably in 2011 when a duo of Pakistani bowlers and the captain were caught cheating in a British tabloid sting operation. Back in India, a more minor spot-fixing hit the IPL during the 2012 tournament, when five players were banned.

Although betting on cricket was officially banned, I had often watched wealthy Indians place discreet wagers on the sport. Local tabloids often carried racy stories about the betting gangs, operated by Mumbai's criminal underworld but controlled by Indian gangsters in exile in Dubai or Pakistan: 'The mastermind is sitting abroad,' as Commissioner Kumar put it after Shanthakumaran Sreesanth's arrest. Yet, widely known though all this was, it was only Operation U-Turn that brought the corrosive effects of betting rushing into public view.

Attention focused at first on the way fixing worked, and how a player like Sreesanth might have been lured into it. The IPL's format was ideal for betting, with a freewheeling atmosphere in which executives, sponsors and hangers-on all fraternised with players and officials. The cricketers had sizeable retinues of their own: the associates, managers, handlers, trainers and stylists that signified their status as tournament royalty. Information economies built up around teams, in which friends would call insiders seeking gossip, or swap stories in the bar of the team hotel. Any tip could be useful to those setting odds, from line-ups and injuries to team tactics and pitch conditions. The better the information, the better the return, hence why bookies and high-rollers sometimes took the riskier step of bribing cricketers directly, at first paying a little for information, and then, if the player seemed willing, taking things a step further and asking them to perform, or not, to order. 'The bookies often pay off the players and referees around the competition, in the hotels and the bars,' I was told by Chris Eaton, director at the International Centre for Sport Security, a Qatar-based group that tracked illegal betting. 'It might be a honeypot with a girl, or it could just be cash. It's a slow professional process . . . and, given India's growth over the past five years, the size of this illegal market is growing like crazy.'

Even with plenty of speculative media coverage, it was hard to penetrate the mysterious and understandably secretive illegal betting industry that these tips fed. The best account came via Ed Hawkins, a betting expert and writer, whose book *Bookie Gambler Fixer Spy* gave a gripping exposé of the seedy underbelly of cricket gambling. Hawkins managed to befriend a handful of minor Indian bookmakers, travelling to remote towns to watch them set up impromptu betting shops.[13] Armed with laptops and dozens of mobile phones, they sat in otherwise empty hotel rooms, fielding calls from punters as matches began.

The wider system in which these bookies operated was run by a handful of larger betting syndicates, who set the odds and provided capital, working with teams of freelance bookies around the country. Word of mouth and trust made the system work; punters used bookies they knew; no cash changed hands and accounts would be settled later. The common view was that high-rollers could win small fortunes by fixing small, low-probability elements of matches – paying a bowler to produce a no-ball in a particular over, for instance – and betting heavily on that outcome. But the reality was more subtle, Hawkins told me, with only a few types of wagers. The most popular was known as a 'bracket' bet: a wager in which customers guessed the score after a particular period of play, such as the first six overs. 'If Sreesanth did what they say he did, it looks like a classic example of a bracket fix,' he said.

None of this explained why Sreesanth himself had been drawn in, although even his associates did not seem entirely surprised that the tempestuous sportsman had ended up in trouble. As much as for his impudent wicket-taking celebrations, Sreesanth was known in India for one incident: 'Slapgate'.[14] Towards the end of a match in the IPL's debut season he was struck in the face by Harbhajan Singh, a burly Sikh spin bowler, known affectionately as the 'Turbanator', for both his religious headgear and his no-nonsense cricketing style. Sreesanth walked off the pitch, tears streaming down his cheeks. The cause has never been more than tabloid speculation, but it came to symbolise Sreesanth's image: a brat and a cry-baby whose petulance made him unpopular with teammates, including the then India captain, Mahendra Singh Dhoni.

'Everyone knew Dhoni hated him,' an IPL executive told me. 'In fact, all the players hated him.' Those who knew him well described a different side: gregarious, generous to a fault and fun to be around, with a strong traditional, religious streak. But he was insecure and attention-seeking too, according to a close friend from well before the bowler's entry into the stratosphere of Indian sporting celebrity. 'He used to compare himself to Michael Jackson, which I used to think was mad, but Michael Jackson was one of his idols,' the friend said. 'When you think about it, they were a bit the same, though: worshipped in one way, hated in others, surrounded by these weird people, and both a bit bat-shit crazy.'

Isolated from his teammates, Sreesanth instead stayed in five-star hotels with an ever-expanding court of hangers-on. The coterie provided at least a measure of structure in an otherwise rootless lifestyle, moving from city to city for games and training, and living out of half a dozen suitcases. It was an existence that combined periodic sporting exhilaration and bouts of excess with long stretches of boredom, yet all set against a bewildering backdrop of permanent public adoration. 'Sree had his lackeys around him constantly, and I always wondered how they could afford to be with him, given they had no jobs of their own,' his friend said. Eventually it became clear the cricketer funded them himself, paying for air tickets and hotel rooms, handing out bundles of cash for expenses, and inviting them to the glamorous parties at which cricketers of his stature were feted. 'It's hard to describe the madness that went on around them all the time, the huge crowds that appeared in an instant as soon as they went outside. It just never stopped,' his friend told me. And it was exactly in this kind of chaotic, carnival atmosphere that it was possible to imagine an impressionable young man, intoxicated by fame and money, gradually being talked into actions he might later regret.

Sreesanth spent the best part of a month in custody after his arrest, mostly in New Delhi's infamous Tihar jail. At first the police said he had given a full confession. Later he emerged on bail and protested his innocence. After Operation U-Turn, journalists at first questioned the lax culture of Lalit Modi's IPL, in which efforts to detect cheating were virtually non-existent. But after Gurunath Meiyappan's arrest their focus changed to the teams and their owners, not least when the head of the Rajasthan Royals franchise also confessed to betting on IPL matches. Meiyappan's arrest also drew Narayanaswami Srinivasan into the controversy directly, as angry fans began to blame the sport's most senior administrator for the mess in which the game now found itself. Rolling news outlets covered almost no other story for weeks, treating each small development as a ground-shaking outrage. Times Now, the country's most-watched English news channel, made particular efforts to castigate Srinivasan, as its pugnacious frontman Arnab Goswami led calls for the BCCI head to resign.

Not a man at ease with the media, Srinivasan sought at first to deflect attention from his son-in-law. Press reports suggested Meiyappan ran the Chennai team. Srinivasan denied this, suggesting he had no formal role, a claim many observers found unconvincing. 'The simplistic explanation was given that Gurunath [Meiyappan] was just an enthusiast,' I was told by Ajay Shirke, a courteous businessman turned BCCI administrator, and a sometime Srinivasan ally in the ever-changing politics of Indian cricket administration. 'But then why had he been there at every auction representing the team, why had he been notified in our official documents as the team principal, and what is he doing in the dugout with the players? To me it really looked like they are just trying to cling onto power.' Sensing he was losing control, Srinivasan changed tack. At a bad-tempered press conference a few weeks later, he tried to draw a line under the scandal. But the more he stonewalled, the more it looked like he was trying to stop questions turning to his own overlapping roles and the conflicts of interest they brought with them. A power struggle began, as Srinivasan launched a rearguard action to keep his job.

THE DON

If Lalit Modi was cricket's impresario, Srinivasan was its powerbroker. In the IPL's floodlit glare it was easy to think that the rush of money had entirely reinvented the sport. But underneath the power structures of old remained largely unchanged, inherited from an earlier era when the game was run by 'men of middling talent and limited ambition, serving usually in honorary capacities and concerned chiefly to insure cricket against change,' as Gideon Haigh once put it.[15]

Influence in this old world of Indian cricket, as Modi discovered, actually came via control of state-level boards, the bodies one step down the pyramid from the BCCI: the Rajasthan Cricket Association, the Maharashtra Cricket Association and so on. Some of these were little more than family dynasties, with fathers passing control to their sons. Others were vassals of local businesses, as with Srinivasan's India Cements group, whose financial support to struggling clubs and cash-strapped players had helped him to take control of the Tamil Nadu Cricket Association, the body which formed the power base from which he launched his efforts to control the sport. This edifice of cricketing power was democratic to a degree, at least in the narrow sense that anyone aspiring to national prominence had to take care of those below them, creating networks of patronage through which the game's growing largesse could be channelled in exchange for votes. 'The [BCCI] elections every September are such sordid affairs that Caligula would have been proud,' the editor-in-chief of cricket magazine *Wisden India*, Dileep Premachandran, once wrote. But this was Srinivasan's true forte: the weighing of votes, and the discovery of what men needed to be given in return.

In person he was far from imposing: medium height and heavy-set, with a weary, jowly look and greying hair slicked back with oil. Where Lalit Modi was full of pyrotechnics, Srinivasan – or just 'Srini' as people generally called him – talked slowly and tersely, his voice coming in a low growl. Also unlike Modi, he was at least motivated by a longstanding passion for the sport. People talked well of him in Chennai, where the Srinivasans were pillars of a conservative establishment and admired for the free sports kits they handed out to school teams and the jobs they found for retired players. His early years in business were not easy, including a long clash with his uncle over the family cement empire, a skirmish cited by some as the wellspring of his instincts for bureaucratic control. He was wealthy, in an understated southern Indian way, and a conservative of firm Hindu faith, often sporting a red tika on his forehead.

Srinivasan became BCCI president two years before Operation U-Turn, having built up his base first as treasurer, then secretary, the position from which he oversaw Lalit Modi's suspension. He operated mostly from Chennai, flying by private jet for meetings in Mumbai. Power within the BCCI came via the slow turn of committees, an environment to which Srinivasan proved thoroughly well suited. The finance committee was his particular fiefdom, where he held sway through his mastery of agendas and minutes, but also by knowing exactly where all money went, and to whom. It was this capacity for brutal bureaucratic management that proved to be his true talent, according to essayist Rahul Bhatia. 'He always prepared well for meetings, he could think like an accountant, he kept his advisers close, and almost never failed to ensure that his supporters were happy and well-rewarded,' Bhatia wrote in a profile in *The Caravan*.[16]

Operation U-Turn broke at a time of wider national disquiet: mid-2013, a moment of swirling anxiety about corruption, when public disgust over the country's various telecoms and mining scandals was much in the air. Yet rather than a practitioner of outright dishonesty, Srinivasan's own role was more as a ringmaster of patronage. Cricket's rising economic heft brought in unheard-of sums; he steered it down to the right places, ensuring that he won future votes in turn. It was a deceptively simple mechanism of control, in which the game's various factions – regional administrators, cricketers, ex-cricketers, commentators and grandees – were kept in line through a web that distributed generous rewards. 'No Medici controlled Florence as comprehensively as the BCCI controlled cricket,' as Indian commentator Mukul Kesavan once put it.[17] 'During his [Srinivasan's] reign most living things in cricket's jungle became the Board's creatures, bound by contract, muted by money and sworn to servility.'

India's local boards were hardly known for good governance, but they were generally viewed as the cleanest in a tawdry line-up of Indian sporting bodies, and without question the most professional. 'Srini's gig was always about control,' I was told by a former official at the International Cricket Council (ICC), the global body Srinivasan would eventually be appointed to run in 2014. 'But he is not dishonest . . . He made the system work. Srini has never enriched himself, and in my view it has cost him a good amount of money.' As outrage over U-Turn grew, Srinivasan's instincts were to dig in, cashing in the support this patronage had built. 'He seems to be very organised, very controlling,' Kesavan told me later. 'He genuinely thinks that he can get away with virtually anything by squaring the politicians . . . that if they all buy in, nobody is really going to worry about conflict of interest.'

Maintaining this political support was now imperative if Srinivasan was to have any hope of survival. Cricket's sheer prestige drew big-name politicians to the BCCI, a few out of devotion to the game, but most for the many other opportunities it provided. Among the most prominent were Arun Jaitley, a wily lawyer who became Narendra Modi's finance minister, and Sharad Pawar, a forceful Maharashtrian satrap, notable both for his reputed cunning and personal wealth. Even Narendra Modi, no noted lover of cricket himself, had been president of the Gujarat Cricket Association for five years until his election as prime minister in 2014, before handing the job over to Amit Shah, his closest political ally. (Narendra Modi and Lalit Modi are not related.) In his own way, Srinivasan learned to keep close to all of these men, and adroitly managed to navigate their various shifting alliances. So long as they continued to back him, Srinivasan assumed his position was safe. But as the howls from the talk shows grew louder, and the op-eds demanding his resignation grew more frequent, even that faith was thrown into doubt.

Srinivasan had not been accused of personal wrongdoing: few thought so terse a man had been laying wagers and gossiping with bookies, as his arrested son-in-law was alleged to have done. He stressed his own innocence in interviews, doing little to disguise his anger at what he described as 'trial by media'.[18] But critics asked, reasonably enough, whether he could preside over a fair investigation into the aftermath of Operation U-Turn, given his various overlapping roles as owner, regulator and relative.

As the scandal grew, attention focused ever more on the broader problem of conflicts of interest. Srinivasan controlled the body that owned the IPL, and hence the many revenues it produced. As head of the BCCI, he also distributed much of that money downwards to supplicants in the lower orders of the game. As chairman of India Cements he was not simply an IPL team owner, albeit indirectly, but also a major sponsor too. His backing for the Chennai Super Kings proved to be especially problematic, given that it was formally against the rules for BCCI office holders to own teams when the franchise bidding first took place. The conflicts between Srinivasan's roles were so striking that they almost seemed to excuse the many other smaller examples of patronage that riddled the lower reaches of the game. Yet for all the self-evident conflicts his web of interests represented, Srinivasan ploughed on. Using just the kind of clever backroom manoeuvre his critics loathed, he cleaned up one of his problems with the Chennai Super Kings a year later, by having the BCCI's constitution changed retrospectively, in the process making it legal for IPL team owners to be cricket administrators too.

Events came to a head during a BCCI crisis summit in a plush conference room at the Sheraton Park hotel in Chennai in early June, a few weeks after U-Turn had begun. Srinivasan ran proceedings, first pushing through agenda items unrelated to the scandal, then trying to paint himself as the only man with the authority to help the BCCI ride it out. Yet such was the clamour for his head that even the board's loyalists were unnerved. By the meeting's end a compromise had been struck: Srinivasan agreed to step aside, at least temporarily, until an investigation had been completed. In the days that followed, the BCCI announced a raft of minor clean-up measures, prohibiting team owners from mingling with players, banning post-match parties, and promising an end to pitch-side cheerleaders. An inquiry run by two judges from Chennai was set up by the BCCI. Meanwhile India's Supreme Court also became involved, establishing a commission of its own. The BCCI's panel came back first, revealing to no one's surprise that Srinivasan had done nothing wrong – a 'clean chit' that, in his own mind, gave the BCCI's president the excuse he needed to begin planning to retake control.

While the domestic scandal raged, Srinivasan's position was complicated further by India's growing role abroad. A year after U-Turn began he was elected as head of the ICC, a position from which he presided over a notorious carve-up that gave India, England and Australia – cricket's 'big three' – an outsize share of future television revenues, with India taking most of all. Indians made up the majority of cricket's fans, and contributed well over half of its revenues. Operations in smaller nations like New Zealand and the West Indies were kept afloat only by the rights they sold during Indian tours. India felt it had been bossed around for too long in a sport run until relatively recently along neo-colonial lines from London and Sydney. Hopelessly divided over how to sort out the problems in its domestic game, India's cricket establishment was firmly united in believing that its own position as cricket's sole hyperpower should be recognised internationally, and that India should in turn be given a greater say over the global game itself.

The take-it-or-leave-it style in which Srinivasan announced his ICC deal sparked a backlash, however. Cricket's minnows, already sensitive to Indian bullying tactics, were furious, while fans reacted badly too. A low-budget 2015 documentary called *Death of a Gentleman*, made by two young cricket fans, won wide acclaim for decrying the corrupting influence of money. Srinivasan allowed himself to be interviewed for the film, and was felt by many to have come off looking shifty and evasive.

'India has ended up with a special gift: the clout to shape an entire sport,' wrote Lawrence Booth, editor of cricket bible *Wisden*, around the same time. Instead, Booth argued, India's pre-eminence appeared to be resulting in a new kind of 'Twenty20 nationalism' marked mostly by 'the growth of private marketeers and high-level conflicts of interest'.[19] Many fans worried about the BCCI's new style of muscular diplomacy, with its mixture of brute financial considerations and unabashed India-first attitude. More than anything, the ICC episode suggested that the administrative style of Srinivasan's BCCI, with all of its attendant money-spinning deals and backroom bust-ups, was now being transferred up to the global stage as well.

Back at home, a different power battle raged, as the old BCCI establishment turned to the courts to try and contain the fall-out from U-Turn. The first commission established by the Supreme Court reported later in 2014, clearing Srinivasan, but finding that Gurunath

Meiyappan had been involved in illegal betting. The court then launched a second investigation, led by a retired judge, with a broader remit to reform cricket's governance. The court gave Srinivasan's attempts to return short shrift too, with one judge describing his machinations as 'nauseating'.[20] Eventually the judges prevailed, stopping Srinivasan from standing at the BCCI's next elections in 2015 and in effect barring his return as chairman.

Later that year the BCCI sacked Srinivasan from his role at the ICC as well, as if sensing the waning powers of their once-dominant former master. The Supreme Court's commission then launched a radical over-haul, banning politicians from holding office in the governing body and suspending both the Rajasthan Royals and the Chennai Super Kings from the IPL for two years. Eventually, in early 2017, its patience exhausted, the court also in effect sacked the BCCI itself, installing a temporary four-person committee of grandees to run the game, which included Ramachandra Guha among its members. As if the parallels between cricket's corruption scandal and those that plagued India more broadly were not clear, the court picked Vinod Rai, the government's crusading former auditor, as the body's new chair.

Almost no one emerged from the aftermath of Operation U-Turn with much credit. Shanthakumaran Sreesanth was banned for life and never played competitive cricket again, although the trial court in Delhi dropped all charges against him in 2015 for lack of evidence. Gurunath Meiyappan was found guilty of bringing cricket into disrepute and banned from the game as well. Lalit Modi remained in London. Openly and vocally aggrieved, and having lost little of his capacity to attract attention, he lobbed incendiary allegations on Twitter against political enemies and one-time cricketing allies alike. Srinivasan returned to Chennai and kept out of sight, keeping a careful hold over his cricket board in Tamil Nadu, and waiting to see if the national tide might shift again in his favour.

Modi's and Srinivasan's contrasting styles were clear from their respective exiles. Yet as the game struggled to escape their twin legacies, their common traits became clearer too. Both enjoyed hereditary wealth, born of families with businesses in regulated industries – cement and cigarettes respectively – where success rested on influence and political connections. Both were dismissive of the amateurism of the old guard and had worked industriously to overthrow it. Both grasped instinctively the shifts India's economic rise would unleash and foresaw how they would come to change cricket. And both, at once innovators and old-fashioned wielders of power, were brought down by changes they themselves had unleashed.

After a decade of scandal, judging the present state of Indian cricket is difficult. On its own terms the IPL remains a gigantic success. At height of the U-Turn furore, some wise heads predicted the tournament would have to be scrapped. But it has since bounded onwards, with each iteration bigger and more lucrative than the last. Even during the crisis, its supporters were phlegmatic about allegations of cheating. 'The Indian public's memory is very short, and next season a lot of this will be forgotten,' I was told then by Harsh Goenka, a respected industrialist, who had tried to buy an IPL franchise. 'Sadly it's a bit like [US televised] wrestling. Everyone knows that it is fixed, but you don't know the actual result, and so it's still exciting. And while some wrestling is one hundred per cent fixed, maybe the IPL is just one per cent fixed. So people will still go, that's how it is.' Even so, the fall-out from the Modi and Srinivasan years left its mark. Today's IPL is more carefully run: the cheerleaders are still there, but the after-match parties are tamer, and much more has been done to combat the temptations of betting.

For all their grumbling, cricket purists have much to thank the tournament for as well. Before India's ascendancy cricket was stuck in a gentle but inevitable decline, dominated by a five-day product that bored rigid all but its most committed fans. The IPL's popularity finally convinced a hidebound establishment that it had to change, and also provided a popular, lucrative model on which to base its renaissance. In India, all those various TV deals and sponsorship contracts have now built better stadiums and provided more money for local clubs, as well as bumper pay packets for players. Unimaginable as it might now seem, as late as the 1960s cricketers in India were paid just Rs 250 to play a five-day test match – a *per diem* rate of Rs 50. If the team performed well, and won in four days, they were docked a day's wages.[21] There seems little reason to look back on those years of straitened amateurism with nostalgia. 'There is something genuine about the outrage that people like Srinivasan feel when they are accused of being predatory or rent-seeking,' Mukul Kesavan told me, suggesting that the men who revolutionised cricket felt that the positive side of their contribution had not been fairly recognised.

Yet India's cricketing rise, and the brash and bankable version of the game it spawned, remains deeply problematic. Whether you took him seriously or not, Lalit Modi's vision of a game run along free-market lines and governed by transparent rules self-evidently did not come to pass. Modi thought the IPL could become a blemish-free Indian success story, a kind of sporting version of the country's largely corruption-free IT outsourcing industry. But instead the first decade of the IPL ended up far closer in character to the darker corners of the industrial economy, with its power politics and rife with accusations of cronyism and powerful tycoons carving up the game's riches between themselves. In this, Indian cricket is not alone: the governance of the game in England and Australia has had its share of embarrassing episodes. But India's game is now on a different scale from those lesser powers. Cricket administration in India has long suffered from conflicts of interest, but those mattered little when the interests themselves were so minor. As the financial rewards swelled, a culture of opaque governance and overlapping became a serious problem, and one the game is yet fully to solve.

This system of entrenched patronage and influence proved just as difficult to reform in cricket as elsewhere. The irony that the Supreme Court had to call on an outsider like Vinod Rai to fix the game was lost on no one. There was a further similarity: in trying to clear up corruption in industries like iron ore, India's courts felt they had no option but to ban mining entirely. Now in cricket, too, it seemed there was nothing to be done: so rotten had it grown that the judges decided they had no choice but to shut down the BCCI's system entirely, if there was to be a chance to cleanse it. It was hard to feel sympathy for Srinivasan, a man who ran cricket as client state. But the manner of his defeat at least reflected a deeper and more positive change, and one that showed Srinivasan himself had misread the kind of country India was becoming. It remains to be seen if the sport can be run along more open and transparent lines, free of the blatant conflicts of interest of old. But the publicity after U-Turn, and the glare of the media that came with it, at least made it clear that the old world was no longer tenable.

Later in 2013, after he had temporarily stood down, Srinivasan tried to clear his name by appearing on *Frankly Speaking*, an interview show hosted by Times Now anchor Arnab Goswami. Srinivasan seemed flustered as the presenter peppered him with questions. 'You have the benefit of the television, you have the media,' he complained at one point. 'You can say what you like. I don't have a channel.'[22] A few weeks after U-Turn began, Srinivasan snarled much the same complaint during a combative press conference. 'I would request you all to be wary of trial by media,' he said. 'TV news channels have been carrying unverifiable statements devoid of truth.'[23] But complain as he might, Srinivasan never did find a way to respond to this new world of accountability, with India's ferocious media at its fore. The public's outrage was too strong; India's courts were too active; the glare of the media was simply too fierce. When demands for public legitimacy were set against the squalor of backroom deals, there was now only one winner.

Television anchor Arnab Goswami is India's best-known and most-controversial broadcaster, often inviting six or more guests to shout over one another on his popular evening talk show.

CHAPTER 11

THE NATION WANTS TO KNOW

MUCKRAKER-IN-CHIEF

One moonless night in September 2016, a small band of Islamist militants crossed from Pakistan into India, and attacked an army base near Uri, a village in the state of Jammu and Kashmir. The assault left seventeen Indian soldiers dead.[1] Nearly two weeks later, Indian paratroopers hit back, launching what were described as 'surgical strikes' against terrorist camps across the line of control that divides Kashmir between the two nations, both of whom claim it as their own. The attack was hailed as a triumph by India's army, which held an uneasy peace in the area, often accusing its neighbour of helping militants to conduct cross-border raids. A wave of nationalist fervour swept through social media, while news channels showed clips of jubilant men on street corners, waving tricolour flags. But few could match the endorsement from television anchor Arnab Goswami: 'The entire country is celebrating this evening,' he told viewers of in a patriotic special Times Now broadcast, encouraging supportive tweets with the tag #IndiaStrikesBack. In thunderous form, he chided Pakistani duplicity and praised India's *jawans*, who were reported to have killed thirty militants or more. There were few hints of journalistic objectivity. 'We here at Times Now support the surgical strikes,' Goswami said twice in the first three minutes of the broadcast alone.

That night's programme was typical of Goswami's high-octane style, mixing a rush of jingoism with flashy graphics and breathless presentation. His regular show – *The Newshour with Arnab Goswami*, to give it its full title, airing at 9 p.m. on weekdays – was India's most-watched English-language political broadcast. It was here perhaps more than anywhere that India tuned in to get views on its many public scandals, from the season of scams to corruption in the IPL. Its host's hectoring style transformed Arnab, as he is generally known, into the country's best-known broadcaster, and one of its most controversial public figures.

As editor-in-chief of Times Now, Goswami was widely credited with fashioning a new and aggressive reporting style, in a country where rolling news channels were still barely a decade old. Yet dozens of competitors now vied for these same viewers' attention, most of them by mimicking Goswami's own pacy delivery and monomaniacal obsession with breaking news. Lampooned by local comedians and Bollywood movies, this hyperventilating persona had even gained some measure of international notoriety. British comic John Oliver featured clips of Goswami's abrasive questioning on his own US talk show in 2014, suggesting with some incredulity that India had managed to spawn a news style even more excessive than Fox News.[2]

India's media landscape is large and complex, with more than eighty-two thousand newspapers and nearly nine hundred TV channels,[3] mostly in languages other than English. It boasts a venerable print tradition, and in the *Times of India*, the world's most-read English newspaper.[4] Yet as tens of millions bought their first television set in the years after 1991, the balance of power swung away from print and towards broadcast. Times Now, which launched in 2006, stood out for the nationalistic tinge to its coverage, not least in Goswami's habit of inviting Pakistani guests onto his show, only to brusquely shout them down. But the anchor became a household name more for his campaigning style and ear for simmering middle-class anger. Beginning with the Commonwealth Games scandal in 2010, and intensifying throughout the season of scams, *The Newshour* laid into a familiar cast of villains, from dishonest government ministers and dodgy business cronies to corrupt cricket administrators. Channels in Hindi pulled in more viewers, but Times Now's appeal to English-speaking urbanites gave it outsize importance. And as his approach won viewers, so Goswami's political pulling power grew too, securing the two most coveted interviews of the 2014 election: a faltering performance from Rahul Gandhi and a more assured display from Narendra Modi.

Goswami's power was all too readily acknowledged by those he targeted. 'It was basically Arnab who started it, everybody else jumped to the bandwagon,' I was told in London by Vijay Mallya, who blamed the anchor for portraying his sudden departure to the UK as a flight from justice. Even the publicity-wary Mukesh Ambani, speaking in a rare interview of his own in 2016, confessed to being a regular *Newshour* viewer.[5] Through all this, Goswami became India's most feared watchdog, a one-man judge, jury and national moral arbiter. His favoured catchphrase – 'The nation wants to know!' often yelled at guests midway through interviews – became a byword for India's newly assertive fourth estate.

As foreign money poured into media ventures, new channels like Times Now reflected the churn of the post-liberalisation years. But they helped to create it too, taking their place alongside the other independent democratic institutions that began to investigate corruption and challenge old hierarchies, from activist judges and government auditors to anti-corruption charities using freedom-of-information laws to ferret out wrongdoing. To his admirers, Goswami was a muckraker in the noble tradition of the campaigning magazines of late nineteenth-century America, which picked fights with corporate monopolies and corrupt politicians. Yet his influence was just as often lamented by those who saw in him echoes of the fearmongering 'yellow journalism' of US publisher William Randolph Hearst. In 2012, liberal academic Madhu Kishwar laid out this broader critique in an open letter, comparing Goswami's show to a kangaroo court in which its host ignored 'the necessary dividing line between journalist and crusader'.[6] In Goswami's style, critics saw an Indian variant of what became known later as 'post-truth' politics, in which the nightly clash of guests deepened social divisions but added little to public understanding.

I arranged a meeting with Goswami over lunch in late 2014, settling down the night before to watch a full edition of *The Newshour* in preparation. The topic was a court case in the ongoing IPL cricket scandal, a story that Goswami had pursued doggedly over the preceding two years. The show began in bravura style: 'Will he be sacked?' he thundered in his opening section, attacking Narayanaswami Srinivasan, who at the time still hoped to return as the head of Indian cricket. Wearing a dark suit and looking grimly serious, Goswami accused 'shameless' administrators of 'cheating the people, cheating you and me'.

Pausing, he addressed the audience directly, his voice rising sharply: 'Will *you* watch a tournament which has fallen so low?'

From there events descended rapidly into a familiar form of bedlam, as the host called out 'Let's debate!' and introduced eight guests in turn. None were in a studio: for all its relentless pace and seizure-inducing graphics, *The Newshour* was a low-budget affair, and many of his inter-viewees joined from their workplaces or shambolic offices at home, with bookshelves and plant pots as backdrops. That night's star turn was Vindu Dara Singh, a small-time actor who had been arrested on suspi-cion of illegal betting during the cricket scandal back in 2013, before being released on bail. (His trial remained pending at the time of writ-ing.) He was interviewed in front of an anonymous brown curtain, making it look as if he had agreed to appear from inside a photo booth.

Amid the chaos, Goswami played ringmaster and orchestrator, barracking his invitees and setting one against the other. Sometimes all eight appeared at once: a row of four boxes along the top of the screen, and four more along the bottom, with a special double-height box for Goswami on the left. When he interrogated a guest head to head, there would be just three boxes: the host on the left, the interviewee on the right, and a middle box showing dramatic stock footage of players being arrested or IPL executives fleeing from cameramen. Red and blue graphics whizzed around, enveloping whoever was speaking in a barrage of flashing words and colours.

Although no actual news was being broken, the word 'BREAKING' was almost never absent from the screen. The disorder was interrupted only for commercial breaks and periodic Goswami mini-monologues: 'What is at stake tonight is our love of cricket,' he said at one point, as the hashtag #SackIPLChief whooshed across below. Towards the end he peppered Dara Singh with questions, shouting down the actor's attempts to answer and jabbing his finger in the air. Eventually, Dara Singh ripped off his microphone and walked out, leaving only the brown curtain in shot, and providing a moment of satisfying catharsis for host and viewer alike. The spectacle was exhilarating but exhausting, and by the end I felt in need of a lie-down. More alarmingly, after watching for an hour, I was little the wiser as to the basic facts of that day's developments.

When we met the next day, the difference in his appearance was jarring. Then just in his early forties, Goswami in person looked far younger and softer than he did on screen. The sharp suit was replaced by a casual black shirt and dark blue jeans. The hair gel he wore on screen was absent too, leaving a thick black fringe to flop forward over hipsterish square black glasses. Also gone was the overbearing voice, as he told me quietly about a recent trip to Oxford, where he had given a speech about the state of Indian media, and where he had once studied for a Master's in social anthropology. At once charming and thoughtful, and scrupulously polite throughout, his was a mild-mannered alter ego fit for a superhero comic, as if I'd planned to meet Superman and Clark Kent showed up instead.

We met in a fancy hotel not far from the Times Now studio in midtown Mumbai, surrounded by half-finished glass towers and the hubbub of traffic. Goswami lived down the road with his wife and young son, preferring life in the financial capital to New Delhi, whose culture of intrigues he claimed to despise. Living in Mumbai was mostly a personal and family decision, he told me, but a political one too. More than anything he styled himself as an outsider to the capital's journalistic establishment, whom he referred to witheringly as the 'Lutyens crowd', a reference to the incestuous geographical heart of Delhi, where many of the country's most powerful politicians, business leaders and senior media figures tended to live.

As if to confirm his iconoclastic image, Goswami walked out of Times Now in late 2016, a few months after his broadcast on the attacks at Uri, and announced plans to set up a channel of his own. He called it Republic TV and launched it about six months later. The move was partly about control: Times Now was owned by Bennett, Coleman & Co., a powerful media conglomerate, which also ran the *Times of India*. Goswami was by now an industry giant, but he was also merely an employee, and one who had to defer to the company's powerful owners. There were broader ambitions too, one of which he hinted that day in Mumbai. India's media now acted as a watchdog against domestic corruption, he told me, but it would soon go on to take a much larger global role, by creating international broadcasters that would rival the likes of Al Jazeera or CNN. 'So many Indians speak English that we will be the media capital of the world,' he told me, giving just the briefest flash of the kind of hopelessly grandiloquent statements he trotted out each evening on air. 'India, with its competence and technology, with English, with the fact that we are a very vibrant democracy, we are going to be the global media powerhouse.'

SUPER PRIME TIME

India's TV news boom began on 5 February 1995, as Prannoy Roy, a sober-sounding presenter in a cream-coloured suit, first introduced *The News Tonight* – and ran instantly into trouble. 'On the very first night of our news broadcast I was anchoring and decided to show off a little,' Roy recounted of his debut bulletin, the first in India to be produced by a private company. 'As we went on air, I looked at my watch and said: "It's eight o'clock and this news comes to you live." Someone in the PM's office heard the word "live" and threw a fit.'[7]

After years of pressure India had finally allowed a private sector production house to make a news programme for the state-owned Doordarshan. But cautious politicians thought an actual 'live' broadcast a step too far, forcing Roy to record the evening's show ten minutes before it went on air. But by then the principle had been established: that night New Delhi Television, NDTV, made a crack in the government's long-running broadcasting monopoly, which others would soon begin to widen. Another private operator ran a live night-time news bulletin on its own channels for the first time later that year. In under a decade dozens of rolling-news operators had launched, operating in English and other major languages, including NDTV's own rolling-news channel, NDTV 24x7, in 2003.

India's news pioneers were scrappy affairs, broadcasting from make-shift studios and operating on tiny budgets. But founders like Roy, who set up NDTV as a production company in 1988 alongside his wife Radhika, were ambitious, seeing in their young medium a chance to replicate the ideals of education and objectivity articulated by public service broadcasters like the BBC. They attracted eager young journalists: Arnab Goswami joined NDTV in 1995 and was promoted rapidly. A generation of news anchors grew up in the same mould: Rajdeep Sardesai, who was Goswami's boss, and who also left in 2005 to found rival rolling-news outfit CNN-IBN; or Karan Thapar, a dapper, plummy-voiced presenter, on whose serious and thoughtful evening discussion programmes I would occasionally appear as a guest commentator.

More than anyone, though, it was the Roys who embodied the sector's youthful hopes: grand, high-minded Delhi insiders; media radicals but also establishment stalwarts; a power couple who saw broadcasting as a progressive endeavour, an opportunity to shape the nation. Put another way, Prannoy and Radhika Roy stood for almost everything that Goswami would later react against.

This was partly personal. Goswami moved to NDTV after his first job as a junior editor at *The Telegraph*, a newspaper in Kolkata. Over the next decade he became one of the channel's more prominent faces, ending up as a senior editor and presenter of his own show, also called *The Newshour*. But his tenure was not always happy, especially towards the end, as he grew dissatisfied with his position as second-tier host, and chafed at Sardesai's position as the network's unquestioned star performer.

The offer to establish a new channel for India's most powerful media group, which arrived when he was only in his early thirties, would have been hard to turn down under any circumstances. But beyond his brewing resentment, Goswami's move to launch Times Now was also born of growing disagreement over style. 'The standard bulletin, with a political story in the beginning, a sports story somewhere in the middle, and an entertainment or 'back-of-the-book' feature at the end, was a very nineties way of doing it,' he told me when we met over lunch. 'When a person turns on he's not going to wait for one hour for you to run the particular news package. So we focused a lot more on events as they were happening.'

Times Now was far from an immediate hit. As editor-in-chief, Goswami masterminded news coverage during the day, before taking to the studio for his own show at night. Alongside the usual staples of cricket and Bollywood, the channel began as a mishmash of politics and business, mixing news with features, and drawing weak ratings. For months after its launch rumours swirled that Goswami was struggling to retain the confidence of Bennett, Coleman & Co.'s powerful media baron proprietors, the brothers Vineet and Samir Jain. 'He grew unsettled, unpredictable and deeply insecure,' according to an account by journalist Rahul Bhatia. It was a stressful period, and one that helped Goswami win a reputation for treating his subordinates harshly. 'Away from the eyes of the millions who watched him, his behaviour consisted of throwing things, kicking chairs and, in one instance, dislocating his own shoulder during an argument with an executive producer.'[8]

The channel found its footing only gradually, first ditching the corporate coverage, then following Goswami's instincts for more emotional stories involving human interest, or more likely human suffering, which in India remained sadly plentiful. With fewer resources than his rivals, he focused on fewer stories too, flooding in reporters and outside broadcast vans to capture gripping live footage, and reporting relentlessly in the hope of turning otherwise minor episodes into national events. Some involved social injustice: issues of caste violence or the treatment of women, for instance. But just as often it was misfortune in a simpler sense: a collapsed building in the suburbs, a hospital providing shoddy care, or Indian citizens being treated shabbily in Australia or America; ordinary situations of suffering or inconvenience, for which someone in authority needed to be held quickly and brutally accountable.

Over lunch, Goswami told me that he took particular pride in finding 'stories of individual loss, individual tragedy' that would otherwise have 'been buried in the inside pages of a newspaper'. He pushed these as news during the day, then rammed them home on his discussion show later in the evening. The new style worked a treat: within a few years, he was able to say that Times Now had beaten its great rival NDTV in the ratings, a claim Goswami has never since tired of repeating.

One Saturday in 2016, I watched Goswami deliver a barnstorming talk at a book festival in Mumbai. He recounted a story of his early days at Times Now, when a foreign journalist had lectured him on 'the basic rules of reporting', namely the need to stay impartial and avoid expressing your own opinions. 'Why, for God's sake, should we not express our opinion?' he shouted at the audience. He then went on to list the national outrages on which his channel had made its views clear – the Commonwealth games scam, the 2G scam, the mining scam, the IPL – drawing loud, sustained applause from the crowd.

Moments that combined the drama of breaking news with this brewing sense of national outrage were his particular gift, with the 2008 Mumbai terror attacks an especially formative moment. 'I think we did about 100 hours of coverage, and I anchored about 75, 80 hours,' he recalled of the days when Pakistani militants killed more than 160 people in a dramatic series of assaults, culminating in a shoot-out at the city's famous Taj Mahal Palace hotel. Dropping all commercial breaks, Goswami barely left the studio for days. His indignant coverage drew in viewers, channelling first anger at Pakistani support for the attacks, and then a rising sense of middle-class humiliation over the state's incompetent response, in which militants armed with sub-machine guns had been countered by police wielding batons and old-fashioned rifles. The city's armed response teams had been provided with AK-47s, but no bullets had been bought for three years.[9]

This intuitive sense for middle-class indignation also lay behind Goswami's singular focus on corruption. He was far from the first Indian journalist to make a name for himself on the topic: as editor of the *Indian Express*, Arun Shourie fought memorable battles with Dhirubhai Ambani in the mid-1980s, and, alongside *The Hindu*, helped to expose the Bofors arms scandal a few years later. Yet these journalists of the old school mostly did their work through gradual, painstaking reporting. Goswami broke his fair share of scoops too, but his journalistic mission strayed far beyond that narrow task. Instead, he wanted to act as a cheerleader for the nation's new wave of anti-corruption protests, which began in 2011. For an audience born in more deferential times, there was something undeniably thrilling about watching Goswami in full spate, tearing strips off authority figures. He had a knack for articulating what viewers were already thinking. 'His pronouncements are rooted in everyday frustrations,' as Rahul Bhatia put it. 'Why is Pakistan dithering? Why can't Australians admit that they're racist? Why is the government indifferent to the middle class? Who is responsible for all this?'[10]

Goswami's populist instincts came partly from his own background, growing up first in the rural state of Assam in India's isolated northeastern region. His family moved often when he was young, following his father's army postings. He studied later at a well-regarded college in New Delhi, although not one of the very best. Comfortable but not privileged, it was an upbringing that later fed his sense of himself as an outsider. It was at school, however, that he first discovered a passion for public speaking. 'Since I was ten or eleven years old I have been debating,' he told me. 'So when you debate you really debate. It's points versus points, your points versus mine.' Goswami often cites these youthful parliamentary debating tournaments as his early training ground for television, a deft claim, in that it roots his belligerent style in an activity most people would instinctively admire. Yet his persona undeniably retains the imprint of those early contests, whose young participants are drilled to find extreme and eye-catching arguments, and then assert them as forcefully as possible, whether they actually happen to believe in them or not.

In 2016, not long before he quit Times Now, I went to watch *The Newshour* being recorded. The studio's entrance was partially hidden along a narrow side street in Lower Parel, a disorderly neighbourhood in midtown Mumbai that had once been filled with textile mills, but was now equal parts commercial hub and chaotic permanent building site. Goswami looked relaxed when I arrived at around 7 p.m., dressed in a knee-length orange *kurta* over black jeans and sneakers, with his dark hair flopping loosely over his forehead.

The studio was surprisingly cramped: two dozen young journalists crowded round a central news desk packed with monitors, hammering silently at their keyboards, before occasionally shouting at one another across the room. The decor matched the channel's colours: blue and red chairs sat at blue and red desks on top of a blue and red carpet. A single flash of orange ringed the main desk, bearing the slogan 'WE CHANGED THE NEWS'. There was a noticeboard in one corner covered in A4 sheets, advertising the channel's successes. One read: 'Credibility Brings Supreme Leadership'. It pictured Goswami, looking serious with his arms folded, next to a pie chart that showed Times Now's audience share at a dominant fifty per cent, lording it over NDTV, which had barely half as much.

Goswami was easily the oldest employee, and eyes turned whenever he emerged from his office and paced through the studio, firing questions about that evening's line-up. The hubbub increased as 9 p.m. approached. '*Challo*! Breaking! Breaking breaking!' one producer shouted with about fifteen minutes to go, as news filtered through about a developing spat between India and Pakistan. Until then Goswami was to lead the programme with a political squabble in the state of Uttarakhand, although he seemed unenthused about the story, searching for a better option. Now a frantic debate began. 'I want to see the visuals again,' shouted another producer. 'Are we going with that story or not?!' yelled a third.

With just a few minutes to go Goswami, still dressed in his *kurta*, dashed off suddenly into a backroom, and then emerged a minute or two later into the lights of the studio. I turned to watch on a monitor: the introductory credits announced that 'SUPER PRIME TIME' had begun. The camera panned in on the host, who sat transformed, dressed in a dark blue tie, matching blue shirt and sharp black suit, his hair now slicked back. The phrase 'INDIA REJECTS PAK VIDEO CLAIM' burst onto the screen, as Goswami launched into a fiery monologue about Pakistan's decision to release footage supposedly showing the confession of a captured Indian spy – a minor diplomatic kerfuffle, but now firmly that night's top story. Later, still on Pakistan, Goswami moved on to a rowdy discussion segment called the 'burning question', which was signified by the appearance of flickering digital flames all across the bottom of the screen.

Such theatrics make it easy to lament the state of Indian television news, and many in the country do just that. Rajdeep Sardesai, a more self-critical figure than his main rival, has lamented his industry's obsession with the 'three Cs' – crime, cinema and cricket – describing them as a 'triple-headed deity at whose altar the industry worships'.[11] More telling is what newspaper editor T. N. Ninan dubbed the rise of 'vigilante TV', with Goswami as its leader. 'Impartiality is for the clubby Prannoy Roys of the world,' as Ninan put it. 'TV news Rottweilers in attack mode have proved for many to be as riveting as any soap opera. Breaking news is now about smashing reputations.'[12]

Many also blame Goswami for a wider decline, given the way his style has been copied not just by other channels in English, which reach barely a tenth of the population, but also by those in Hindi and other languages, which are now often even more tabloid in orientation. Either way, the rapid increase in the quantity of political news has clearly not resulted in a broader political consensus. The basic details of important national events – the role of Narendra Modi in the Gujarat riots of 2002, for instance – often remain fiercely contested. 'In India, the problem is nothing is ever really true,' I was once told by Jonathan Shainin, an American who worked for years as a magazine editor in New Delhi. By this, Shainin meant that the extraordinarily adversarial nature of public discussion, most obviously on television, often seemed to make even minimal factual agreement impossible. 'Long before we all became interested in "fake news", it was right there, you know? India was kind of the pioneer.'

There is something exhilarating about India's raucous news media, especially when viewed next to its staid and timid competitors in many other Asian countries. The press is not exactly free – it ranked just 136th in the 2017 World Press Freedom list published by the charity Reporters without Borders – but it is often fearless.[13] The print industry is thriving, with rising readership especially in languages other than English, in clear contrast to the struggling newspaper empires of the West. Most TV news channels lose money, but broadcasters in general are handily profitable, and reach an audience of more than three quarters of a billion, easily the largest of any country outside China.[14] The media also played an undeniably important role in helping to bring to an end the scandals that plagued India in the early part of this decade.

Still, when we met, I pushed Goswami on the downsides of his combative style, and especially the trade-off between attracting attention and accurate reporting. Mostly he declined to admit that any such tension existed, describing his style simply as 'a more aggressive' form of traditional journalism. 'The idea is not to impose your point of view on anyone,' he told me. 'The idea is to generate [and] elicit the strongest and best response.' He rejected, in particular, the comparison with outlets like Fox News, denying the US channel had been an inspiration. 'People may want to flatter themselves thinking that this has evolved from some inspiration from America,' he argued. 'We have our own cultural editorial style, our syntax, our own grammar. And I've never watched much of these channels.' It was hard to tell if this was strictly speaking accurate. '[Goswami] has said to me that he has followed the Fox News model in many ways,' I was told by the head of one media organisation around the same time.

As much as on this uncompromising style, Goswami's popularity also rested on a kind of moral authenticity, in an industry that itself had struggled to win public trust. Although it reported forcefully on corruption, Indian media had struggled to avoid the perception that it too had become corrupted, given the widespread problem of what was known as 'paid news', corporate or political interests gaining or removing coverage for cash. It is hard to know the extent of this problem, although industry figures often told me it was widespread. More broadly, Indian proprietors still cheerfully jumble up adverts, editorial and paid-for 'advertorial', with the latter especially prominent in news stories related to upcoming Bollywood releases.

Vineet Jain, one of the brothers who own both Times Now and the *Times of India*, displayed a notably relaxed attitude to editorial standards. 'We are not in the newspaper business,' he once told the *New Yorker*. 'If ninety per cent of your revenues comes from advertising, you're in the advertising business.'[15] There were anxieties too about the influence of big business on media ownership, most obviously when Mukesh Ambani took over the company that owned CNN-IBN in 2014. Shortly after the tycoon's purchase, Goswami's rival Rajdeep Sardesai, the channel's editor, resigned, along with a number of other senior executives.[16]

Perhaps the most damaging episode came a few years earlier, when police recordings were leaked of conversations involving Niira Radia, a public relations guru, whose clients included both Ambani and Ratan Tata, patriarch of the Tata group. The ensuing 'Radia tapes' scandal engulfed a number of senior journalists by appearing to expose a world in which business and political rivals attacked one another anonymously through the press, aided by supposedly impartial reporters. The farrago provided particular succour to Goswami, who used it repeatedly to lambast the 'Lutyens' elite and the cosy links they maintained with corporate and political powerbrokers. 'It's downright shameful,' Goswami wrote to his staff when the tapes emerged, in a memo that was quickly leaked. 'No gifts, no favours, no lobbying, no free dining and wining,' he warned his own staff. 'If I hear of any, we will come down hard.'

Goswami's ability to avoid any taint of corruption only added to his popular appeal, allowing him to paint himself as the master of an uncomplicated evening morality plan. Times Now launched in a moment of economic change, in which many old certainties were being upturned. Yet as India seemed to be losing its moral bearings, with venerated business houses beset by scandals and politicians mired in corruption, Goswami provided a measure of moral clarity. It was a style even his competitors admitted was effective. 'Arnab is very smart, he is very good, he is very quick on the draw, he is infuriating if you don't like his views, but he is very, very good,' the editor Shekhar Gupta once told me. It helped that Goswami seemed to revel in his position as moral arbiter too. 'I don't believe in creating an artificial consensus,' he told me. 'If there is something wrong, you can ask yourself two questions: "Why did it happen? Will the people who did it go unpunished?"' He added: 'I've often said this: that, in a choice between right and wrong, black and white, the facts that stare you in your face, will you not take a side on what is right?'

BATTLE HYMN OF THE REPUBLIC

About a month after he quit Times Now, I met Goswami again in Mumbai. At the time he had said little about his plans to launch a new channel, although he was clearly busy. He would fly back from meetings in New Delhi on Saturday afternoon, he told me over the phone, and then go straight to meet Uddhav Thackeray, the head of the Shiv Sena, the right-wing political party that had run Mumbai for a generation or more. I should come to Thackeray's home, he said, from where we could talk in the car as he drove downtown to give a speech.

The Thackeray house had been notorious. A tightly guarded mansion called Matoshree, in an enclave not far from the airport, it had belonged to Thackeray's father, Bal Thackeray, the Shiv Sena's founder and leader, until his death a few years before. A newspaper cartoonist turned politician, the elder Thackeray was a dominant figure on the Mumbai political scene. Those years saw ill feeling towards migrants, and occasionally mob violence that shut down the entire city. Matoshree was his seat of power, the place where he received visitors and dispensed justice, sitting on a throne engraved with two golden lions. As he plotted his own channel, Goswami felt the need to pay respect to Thackeray's son, who now controlled his father's party, and many felt the city as well.

It was a sunny December afternoon as I strolled past the twin machine gun posts at the entrance and headed into the colony beyond. Filled with sleepy old bungalows, the street provided a rare moment of calm amid the clamour of Mumbai, with no traffic to speak of and the distant sound of birdsong up above. For all its fearsome reputation, Matoshree, which stood at the end of the lane on the left, was unassuming: a four-storey home with an A-shaped roof that would not have looked out of place in a central European suburb, barring the orange flags on its high perimeter walls, and the fleet of luxury saloons with blacked-out windows parked at the front. Armed guards ushered me through the security gates and into a largely empty ground-floor reception area, with hundreds of cream-coloured plastic chairs stacked up to one side. A life-size photograph of the deceased leader, dressed all in white except for a generous red bindi daubed on his forehead, stood propped against the back wall. His old throne sat unused in a corner, its twin golden lions looking badly in need of a polish. A garland of marigolds lay abandoned on the seat.

Goswami and Thackeray emerged looking relaxed about ten minutes later, and after brief pleasantries, Goswami ushered me back outside towards his car, a modest saloon. The afternoon light was fading as we pulled back out down the lane, and his driver turned left onto the main road, rejoining the blaring rush of evening traffic. Sitting in the back seat, Goswami was dressed stylishly in a dark shirt. His hair was bushier than I remembered, as if he had dared to let it to grow long now he was no longer on air each evening. He missed the nightly thrill of broadcasting, he admitted, but had been kept busy meeting potential financial backers, hiring journalists and jumping through regulatory hoops to get his planned new channel off the ground. His departure from Times Now had been front-page news. But intense outside interest in his new venture didn't bother him, he said, nor did the bad blood it left behind with his former employees, who had even begun court proceedings demanding he no longer use his favoured 'the nation wants to know' phrase on his new channel.[17] 'It's exhilarating,' he told me as we pulled onto the city's Sea Link bridge and began speeding south, the skyscrapers of midtown glinting off to our left. 'When you're in a steady ship, it's boring.'

I asked why he'd quit. Goswami sidestepped, talking animatedly about how his new channel would respond to wider forces, not least a bulging population of young Indian smartphone users, who he said were no longer interested in watching broadcast television. Tens of millions were coming online this way each month, he said. TV stations were losing advertisers. Print publications, while ostensibly healthy, were under pressure as well. Newspapers were still delivered to readers' homes each morning, but advertisers were beginning to cotton onto the industry's dirtiest secret, namely how many of these went unopened and thus unread. Eventually even the young men paid a pittance to squeeze broadsheets under front doors in cities like Mumbai and New Delhi would want to find better jobs. 'The day the delivery boy goes out of the print industry, print ends,' Goswami said. 'It's not going to be a gradual thing. It's going to be a cliff edge.'

By contrast, his own new venture would be a largely digital affair, designed for social-media-savvy twenty-somethings as much as political news obsessives. Goswami explained all this in a quiet voice as we rumbled south, addressing me often by my first name, a subdued style that I had come to recognise as part of his studiously calm off-screen personality. Yet from time to time he became visibly excited too. 'I'll do it. It's a bloody exciting road, *yaar*!' he said at one point, thumping his hand against the seat between us for emphasis. 'Only we can do it, James. Only we!' he added with patriotic gusto. 'We are the only democracy that is English speaking, has technology, has young people, right? Only we. There's nowhere in the world you can do this!'

Behind the optimism there was still the sound of scores being settled. Goswami spoke respectfully of his old employers, but the frustrations he had felt as an underling to the Jains were clear. At Times Now he had run a news channel that was his in every way except the one that really mattered: ownership. Now he had the chance to launch a new venture that was his entirely. The idea of being a proprietor – and thus, in his own way, a tycoon – seemed to fit his personality. Rivals like Rajdeep Sardesai cherished their reporting backgrounds, returning often to rural villages and distant states to look into stories. They tried to build intellectual reputations too, writing books on national politics and firing off op-eds on the issues of the day. Goswami bothered little with any of this, rarely leaving the newsroom. It was this mastery of the studio that had made him India's most recognised journalist, albeit one who still insisted on portraying himself as a rank outsider. 'It is now a David–Goliath fight, I am up against behemoths of Indian media,' he said at one point, without naming any in particular. 'Professional journalists in India are not expected to play the big game. They are expected to loyally serve the existing media organisations.' His ire at his competitors – 'My bigger battle, James, is with the Lutyens group' – had, if anything, become more pronounced.

The new channel also provided a vehicle for Goswami's global ambitions. He'd been to Moscow, he said, to visit Russia Today, the Kremlin-backed operation known for its anti-American views. He'd watched the rise of Al Jazeera too. The fact that India had nothing similar seemed shaming. 'We are present everywhere in the world, from garment exports to software. But we have no presence globally in the media,' he told me, as we crawled south through the city. 'Everything we do henceforth in media has to be about scaling up . . . and about our soft power. Our reach in the world.' The narrowness of domestic media seemed to irk him, with its scant global coverage and particular local obsessions: international politicians of vaguely Indian descent, *desi* Indians abroad who had done well in their particular fields, or the predicaments of

Indian tourists or students in foreign countries; all genres Goswami himself had done much to popularise. 'Why is it that when I seek an interview with Donald Trump, I'm only going to ask "Mr Trump, what message do you have for Indians?"' he said. 'An Indian journalist, interviewing an American statesman, does not have to be about what you're going to do for India. It's wrong, James. What we have done to Indian media is wrong.'

There was something captivating about this global vision. Given time, Goswami was surely right: somebody in India would indeed one day launch a global news channel, which could well go on to take its place alongside the BBC or CNN. But the ambition still sat oddly next to Republic itself, which, when it launched six months later, was if anything even more narrowly parochial than its domestically obsessed predecessor. Republic's style and content mimicked the bombast of Times Now, only much more so. The graphics were in different colours, but they whizzed around just as rapidly. In one early episode of his own show – which still aired at 9 p.m., and was still called *The Newshour* – Goswami crammed a full dozen guests on screen, achieving a new level of stupefying incomprehensibility. Of the channel's promised digital innovations, there were few to be seen.

The most striking change involved the channel's politics, which were more obviously populist and nationalist than before. Goswami launched with a flimsy exposé targeted at Shashi Tharoor, the debonair Congress politician. Debates about Kashmir proved enduringly popular, allowing Goswami to rail against two favoured enemies at once: duplicitous Pakistanis on the one hand, and disloyal liberals on the other, for suggesting that India, with its heavy military presence and grim human rights record, might bear some responsibility for the Muslim-majority state's outbursts of violence. 'We represent the REAL INDIA,' Goswami wrote during a discussion on Reddit, not long before Republic's launch. 'All Indians should be pro-military and pro-India. If that makes us right wing, then so be it.'[18]

Goswami's tilt to the right solved a wider problem created by Narendra Modi's election. His Times Now heyday came amid the scandals of the Congress era, most obviously in 2011, when he tapped the spirit of the Arab Spring and supported the various anti-corruption protests that commentator Sadanand Dhume dubbed 'India's mini-Tahrir Square moment'.[19] Back then *The Newshour* still involved plenty of Pakistan-bashing, but its host's favoured quarry was unscrupulous and hypocritical politicians. Modi's arrival complicated this narrative. For a start, the BJP leader put a stop to most of the mega-scams, drawing oxygen away from the most important source of Goswami's appeal. Modi's government was closer to Goswami's own brand of nationalism too, with tough views on security and uncritical support for the military. Finding his political room for manoeuvre narrowing, the suspicion was that Goswami had decided to throw his lot in with India's new prime minister, abandoning in the process the more socially liberal views that had marked his earlier career.

This impression deepened when news of Republic's financial backers leaked out. The largest was Rajeev Chandrasekhar, a telecoms tycoon and independent member of India's upper house, although one generally supportive of the BJP.[20] Another was Mohandas Pai, a cerebral technology executive, who often lambasted liberals on Twitter.[21] Goswami denied he had drifted to the right, telling me he had no 'consistent' political views. 'People can't typecast me. They can't call me a right-winger because I'm socially liberal,' he said in the car. To prove the point, he gestured out of the window towards the Haji Ali Dargah. A run-down fifteenth-century mosque and mausoleum, it stood on a small island just off the coast, accessible only by foot and illuminated by floodlights as we drove past. 'My biggest campaign before my resignation has been the right to pray,' he said of programmes badgering authorities to allow women access to religious sites, including the Haji Ali.

Goswami displayed his liberal views later that evening, when we finally arrived at Mumbai's press club for an awards ceremony run by an LGBT rights group. He was to give a speech attacking Section 377 of India's Victorian-era penal code, which banned homosexual acts and which he had criticised frequently on his show. I had expected a glitzy affair with film stars and media personalities. But the gathering was meagre, with an audience of barely fifty activists sitting in front of a makeshift stage, including a handful of transgender *hijras* in colourful saris. We arrived an hour late, but the organisers greeted Goswami as an old friend, thanking him for his support. He went on to give a speech which was at once powerful and touching, talking about his own belief in social tolerance and how he had tried to use his own channel to raise the issue. The applause as he sat down was warm and generous.

Whatever his own politics, Goswami guarded his views on Modi carefully. When we met the first time in 2014 I had asked him directly what he thought of him. He would say only that the prime minister had a 'strong media presence' and was an 'effective communicator'. I asked the same question during our car ride and he was similarly evasive, saying only that he and Modi shared a similar distaste for New Delhi's political establishment. This was true enough: Modi often accused the press of treating him unfairly, sometimes calling journalists 'news traders' during speeches.[22] He was known to be especially critical of the English-speaking media, including channels such as NDTV, a grudge that dated back to their harsh coverage of the violence that swept through Gujarat in 2002. Yet despite Goswami's denials, it was hard not to imagine a certain affinity between the two men: both self-described outsiders, both disdainful of traditional New Delhi elites, and both ardent nationalists, keen on projecting unashamed Indian power abroad. Modi was a made-for-television politician, an accomplished orator with a knack for memorable sound bites and an eye for visual theatre. It came as no surprise in 2016 when he picked Goswami to host his first post-election set-piece interview, just as he had during the campaign itself.[23]

Goswami and Modi were right in one sense: many senior Indian journalists were indeed liberal in their outlook, broadly supporting the old-style secular nationalism of Jawaharlal Nehru and fretting about the rise of an assertive Hindu identity under the BJP. Republic was also just one example of a tilt to the right in the media. Other channels, forced to respond to Goswami's style, began to serve up a diet of nationalist outrage. Right-wing commentators, once rare on screen, became more common.

This political shift was most marked online, where social media was awash with Modi supporters, known to their detractors as *bhakts*, a Hindi word typically used to describe unquestioning religious devotees. Normally young men, and always staunch Hindu nationalists, the *bhakts* swarmed coverage they disliked, using the term 'presstitutes' to attack less favoured journalists. Anchors such as Rajdeep Sardesai and Barkha Dutt were among their most prominent targets. Goswami, by contrast, was a hero, with clips of his performances shared proudly online. 'There can never be enough nationalism,' Goswami said prior to Republic's launch. 'We have forces that are trying to divide and break

India from within. No nation can be soft on anti-nationals.'[24] That phrase – 'anti-national' – became a common slur after Modi's election, tarring everyone from Kashmiri peace activists to former central bank governor Raghuram Rajan. Goswami dropped it in liberally on his show.

Although Goswami was its most prominent advocate, this criticism of India's old elites spread well beyond the news media. About a year after Modi's election, I met Amish Tripathi, a former banker turned author of a trilogy of mythological thrillers inspired by the Hindu god Shiva. Tripathi, or just Amish, as his name appeared on his book covers, had become a central figure in a new wave of commercial fiction, aimed at a mass market which preferred potboilers and campus romances to high-minded literature. His trilogy shifted over two million copies, the fastest-selling series in Indian publishing history, retelling stories of Shiva's adventures in a brisk page-turning style.

In person, Amish was gentle and thoughtful, but also critical of local publishers, who he said churned out high-minded novels by writers like Arundhati Roy and Salman Rushdie, but produced little to the tastes of ordinary readers. 'The Indian publishing industry, until around ten years ago, was Indian in name only,' he told me. 'It was more of a British publishing industry that happened to be based in India.' Tripathi's books were not obviously right wing; their gods and heroes were in fact often surprisingly liberal. But he echoed Goswami's criticism of the 'old elites of Lutyens Delhi and south Mumbai', and shared his hope that Indian media would soon grow comfortable with a more robust form of nationalism.

Yet while some welcomed this turn, others worried that India's media was becoming cowed and uncritical of its new government in particular.[25] 'With Hindu nationalists trying to purge all manifestations of "anti-national" thought from the national debate, self-censorship is growing in the mainstream media,' Reporters without Borders said in its 2017 report. There were wider worries about creeping media restrictions under Modi too, partly through the use of repressive colonial-era libel and sedition laws. In 2017, police raided the offices of NDTV, as well as the home of Prannoy and Radhika Roy. Although ostensibly an investigation into a disputed bank loan, many viewed the raid as politically inspired. The year before, the channel was threatened with being taken off air for a day, after the government accused it of damaging national security via live coverage of a militant attack on an army base in Kashmir, similar to the assault in Uri.

Goswami himself seemed untroubled by all this, comfortable perhaps in the fact that his own politics were closer to those of the national mainstream than those of either his rivals or his critics. 'It has to be done! And we have to do it now!' he exclaimed suddenly back in the car, as if energised at once by his news channel plans and his pugilistic vision for what Indian media could become. 'You see India is on the upsurge. We are doing dramatic things!'

As I left Goswami later that night, I still found it hard to square his flamboyant, rabble-rousing performances on screen with the reasoned and introspective manner he typically displayed off it. Yet in barely five years he had led a revolution in Indian news television, one that seemed sure to have long-lasting consequences. His was a revolt not just against an old establishment, but also against an old idea of India. This was held dear by an older generation of journalists, who hoped that a more cerebral and reflective public sphere could in turn bring about greater social harmony. It was a vision that had gradually been eroded in the decade either side of Modi's election victory. 'On the whole, the credibility he lends to the nationalist cause is such that there is little distinction between Goswami and the state,' as former journalist and poet C. P. Surendran wrote after the launch of Republic.[26] Ultimately, however, Goswami and those who supported him were playing on a field that others had created, and upon which a new brand of nationalism was becoming ever more dominant. And more than anyone else, the most important creator of that field was Narendra Modi himself.

Narendra Modi meets US President Barack Obama in 2015, but is widely mocked for wearing a dark blue Savile Row suit monogrammed with golden pinstripes that spelled out his own name.

CHAPTER 12

THE TRAGEDIES OF MODI

THE ROCKSTAR

Narendra Modi settled down at home one Monday morning in June 2016 and prepared to defend his record. It was to be his first set-piece television interview since taking office two years earlier, fielding questions from an unusually deferential Arnab Goswami. Inside, the scene looked at once domestic and confrontational, as the two men sat opposite one another in identical wooden armchairs, close enough to touch toes. Their venue was a spacious sitting room at what was then still one of India's most famous addresses: the prime minister's official residence at 7 Race Course Road. The name changed a few months later, when a BJP parliamentarian complained that the old colonial name did not 'match Indian culture'.[1] Modi now lives at 7 Lok Kalyan Marg instead.

'I was completely new in the job. Delhi was new for me,' Modi said at first, reminiscing on those earliest days, when he moved into the complex of squat bungalows that Indian leaders called home. 'I was not experienced about this place; I had not even been an MP.'[2] Dressed in a cream *kurta*, his white beard neatly trimmed, the prime minister gave detailed answers in Hindi for more than an hour. At times he rambled on, respectfully uninterrupted, describing the intricacies of policy schemes and recounting a meeting with a ninety-year-old woman who had been forced to sell her four goats to raise funds to build a toilet. At other moments he was curt, displaying flashes of irritation, especially with his critics in the press. 'If someone would want to know Modi through the eyes of the media, then he would be disillusioned about which Modi is the real Modi,' he said at one point, referring to himself, as he often does, in the third person. Goswami pressed gently towards the end, asking whether Modi's various economic plans now risked being overshadowed by the 'communal agenda' pushed by zealots within his party's radical Hindu wing. 'I fought elections on the issue of development,' Modi replied bluntly. 'I believe that the solution to all problems is in development.'

Those development ambitions remain daunting. The average Indian earned about $1,600 a year when Modi won his landslide in 2014, lagging far behind Asian countries such as China or Malaysia, with roughly $8,000 and $11,000 apiece.[3] Some projections suggest India will reach roughly double its current income level by 2025, placing it firmly among the middle tier of what the World Bank calls 'lower-middle-income' economies.[4] With luck, within another decade or so, it should reach the level China has attained today. But when people talk airily about India's 'rise', they are really referring to the stage after that, which could come around the middle of this century, when the country closes in on that magic threshold coveted by all poorer nations: a 'high-income' economy, meaning one in which the average person earns $12,236 or more.[5]

Put like this India's future sounds straightforward, with an almost inevitable sense of upward progress, but it still presupposes the kind of sustained expansion that almost no country has ever managed. Brazil produced a brief but stellar run in the late 1960s and early 1970s, growing at around eight per cent a year. Beginning in 1985, Thailand was the world's fastest-growing nation for the best part of ten years.[6] But neither of these countries, nor indeed any other large economy bar China, has ever sustained such rates for more than a decade.[7] Most never come close. China's extraordinary performance gives false hope to other developing countries. It was a dazzling trick, but not one anyone has managed to repeat.

The human scale of India's future remains equally intimidating. 'There are eight hundred million people below the age of thirty-five in our country,' as Modi told Goswami, talking of their hunger to find modern, well-paying jobs. Too many Indians were stuck in low-skill professions, he admitted, toiling away in positions their children would no longer want. 'More than three crore [thirty million] people work as washermen, barbers, milkmen, newspaper vendors and cart vendors.'

Yet Modi's hopes of meeting the aspirations of his vast and youthful people meant first navigating a trio of perilous economic transitions, all of which now stand at best half completed.

The first challenge is demographic, as India grapples with a population bulge that will deposit at least ten million young people into its labour market every year for decades, all looking for jobs that presently do not exist.[8] The second involves urbanisation, as hundreds of millions more look to leave rural poverty for new urban opportunities, straining the country's already teeming cities. A third relates to the development of manufacturing, a crucial ingredient in the recipe for economic development, but an area where India has long struggled. And all of this is without wrestling with the twin challenges Modi himself placed at the heart of his governing agenda: ending corruption and lifting up those he called 'the poorest of the poor'.

Whichever path is taken, this journey will not be easy. Yet if India can complete it, with an estimated population of 1.7 billion by the middle of this century, it will bring more people into conditions of moderate prosperity than any country in history.[9] India would also be the first major world economy to do this as a democracy, rather than turning democratic as it grew prosperous, as happened in America and Britain, or, like China, not being a democracy at all. 'Long years ago, we made a tryst with destiny, and now the time comes when we shall redeem our pledge,' Jawaharlal Nehru said on the evening of 14 August 1947, as his country stood ready to cast aside the injustices of British colonial rule.[10] 'India stands forth again, after long slumber and struggle, awake, vital, free and independent.' By 2047, as its people celebrate their centenary, India has a chance to fulfil that destiny: to become history's second democratic superpower and a beacon for free peoples around the world.

Modi's admirers like to see him in just these historic terms, as the man destined to take a nation beset by graft and poverty and wrestle it doggedly towards greatness. 'The prime minister is doing for India what Teddy Roosevelt did for America, moving us away from the Gilded Age and towards a new Progressive Era,' Jayant Sinha, the BJP minister, told me in 2015. The comparison was bold but also carefully made: Roosevelt, the macho reformer, anti-corruption campaigner and trust buster, held the presidency for seven years from 1901 and ended up immortalised in stone alongside Washington, Jefferson and Lincoln on Mount Rushmore. Placing Modi in such company sounded fanciful. But in 2019, when

India is next set to go to the polls, he has a good chance of winning a second national victory, and then going on to become the fourth prime minister to serve ten years in office, after Nehru, Indira Gandhi and Manmohan Singh.

Modi's depiction of his early naivety as prime minister – 'Delhi was new for me' – needs to be treated with a touch of scepticism. A three-term chief minister from one of India's most important states, he understood the capital's intricacies and power plays well enough. He had lived there as a younger man too, first as an RSS loyalist, then as a BJP apparatchik. Yet he was still an outsider, who grew up far outside the country's elite and whose popularity stemmed partly from his opposition to it. His ascent then carried added symbolism: a self-made politician in a nation beset by dynasties, whose successes embodied a certain, rarely realised vision of Indian social mobility. Modi played up his youthful *chai-wallah* image for political ends, but there remained an undeniable power in his life story: the poor lower-caste boy from Vadnagar who rose to lead a nation.

Just as importantly, Modi's victory in 2014 rebuffed the notion that India itself had grown ungovernable, as if its turbulent democracy had become such a drag on its economy that it could not follow China's rapid process of development. For all of its economic vitality since 1991, India's political system had grown noticeably weaker. The authority of both the Congress and BJP had ebbed, stolen away by more vital regional rivals, while wobbly coalition governments in New Delhi took on the air of a permanent constitutional feature. Modi's victory, with its stunning and unexpected scale, reversed all this and brought power coursing back into the national capital. Once in office he proved a largely effective administrator, ending almost entirely the grand scandals that had so bedevilled his immediate predecessor. His sense of purpose transformed the country's image abroad too, convincing many that India was retaking its place among the great powers. Some saw an even grander geopolitical moment, heralding the end of an international system in which only America and China counted as truly global players. 'Modi has given birth to a truly multipolar world,' as former Singaporean diplomat Kishore Mahbubani put it in 2015, one year after Modi's election.[11]

1,200 YEARS A SLAVE

For all his popularity, Modi remained a deeply unsettling figure in Indian public life, a place he had held ever since the bloodshed that swept through Gujarat in his earliest days as chief minister. In the years after 2002 he pledged himself to the cause of economic development, and denied firmly any lingering, covert agenda to 'Hinduise the nation', in the words of Vinayak Savarkar, the Hindutva ideologue who had once been an important intellectual influence.[12] 'Development is also the solution to the tension that people talk about,' as Modi put it, in answer to a question from Arnab Goswami about enmities stirred up by extremist Hindus. 'If we provide employment to people, if we ensure there's food on their plates, if we provide them with facilities and give them education, all the tension will end.'

Fears that Modi's arrival in New Delhi would prompt an upsurge in sectarian savagery proved unfounded. Indeed, the richer India has grown, the less violent it has generally become, with steadily declining rates of communal rioting over recent decades.[13] Even so, since 2014 there has been a growing drumbeat of alarming episodes involving Hindu chauvinists, almost all of whom are staunch Modi supporters. Some have involved symbolic strikes against secularism: removing Nehru's name from school textbooks, for instance, or banning works on Hinduism by liberal Western scholars, whose ideas were said to offend mainstream sensibilities.[14] Others have featured jingoistic campaigns against 'anti-national' elements, from students to human rights activists, and even those who resist chanting patriotic slogans or standing when the national anthem is played in cinemas.

There was then particular animosity directed at Islam, beginning with trumped-up campaigns against what was often called 'love jihad', in which Muslim men were accused of using surreptitious marriage proposals as a tool for the conversion of Hindu women. In 2015, around a year before they changed the name of Modi's own street, authorities in New Delhi changed another major artery, Aurangzeb Road, renaming it after the country's revered former president, Dr A. P. J. Abdul Kalam. The decision swapped one Muslim icon for another, but still removed a prominent symbol of the capital's Islamic heritage under centuries of Mughal rule. More prominent still was a spate of violent campaigns to protect cows, which are considered sacred by conservative Hindus.

Some involved legal changes, for instance to tighten rules governing slaughterhouses, most of which are run by Muslims. But at their worst they devolved into Islamophobic thuggery, leading to a rash of murders and lynchings conducted by *gau-rakshaks* (cow protectors) against those suspected of eating or selling beef.

None of this was caused directly by Modi, or indeed condoned by him. But almost all these incidents were linked in one way or another to a constellation of fanatical Hindu groups that had grown bolder after Modi's arrival, most notably the RSS, whose leaders remained tied closely to his government. Sometimes Modi spoke out against these forces of division, but he generally did so reluctantly and belatedly, as if unwilling to dress down his more fervent supporters. For all his undoubted rhetorical skills, he also almost never deployed them to win over worried liberals, or to reassure minorities fearful about the rise of newly partisan Hinduism. Instead, his speeches preached a gospel of growth while dropping in dog whistles that only the attentive would hear. 'Almost for 1,000 to 1,200 years we were slaves,' he told a cheering crowd of well-heeled diaspora Indians at New York's Madison Square Garden in 2014.[15] The implication was clear: Indians were subjugated not just during British rule but also under the various Muslim empires that preceded it. Only now under Modi were they – meaning the long-suffering Hindu majority – becoming free.

Even more than Modi himself, liberal critics were alarmed by Amit Shah, a tall and heavy-set politician who was both BJP president and the prime minister's enforcer. An adept strategist, Shah won a Machiavellian reputation, both for his acute grasp of the intricacies of caste politics and for his unerring ability to use them for electoral purposes. His talents in this second domain were such that the Election Commission of India took the unusual step of banning him from making public speeches in the run-up to the 2014 election, as punishment for a series of earlier inflammatory remarks.[16] Ugly though they were, Shah's methods were also effective, scripting for Modi a run of state-level election triumphs, notably his crushing Uttar Pradesh win in early 2017, which left the BJP in a position of unprecedented national dominance.

More than a decade younger than his mentor, Shah met Modi first through the RSS as a teenager. A framed picture of Savarkar, their mutual inspiration, hangs in his home in New Delhi.[17] His notorious public image stemmed from his time as a powerbroker in Modi's Gujarat administrations. As the state's home minister he was accused of involvement in extrajudicial police killings, and spent three months in jail in 2010. The case against him eventually collapsed, but not before it buttressed the reputation as henchman and hardliner that he would later take with him to New Delhi.[18] In person, as I discovered when I met him briefly in UP, Shah shared many of his boss's traits, not least a distrust of the media and hostility to questioning. In his public speeches, he stuck mostly to Modi's script of economic development. But there was also clear logic to his methods, which stirred up religious passions as an election-winning tactic. Hindu voters were divided by caste, region and language. Modi's electoral odds improved greatly when they were united – an approach that political scientists like Ashutosh Varshney dubbed 'Hindu consolidation'.[19]

The BJP was far from the only party to play politics with communal identity: 'The Congress is opportunistically communal while the BJP is ideologically communal,' as writer Mukul Kesavan once put it.[20] But whatever its ideological leanings, in practice the BJP most often used communal tactics to build common cause against non-Hindus, Muslims in particular. 'If land is given for cemetery in a village, it should be given for cremation ground also,' the prime minister thundered at a mass rally in UP as the 2017 state election campaign began, making reference to the funerary practices of Christians and Muslims on the one hand and Hindus on the other.[21] 'If electricity is supplied during Ramzan [Ramadan], it should be supplied during Diwali also,' he went on. 'There should not be discrimination.'

What appeared to be a plea for equality was actually a transparent wedge issue, likely to agitate Hindus who feared Muslims were being given special government treatment. Shah had already made a series of earlier incendiary speeches, one of which claimed that Hindus in one UP town were being ejected forcibly from their land.[22] Modi's svengali showed a particular gift for making Hindus feel as if they were under threat from shadowy outside forces, most linked in some way to Islam. What many feared in Modi they saw clearly enough in his most trusted lieutenant: a talent for rough-and-tumble politics and a radical ambition to reimagine India as a Hindu nation.

One hundred and seventy-one million people voted for Modi in 2014.[23] It is hard to know how many did so enthusiastically and how many were to some degree reluctant, viewing the BJP leader as their least-worst option, or feeling some degree of alarm at the company he kept. Modi's political family still included the RSS and its even more fanatical acolytes, all of whom campaigned openly for a Hinduised society. Yet it was Modi alone who took these ideas and remixed them with wider appeal. The Hindu nationalism of old was, if not entirely a fringe ideology, then at least a minority one. Before him the BJP had held power in New Delhi on only a handful of occasions. The party's power base was restricted to particular stretches of Hindi-speaking northern and western India, while its more militant adherents were viewed mostly as cranks. Modi was different: he took Hindu national-ism and fashioned it into something popular.

At the heart of this appeal lay an ability to fuse the modern and the authentically traditional. Modi's religious background was unimpeach-able, but he built alongside it a broader coalition that reached from lowly villages and slums to the plush homes of the business elite, who were typically reliable BJP voters. His speech at Madison Square Garden had all the trappings of a contemporary rock concert. But his delivery that day was more impressive for coming in the middle of a nine-day fast, where he was said only to have drunk lemonade and tea, even during a formal dinner at the White House.[24] His speeches touched on themes of ambition, talking about the importance of finding jobs and enjoying material comforts. But his public statements were also laced with allusions to Hindu mythology and examples of quirky village wisdom. 'Plant five trees to celebrate a daughter's birth, they will fetch you the funds for her marriage,' he once wrote on Twitter, the point being that the timber could eventually be harvested to pay for a gener-ous wedding ceremony.

Where earlier prime ministers appeared indecisive, Modi was reso-lute, with a particular flair for communication. Even his penchant for colourful outfits brought a dash of glamour to a country long used to politicians in dowdy, hand-spun white cotton. There was an undeniable masculinity about his appeal: the man who boasted of his '56-inch chest', launched surgical strikes against Pakistan and stubbornly refused to apologise for his role in the violence of 2002. This muscular firmness seemed to hold particular allure for younger men, like Vivek Jain, the bank worker I met during Modi's 2014 election day celebrations in Gujarat. Yet it was an incongruous kind of attraction too, given that it

rested in large part on the implied virility of a leader who, were his official biography to be believed, had never actually had sex.

Modi's taste for flashiness sometimes got the better of him. In 2015
he met President Barack Obama resplendent in a dark blue Savile Row
suit, with gold pinstripes repeatedly spelling the words 'NARENDRA
DAMODARDAS MODI'. The costume was widely mocked for its expense
and vanity. A rare public relations stumble, it was this episode that
gifted his opponents the slogan '*suit boot ki sarkar*', meaning a rotten
regime run by the prime minister and his elegantly tailored cronies.[25]
Modi recovered only by selling the offending item off for charity, in the
process raising Rs 43 million ($672,000) and winning a Guinness World
Record for 'the most expensive suit sold at auction'.[26] Such missteps
remained rare, however. Half way through his term in office, at a
moment when many leaders find themselves at a low ebb, data from the
Pew Research Centre suggested that nine in ten Indians viewed their
prime minister positively, making him easily the most popular leader of
any major global power.[27]

The broader point was that Modi was neither a born-again technocrat nor a recovering Hindu zealot. Rather he was both those things,
and he made their mix uniquely attractive. He proved politically canny
in other ways, not least by adopting secular symbols. As well as lauding
Gandhi in speeches, he adopted the Mahatma's rounded glasses as the
logo for *Swachh Bharat*, his campaign for public cleanliness. A devotee
of early-morning stretching exercises, Modi launched International
Yoga Day in 2015 with a gigantic public demonstration that brought
some thirty-five thousand onto the streets of New Delhi, winning a
further Guinness World Record.[28] There were dozens more displays
around the world, in an event that played a useful political double
purpose: on the one hand displaying a new kind of Indian soft power,
on the other firmly reclaiming a practice, rich in symbolism for Hindus,
that had grown worryingly entangled in the secular lifestyles of the
West.

The yoga event was typical of Modi's ability to appeal to both traditional values and contemporary frustrations. The anti-corruption
protests of 2011 erupted partly as a conduit for middle-class anger
about governance. But they also spoke to wider disappointment at the
amateurishness of the Indian state: the sense of shame that flowed from
nationwide power cuts or delayed journeys in dilapidated trains or

being shaken down for bribes by minor public officials. It was an anger that Modi shared. His was a vision of India with wide highways, solar parks and bullet trains; a country in which things were achieved and people got on, as he himself had done.

This appeal came across most clearly when he toured abroad, a process that shared more in common with a pop star than a politician. Madison Square Garden hosted his first big foreign rally in 2014, in an event freighted with extra symbolism, given that Modi's arrival in New York that September marked the end of his exclusion from America in the aftermath of 2002. Nearly twenty thousand packed in to see him perform, the kind of crowd almost no global leader could match. Similar spectacles followed in Sydney, Silicon Valley and London, where sixty thousand jammed into Wembley Stadium on a brisk November night in 2015, with Prime Minister David Cameron as his warm-up act. Modi revelled in the attention.

The Indian diaspora were far from united in their admiration for the BJP. Most Indian-Americans tended to vote for the Democrats, while British Indians historically favoured the Labour Party. Yet there was still undeniable Modi enthusiasm among a certain kind of émigré, typically upper-caste Hindus who had found success abroad and wanted the same to be possible back home. Modi deftly exploited these feelings, first filling his audiences with pride in their motherland, then subtly needling their grievances at its present condition. Yet for those Indians packed into foreign stadiums or watching back at home, there was a simpler reaction too: to see their prime minister up on stage, being cheered as a global superstar, was to suggest that India itself might soon achieve that same status too.

BRAVE NARENDRA

Modi runs India from a pale red sandstone building, tucked almost out of sight towards the end of the government secretariat complex on New Delhi's Raisina Hill. There are few outside hints of its importance, beyond a single checkpoint and a small red sign reading 'Prime Minister's Office: Gate No. 5'. Inside there are layers of security checks, one involving an old dresser into which visitors surrender their phones. The corridors beyond are eerily empty, except for pairs of camouflaged soldiers, who stand quietly at doorways in blue caps, bearing conspicuous automatic weapons.

A grand staircase curves up towards Modi's office and the nearby room where India's cabinet meet. The upper-floor balconies are draped in a thin mesh to stop marauding monkeys breaking in. There is no central heating, so civil servants keep portable electric heaters handy for the colder months. Modi is often pictured presiding over wintertime meetings wearing a warm jacket and thick woollen scarf. For a leader known to love technology the place is curiously antiquated, with barely a computer or flat-screen television in sight. It is all too easy to imagine the same draughty hallways in colonial times, when the viceroy had offices there, just over the road from his sumptuous imperial residence.

Those who work with Modi speak admiringly of his energy: a man who rises before dawn and has been never known to take a holiday. 'He is a workaholic,' one civil servant told me when I visited the building in the summer of 2017. 'Mostly he starts at 7 a.m., and works fourteen-hour days.' Officials remark less on his intellect – although he is said to be clever – and more on his endurance, as he sits through gruelling late-night PowerPoint briefings. In public Modi is flamboyant: a maker of speeches and an entertainer of crowds. But in private he sits impassively: a good listener, who sucks up detail, asks pointed questions and displays prodigious acts of memory, dredging up details from many months before. He has few distractions, with an estranged wife and neither children nor grandchildren. Instead, his companions are administrators: the joint secretaries, deputy secretaries and officers on special duty with whom he shares the Prime Minister's Office – or just 'PMO' – many of whom have worked for him loyally since Gujarat. 'It's monastic, but that's because he has a lot of time for bureaucrats,' I was once told by Arvind Subramanian, the government's chief economic adviser, who spoke glowingly about his boss. 'As a person who is interested in decisions, development and making sure that he gets all the structures and decision-making in place, I think he's quite extraordinary.'[29]

Whether there is another, softer side to Modi is hard to tell. A noted raconteur in his *pracharak* days, there are still flashes of humour in his speeches and genuine warmth in the bear hugs with which he envelops visiting foreign leaders. In public he has his quirks, not least an enduring love of corny acronyms. 'My mantra is: IT + IT = IT,' he told an audience in 2017, explaining that the slogan meant 'Information Technology + Indian Talent = India Tomorrow'.[30] When meeting Israel's Benjamin Netanyahu later the same year he unveiled the slogan 'I4I', or 'India for Israel and Israel for India'.[31] In meetings, he displays an autodidact's mastery of niche subjects, with interests ranging from animal husbandry to rural irrigation, many of which he picked up while running his home state. Modi's approach to government prom- ises unparalleled transparency, with his YouTube channels, hologram appearances and tens of millions of Twitter followers.[32] But of the man behind the mask there is nothing, beyond an inscrutable sense of 'Modi's unwillingness to be known', as one account from his time in Gujarat put it.[33]

As prime minister, Modi is even more guarded, a fact he occasionally appears to regret. 'Earlier when I used to make speeches, I would make them so humorous,' he told Arnab Goswami, before blaming India's journalists in general terms for their habit of distorting his remarks. 'There is no humour left in public life because of this fear. Everyone is scared.'[34] That same fear certainly extends to those who work under him, who are careful never to show even a hint of disloyalty. In New Delhi, tales of prime ministerial control have grown legendary, extend- ing to matters both weighty and trivial. One example of the latter involves Prakash Javadekar, then a junior BJP minister, who is said to have received a surprise phone call one day on the way to the airport. He listened bemused as an official in Modi's office upbraided him, having somehow discovered that the minister was leaving on an official trip dressed in jeans, rather than a formal suit.[35] Javadekar denied the story but it circulated widely anyway, both as an example of the prime minister's widely suspected megalomania, and as a warning to others that no perceived infraction, not matter how minor, could escape Modi's all-seeing gaze.[36]

When he entered office, Modi pledged to push power away from Delhi and back down towards the people. Yet in practice he has proved to be an arch-centraliser, drawing decisions upwards to the PMO, as if measuring himself against the complexities of running so vast a nation. Before his election some observers predicted that Modi would become a market-friendly kind of reformer, keen to push back the boundaries of an over-mighty government. Instead, as it had been in Gujarat, his chosen self-image was of a kind of no-nonsense chief executive, but one perfectly at ease wielding state power. 'The PM admires Lee Kuan Yew, and his attitude is a bit like the chewing gum ban,' one of Modi's more senior advisers once told me, referring to Singapore's first prime minister and the kind of autocratic crackdowns for which he was famed. 'The point of the ban wasn't that Lee cared about gum. It was that he wanted to show that the government was in charge, down to the smallest detail. In India, when things are always so up in the air, that's what he [Modi] wants to do too.'

His record of economic control is on the face of it impressive. Growth has purred along at levels most other world leaders would envy. India's historically rocky finances have become stable, while its haywire inflation has gradually fallen. Power cuts have grown rarer, foreign investment rules have been liberalised, and a few costly subsidy programmes have been trimmed back. The prime minister has proved especially indefatigable in the production of initiatives: *Swachh Bharat*, to clean streets and build indoor toilets; 'Digital India', to boost online access; and 'Skill India', to train workers. There are to be a hundred 'smart cities', and a new $3 billion scheme to cleanse the sacred but filthy river Ganges. Most important is 'Make in India', a flashy programme aiming to jump-start India's struggling export sector by courting multinationals and fixing rules that have made it hard to run factories. A long-awaited national sales tax, the GST, has been brought in too, part of an effort to turn India into a single subcontinental economy, rather than a collection of twenty-nine separate states. Foreigners are pumping in record investment while big multinationals – Alibaba, Amazon, Apple, Foxconn, Uber, Vodafone – talk up their Indian futures.

Yet there is also an odd pattern to Modi's rule, in which a leader who revels in his own strength has turned out not to be terribly courageous. From the start there was no 'team of rivals', as he fashioned a cabinet filled largely with also-rans. Economists have harped on about the need for structural economic reforms, for instance by making it easier to hire workers, buy land or pay taxes. But all these fights involve bruising battles, and Modi has more often decided to hoard his political capital instead. This timidity is evident in his dealings with state governments too, many of which are run by chief ministers from his own political party, and owe much of their popularity to the prime minister himself. When he has picked a major fight, as with his bold demonetisation experiment, the results have often turned out to be little short of disastrous.

Efforts to change land and labour laws have stalled and been kicked downwards to the states. A vast army of cheap labour, which ought to be one of the country's greatest blessings, has gradually come to be viewed as a curse. India needs to create at least ten million jobs a year for the army of young people arriving in its labour market. Instead it is creating almost none.[37] Rather than an east-Asian-style export boom, manufacturing's share of output has barely budged. Fearful domestic manufacturers have begun shunning youthful workers in favour of robots. As time ticks onwards Modi's many targets – to train half a billion workers, bring power to every village, and dramatically raise manufacturing export levels – remain far out of reach. Promises to canter up to fiftieth place in the World Bank's 'ease of doing business' rankings have proved hopelessly ambitious.[38] Meanwhile, the holy waters of the Ganges flow onwards to the sea as putrid as ever, and Modi's government appears powerless to stop the thick, acrid pollution that chokes New Delhi each winter.

It didn't take long before doubts began to set in. Arun Shourie, a brainy ex-BJP minister and one-time Modi admirer, put these most waspishly. 'When all is said and done,' he wrote in 2015, 'more is said than done.'[39] Modi's many initiatives have a habit of delivering much less than they promised. Plans to reform the state have gone the same way. The prime minister made his name back in Gujarat by shaking up struggling public sector enterprises, cutting costs and hiring in better management. During 2014's election he promised 'maximum governance, minimum government', a phrase that raised hopes that a wave of privatisations would soon reshape a sclerotic state. But in office Modi has proved cautious, avoiding big shifts in the public sector, which still accounts for one sixth of economic output and employs millions of potentially restive workers.[40] Some of the more liberal voices around the BJP argued for steep cuts to Congress-era welfare schemes, which subsidise everything from rural jobs to food distribution.[41] Modi ignored most of these ideas too.

Modi's tenure has included many promising initiatives, including both the GST and Aadhaar, a vast biometric identity card system, which has helped hundreds of millions access better government services. His allies claim further, bolder measures are not feasible. The BJP holds a majority in parliament's lower house, but not the upper, so laws cannot be rammed through. Instead Modi has to bargain with awkward state governments, while also grappling with other powerful forces which often block economic change in India, from trade unions and farmers to small businesses. This is the reason India is often described as having a weak state but a strong society: a social order that 'successfully curbed and blunted the ambitions of political power, and made it extraordinarily resistant to political moulding,' as academic Sunil Khilnani once put it.[42] The BJP once before ran a government that pushed economically liberal ideas, only to lose an election in 2004 that it was widely expected to win. Modi has learned that lesson. He governs as a populist, in the sense that he enjoys being popular, and has steered clear of divisive 'big bang' reforms. Over a decade and a half in public life he has never once lost an election. He does not intend to start now.

The most dispiriting episodes have occurred when Modi had easy opportunities to push forward with development reforms and yet still opted not to do so. One came after his sweeping election victory in UP in 2017, when he picked Yogi Adityanath, a radical Hindu preacher, as the state's next chief minister. The move shocked even seasoned political observers. I had met Adityanath at his temple complex in the depressed eastern city of Gorakhpur at the height of the election campaign, about a month before his appointment.[43] Outside the scene was peaceful: elderly *sadhus* sat praying on the floor of buildings nearby, while the scent from the temple's flower gardens wafted through the air. Inside, Adityanath sat alone on a saffron-coloured couch at the front of a large windowless meeting room, wearing his trademark orange robes.

Shaven headed and in his mid-forties, he spoke that morning in calm, measured tones, sitting below a large portrait of one of his predecessors as chief priest. But the previous evening I had watched as he whipped up a crowd of hundreds of frenzied supporters at a nearby street rally, blaming the city's many problems on an influx of poor workers from nearby states. Adityanath showed little interest in economics, preferring fiery anti-Muslim speeches and divisive cow protection campaigns. Over two decades he had used these talents to move from firebrand priest to political powerbroker, founding his own vigilante group and rising to become a BJP member of parliament in New Delhi.

After the fact, Modi's supporters made various excuses following the appointment, saying the prime minister was simply responding to the preacher's local popularity, and stressing that his administration would still push improved economic management. Yet having just won a thumping election victory, and with his personal authority at its zenith, Modi still picked a man who delighted Hindu extremists but dismayed economic and social liberals alike. He could easily have spent some of his political capital and installed a more qualified figure, capable of grappling with the state's vast problems of joblessness and poverty. The decision was explicable only in raw electoral terms, although it was no less dismal for that: Modi wanted to win UP in 2019's national election and he knew Adityanath would help him to consolidate his Hindu base in the state. The appointment was one further example of a pattern that has marked Modi's period in power. In New Delhi, he has struck terror into ministers and bureaucrats alike, and appears to be able to get them to do almost anything he wants. But when it comes to confronting hardliners within his own party, those same powers of intimidation and persuasion mysteriously vanish.

A second example came with the downfall of Raghuram Rajan, following his surprise resignation in the middle of 2016.[44] Rajan by that point had led India's central bank for nearly three years, battling inflation and beginning to bring problems of bad bank debts under control. Yet as governor of the Reserve Bank of India he also spoke out on an eclectic range of further topics, including one notably pointed address in October 2015. In front of an audience at his *alma mater*, the Indian Institute of Technology in Delhi, Rajan gave what amounted to a full-throated economic defence of social liberalism. 'India's tradition of debate and an open spirit of enquiry is critical for its economic progress,' he told the assembled students. 'Tolerance means not being so insecure about one's ideas that one cannot subject them to challenge.'[45]

Whether or not he intended this as a direct jibe against Modi, that was how India's media took it, splashing the speech in the next day's headlines. Some of the prime minister's more extreme allies – including those in the RSS, who were never keen on Rajan to begin with – were incensed, viewing the speech as a direct challenge to their leader's authority. A whispering campaign began. Subramanian Swamy, a clever but intemperate BJP parliamentarian, dusted down his anti-national playbook and went on the attack, questioning Rajan's decision to spend most of his career teaching in the United States and implying that his belief in Western economic ideas somehow outweighed his loyalty to his country. In a phrase that became quickly infamous, Swamy in May

2016 described the central bank chief as 'mentally not fully Indian', and called for him to be sacked.[46] One month later, in effect, he was.

Behind the scenes Rajan had asked to serve a second term, as he made clear later in his resignation letter. But one official aware of his discussions told me that he had also asked for the flexibility to serve only part of that term, as some of his predecessors had done before him. This provided a face-saving excuse for Modi's team to ask Rajan to leave, arguing that they wanted a candidate for a full three-year term. Yet such technicalities did little to hide the truth of the situation, which is that Rajan was fired. This was not because of personal animus towards Modi. Indeed, those familiar with their dealings say the two men actually got on reasonably well during their regular meetings. Modi also went out of his way to be complimentary after he left. 'Raghuram Rajan's patriotism is no less than any of ours,' he told Arnab Goswami in their interview. 'He is a person who loves the country.' Rather Rajan was kicked out because he crossed a line with Modi's hardcore supporters, with whom Modi himself refused to disagree. The result was the needless departure of one of India's most able advocates for economic reform, making the battle for India's future, and attempts to push back the forces of corruption and vested economic interests, that little bit harder to win.

INDIA AFTER MODI

Narendra Modi is not a man given to displays of doubt, although he did describe the process of wielding power in curiously self-involved terms. 'I have given myself completely. I've been successful in pulling my entire government,' he told Arnab Goswami, as their interview drew gently to a close. Goswami then posed one final question, asking the prime minister if he might share the anxieties that kept him awake at night. 'I don't live under the burden of worries,' he replied. '[But] I can't leave the country helpless . . . For all good and bad things, it is my responsibility.'

Hopes that these responsibilities of office would transform Modi into a socially tolerant economic reformer were always naive. His personal conversion to the cause of development is sincere, and few doubt the indefatigable energies he has brought to the task of governing. But the fiery teachings of his youth, and the world view they inspired, remain deeply lodged. Then there are simple questions of politics, as Modi seeks to balance his hopes of delivering unpopular structural reforms against the odds of a handsome future re-election win. Yet even these goals, central though they may be, are subsumed within a larger ideological project: the destruction of Congress as a political force, and its left-of-centre, secular ideology along with it. In this final task Modi has proved strikingly successful. His victory in 2014 dealt Congress, for so long India's natural party of government, a crushing and perhaps irreparable blow. Certainly the party has shown few signs of recovery in the years since its defeat, as it staggers along under Rahul Gandhi's ponderous and diffident leadership.

The tolerant vision that Mahatma Gandhi and Nehru held dear had been in retreat long before Modi. In truth its decline began not with the BJP but with Nehru's own daughter, Indira Gandhi, who as prime minister during the 1970s moved to strike deals with any number of caste and community groups, trading her party's ideals to sustain, at least for a while, its grip on power. Modi's arrival nonetheless represented a new and fundamental threat to the secular ideals India's founding fathers held dear. He went on to become the nation's most forceful prime minister since Indira Gandhi herself, an achievement that, given her authoritarian leanings, should have been as alarming as it was flattering.

Far from being an economic liberal, the longer he stays in office, the clearer his comfort with state power becomes. He is the kind of leader Americans would call a big-government conservative. Yet here Modi faces a different problem, namely the limitations of the institutions he controls. India's state has often proved strikingly competent, from its ability to run vast elections to its timely response to natural disasters. It boasts many creditable institutions too, including the country's central bank and its best universities. But more often than not these are isolated examples of proficiency. India's slow-moving legal system, by contrast, had thirty-three million pending cases, as the head of the Supreme Court complained in a tearful speech in 2016.[47] At its current pace, another judge has suggested, the backlog would not be cleared for three centuries.[48] Meanwhile, New Delhi's thick smog, now widely agreed to be worse even than Beijing's, stands as a choking testament to the state's inability to balance the aims of economic growth, environmental sustainability and public health.

The PMO's pink sandstone corridors house one of the more highly functioning parts of India's system, staffed by a small band of elite civil servants, whose efforts do much to hold a creaking government machine together. Yet Modi's habits of centralisation mean even they are overloaded. As I walked back into the sunshine after my visit, the contrast with New York's Michael Bloomberg popped into my head. As mayor, Bloomberg worked from a cubicle in a modern open-plan office space known as the 'Bullpen'.[49] Stacked with computers and data displays, the place was designed to facilitate easy communications and allow its leaders to make quick decisions, with a particular focus on sucking up real-time data about the state of the city's public services. By contrast, Modi governed a vastly larger population from an office that seemed stuck in the Victorian era, sitting above a governing machine that conducted its business by shuffling around paper 'files', in which pending decisions were slipped quietly inside green cardboard folders and bound up with string. Modi's harsher critics often accused him of excessive use of state power. Inside the machine, it was amateurism rather than authoritarianism that appeared to be the greater threat to India's future.

Historian Ramachandra Guha has called India's an 'election only' democracy, meaning that the majestic spectacle of its elections hides a less impressive reality in the years in between.[50] Part of the problem is that India itself, for all the lofty ideals of its constitution, has never actually made the transition to becoming a full liberal democracy, with public institutions capable of guarding in every respect the civil and political rights of its many peoples. Yet it was never exactly an 'illiberal democracy' either, in the sense of the phrase coined by author Fareed Zakaria to describe the likes of Turkey and Russia, which hold elections but then actively deny their citizens many important constitutional protections.[51] For his critics, the worry was that under Modi India would gradually join this same chorus, drifting towards full illiberal-democracy status, with its secular foundation replaced by some kind of new Hindu majoritarian vision. Before Modi, the worry was that India's state was incapable of enforcing the liberties its laws carefully enshrined. Now many feared its leadership did not actually want to enforce them.

These threats of illiberalism should not be exaggerated. Relations between India's religions and castes have often been far worse than they are today. Nothing during Modi's tenure in New Delhi comes close to the violence that swept India after the destruction of the Babri Masjid in 1992, or indeed the Gujarat pogrom a decade later. Both ruptures appeared to leave the nation's secular fabric irretrievably torn, yet after both it was patched back together to some degree. Modi does carry with him the baggage of communal division, but many earlier BJP leaders were more extreme, while there are plenty of alarming figures among the party's current senior leadership, Yogi Adityanath among them. Modi's critics might well ponder whether any of India's crop of plausible alternative leaders would prove more palatable.

Modi has also never pretended to be a liberal leader, so it should be no surprise that he has failed to govern as one. Instead, he and his lieutenant Amit Shah are tacticians, who understand the powerful role identity politics can play in winning popular support when they need it. Modi's dramatic experiment with demonetisation showed equally clearly his willingness to push extreme populist measures. Yet any future decision to pursue a more overtly Hindu nationalist political strategy would still carry significant political risks. For all of Modi's present popularity, India's voters have often moved away from political leaders who appeared to whip up communal discord for brazenly self-interested reasons. In this way there is some hope that the safety valve of democracy itself will guard against a new era of wrenching division. 'India's semi-liberal democracy has survived because of, not despite, its strong regions and varied languages, cultures and even castes,' as Fareed Zakaria put it.

Yet the risks of rising illiberalism should not be downplayed either. The appeal of Hindu nationalism has grown in strength partly because of Modi himself, but also because of the thick sense of identity it provides in a country buffeted by the uncertainties of globalisation. India's rising prosperity offers no special defence against this rise of a slippage into majoritarianism. Modi's Gujarat, one of the country's richest and most industrialised states, also suffers from one of its most wretched records of caste and communal disharmony.

Even if Modi wanted to step away from the more extreme elements within his political coalition, he remains stuck in a deeper political bind. Congress politician Shashi Tharoor has described it as 'the fundamental contradiction Mr Modi faces, of advocating, as prime minister, liberal principles and objectives whose fulfilment would require him to jettison the very forces that have helped ensure his electoral victories'.[52] By this, Tharoor means that there is at least a part of Modi that knows he ought to avoid sectarian distractions, given that these are likely to get in the way of his hopes of expanding and modernising India's economy.

But with the next election looming, he also knows that the RSS and their millions of footsoldiers could well mean the difference between an unexpected defeat and a second Modi triumph. It is far from clear that Modi yearns to slap down the dogmatists and bigots within his own ranks, but he has found himself bound to them by political expedience nonetheless.

As he prepares for re-election, and a second term thereafter, the risk is that Modi will follow the path commonly charted by other conservative nationalists before him. In their own ways both Vladimir Putin in Russia and Recep Tayyip Erdoğan in Turkey took power by promising economic reform and hinting that they might move their countries in more liberal directions.[53] But rare is the strongman leader who grows less autocratic the longer he stays in office. Liberals like Raghuram Rajan argue that development and social tolerance are reinforcing, which is indeed a persuasive argument in the long run. But viewed through the lens of short-term politics – the brief five-year cycle of an election, most obviously – there is no obvious reason this has to be the case. It is quite plausible to imagine that a leader like Modi with sharp populist instincts, who is both facing waning popularity and conscious of the need to push on with economic reforms, might decide to whip up nationalist sentiment to bolster his own support. Here the risk is not that Modi will weigh up a choice between nationalism and reform. It is that he will determine that these are twin and reinforcing projects that have to be pursued in tandem.

This same balance of risks underpins the bargain many felt they struck when voting for Modi himself. Some, like Rajan, went to work for him, despite personal reservations about his Hindu nationalist baggage. Others held their noses and voted for the BJP, calculating that Modi's promises of development were worth the dangers of the potential social upheaval that he might bring. 'I was aware of the risks,' as Gurcharan Das, a socially liberal author and ex-businessman, said of his own voting decision in 2014.[54] 'Modi was polarising, sectarian and authoritarian. But I felt the risk in not voting for him was greater.'

These, then, are the tragedies of Modi. The first: that such a bargain had to be struck in the first place. In 2014, many voters were forced to conclude that a personally honest and economically reform-minded leader was the best that India could hope for, even if his election came with the risks of political schism. This choice was made because the desired alternative – a leader who was popular, honest, economically imaginative, but also statesmanlike, untainted by violence, and willing to place issues of identity and faith outside the public square – was now in India almost impossible to imagine. The second: that Modi, a man of such great persuasive abilities, has consistently declined to speak up in defence of the kind of social tolerance that, in the long run at least, ought to have provided the surest footing for his own stated economic objectives. And then the third: that having struck this devil's bargain, and chosen the hope of reform over the risk of polarisation, those same voters have found their hopes of economic development at best half delivered – as Modi has proved to be a far less courageous and radical leader than they had hoped.

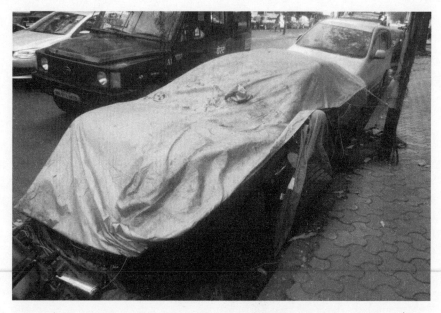

The mysterious Aston Martin, abandoned in the middle of the night, sat under a grey plastic sheet outside Gamdevi police station for months after the crash.

A PROGRESSIVE ERA?

I left India early one Saturday morning in spring 2016. My wife and I closed the door on our empty apartment and took the lift down with our infant son, born in a nearby hospital nearly two years before. As the sun rose higher we drove out through southern Mumbai, racing along the curve of Marine Drive and passing the empty sands of Chowpatty Beach. Soon we hit Pedder Road, where Antilia came into view up on the right hand side. A few minutes later we crossed the spot where its owner's Aston Martin had finally come to rest. I never did find out what became of the car. One afternoon in 2014, many months after the crash, I happened to drive past Gamdevi police station, expecting to see a familiar silhouette standing outside. But on that day both the car and its grey plastic cover were gone. Inside the station, an officer shrugged and said he didn't know where the wreck had ended up.

Five years earlier I had flown into Mumbai's old airport, a decrepit and congested concrete warren. On that last Saturday we left through the new Terminal 2, its exterior an elegant half-moon, painted in brilliant white. To many, the airport symbolised what was going right with India. Mumbai's elite certainly viewed it with thinly disguised elation, as if their city had finally shed a shaming indictment, with its hour-long entry lines and third-world interiors. Rather than snaking through choked streets, passengers now arrived via the Sahar Elevated Access Road, a purpose-built 2-kilometre stretch of raised six-lane highway, and perhaps the nicest road in all of India. Inside, the building was efficient and stylish, with soaring ceilings supported by pillars resembling the feathers of a peacock, the national bird. Yet the city's infamous slums still pushed right up against the airport's fence, while even the highway marked a curious kind of progress: a public facility that only the most prosperous would ever be able to use.

In early 2014, just before the new terminal opened, I called Katherine Boo, an American writer who had lived for a time in Annawadi, one of a clutch of shanty towns that ring the airport's perimeter. *Behind the Beautiful Forevers,* her book from 2012, laid out a searing portrait of the traumas and injustices these residents faced. She was back in Mumbai for a spell on the day I rang, visiting some of those she had met during her research. The airport's mysterious constructions had attracted plenty of local attention. 'People in the slums are watching, amused, as the crews do the frantic work installing full-grown gardens, painting walls and making improvements for the prime minister,' she told me, just a few days before India's leader arrived formally to inaugurate the building.[1]

The gap between those inside that fence and those outside remained unbridgeably vast. Residents in places like Annawadi were unlikely to find jobs at the airport, let alone ever have enough money to enter as passengers. 'City planners sweat to make their terminals grand by global standards,' Boo told me. 'There's always a vague, tertiary hope that some of the magic dust will settle upon the struggling locals, but they don't see much of that.' Brijesh Singh, a slum-dweller who lived in a tiny one-bedroom house nearby, marvelled at the new lines of lush, green palm trees along the elevated road, recently installed by labourers toiling high above his head. 'Now it's Singapore, up there on the expressway!' he said. 'It would be interesting to see the inside [of the airport], but we will look from the outside.'

Having left and moved to Singapore myself, I began to think more about India and its future. On the one hand its development aims are straightforward: first to cement its position as a firmly middle-income parliamentary democracy, then to enter the ranks of advanced econo-mies at some stage after the mid-point of this century. Yet until it grapples with the three challenges outlined in this book – inequality and the new super-rich, crony capitalism, and the travails of the industrial economy – the path to achieving those goals will remain uncertain.

In 2008, at the height of the go-go years, Raghuram Rajan posed a basic question about the super-rich: is there a threat of an Indian oligarchy? At the time his answer was 'Yes'. Back then, billionaire wealth grew unchecked, from Vijay Mallya's raucous parties to the *nouveau riche* grandeur of Antilia, leading many to fear a Russian-style carve-up. A decade later that threat has receded, at least to some degree. Few of India's tycoons fell to earth as spectacularly as Mallya, but the after-shocks of the season of scams still left many powerful industrialists diminished. The old system, with its political favours and risk-free bank loans, came under intense scrutiny, not least from Narendra Modi himself. Even the word 'oligarchy', with its suggestion of a closed elite that held power in perpetuity, proved an imperfect description of India's hurly-burly business scene. Mukesh Ambani's perennial position on top of the billionaire rankings gives an impression of unfaltering supremacy. But it has been just as common to see old dynasties decline and new figures like Gautam Adani rise up to take their place. In all this, India actually looks very little like Russia.

Whatever else you think of him, Modi has also reset the balance of power between politics and business. When I met him in London, Vijay Mallya described the speed at which India's new prime minister shut down the political access he and his fellow tycoons had long enjoyed. Yet even while crediting Modi with curbing corruption, Mallya expressed frustration with what he said was a new suspicion of entre-preneurs in New Delhi. 'Modi's narrative now very clearly is: "I was a tea seller. I'm now prime minister. I'm the champion of the poor. I'm going to screw the rich, screw the dishonest, and spread the impression that every rich man is dishonest too,"' he said. During demonetisation, Modi's rhetoric took an especially sharp turn. 'With what we have done, the rich need pills to go to sleep,' the prime minister said in 2016, just after the note ban came in.[2]

In fact, India's ultra-wealthy are thriving. The ranks of its billionaires have kept swelling, while the fortunes of the merely very rich continue to shoot up as well. In many ways this should be welcomed. India needs affluent entrepreneurs, a point recognised even by left-wing thinkers. 'There is something a little deceptive about focusing on the very rich,' I was once told by Amartya Sen. 'Having lots of rich people is not always a big problem so long as they get no special favours and pay fair taxes.' The problem is that these increases in wealth have turned India into one of the world's least equal countries. Without action, this gap between rich and poor – between those inside the airport fence and those outside it – is only likely to widen. Perversely, the closer India comes to its ambitions of near-double-digit growth, the faster this will happen.

It is unfair to blame these trends on Modi, although he has done little to reverse them. Yet there will be grim consequences if they continue unabated. Those Latin American economies with the widest social divides have proved less economically stable and more likely to get stuck in the 'middle-income trap', in which poorer nations achieve moderate prosperity but fail to become rich.[3] The more successful countries of east Asia, by contrast, grew prosperous while managing to stay broadly egalitarian, partly by building basic social safety nets. Of the two models, it seems clear which India should want to follow.

Inequality has complex causes, so making progress will not be easy. But there are still basic steps that would help. Sen is right to push basic education, health and pension provision for those at the bottom of the social ladder, all areas in which Modi's government has promised much but delivered surprisingly little. At the top, it means greater focus on raising tax, especially from the wealthy. This does not mean attacking the rich, but it does mean ending the ridiculous situation in which only one per cent of Indians pay any income tax at all, and barely 5,000 people do so on earnings above Rs 10 million ($155,000).[4] In America, 'millionaires and billionaires' are often called on to pay their fair share. Until the same happens in India, it is hard to see how a fairer society can be built.

On corruption, India's progress has at first glance been good. The old mega-scams have stopped, partly because valuable natural resources contracts are now auctioned off. Various recently introduced measures should help to curb fraud too, from the goods and services tax launched in 2017, to plans linking state welfare programmes to bank accounts via Aadhaar, the biometric identification system.[5] Most importantly, India's democratic institutions are newly alert. At our meeting in Singapore, Vinod Rai, the crusading former auditor, was upbeat. 'The media and citizens at large are far more vigilant about corruption,' he told me. 'I don't think we can go back.'

Yet there remains a danger of complacency. Kickbacks still dominate swathes of public life, from land purchase to municipal contracts. Criminal probes have dragged on, with almost no one sent to jail. State and city governments are just as venal as ever, while surveys say India remains the most bribe-ridden nation in Asia.[6] Then there are deeper problems. 'For any society to lift itself out of absolute poverty it needs to build three critical state institutions: taxation, law and security,' according to Oxford economist Paul Collier.[7] All three in India – the revenue service, the lower levels of the judiciary and the police – still suffer endemic graft. Perhaps most importantly, the country's under-the-table political funding system remains largely untouched. This is understandable: Modi wants to win re-election in what is sure to be the costliest national poll in Indian history, and he needs to raise money to do so. But cronyism will never be properly fixed until the problem of 'money power' is fixed too, starting with the full auditing of party finances and ending with some kind of transparent or publicly funded system.

Much of the current corruption drop-off is also a function of fear, not least the trepidation inspired by Modi himself. The prime minister's efforts have had tough economic consequences. This was certainly the case during demonetisation, which did much to harm growth but little to curb graft. Corruption anxieties have depressed private sector investment rates too.[8] Yet whatever its pluses and minuses, Modi's leadership is also temporary. His successors may well be less censorious about corruption, hence it is important to introduce wider measures to combat graft, rather than relying only on honest leadership. This matters because cronyism is sure to recur in new forms as India develops. At its most basic level, graft is a function of growth, meaning that it will re-emerge when the economy expands strongly. This is especially true in areas like infrastructure, where estimates suggest India must invest around $4.5 trillion over the next two decades.[9] Without careful management, spending on this scale will provide ample scope for grand corruption to return.

Corruption plagues developing countries, not because their people are immoral but because it is often useful. At its best, graft can oil the wheels of progress, as political leaders gift economic rents to favoured businesses, which is what happened in the 'developmental states' of east Asia. The proceeds of corruption can also bind together otherwise unstable social groups, as Samuel Huntington described in *Political Order in Changing Societies*.[10] Here India has been a textbook example, as kickbacks have helped politicians to build infrastructure projects, while revenues extracted from corruption have united political coalitions in New Delhi. Elsewhere, the proceeds of patronage have given caste groups and other minorities a stake in the wider economy.

India therefore faces a choice. For a decade after 2004 it enjoyed rocketing growth but at the cost of sky-high corruption. More recently corruption has fallen, but growth has fallen along with it. Many now dream of rapid, graft-free expansion. But this is largely a fantasy: 'The optimal level of corruption will not, in practice, be zero,' as Robert Klitgaard wrote in *Controlling Corruption*.[11] By this he means that the cost of wiping out profiteering would require unacceptable collateral damage. 'Fight corruption too little and destroy the country,' as one Chinese communist leader is supposed to have said. 'Fight it too much and destroy the party.'[12] Instead, there is likely to be a continuing trade-off, in which India will struggle to deliver the two things Modi has promised above all: very rapid growth and very little graft.

A better approach is to push institutional anti-graft reforms, such as the earlier decision to auction off rights to natural resources, which can help keep corruption under control while allowing growth slowly to return. This in turn should form part of a broader set of changes that are described in India as a transition from a 'deals-based' to a 'rules-based' model of capitalism, meaning one whose rules allow little political and bureaucratic discretion over public resources.[13] Yet even this will be far from straightforward. Francis Fukuyama describes this shift away from a 'patrimonial' state, meaning one marked by corruption and clientelism, as the defining challenge for all developing nations. '[It is] much more difficult', he writes, 'than making the transition from an authoritarian political system to a democratic one.'[14]

This balance of growth and corruption then lies at the heart of the struggles of India's industrial economy. The problems of indebted conglomerates and ailing banks were well known when Modi arrived in office. Yet progress towards fixing them has been slow, leaving India facing a lost decade of investment. Beyond Vijay Mallya, few errant tycoons have been pursued aggressively by the authorities. Instead, many now lead zombie companies that have struggled to repay their debts, including GVK, the Andhra Pradesh conglomerate which built Mumbai's shiny new airport terminal. Modi's administration introduced some important measures to help, including a new bankruptcy laws and a series of bank recapitalisations. But more radical options have been ignored, notably privatisation of struggling public sector lenders, leaving India with one of the most state-dominated banking systems of any large economy outside China. It is an irony of Modi's tenure that a prime minister so obsessed with infrastructure projects has been unable to create the conditions in which more could be built. A better option would be some kind of grand bargain, in which tycoons, banks and politicians share the pain of putting right the festering problems created in the boom years.

Here Raghuram Rajan's warnings about oligarchy were as much about the threat of poorly functioning markets as they were about vested interests, given that India's old, corrupt system of industrial investment has clearly broken down, but a new alternative is yet to emerge to replace it. When I spoke to Rajan at the Reserve Bank of India, he sketched out a rough way forward. 'If one was a dictator, you would work on improving public services to break the nexus [between business and politicians] and reduce the level of corruption,' he told me. 'And you would also work directly on trying to reduce the concentration of economic power by increasing competition.' This was the same basic point made in 2011 when Ashutosh Varshney and Jayant Sinha, a left-leaning academic and a centre-right businessman respectively, co-wrote their article about their country's new Gilded Age. 'It is time for India to rein in its robber barons,' they argued. The best part of a decade later, their call for firm action against entrenched corporate power remains largely unanswered.

These problems then focus attention on one final critical barrier India faces: government itself. The crony capitalism of America's Gilded Age ended when rampant nineteenth-century clientelism was curbed by impartial, meritocratic twentieth-century public administration. The kind of concentrated power built up by tycoons like Cornelius Vanderbilt was undone through the introduction of new anti-trust law and competition policy. Improvements in basic public services gradually broke the grip of political patronage, a process that developed over many decades after the Gilded Age itself, culminating only with the New Deal of the 1930s.

In India's case, similar breakthroughs will require a focus on what is often called 'state capacity'.[15] Ending corruption is part of this battle, but it also involves the more complex objective of building a state machinery able to create and implement wise public policies, while remaining impartial between different social groups. That this can be done is clear from the case of China, which achieved huge social and economic progress while also being amazingly corrupt, largely because its machinery of state is so capable. 'The most important political distinction among countries concerns not their form of government but their degree of government,' as Huntington wrote in the 1960s.[16] The risk is that without sharp improvements in state capacity, rapid economic expansion can rip societies apart, resulting in upheaval and social division.

India's state capacity problems are glaring, a point brought home to me by Shekhar Gupta during my trip to Uttar Pradesh in 2017. We spent many days driving around the east of the state, bouncing along potholed roads in one of India's poorest corners. There were fewer signs of the dire problems of hunger and abject poverty that dogged the country a few decades earlier. Young people generally went to school and found some kind of basic job. They also had mobile phones and modern clothes and lived in brick homes, not mud-walled huts. Yet at the same time they lacked reliable water and electricity, while their streets had no sewerage or rubbish collection. They suffered ill health, because medical care was haphazard, and poor education, because the local schools were hopeless. 'Indians are living behind their means' was Gupta's way of putting it. 'There was an old poverty where you did not have enough to eat. The new poverty is getting some development but not all, because municipal administration is weak.'

This sounds mundane, but developing nations can only sustain high growth by updating their government machinery. 'Without major changes to its institutions, my big conclusion is that India's rapid growth is unsustainable,' Dani Rodrik, the Harvard development economist, once told me. Bureaucrats in New Delhi need to get out of the business of owning airlines and coal mines, and into the business of regulating them. More generally, India's state must become more skilled at creating and managing markets, while building the kind of infrastructure that can deliver basic public services. In the aftermath of liberalisation, India has suffered from an enduring delusion that it might move rapidly from poverty to advanced-economy status, often by using technology to 'leapfrog' towards a modern form of competitive capitalism. These hopes are understandable, but often they are also a distraction from the tedious business of building the kind of government institutions that make economic advancement most likely.

The need for a government with east Asian levels of competence is all the more urgent, given that India is now unlikely to mimic east Asian models of growth. Without exception, every Asian nation that has clambered from poverty up towards high-income status has done so in the same way: by developing an expertise in manufactured goods, and then exporting to world markets. India's development has a back-to-front look to it, with its historically weak manufacturing but vibrant services, especially in areas like technology outsourcing. Modi's attempts to rebalance this have made some headway, but replicating exactly the paths of countries like China and South Korea still seems unlikely. Instead, India must chart a hybrid economic model of its own. Whatever happens, it cannot rely on a handful of profitable service sectors alone, a model that would leave it looking more like an oil emirate than an east Asian tiger.

This all sounds daunting, but there are still many good reasons for optimism. India is the world's largest remaining emerging market, a fact that should continue to attract investment from abroad. Although they do not function perfectly, its liberal institutions – from courts and regulators to the media and political parties – can provide a solid basis for future growth. Chaotic though it might look, its electoral democracy is a source of stability, especially when compared to its autocratic rival in communist China. Put another way, of the two Asian giants, it is much easier to imagine India retaining roughly the same political set-up fifty years from now.

Then there is the untapped potential of India's people. After my family and I left Mumbai's airport in 2016, we settled down in Singapore, a country with a notably successful Indian diaspora population. It is a pattern familiar from dozens of other countries. Entrepreneur Manish Sabharwal once told me a story about his own move to study in the United States in the mid-1990s. After spending a first freezing winter in Philadelphia, he was surprised: 'I realised that the Americans at my school weren't actually smarter than the Indians, so I had to ask why were they richer than us?' he told me, sitting in a hotel in Bangalore. The more he travelled around the US, the more he found that diaspora Indians enjoyed great economic success, as they did elsewhere around the world. 'My conclusion was simple, namely that if we could only make government work at home roughly as well as it did in all these other places, the talents of the Indian people would do the rest.'

This is what happened in the United States more than a century ago. The decades that followed America's Gilded Age were known as the

Progressive Era, a moment in which anti-corruption campaigns cleaned up politics and the middle classes exerted control over government. It was a period that left lasting and positive effects at home and abroad. In much the same way, India now stands at the threshold of the kind of superpower status it will eventually achieve. As democracy falters in the West, so its future in India has never been more critical. There is no reason why the excesses of the last decade should re-emerge and turn India into a saffron-tinged version of Russia. Instead, with good judgement, India's new Gilded Age can blossom into a Progressive Era of its own, in which the perils of inequality and crony capitalism are left decisively behind. India's ambition to lead the second half of the Asian century – and the world's hopes for a more democratic, liberal future – depend on getting this transition right.

ACKNOWLEDGEMENTS

I first visited Mumbai in 2007, developing an instant fascination for the place that I've never been able to shake since. From that very first trip I still owe a debt to Anand Giridharadas, who sat for hours answering questions over coffee in Indigo Deli, before taking me out to my first meal at Trishna, the city's legendary seafood joint. The same is true of Pablo Jenkins, who let me share his room at the YMCA in Colaba, just a few streets away from the apartment where I would later come to live. Here I should mention Suketu Mehta, too, whom I have never actually met, but whose book *Maximum City: Bombay Lost and Found*, which a friend suggested I read during that early visit, did as much as anything to excite my interest in the metropolis that would become my home five years later.

Back in London, when I joined the *Financial Times* in 2010, my wife and I would often sit around our kitchen table pondering possible future postings as a foreign correspondent. The idea of moving to Mumbai excited me most of all, and it was perhaps a kind of fate that a job in the bureau there came free barely a year after I'd joined the paper. In the years since I have come to owe many debts to my colleagues and friends at the *FT*, but my thanks are due in particular to its editor, Lionel Barber, who took a sizeable gamble sending me off to cover business and finance in a city I barely knew, while gracefully in the process ignoring my lack of experience as a corporate reporter. I'm grateful also to Alec Russell, for encouraging me to go; to James Lamont and Victor Mallet, for being welcoming when I arrived; and later to Ed Luce, for suggesting that my thoughts on the place might in time make something longer than a newspaper article.

Having turned up in India in 2011, I was lucky enough to share the *FT*'s ramshackle bureau – up four flights of wooden stairs and above a sari shop – with an array of wonderful colleagues, including: Avantika Chilkoti, David Keohane, James Fontanella-Khan, Neil Munshi, Mahinda Gupta, Kanupriya Kapoor, Andrea Rodrigues, and Darshan Salvi. Later, I was equally grateful to the Lee Kuan Yew School of Public Policy in Singapore, who provided me a berth while I wrote my manuscript, and then a more permanent home when it was finished – in particular to Kishore Mahbubani, Danny Quah and Kanti Bajpai.

A book of this sort involves many intellectual debts, and my living room shelves are packed with books by authors whose ideas have shaped my own in ways small and large. On the latter front I owe a particular appreciation to Jayant Sinha and Ashutosh Varshney, whose original article on the idea of an Indian Gilded Age first got me thinking about the power of the country's super-rich, even before I had arrived in their country. Many others have since debated variants of that same topic, and over the years I have taken inspiration from the writing of Rana Dasgupta, Siddhartha Deb, Patrick Foulis, Devesh Kapur, Sunil Khilnani, T. N. Ninan, and Michael Walton.

Writing a book is a distressingly solitary task, but preparing to write one remains mercifully sociable. This is fortunate, given India is a bewilderingly place, and one whose many and ever-changing intricacies often leave a perpetual sense of uncertainty. To the extent that I ever overcame this feeling, it was because of the generosity of friends, who let me pester them on the issues about which I remained confused.

In particular, my understanding has been helped immeasurably by conversations with Reuben Abraham, Swaminathan Aiyar, Mukulika Banerjee, Jagdish Bhagwati, Sanjay Bhandarkar, Surjit Bhalla, Sidharth Bhatia, Katherine Boo, Praveen Chakravarty, Sajjid Chinoy, Gurcharan Das, Gaurav Dalmia, Gerson da Cunha, William Dalrymple, Ridham Desai, Sadanand Dhume, Amitabh Dubey, Naresh Fernandes, Anant Goenka, Harsh Goenka, Anthony Good, Ramachandra Guha, Nisid Hajari, Ishaat Hussain, Zahir Janmohamed, Akash Kapur, Bharat Kewalramani, Jaideep Khanna, Parag Khanna, Kumar Iyer, Mukul Kesavan, Manjeet Kripalani, Rajiv Lall, Pratap Bhanu Mehta, Brijesh Mehra, Saurabh Mukherjea, Anant Nath, Sanjay Nayar, Nandan Nilekani, PJ Nayak, Nitin Pai, Anuvab Pal, Deepanjana Pal, Jay Panda, Nick Paulson-Ellis, Basharat Peer, Stanley Pignal, Eswar Prasad, Naman

Pugalia, Raghuram Rajan, Vinod Rai, Adam Roberts, Alan Rosling, Vijay Sankar, Amartya Sen, Neelanjan Sircar, Ruchir Sharma, Arun Shourie, Arvind Subramanian, Mark Tully, Siddharth Varadarajan, Gilles Vernier, and Adil Zainulbhai.

Reading drafts is probably the greatest burden an author can place upon their friends, yet many of mine still gave generously and uncomplainingly of their time, skimming chapters and giving kindly feedback on messy early drafts. In particular, I am indebted to: Sebastian Abbot, Sara Abdo, Rahul Bhatia, Bilal Baloch, Anirudha Dutta, Raghu Karnad, Madhav Khosla, Henry Foy, Barney Jopson, Neelkanth Mishra, Supriya Nayer, Gautam Pemmaraju, Sanjeev Prasad, Niranjan Rajadhyaksha, Mihir Sharma, Jonathan Shainin, and Milan Vaishnav.

Elsewhere I owe thanks to a handful of other friends who helped me out in one way or another during my research, especially: Sriparna Ghosh, Mahesh Langa, Will Perrin, Fran Sainsbury, Catherine Casey, Raman Nanda, Holly Edgar and Kiran Stacey. Extra special gratitude is due to my tireless researcher, Mariyam Haider, who conscientiously checked references, dug out facts, fiddled with footnotes and told me nicely when the story was in danger of getting dull.

Books only get made if someone is willing to take a punt on half-formed ideas, and to that end I am grateful to my three publishers: Oneworld, Random House and HarperCollins. As a first-time author, I feel immensely lucky to have found a team at each that supported my work unstintingly. In particular, it has been a pleasure working with Sam Carter, Jonathan Bentley-Smith, Tim Duggan, Will Wolfslau and Udayan Mitra. More than anyone, I was fortunate to have in Toby Mundy a generous and supportive agent, without whose good humour and encouragement my original proposal would certainly never have been written, and the resulting book probably would never have been finished.

Throughout this process, however, no one did more to support my writing than my wife, Mary. She was game enough to move to India in the first place, becoming my companion throughout the biggest adventure of both of our lives. She proved enthusiastically supportive from the first moment the idea of writing a book began to take shape, and in the years since has shouldered more burdens than was reasonable, not least as I slunk off in the early hours of the morning to write. I will always feel grateful that she gave me her hand, as well as for the fact that she is the best proofreader and editor I know. To her, my love and thanks are owed most of all.

Neither of my two children – Alexander, who was born in India, and Sophie, who arrived in Singapore just a few days after I had handed in my first draft – are old enough to know the debt I owe their mother. Yet hopefully in later life they might come to forgive their father for his moments of book-related distraction during their earliest days, and to understand that they both provided a source of joy and inspiration throughout the writing process. Lastly, I remain grateful above all to my parents, who gently encouraged my desire to write from a young age, and whose bottomless support throughout my life I value above all. With enduring affection, this book is dedicated to them.

BIBLIOGRAPHY

Acemoglu, D. and Robinson, J. A. *Why Nations Fail: The Origins of Power, Prosperity and Poverty*. London, Profile, 2012.

Adiga, A. *The White Tiger: A Novel*. New York, Free Press, 2008.

Aiyar, S. *Accidental India: A History of the Nation's Passage through Crisis and Change*. New Delhi, Aleph, 2012.

Alvaredo, F., Atkinson, A. B., Piketty, T. and Saez, E. 'The Top 1 Percent in International and Historical Perspective'. *Journal of Economic Perspectives*, 27(3), 2013.

Anand, A. *One vs All: Narendra Modi – Pariah to Paragon*. Chennai, Notion Press, 2016.

Astill, J. *The Great Tamasha: Cricket, Corruption and the Turbulent Rise of Modern India*. London, Bloomsbury, 2013.

Baisya, R. K. *Winning Strategies for Business*. New Delhi, Response, 2010.

Bal Narendra. Childhood Stories of Narendra Modi. Ahmedabad, Rannade Prakashan, n.d.

Bertrand, M., Djankov, S., Hanna, R. and Mullainathan, S. 'Obtaining a Driver's License in India: An Experimental Approach to Studying Corruption'. *Quarterly Journal of Economics*, November 2007, pp. 1639–76.

Bhagwati, J. and Panagariya, A. *Why Growth Matters: How Economic Growth in India Reduced Poverty and the Lessons for Other Developing Countries*. New York, PublicAffairs, 2013.

Boo, K. *Behind the Beautiful Forevers: Life, Death and Hope in a Mumbai Slum*. New Delhi, Konark, 2011.

Booth, L., ed. *Wisden's Cricketers' Almanack 2012*. London, Bloomsbury, 2012.

Bremmer, I. and Keat, P. *The Fat Tail: The Power of Political Knowledge for Strategic Investing*. Oxford University Press, 2010.

Chakravarty, P. and Dehejia, V. 'India's Income Divergence: Governance or Development Model?', Briefing Paper 5, IDFC Institute, 2017.

Chancel, L. and Piketty, T. 'Indian Income Inequality, 1922–2014: From British Raj to Billionaire Raj?' World Wealth and Income Database Working Paper 2017/11, July 2017.

Chande, M. B. *Kautilyan Arthasastra*. New Delhi, Atlantic, 1998.

Chaturvedi, S. *I Am a Troll: Inside the Secret World of the BJP's Digital Army*. New Delhi, Juggernaut, 2016.

CMS Transparency. 'Lure of Money in Lieu of Votes in Lok Sabha and Assembly Elections: The Trend 2007–2014'. New Delhi, Centre for Media Studies, 2014.

Damodaran, H. *India's New Capitalists: Caste, Business, and Industry in a Modern Nation*. Basingstoke, Palgrave Macmillan, 2008.

Das, G. 'India: How a Rich Nation Became Poor and Will Be Rich Again'. In L. Harrison and P. Berger, eds, *Developing Cultures: Case Studies*. New York, Routledge, 2006.

Das, G. *India Grows at Night: A Liberal Case for a Strong State*. London, Penguin, 2013.

Dasgupta, R. *Capital: The Eruption of Delhi*. New York, Penguin, 2014.

Debroy, B. and Bhandari, L. *Corruption in India: The DNA and the RNA*. New Delhi, Konark, 2012.

Debroy, B., Tellis, A. and Trevor, R. *Getting India Back on Track: An Action Agenda for Reform*. New Delhi, Random House, 2014.

Denyer, S. *Rogue Elephant: Harnessing the Power of India's Unruly Democracy*. London, Bloomsbury, 2014.

Dhingra, P. *Life behind the Lobby: Indian American Motel Owners and the American Dream*. Stanford, CA, Stanford University Press, 2012.

Drèze, J. and Sen, A. *An Uncertain Glory: India and Its Contradictions*. London, Allen Lane, 2013.

Encarnation, D. J. *Dislodging Multinationals: India's Strategy in Comparative Perspective*. Ithaca, NY, Cornell University Press, 1989.

Fitzgerald, F. S. *The Great Gatsby*. Toronto, Aegitas, [1925] 2016.

Friedman, T. L. *The World is Flat: The Globalized World in the Twenty-First Century*. London, Penguin, 2006.

Freund, C. *Rich People Poor Countries: The Rise of Emerging-Market Tycoons and Their Mega Firms*. Washington, DC, Peterson Institute for International Economics, 2016.

Fukuyama, F. *The End of History and the Last Man*. New York, Free Press, 2006.

Fukuyama, F. *Trust: The Social Virtues and the Creation of Prosperity*. New York, Free Press, 1995.

Gandhi, A. and Walton, M. 'Where Do India's Billionaires Get Their Wealth?' *Economic and Political Weekly*, 47(40), 2012.

Ghosh, J., Chandrasekhar, C. P. and Patnaik, P. *Demonetisation Decoded: A Critique of India's Currency Experiment*. Abingdon and New York, Routledge, 2017.

Ghosh, S. *Indian Democracy Derailed: Politics and Politicians*. New Delhi, APH, 1997.

Gill, S. S. *The Pathology of Corruption*. New Delhi, HarperCollins, 1999.

Giriprakash, K. *The Vijay Mallya Story*. New Delhi, Penguin, 2014.

Global Wealth Databook 2016, Credit Suisse, November 2016.

Global Wealth Report 2016, Credit Suisse, November 2016.

Gomez, E. T. *Political Business in East Asia*. London, Routledge, 2002.

Gowda, M. V. R. and Sharalaya, N. 'Crony Capitalism and India's Political System'. In N. Khatri and A. K. Ojha, eds, *Crony Capitalism in India: Establishing Robust Counteractive Institutional Frameworks*. Basingstoke, Palgrave Macmillan, 2016.

Guha, R. *A Corner of a Foreign Field: The Indian History of a British Sport*. London, Picador, 2003.

Guha, R. *India after Gandhi: The History of the World's Largest Democracy*, rev. ed. London, Pan Macmillan, 2011.

Guha Thakurta, P., Ghosh, S. and Chaudhuri, J. *Gas Wars: Crony Capitalism and the Ambanis*. New Delhi, Paranjoy Guha Thakurta, 2014.

Gupta, A. and Kumar, P. 'India Financial Sector: House of Debt'. Credit Suisse, 2 August 2012.

Gupta, A., Shah, K. and Kumar, P. 'India Financial Sector: House of Debt Revisited'. Credit Suisse, 13 August 2013.

Hamid, M. *How to Get Filthy Rich in Rising Asia*. London, Hamish Hamilton, 2013.

Hausmann, R., Pritchett, L. and Rodrik, D. 'Growth Accelerators'. *Journal of Economic Growth*, 10(4), 2005, pp. 303–29.

Hawkins, E. *Bookie Gambler Fixer Spy: A Journey to the Heart of Cricket's Underworld*. London, Bloomsbury, 2013.

Hofstadter, R. *The Age of Reform: From Bryan to FDR*. New York, Knopf, [1955] 2011.

Hoornweg, D. and Pope, K. 'Socioeconomic Pathways and Regional Distribution of the World's 101 Largest Cities'. Global Cities Institute Working Paper 04, January 2014.

Howe, I. *The American Newness: Culture and Politics in the Age of Emerson*. Cambridge, MA, Harvard University Press, 1986.

Human Rights Watch. ' "We Have No Orders to Save You": State Participation and Complicity in Communal Violence in Gujarat'. *Human Rights Watch*, 14(3(C)), 2002.

Huntington, S. P. 'Democracy's Third Wave'. *Journal of Democracy*, 2(2), 1991, pp. 12–34.

Huntington, S. P. *Political Order in Changing Societies*. New Haven, CT, Yale University Press, 1968.

Jacob, P. *Celluloid Deities: The Visual Culture of Cinema and Politics in South India*. Lanham, MD, Lexington, 2008.

Jaffrelot, C., *The Hindu Nationalist Movement and Indian Politics: 1925 to the 1990s: Strategies of Identity-building, Implantation and Mobilisation (with Special Reference to Central India)*. London, C. Hurst & Co., 1996.

Jaffrelot, C. 'The Modi-Centric BJP 2014 Election Campaign: New Techniques and Old Tactics'. *Contemporary South Asia*, 23(2), 2015, pp. 151–66.

Jain-Chandra, S., Kinda, T., Kochhar, K., Piao, S. and Schauer, J. 'Sharing the Growth Dividend: Analysis of Inequality in Asia'. International Monetary Fund Working Paper 16/48, March 2016.

Jayyusi, S. K., ed. *The Legacy of Muslim Spain*. Leiden: Brill, 1992.

Jeffery, R., Jeffrey, C. and Lerche, J. *Development Failure and Identity Politics in Uttar Pradesh*. New Delhi, Sage, 2014.

Joseph, J. *A Feast of Vultures: The Hidden Business of Democracy in India*. Noida, HarperCollins, 2016.

Joshi, V. *India's Long Road: The Search for Prosperity*. New Delhi, Haryana, 2016.

Kahneman, D. *Thinking, Fast and Slow*. New York, Farrar, Straus and Giroux, 2011.

Kang, J. W. 'Interrelation between Growth and Inequality'. ADB Economics Working Paper 447, August 2015.

Kaplan, R. D. *Monsoon: The Indian Ocean and the Future of American Power*. New York, Random House, 2010.

Kapur, D., Mehta, P. B. and Vaishnav, M., eds. *Rethinking Public Institutions in India*. New Delhi: Oxford University Press, 2017.

Kapur, D. and Vaishnav, M. 'Quid Pro Quo: Builders, Politicians, and Election Finance in India'. Center for Global Development Working Paper 276, December 2011

Khan, M. H. and Jomo, K. S. *Rents, Rent-Seeking and Economic Development: Theory and Evidence in Asia*. Cambridge, Cambridge University Press, 2000.

Khanna, J. and Johnston, M. 'India's Middlemen: Connecting by Corrupting?' *Crime, Law and Social Change*, 48(3–5), 2007.

Khatri, N. and Ohja, A. K. 'Indian Economic Philosophy and Crony Capitalism'. In N. Khatri and A. K. Ojha, eds, *Crony Capitalism in India: Establishing Robust Counteractive Institutional Frameworks*. Basingstoke, Palgrave Macmillan, 2016.

Khilnani, S. *The Idea of India*. New Delhi, Penguin, 1999.

Klitgaard, R. *Controlling Corruption*. Berkeley, University of California Press, 1988.

Kumar, A. *The Black Economy in India*, rev. ed. New Delhi, Penguin, 2002.

Kumar, A. 'Estimation of the Size of the Black Economy in India, 1996–2012'. *Economic and Political Weekly*, 51(48), 2016.

Kumar, A. *Understanding the Black Economy and Black Money in India: An Enquiry into Causes, Consequences and Remedies*. New Delhi, Aleph, 2017.

McDonald, H. *Mahabharata in Polyester: The Making of the World's Richest Brothers and Their Feud*. Sydney, University of New South Wales Press, 2010.

McKean, L. *Divine Enterprise: Gurus and the Hindu Nationalist Movement*. Chicago, University of Chicago Press, 1996.

Maddison, A. *The World Economy: A Millennial Perspective*. Paris, Organisation for Economic Co-operation and Development, 2001.

Maiya, H. *The King of Good Times*. Scotts Valley, CA, CreateSpace, 2011.

Marino, A. *Narendra Modi: A Political Biography*. Noida, HarperCollins, 2014.

Mehta, N. *Behind a Billion Screens: What Television Tells Us about Modern India*. Noida, HarperCollins, 2015.

Michelutti, L. and Heath, O. 'Political Cooperation and Distrust: Identity Politics and Yadav–Muslim Relations, 1999–2009'. In R. Jeffery, C. Jeffrey and J. Lerche, eds, *Development Failure and Identity Politics in Uttar Pradesh*. New Delhi, Sage, 2014.

Ministry of Finance, Government of India, *Economic Survey 2016/17*.

Misra, R. P. *Rediscovering Gandhi, vol. 1: Hind Swaraj – Gandhi's Challenge to Modern Civilization*. New Delhi, Concept, 2007.

Mukhopadhyay, N. *Narendra Modi : The Man, the Times*. Chennai, Tranquebar Press, 2013.

Myrdal, G. *Asian Drama: An Inquiry into the Poverty of Nations*. New York, Pantheon, 1968.

NDTV. *More News Is Good News: Untold Stories from 25 Years of Television News*. Noida, HarperCollins, 2016.

Nehru, J. *Toward Freedom*. New York, John Day, 1941.

Neider, C., ed. *Life As I Find It: A Treasury of Mark Twain Rarities*. New York, Cooper Square Press, 2000.

Ninan, T. N. 'Indian Media's Dickensian Age'. Center for the Advanced Study of India Working Paper 11-03, December 2011.

Ninan, T. N. *The Turn of the Tortoise: The Challenge and Promise of India's Future*. Gurgaon, Allen Lane, 2015.

Oldenburg, P. 'Middlemen in Third-World Corruption: Implications of an Indian Case'. *World Politics*, 39(4), 1987, pp. 508–35.

Painter, J., ed. *India's Media Boom: The Good News and the Bad*. Oxford, Reuters Institute for the Study of Journalism, University of Oxford, 2013.

Pal, M. 'Haryana: Caste and Patriarchy in Panchayats'. *Economic and Political Weekly*, 39(32), 2004, pp. 3581–3.

Palepu, K. and Khanna, T. *Winning in Emerging Markets: A Road Map for Strategy and Execution*. Boston, Harvard Business Press, 2010.

Panagariya, A. *India: The Emerging Giant*. New York, Oxford University Press, 2010.

Pei, M. *China's Crony Capitalism: The Dynamics of Regime Decay*. Cambridge, MA, Harvard University Press, 2016.

Phongpaichit, P. 'The Thai Economy in the Mid-1990s'. In D. Singh and L. T. Kiat, eds, *Southeast Asian Affairs 1996*. Singapore, ISEAS–Yusof Ishak Institute, 1997, pp. 369–81.

Piramal, G. *Business Maharajas*. New Delhi, Viking, 1996.

Price, L. *The Modi Effect: Inside Narendra Modi's Campaign to Transform India*. London, Hodder and Stoughton, 2015.

Pritchett, L. 'Is India a Flailing State? Detours on the Four Lane Highway to Modernization'. HKS Faculty Research Working Paper RWP09-013, John F. Kennedy School of Government, Harvard University, May 2009.

Przeworski, A. 'Capitalism, Development and Democracy'. *Brazilian Journal of Political Economy*, 24(4), 2004, pp. 487–99.

Quraishi, S. Y. *An Undocumented Wonder: The Great Indian Election*. New Delhi, Rainlight, 2014.

Raina, R. C. and Chaudhary, M. 'Television Broadcasting in India: Empirical Growth Analysis since 1959'. *IMS Manthan*, 6(2), 2011, pp. 167–81.

Rajakumar, J. D. and Henley, J. S. 'Growth and Persistence of Large Business Groups in India'. *Journal of Comparative International Management*, 10(1), 2007.

Rajan, R. *Fault Lines: How Hidden Fractures Still Threaten the World Economy*. Noida, CollinsBusiness, 2012.

Rajan, R. and Zingales, L. *Saving Capitalism from the Capitalists: Unleashing the Power of Financial Markets to Create Wealth and Spread Opportunity*. Princeton, NJ, Princeton University Press, 2004.

Rajan, R. G. and Zingales, L. 'Which Capitalism? Lessons from the East Asian Crisis'. *Journal of Applied Corporate Finance*, 11(3), 1998.

Ray, S. G. *Fixed! Cash and Corruption in Cricket*. Noida, HarperSport, 2016.

Rorty, R. *Essays on Heidegger and Others: Philosophical Papers*. Cambridge, Cambridge University Press, 1991.

Rorty, R. 'Unger, Castoriadis, and the Romance of a National Future'. In *Essays on Heidegger and Others: Philosophical Papers*. Cambridge, Cambridge University Press, 1991.

Rumford, C. and Wagg, S., eds. *Cricket and Globalization*. Newcastle upon Tyne, Cambridge Scholars, 2010.

Schumpeter, J. *Capitalism, Socialism and Democracy*, 3rd ed. London, George Allen and Unwin, 1950.

Sharma, R. *The Rise and Fall of Nations: Forces of Change in the Post-Crisis World*. New York, W. W. Norton, 2016.

Sridharan, E. 'India's Watershed Vote: Behind Modi's Victory'. *Journal of Democracy*, 25(4), 2014, pp. 20–33.

Srinivasan, T. N. and Tendulkar, S. *Reintegrating India with the World Economy*. Washington, DC, Institute for International Economics, 2003.

Stiles, T. J. *The First Tycoon: The Epic Life of Cornelius Vanderbilt*. New York, Alfred A. Knopf, 2009.

Studwell, J. *How Asia Works: Success and Failure in the World's Most Dynamic Region*. London, Profile, 2013.

Sukhtankar, S. and Vaishnav, M. 'Corruption in India: Bridging Research Evidence and Policy Options'. India Policy Forum, 11 July 2015, pp. 193–261.

Thakur, P. *Dr. Vijay Mallya's Kingfisher: The King of Good Times and Latest Turbulence*. Mumbai, Shree Book Centre, 2012.

Tharoor, S. *The Elephant, the Tiger, and the Cell Phone: Reflections on India in the Twenty-First Century*. New Delhi, Viking, 2007.

Twain, M. and Warner, C. D., *The Gilded Age: A Tale of To-Day*. Hartford, CT, American Publishing Company, 1873.

Varshney, A. *Ethnic Conflict and Civil Life: Hindus and Muslims in India*. New Haven, CT, Yale University Press, 2002.

Vaasanthi. *Amma: Jayalalithaa's Journey from Movie Star to Political Queen*. New Delhi, Juggernaut, 2016.

Vaishnav, M. *When Crime Pays: Money and Muscle in Indian Politics*. New Haven, CT, and London, Yale University Press, 2017.

Vanderbilt, A. T. II, *Fortune's Children: The Fall of the House of Vanderbilt*. New York, Morrow, 1989.

Varshney, A. 'India's Watershed Vote: Hindu Nationalism in Power?' *Journal of Democracy*, 25(4), 2014, pp. 34–45.

Varshney, A. and Sadiq, A. *Battles Half Won: India's Improbable Democracy*. London, Viking, 2013

Wade, R. 'The System of Administrative and Political Corruption: Canal Irrigation in South India'. *Journal of Development Studies*, 18(3), 1982, pp. 287–328.

Wit, J. de. *Urban Poverty, Local Governance and Everyday Politics in Mumbai*. New Delhi, Routledge, 2017.

Zubrzycki, J. *The Last Nizam: The Rise and Fall of India's Greatest Princely State*. Sydney, Picador, 2006.

NOTES

PROLOGUE

1. Vinay Dalvi, 'Aston Martin in Rs 4.5 Cr Pile-up on Mumbai's Pedder Road', *Mid-day*, 9 December 2013.

2. Gayatri Jayaraman, 'Nobody crashed the Aston Martin', *India Today*, 19 December 2013.

3. Mustafa Shaikh, 'Car Was Not Driven by Chauffeur: Witness', *Mumbai Mirror*, 10 December 2013.

4. Somendra Sharma, 'Speeding Aston Martin hits Audi and Elantra; driver abandons car, flees', DNA, 9 December 2013.

5. Robin Pagnamenta, 'Bombay Mix: warning lights flash at model village', *The Times*, 20 January 2014.

6. 'Aston Martin case: Complainant identifies Reliance firm driver', Press Trust of India, 25 December 2013.

7. 'ID surprise in Reliance hit-and-run', *The Telegraph*, 26 December 2013.

8. Mustafa Shaikh, 'Car Was Not Driven by Chauffeur: Witness'.

9. Somendra Sharma, 'Young driver was whisked away by escorts', DNA, 9 December 2013.

10. 'Aston Martin Crash: RIL Worker Identified as Driver', *Hindustan Times*, 26 December 2013.

11. 'Aston Martin hit and run: driver nailed', *The Free Press Journal*, 26 December 2013.

12. Arunabh Saikia, 'The Car Crash That Never Was', News Laundry, 12 December 2013.

13. Naazneen Karmali, 'The Curious Incident of Mukesh Ambani's Aston Martin in the Night-Time', *Forbes*, 2 January 2014.

14. 'Mumbai Police Chases Whodunnit in Aston Martin Car Crash', *Business Standard India*, 13 December 2013.

15. 'Driver owns up to Peddar Road car crash', *Times of India*, 11 December 2013.

16. https://twitter.com/omarabdullah/status/410979217711452160

INTRODUCTION

1. 'Special Feature: Residence Antilia', *Sterling*, July 2010.

2. 'In Pictures: Inside The World's First Billion-Dollar Home', *Forbes*, 30 April 2008.

3. Cathal Kelly, 'Billion-dollar home has parking for 168', *The Star*, 14 October 2010.

4. Rajini Vaidyanathan, 'Ambanis Give First View inside "World's Priciest House" in Mumbai', BBC News, 18 May 2012.

5. Naazneen Karmali, 'India's 100 Richest 2017: Modi's Economic Experiments Barely Affect Country's Billionaires', *Forbes*, 4 October 2017.

6. Gandhi and Walton, 'Where Do India's Billionaires Get Their Wealth?'

7. Naazneen Karmali, 'For the First Time, India's 100 Richest of 2014 Are All Billionaires', *Forbes*, 24 September 2014.

8. Karmali, 'India's 100 Richest 2017'.

9. *Global Wealth Report 2016*.

10. Gandhi and Walton, 'Where Do India's Billionaires Get Their Wealth?'

11. Maddison, *The World Economy*.

12. Ibid.

13. Joshi, *India's Long Road*, p. 37.

14. Ministry of Finance, Government of India, *Economic Survey 2016/17*, p. 41.

15. In July 2017, data from the Bombay Stock Exchange BSE500 index showed that foreign institutional investors own forty-two per cent of shares which are freely traded, meaning shares which are not owned by the promoters/owners of the companies. Foreign investors own twenty-one per cent of all shares, if those of the promoters/owners are included.

16. 'Press Release: Remittances to Developing Countries Decline for Second Consecutive Year', World Bank, 21 April 2017. India's sent home $62.7 billion in 2016.

17. 'What the World Thinks about Globalisation', *The Economist*, 18 November 2016.

18. Dasgupta, *Capital*, p. 44.

19. Drèze and Sen, *An Uncertain Glory*, p. ix.

20. Raghuram Rajan, 'Is There a Threat of Oligarchy in India', University of Chicago, 10 September 2008.

21. *Global Wealth Report 2016*.

22. Chancel, L. and Piketty, T., 'Indian Income Inequality, 1922–2014'; *Global Wealth Databook 2016*, p. 148.

23. S. Sukhtankar and M. Vaishnav, 'Corruption in India: Bridging Research Evidence and Policy Options', India Policy Forum, 11 July 2015, p. 3.

24. CMS Transparency, 'Lure of Money in Lieu of Votes in Lok Sabha and Assembly Elections', p. 7.

25. Rajesh Kumar Singh and Devidutta Tripathy, 'India Moves Resolution of $150 Billion Bad Debt Problem into RBI's Court', Reuters, 6 May 2017.

26. Hofstadter, *The Age of Reform*, p. 11.

27. T. N. Ninan, 'India's Gilded Age', *Seminar*, January 2013.

28. Twain and Warner, *The Gilded Age*.

29. Francis Fukuyama, 'What Is Corruption?', Research Institute for Development, Growth and Economics, 2016.

30. Jayant Sinha and Ashutosh Varshney, 'It Is Time for India to Rein in Its Robber Barons', *Financial Times*, 7 January 2011.

31. Data compiled by Gapminder.org, which takes India's 2013 GDP per capita data from a cross-country comparison based on 2005 dollars. The comparison was quoted in Dylan Matthews and Kavya Sukumar, 'India Is as Rich as the US in 1881: A Mesmerizing Graphic Shows Where Every Country Falls', *Vox*, 8 October 2015.

32. Tom Mitchell, 'India May Be More Populous than China, Research Suggests', *Financial Times*, 25 May 2017.

33. Hoornweg and Pope, 'Socioeconomic Pathways and Regional Distribution of the World's 101 Largest Cities'.

34. 'India: Data', World Bank, 2016. India's GDP was $2.3 trillion in 2016. The UK's was $2.6 trillion.

35. 'The World in 2050: Will the Shift in Global Economic Power Continue?', PricewaterhouseCoopers, February 2015.

36. Rorty, 'Unger, Castoriadis, and the Romance of a National Future', p. 34.

37. Ibid.

38. Fitzgerald, *The Great Gatsby*, p. 136.

CHAPTER 1: THE RICHEST MAN IN INDIA

1. Rajarshi Roy, 'An Ambani Changes His Family Address', *Times of India*, 16 May 2002.

2. Sarah Rich, 'Perkins + Will's Antilla [sic] "Green" Tower in Mumbai', *Inhabitat*, 25 October 2007.

3. Rob Wile, 'Meet Mukesh Ambani, the Billionaire Owner of the World's Most Expensive Home', *Time*, 27 October 2017.

4. The exact cost of Antilia's construction has never been disclosed. Estimates vary wildly. The $1 billion figure is commonly cited, for instance in Alan Farnham and Matt Woolsey, 'No Housing Shortage Here: Antilia Is the World's Most Expensive House', *Forbes Asia*, 19 May 2008. A 2008 *New York Times* report cited a Reliance spokesman saying the building would cost '$50 million to $70 million' to build.

5. Prabhu Chawla, 'Reliance feud gets murkier by the day, Ambani brothers prepare for possible settlement', *India Today*, 27 December 2004.

6. Joe Leahy, 'Brothers in the News: Anil and Mukesh Ambani', *Financial Times*, 24 October 2009.

7. Piramal, *Business Maharajas*, p. 19.

8. 'Dhirubhai Ambani and Indian Capitalism', *The Financial Express*, 4 July 2003.

9. Paranjoy Guha Thakurta, 'How To Buy Peace, Win Friends And Influence People – Ambani Style', *Outlook*, 30 April 2001.

10. McDonald, *Mahabharata in Polyester*, p. 49.

11. McDonald, *Mahabharata in Polyester*, p. 5.

12. Nasrin Sultana and Kalpana Pathak, 'The Grand Spectacle that is the RIL Annual General Meeting', *Livemint*, 22 July 2017.

13. 'Shourie's 180-Degree Turn with Dhirubhai', *Financial Express*, 7 July 2003.

14. McDonald, *Mahabharata in Polyester*, p. 342.

15. Naazneen Karmali, 'India's 40 Richest', *Forbes*, 15 December 2005.

16. Luisa Kroll, ed., 'The World's Billionaires', *Forbes*, 5 March 2008.

17. Ibid.

18. Diksha Sahni, 'Mukesh Ambani's Luxury Home under Scanner', *Wall Street Journal*, 3 August 2011.

19. Sudhir Suryawanshi, 'This Is No Light Bill', *Mumbai Mirror*, 24 November 2010.

20. Vikas Bajaj, 'Mukesh Ambani's 27-Story House Is Not His Home', *New York Times*, 18 October 2011.

21. James Reginato, 'The Talk of Mumbai', *Vanity Fair*, June 2012.

22. Abbas Hamdani, 'An Islamic Background to the Voyages of Discovery', *The Legacy of Muslim Spain*, vol. 1, p. 274 (Jayyusi ed.).

23. Damian Whitworth, 'Ratan Tata: The Mumbai Tycoon Collecting British Brands', *The Times*, 21 May 2011.

24. James Crabtree, 'Slumdog Billionaires: The Rise of India's Tycoons', *New Statesman*, 5 June 2014.

25. Pei, *China's Crony Capitalism*, pp. 7–8.

26. James Crabtree, 'India's New Politics', *Financial Times*, 25 April 2014.

27. Misra, *Rediscovering Gandhi, vol. 1*, p. 61.

28. James Crabtree, 'Mumbai's Towering Ambitions Brought Low by Legal Disputes', *Financial Times*, 10 October 2014.

29. Stiles, *The First Tycoon*, p. 23.

30. Steve Fraser, 'The Misunderstood Robber Baron: On Cornelius Vanderbilt', *The Nation*, 11 November 2009.

31. Michelle Young, 'A Guide to the Gilded Age Mansions of 5th Avenue's Millionaire Row', *6sqft*, 30 July 2014.

32. Vanderbilt, *Fortune's Children*, ch. 3.

33. Neider, ed., *Life As I Find It*, p. 42.

34. Raghuram Rajan, 'Finance and Opportunity in India', Reserve Bank of India, 11 August 2014.

35. Crabtree, 'India's New Politics'.

36. Amy Kazmin and James Crabtree, 'Ambani Gets Highest-Level Security Cover', *Financial Times*, 22 April 2013.

37. 'Hyper Growth Platforms of Value Creation', chairman's statement, forty-first annual general meeting, Reliance Industries Limited, 12 June 2015.

38. Hemangi Balse, 'The "third man" in the Reliance empire', Rediff, 30 December 2002.

39. 'Faces behind RJio development: Ambani twins lead a trusted team', *Hindu Business Line*, 1 September 2016.

40. 'Four Decades of Serving India', chairman's statement, fortieth annual general meeting post IPO, Reliance Industries Limited, 21 July 2017.

41. James Crabtree, 'The Corporate Theatrics in India of Reliance's Reclusive Tycoon', *Financial Times*, 15 June 2015.

42. 'Jio Not a Punt, Well Thought-Out Decision, Says Mukesh Ambani: Full Transcript', NDTV, 21 October 2016.

43. 'Operationalising Hyper Growth Platforms of New Value Creation for a Prosperous and Inclusive India', chairman's statement, 39th annual general meeting post IPO, Reliance Industries Limited, 1 September 2016.

44. 'Scrap Reliance Jio's spectrum licence: CAG', Press Trust of India, 30 June 2014.

45. 'Auction Rigged, Cancel Broadband Spectrum Held by Reliance Jio, CAG Report Says', *Times of India*, 30 June 2014.

46. 'The Spectrum Auction Was Rigged', *Frontline*, 30 September 2016.

47. 'Union Compliance Communication', Report No. 20, Comptroller and Auditor General of India, 2015, ch. 3.

48. *Gas Wars: Crony Capitalism and the Ambanis*, Ch 1.

49. See, for instance, 'Report of the Comptroller and Auditor General of

India for the year ended March 2015', Comptroller and Auditor General of India, 2016, ch. 14, p. 103.

50. Anand Giridharadas, 'Indian to the Core, and an Oligarch', *New York Times*, 15 June 2008.

51. 'Anil Ambani Sues Mukesh for Rs 10,000 Crore', *Livemint*, 25 September 2008.

52. Swaminathan Aiyar, 'India no more dominated by a handful of business oligarchs', *The Economic Times*, 5 June 2011.

53. 'Deep controversy', *The Economist*, 24 March 2014.

54. 'An Unloved Billionaire', *The Economist*, 2 August 2014.

55. Joseph Schumpeter, *Capitalism, Socialism and Democracy*, p. 82.

56. 'India May Be Challenging Today, but the India of Tomorrow Will Be Fulfilling: Mukesh Ambani', *Financial Express*, 18 March 2017.

57. '12 years after Ambani brothers split, Mukesh to Anil's rescue,' *Hindu Business Line*, 28 December 2017.

CHAPTER 2: THE GOOD TIMES BEGIN

1. Danny Fortson and Oliver Shah, 'Qatari Royals Splash £120m on London Terrace', *Sunday Times*, 28 April 2013.

2. 'Fugitive Vijay Mallya's Extradition Hearing Scheduled for Today in London', *Times of India*, 13 June 2017.

3. Rupert Neate, 'Force India F1 Team Boss Vijay Mallya Arrested in London', *The Guardian*, 18 April 2017; 'Indian tycoon Mallya's yacht impounded in Malta over wage dispute,' Reuters, 7 March 2018.

4. Dilip Bobb, 'The King's Ransom', *Financial Express*, 28 October 2012.

5. Madhurima Nandy and Sharan Poovanna, 'Vijay Mallya's $20 Million "Sky Mansion" in Bengaluru Is Almost Ready. But Will He Get to Live in It?', *Livemint*, 20 March 2017.

6. Aliya Ram, 'India Charges Ex-Kingfisher Chief Vijay Mallya', *Financial Times*, 25 January 2017.

7. Amy Kazmin and Helen Warrell, 'Vijay Mallya Arrested by UK Police', *Financial Times*, 18 April 2017.

8. Suzi Ring, 'Vijay Mallya Says "Keep Dreaming" about "Billions of Pounds",' *Livemint*, 14 June 2017.

9. Amy Kazmin and Naomi Rovnick, 'Vijay Mallya Re-Arrested in Money Laundering Case', *Financial Times*, 3 October 2017.

10. 'Big Bash for Beer Baron', *Hindustan Times*, 27 December 2005.

11. James Boxell, 'Kingfisher Order Gives Welcome Lift to Airbus', *Financial Times*, 16 June 2005.

12. Naazneen Karmali, 'Vijay Mallya Drops out of Billionaire Ranks', *Forbes*, 25 October 2012.

13. Simon Briggs, 'Vijay Mallya in Race to Become an F1 Force', *The Telegraph*, 8 February 2008.

14. Tom Dalldorf, 'Mendocino Brewing's Owner in Financial Quagmire: Billionaire Vijay Mallya under Siege', *Celebrator*, August 2016.

15. Mihir Dalal and P. R. Sanjai, 'How Vijay Mallya Inherited an Empire and Proceeded to Lose It', *Livemint*, 27 February 2016.

16. Maiya, *The King of Good Times*, Introduction.

17. Shekhar Gupta, 'Vijay Mallya Story Is More about Our Easy Embrace of Cronyism', *Business Standard*, 11 March 2016.

18. Heather Timmons, 'Indian Tycoon Spreads His Wings in Aviation', *New York Times*, 21 June 2007.

19. 'Vijay Mallya: The Spirit Shall Prevail', *Times of India*, 22 April 2002.

20. 'Conflict of Interest? Baron on House Panel on Businessman', *Times of India*, 11 March 2016.

21. Dev Kapur, Milan Vaishnav and Neelanjan Sircar, 'The Importance of Being Middle Class in India', Milan Vaishnav Files, 2011, p. 4.

22. Charlie Sorrel, 'World's Lowest Tech Flight Sim in India', *Wired*, 10 October 2007.

23. Tom Peters, 'Sir, May I Clean Your Glasses?', tompeters! blog, October 2009.

24. 'India without Gandhi', *The Economist*, 1948.

25. Nehru, *Toward Freedom*, p. 274.

26. William Dalrymple, 'The Bloody Legacy of Indian Partition', *New Yorker*, 29 June 2015.

27. Baisya, *Winning Strategies for Business*, p. 88.

28. Raghu Karnad, 'City in a Bottle', *The Caravan*, 1 July 2012.

29. Srinivasan and Tendulkar, *Reintegrating India with the World Economy*, p. 16.

30. James Crabtree, 'Game of Thrones with World Chess Champion Vishwanathan Anand', *Financial Times*, 1 November 2013.

31. C. Rangarajan, '1991's Golden Transaction', *Indian Express*, 28 March 2016.

32. 'Secret Sale of Gold by RBI Again', *Indian Express*, 8 July 1991.

33. 'July 1991: The Month that Changed India', *Livemint*, 1 July 2016.

34. Saurabh Sinhal, 'Vijay Mallya Flew Jet First Class to London with 7 Heavy Bags', *Times of India*, 11 March 2016.

35. 'Go Kingfisher', *Siliconeer*, April 2006.

36. Peter Marsh, 'Arcelor and Mittal Agree to €27bn Merger', *Financial Times*, 26 June 2006.

37. Joshi, *India's Long Road*.

38. Scheherazade Daneshkhu, 'Diageo Sues Vijay Mallya over United Spirits Agreement', *Financial Times*, 17 November 2017.

39. Sankalp Phartiyal, 'SEBI Bars Liquor Tycoon Vijay Mallya from Capital Markets', Reuters, 26 January 2017.

40. Ashok Malik, 'The Art of Flying on Froth', *Tehelka*, 30 October 2012.

CHAPTER 3: RISE OF THE BOLLYGARCHS

1. Jim Yardley and Vikas Bajaj, 'Billionaires' Rise Aids India, and Vice Versa', *New York Times*, 26 July 2011.

2. Gowda and Sharalaya, 'Crony Capitalism and India's Political System', p. 140.

3. James Crabtree, 'Gautam Adani, Founder, Adani Group', *Financial Times*, 16 June 2013.

4. Naazneen Karmali, 'For the First Time, India's 100 Richest of 2014 Are All Billionaires', *Forbes*, 24 September 2014.

5. Vinod K. Jose, 'The Emperor Uncrowned', *The Caravan*, 1 March 2012.

6. Piyush Mishra and Himanshu Kaushik, 'Fleet of 3 Aircraft Ensures Modi Is Home Every Night after Day's Campaigning', *Times of India*, 22 April 2014.

7. 'Adani Ports & SEZ Get Environmental, CRZ Nod for Mundra SEZ', Adani media release, 16 July 2014.

8. Rohini Singh, 'Rahul Gandhi's Office Had Requested Jayanthi Natarajan's Ministry to Look into Adani Port and SEZ', *Economic Times*, 24 July 2014.

9. 'Achievements of Ministry of Shipping', National Informatics Centre, Government of India, p. 12, 2016.

10. 'Ancient Stone Anchor May Offer Clues to Indo-Arabian Maritime Trade', *The National*, 23 May 2012.

11. Das, 'India: How a Rich Nation Became Poor and Will Be Rich Again'.

12. Dhingra, *Life behind the Lobby*.

13. Kerry A. Dolan, 'Forbes 2017 Billionaires List: Meet the Richest People on the Planet', *Forbes*, 20 March 2017.

14. Luisa Kroll, 'The World's Billionaires', *Forbes*, 3 October 2010.

15. 'India's 100 Richest Are All Billionaires; Mukesh Ambani Tops List', *Indian Express*, 25 September 2014.

16. Jayant Sinha, 'Share Your Billions with Our Billion', *Outlook Business*, 1 November 2008.

17. Ibid.

18. Bremmer, *The Fat Tail*, p. 196.

19. Rajakumar and Henley, 'Growth and Persistence of Large Business Groups in India'.

20. Thomas L. Friedman, 'It's a Flat World, After All', *New York Times*, 3 April 2005.

21. Richard Waters, 'Business Pioneers in Technology', *Financial Times*, 31 March 2015.

22. *Foreign Affairs*, July–August 2006.

23. James Crabtree, 'India's Billionaires Club', *Financial Times*, 16 November 2012.

24. Raghuram Rajan, 'Is There a Threat of Oligarchy in India?', 10 September 2008.

25. Raghuram Rajan, 'What Happened to India?', Project Syndicate, 8 June 2012.

26. Gandhi and Walton, 'Where Do India's Billionaires Get Their Wealth?'

27. Michael Walton, 'An Indian Gilded Age? Continuity and Change in the Political Economy of India's Development' (unpublished working paper, January 2017).

28. Sharma, *The Rise and Fall of Nations*, ch. 3.

29. Ruchir Sharma, 'Billionaires Can Be Both Good and Bad. Ruchi Sharma Shows How To Tell Apart', Scroll.in, 14 June 2016.

30. Khatri and Ohja, 'Indian Economic Philosophy and Crony Capitalism', p. 63.

31. Alvaredo et al., 'The Top 1 Percent in International and Historical Perspective'.

32. Freund, *Rich People Poor Countries*, p. 3.

33. *Global Wealth Report 2016*.

34. Ibid.

35. Freund, *Rich People Poor Countries*, p. 4.

36. Ibid.

37. 'The Retreat of the Global Company', *The Economist*, 28 January 2017.

38. Jagdish Bhagwati, 'This Is How Economic Reforms Have Transformed India', Hiren Mukerjee Memorial Annual Parliamentary Lecture, 3 December 2010.

39. Bhagwati and Panagariya, *Why Growth Matters*, pp. 44–55.

40. Jagdish Bhagwati, 'Scaling Up the Gujarat Model', *The Hindu*, 20 September 2014.

41. Drèze and Sen, *An Uncertain Glory*, ch. 1.

42. Amartya Sen, 'Quality of Life: India vs. China', *New York Review of Books*, 12 May 2011.

43. Branko Milanovic, 'The Question of India's Inequality', globalinequality blog, 7 May 2016.

44. Nisha Agrawal, 'Inequality in India: What's the Real Story?', World Economic Forum, 4 October 2016.

45. Jain-Chandra et al., 'Sharing the Growth Dividend'.

46. *Global Wealth Report 2016.*

47. Chakravarty and Dehejia, 'India's Income Divergence'.

48. The ADB paper concluded: 'Had inequality not increased, India's poverty headcount would have been reduced from 32.7% to 29.5% in 2008.' Kang, 'Interrelation between Growth and Inequality'.

49. Era Dabla-Norris, Kalpana Kochhar, Nujin Suphaphiphat, Frantisek Ricka and Evridiki Tsounta, 'Causes and Consequences of Income Inequality: A Global Perspective', International Monetary Fund, 15 June 2015.

50. James Crabtree, 'Gautam Adani, Founder, Adani Group', *Financial Times*, 16 June 2013.

51. 'Gautam Adani Kidnapping Case: Underworld Don Fazl-Ur-Rehman Produced in Ahmedabad Court', DNA, 11 August 2014.

52. Deepali Gupta, 'Why India Inc's on the Dance Floor', *Economic Times*, 14 February 2013.

53. Megha Bahree, 'Doing Big Business in Modi's Gujarat', *Forbes*, 12 March 2014.

54. Tony Munroe, 'Billionaire Adani Prospers as Modi Stresses Development', Reuters, 10 April 2014.

55. Shares in Adani Enterprises rose 137 per cent in the year to 16 May 2014, the date of the announcement of Modi's election victory, according to Google Finance.

56. Manas Dasgupta, 'CAG Slams Modi Regime for Financial Irregularities', *The Hindu*, 31 March 2012.

57. P. R. Sanjai, Neha Sethi and Maulik Pathak, 'Adani's Mundra SEZ Gets Environment Clearance', *Livemint*, 16 July 2014.

58. Paranjoy Guha Thakurta, Advait Rao Palepu, Shinzani Jain and Abir Dasgupta, 'Modi Government's Rs 500-Crore Bonanza to the Adani Group', *The Wire*, 19 June 2017.

59. Paranjoy Guha Thakurta, Advait Rao Palepu and Shinzani Jain, 'Did the Adani Group Evade Rs 1,000 Crore in Taxes?', *The Wire*, 14 January 2017.

60. Amrit Dhillon, 'More than 100 Scholars Back Journalist in Adani "Crony Capitalism" Row', *Sydney Morning Herald*, 25 July 2017.

CHAPTER 4: INDIA MODIFIED

1. Milan Vaishnav, 'Understanding the Indian Voter', Carnegie Endowment for International Peace, June 2015.

2. Ullekh NP and Vasudha Venugopal, 'Gujarat Promises Continued, Accelerated and All-Around Progress: Jagdish Bhagwati & Arvind Panagariya', *Economic Times*, 20 June 2013.

3. Vaishnav, 'Understanding the Indian Voter'.

4. K. V. Prasad, 'TsuNaMo Gives BJP Decisive Mandate to Govern', *The Tribune*, 16 May 2014.

5. Pratap Bhanu Mehta, 'Modi's Moment Alone', *Indian Express*, 17 May 2014.

6. Sumegha Gulati, 'In Modi's Vadnagar, ASI Searches for Hiuen Tsang's Lost Monasteries', *Indian Express*, 14 March 2015.

7. 'Selected Indicators 1950–51 to 1999–2000', National Informatics Centre, Government of India.

8. Mukhopadhyay, *Narendra Modi*, p. 196.

9. Prashant Dayal and Radha Sharmal, 'A Loner, Even at the Top', *Times of India*, 31 December 2007.

10. 'Hindus to the Fore', *The Economist*, 21 May 2015.

11. Jaffrelot, *The Hindu Nationalist Movement and Indian Politics*, p. 38.

12. Ibid, p. 100.

13. 'Religion Data: Population of Hindu / Muslim / Sikh / Christian – Census 2011 India', National Census Survey, Census Organisation of India, 2011.

14. Guha, *India after Gandhi*, p. 98.

15. 'The Man Who Thought Gandhi a Sissy', *The Economist*, 17 December 2014.

16. Annie Gowen, 'Abandoned as a Child Bride, Wife of India's Modi Waits for Husband's Call', *Washington Post*, 25 January 2015.

17. Mukhopadhyay, *Narendra Modi*, p. 243.

18. Marino, *Narendra Modi*, p. 26.

19. Ellen Barry, 'Indian Candidate's Biography Has an Asterisk: A Wife, of Sorts', *New York Times*, 10 April 2014.

20. Mukhopadhyay, *Narendra Modi*.

21. 'In Pictures: Narendra Modi's Early Life', BBC, 26 May 2014.

22. Mukhopadhyay, *Narendra Modi*, Ch 3.

23. Kanchan Gupta, 'How Ram Mandir movement shaped Indian politics', *India Today*, 25 December 2017.

24. Ashis Nandy, 'Obituary of a Culture', *Seminar*, May 2002.

25. Jo Johnson, 'Radical Thinking', *Financial Times*, 31 March 2007.

26. 'Report by the Commission of Inquiry Consisting of Mr Justice G. T. Nanavati and Mr Justice Akshay H. Mehta', Home Department, Government of Gujarat, 18 September 2008.

27. Siddhartha Deb, 'Unmasking Modi', *New Republic*, 3 May 2016.

28. 'Gujarat Riot Death Toll Revealed', BBC News, 11 May 2005.

29. Ashutosh Varshney, 'Understanding Gujarat Violence', Social Science Research Council, 2002.

30. Human Rights Watch, '"We Have No Orders to Save You"', April 2002.

31. 'Sanjiv Bhatt: Gujarat Police Officer Critical of PM Modi Sacked', BBC News, 20 August 2015.

32. Martha C. Nussbaum, 'Genocide in Gujarat', *Dissent Magazine*, September 2003.

33. Shashank Bengali and Paul Ritcher, 'US Eager to Forget about New India Premier's 2005 Visa Denial', *Los Angeles Times*, 25 September 2014.

34. Vinod K. Jose, 'The Emperor Uncrowned: The Rise of Narendra Modi', *The Caravan*, 1 March 2012.

35. Heather Timmons and Arshiya Khullar, 'Is Narendra Modi's Gujarat Miracle a Myth?', *The Atlantic*, 7 April 2014.

36. Zahir Janmohamed, 'The Rise of Narendra Modi', *Boston Review*, 28 June 2013.

37. Ashutosh Varshney, 'Modi the Moderate', *Indian Express*, 27 March 2014.

38. Sanjeev Miglani, 'Modi Says Shaken to Core by Gujarat's Religious Riots', Reuters, 28 December 2013.

39. Sruthi Gottipati and Annie Banerji, 'Modi's "Puppy" Remark Triggers New Controversy over 2002 Riots', Reuters, 12 July 2013.

40. Jaffrelot, 'The Modi-Centric BJP 2014 Election Campaign', p. 151.

41. 'Watch Modi's Fiery Attack on Rahul, Sonia in Amethi Live on India TV', IndiaTV/YouTube, 5 May 2014 (https://youtu.be/4ic5To2586s) (accessed 18 December 2017).

42. Ian Buruma, 'India: The Perils of Democracy', *New York Review of Books*, 4 December 1997.

43. Fukuyama, *The End of History and the Last Man*, p. 13.

44. Robert D. Kaplan, 'India's New Face', *The Atlantic*, April 2009.

45. Rohit Trivedi, 'Narendra Modi: Secularism for Me Is India First! We Will Understand Its True Meaning Then Votebank Politics Ends!', www.narendramodi.in, 31 August 2012.

46. James Crabtree, 'Pockets of Wariness amid the Delirium in New Leader's Home State', *Financial Times*, 17 May 2014.

47. '#PMSpeaksToArnab: Read Full Text Here', Times Now, 27 June 2016.

CHAPTER 5: THE SEASON OF SCAMS

1. Douglas Busvine and Rupam Jain, 'Who Knew? Modi's Black Money Move Kept a Closely Guarded Secret', Reuters, 9 December 2016.

2. Suchetana Ray, 'Govt Didn't Have Enough Time to Prepare for Demonetisation: Piyush Goyal', *Hindustan Times*, 3 December 2016.

3. Busvine and Jain, 'Who Knew?'

4. 'PM Modi: "Corruption, Black Money & Terrorism Are Festering Sores"', *The Hindu*, 9 November 2016.

5. 'India's Bonfire of the Bank Notes', *The Briefing Room*, BBC Radio 4, 26 January 2017.

6. 'Union Budget 2017: Full Speech of Finance Minister Arun Jaitley', *Times of India*, 1 February 2017.

7. 'PM Modi: "Corruption, Black Money & Terrorism Are Festering Sores".

8. Rory Medcalf, 'India Poll 2013', Lowy Institute, 20 May 2013.

9. *Corruption Perceptions Index 2016*, Transparency International, 25 January 2017.

10. Coralie Pring, 'People and Corruption: Asia Pacific – Global Corruption Barometer', Transparency International, 2017.

11. 'Deloitte Forensic Protecting Your Business in the Insurance Sector', Deloitte, 2014.

12. 'Rahul Gandhi Tears into Modi's "Suit-Boot Ki Sarkar"', *Times of India*, 21 April 2015.

13. Panagariya, *India*, p. 336.

14. Swaminathan S. Anklesaria Aiyar, 'Paying Record Taxes Is Bliss', Swaminomics, 10 February 2008.

15. Kumar, 'Estimation of the Size of the Black Economy in India, 1996–2012'.

16. 'Narendra Modi in Goa Full Text: Once We Get Clean, We Need Not Worry about Even One Corrupt Mosquito', *Firstpost*, 11 August 2017.

17. 'Teary Eyed Narendra Modi Takes on Rivals, Reaches Out to People on Demonetisation', *Financial Express*, 14 November 2016.

18. James Crabtree, 'Modi Plunders India's Cash. Indians Cheer', *Foreign Policy*, 28 November 2016.

19. William Dalrymple, 'The East India Company: The Original Corporate Raiders', *The Guardian*, 4 March 2015.

20. Gill, *The Pathology of Corruption*, p. 44.

21. Oldenburg, 'Middlemen in Third-World Corruption'.

22. Bhagwati and Panagariya, *Why Growth Matters*, p. 87.

23. Pei, *China's Crony Capitalism*, p. 8.

24. Vaishnav, *When Crime Pays*, p. 31.

25. James Crabtree, 'India: Lost Connections', *Financial Times*, 2 September 2012.

26. Ninan, *The Turn of the Tortoise*, p. 128.

27. 'Report No. 19 of 2010: Performance Audit of Issue of Licences and Allocation of 2G Spectrum of Union Government, Ministry of Communications and Information Technology', Comptroller and Auditor General (CAG), 16 November 2010.

28. Anurag Kotoky, 'Raja, Other Executives Go on Trial; Court Defers Hearing', Reuters, 13 April 2011.

29. Sukhantar and Vaishnav, 'Corruption in India'.

30. Klitgaard, *Controlling Corruption*, p. 75.

31. 'Report No. 7 of 2012–13: Performance Audit of Allocation of Coal Blocks and Augmentation of Coal Production, Ministry of Coal', Comptroller and Auditor General (CAG), 17 August 2012.

32. The CAG produced a draft report in March 2012 estimating the loss at Rs 10.7 trillion (US$167 billion). The final report published in August 2012 lowered that figure to Rs 1.9 trillion (US$29.7 billion). See 'Report No. 7 of 2012–13: Performance Audit of Allocation of Coal Blocks and Augmentation of Coal Production, Ministry of Coal', Comptroller and Auditor General, 17 August 2012.

33. 'Not 1, but 100 Toilet Rolls Bought for Rs 4,000 Each', *Times of India*, 5 August 2010.

34. 'Indian Court Acquits All Accused in 2G Telecoms Case', Reuters, 21 December 2017.

35. James Crabtree, 'India's Supreme Court Declares More than 200 Coal Mining Licences Illegal', *Financial Times*, 25 August 2014.

36. 'Coalgate Brushes Dirtier', *The Economist*, 1 September 2012.

37. Adiga, *The White Tiger*, p. 113.

38. Sunil Khilnani, 'The Spectacle of Corruption', *Livemint*, 16 December 2010.

39. Jyoti and Johnston, 'India's Middlemen: Connecting by Corrupting?'

40. James Crabtree, 'India's Red Tape Causes Trouble for Exporting Cats', *Financial Times*, 21 March 2016.

41. Tadit Kundu, 'Nearly Half of Indians Survived on Less than Rs 38 a Day in 2011–12', *Livemint*, 21 April 2016.

42. James Crabtree, 'Spark of Inspiration', *Financial Times*, 26 July 2016.

43. Bertrand et al., 'Obtaining a Driver's License in India'.

44. Bribe Fighter, 'Driving License without a Driving Test!!', I Paid a Bribe', 14 November 2012.

45. 'Foreign Direct Investment Inflows: A Success Story', Press Information Bureau, Ministry of Commerce & Industry, 19 May 2017. Indian FDI inflows totalled $60.1 billion in the financial year ending 31 March 2017.

46. 'Who to Punish', *The Economist*, 5 May 2011.

47. James Crabtree, 'India Casts Around for More Outrage', *Financial Times*, 29 January 2013.

48. Boo, *Behind the Beautiful Forevers*, p. 28.

49. Huntington, *Political Order in Changing Societies*, p. 69.

50. Khan and Jomo, *Rents, Rent-Seeking and Economic Development*.

51. Studwell, *How Asia Works*, p. 107.

52. 'Doing Business in India', World Bank Group, 2017.

53. Avih Rastogi, 'Inspector Raj for Garment Export Business', Centre for Civil Society, 2002.

54. Aiyar, *Accidental India*, p. 16.

55. Amy Kazmin, 'Drinks Industry: India's Battle with the Bottle', *Financial Times*, 9 October 2016.

56. Shyamal Majumdar, 'Registers and Corruption: Why the "Inspector Raj" Needs to Go!', *Business Standard*, 24 October 2014.

57. Pritchett, 'Is India a Flailing State?'.

58. Debroy and Bhandari, *Corruption in India*, p. 120.

59. Salvatore Schiavo-Campo, Giulio de Tommaso and Amitabha Mukherjee, 'Government Employment and Pay in Global Perspective: A Selective Synthesis of International Facts, Policies And Experience', World Bank, 1997.

60. 'Mandarin Lessons', *The Economist*, 10 March 2016.

61. Victor Mallet, 'Indian Job Ad Receives 2.3m Applicants', *Financial Times*, 19 September 2015.

62. Wade, 'The System of Administrative and Political Corruption'.

63. Wit, *Urban Poverty, Local Governance and Everyday Politics in Mumbai*, section 4.2.

64. James Crabtree, 'Goa Dares to Hope as India Eases Mining Ban', *Financial Times*, 30 April 2013.

65. Ravi Sharma, 'Mine of scams', *Frontline*, 24 September 2011.

66. 'Republic of Bellary', *The Telegraph*, 31 July 2011.

67. James Fontanella-Khan, 'India Lifts Karnataka Iron Ore Export Ban', *Financial Times*, 5 April 2011.

68. Das, *India Grows at Night*, p. 228.

CHAPTER 6: MONEY POWER POLITICS

1. India's 2011 census put Uttar Pradesh's population at 200m. It is now estimated to be in the region of 220m. 'Uttar Pradesh Population Census Data 2011', Census 2011.

2. Varshney, *Ethnic Conflict and Civic Life*, p. 55.

3. Sridharan, 'India's Watershed Vote', p. 28.

4. Pal, 'Haryana'.

5. Michelutti and Heath, 'Political Cooperation and Distrust'.

6. Mohd Faisal Fareed, 'Mulayam's Shocker: Boys Will Be Boys, They Make Mistakes . . . Will You Hang Them for Rape?', *Indian Express*, 11 April 2014.

7. Przeworski, 'Capitalism, Development and Democracy', p. 493.

8. Huntington, 'Democracy's Third Wave', p. 30.

9. Vaishnav, *When Crime Pays*, p. 33.

10. 'India Elections: A Complex Election Explained', *Financial Times*, 7 April 2014.

11. Amy Kazmin, 'Narendra Modi Mocks Economists amid Doubts over Indian GDP', *Financial Times*, 2 March 2017.

12. Gowda and Sharalaya, 'Crony Capitalism and India's Political System', p. 133.

13. S. Rukmini, '400% Rise in Parties' Spend on LS Polls', *The Hindu*, 2 March 2015.

14. J. Balaji, 'Poll Expenditure Ceiling Raised', *The Hindu*, 1 March 2014.

15. 'Munde Admits Spending Rs 8 Crore in 2009 Polls', *The Hindu*, 28 June 2013.

16. 'Assembly Election 2017: Cash, Liquor Seizure Go through the Roof in 2017', Press Trust of India, 26 February 2017.

17. 'Why Tatas, Birlas Use Electoral Trusts to Fund Politics', FirstPost, 10 September 2012. Also see 'Contribution to Political Parties', Press Information Bureau, 27 February 2015.

18. Sanjeev Miglani and Tommy Wilkes, 'On Eve of State Polls, Modi Looks to Clean up Campaign Funding', Reuters, 2 February 2017.

19. Kaushik Deka, 'Now Nail the Netas', *India Today*, 30 November 2016.

20. 'Mamata's Midas Brush', *The Telegraph*, 13 April 2015.

21. Raghvendra Rao, '442 Crorepatis, Richest Worth Rs 683 Crore', *Indian Express*, 19 May 2014.

22. 'Mayawati: Portrait of a Lady', WikiLeaks, 23 October 2008.

23. Janane Venkatraman, 'Mayawati's Cases: A Recap', *The Hindu*, 14 April 2016.

24. Vaishnav, *When Crime Pays*, p. 10.

25. Mehboob Jeelani, 'Under the Influence: Ponty Chadha's Potent Mix of Liquor and Politics', *The Caravan*, 1 November 2013.

26. Cordelia Jenkins and Amaan Malik, 'Ponty Chadha: The Man Who Would Be King', *Livemint*, 30 November 2012.

27. Veenu Sandhu Shashikant Trivedi and Indulekha Aravind, 'Mid-Day Mess', *Business Standard*, 26 July 2013.

28. Anto Antony and Bhuma Shrivastava, 'India Shadow Banker Fights to Keep Empire Built on Poor', Bloomberg Markets, 3 December 2013.

29. Jeelani, 'Under the Influence'.

30. Tony Munroe and Devidutta Tripathy, 'Sahara: Massive, Splashy . . . and Mysterious', Reuters, 26 September 2012.

31. Tamal Bandyopadhyay, 'Sahara Hasn't Done Anything against the Law: Subrata Roy', *Livemint*, 26 April 2014.

32. Suchitra Mohanty and Devidutta Tripathy, 'Sahara Told to Repay Small Investors $3.1 Billion', Reuters, 31 August 2012.

33. Raghuram Rajan, 'Finance and Opportunity in India', Address at Twentieth Lalit Doshi Memorial Lecture, Mumbai, 11 August 2014.

CHAPTER 7: CRONYISM GOES SOUTH

1. Rollo Romig, 'What Happens When a State Is Run by Movie Stars?', *New York Times*, 1 July 2015.

2. Vaasanthi, 'Madras Check', *The Caravan*, 1 April 2014.

3. 'Populism Doesn't Win Polls', *Indian Express*, 8 April 2014.

4. T. N. Gopalan, 'Indian State of Tamil Nadu Gives Laptops to Children', BBC, 15 September 2011.

5. A. S. Panneerselvan, 'The Acid Wears Off', *Outlook*, 25 September 1996.

6. 'Court jails Tamil Nadu CM Jayalalithaa in graft case', Reuters, 27 September 2014.

7. B. V. Shivashankar, 'Jayalalithaa's 10,500 Saris, 750 Slippers, 500 Wine Glasses in Court', *Times of India*, 9 December 2016.

8. 'Jayalalithaa Conviction: 16 Persons Commit Suicide', *The Hindu*, 29 September 2014.

9. Satish Padmanabhan, Dola Mitra and Ajay Sukumaran, 'Winners Take the Decade', *Outlook*, 30 May 2016.

10. K. V. Lakshmana, 'Gold, cellphones, gift coupons: Jaya promises freebies in poll manifesto', *Hindustan Times*, 5 May 2016.

11. Romig, 'What Happens When a State Is Run by Movie Stars?'

12. Ellen Barry and Hari Kumar, 'Suicides Reported in India after Death of Jayalalithaa Jayaram', *New York Times*, 10 December 2016.

13. V. Geetha, 'The Undemocratic Regime of Jayalalithaa', *The Caravan*, 9 December 2016.

14. Jacob, *Celluloid Deities*, p. 212.

15. Vaasanthi, 'Madras Check'.

16. 'Tamil Nadu Gives Tax Sops to Auto Part Makers', Reuters, 23 February 1996.

17. Prachi Salve, 'Jayalalithaa's Legacy: Industrial, Social, Crime Rankings among India's Best', *IndiaSpend*, 6 December 2016.

18. Public Affairs Index: Governance in the Indian States of India, 2016.

19. Mihir Sharma, 'Jayalalithaa's Chief Minister Template Followed by Nitish, Modi', NDTV 6 December 2016.

20. Centre for Media Studies, 'CMS India Corruption Study 2017', 2017.

21. Gomez, *Political Business in East Asia*, p. 37.

22. Annie Gowen, 'Jayaram Jayalalithaa, Powerful Indian Politician Who Broke Gender Barriers, Dies at 68', *Washington Post*, 5 December 2016.

23. 'Largest Wedding Banquet/Reception', Guinness World Records.

24. Robin Pagnamenta, 'Jayaram Jayalalithaa', *The Times*, 10 December 2016.

25. 'Women in India: Tamil Nadu's Iron Lady J. Jayalalithaa', WikiLeaks, 19 March 2009.

26. Robert Byron, 'New Delhi: The Individual Buildings', *Architectural Review*, January 1931, reproduced 25 August 2010.

27. 'MP Who Collapsed in Parliament Admitted to Hospital', *Business Standard*, 13 February 2014.

28. 'Indian Parliament Pepper-Sprayed as MPs Brawl over New Telangana State', Agence France-Presse, 13 February 2014.

29. Shekhar Gupta, 'National Interest: India Stinc', *Indian Express*, 15 February 2014.

30. 'RIPPP', *The Economist*, 15 December 2012.

31. Pratap Bhanu Mehta, 'The Contractor State', *Indian Express*, 2 April 2013.

32. Julie McCaffrey, 'Exclusive: The Last Nizam of Hyderabad Was So Rich He Had a £50m Diamond Paperweight . . .', *The Mirror*, 15 April 2008.

33. Shekhar Gupta, 'India Stinc', *Indian Express*, 15 February 2014.

34. Aparisim Ghosh, 'South Asian of the Year: Chandrababu Naidu', *TIME Asia*, 31 December 1999.

35. B. V. Shiv Shankar, 'Jalayagnam: The Mother of All Frauds', *Times of India*, 16 April 2012.

36. 'Corruption Plagues Andhra Pradesh's Big Ticket Spending Programs', WikiLeaks, 22 October 2007.

37. Supipto Dey, 'Sons of the soil', *Outlook Business*, 5 September 2008.

38. James Crabtree, 'India's Billionaires Club', *Financial Times*, 16 November 2012.

39. Praveen Donthi, 'The Takeover', *The Caravan*, 1 May 2012.

40. 'CAG Finds Grave Irregularities in Land Allotments by YSR Govt', *Business Standard*, 30 March 2012. Also see Sukhantar and Vaishnav, 'Corruption in India', p. 8.

41. Donthi, 'The Takeover'.

42. Mark Bergen, 'Dividing Lines', *The Caravan*, 1 May 2013.

43. Kapur and Vaishnav, 'Quid Pro Quo'.

44. James Crabtree, 'Mumbai's Bloodied Elite', *Prospect*, 17 December 2008.

45. Gowda and Sharalaya, 'Crony Capitalism and India's Political System'.

CHAPTER 8: HOUSE OF DEBT

1. 'Profile: Rakesh Jhunjhunwala', *Forbes*, 15 June 2017; 'The World's Billionaires Index', *Forbes*, 26 March 2012.

2. Rana Rosen, 'No More Room in India's Most Expensive Office', *Livemint*, 17 August 2007.

3. T. C. A. Srinivasa-Raghavan, 'The Economic History of Liberation', *Open*, 22 July 2016.

4. Gupta and Kumar, 'India Financial Sector: House of Debt'.

5. Hamid, *How to Get Filthy Rich in Rising Asia*, p. 180.

6. Ajit Barman and Biswajit Baruah, 'Not Hyper-Critical, I Want to Be Hyper-Objective: Ashish Gupta, MD Equity Research, Credit Suisse', *Economic Times*, 21 June 2013.

7. James Crabtree, 'Concerns Grow over Indian Industrials' Debt Burdens', *Financial Times*, 14 August 2013.

8. James Crabtree, 'Lackadaisical Indian Bank Set for Shake-Up under New Leader', *Financial Times*, 8 December 2013.

9. Kahneman, *Thinking, Fast and Slow*, p. 250.

10. Paranjoy Guha Thakurta and Aman Malik, 'From Adani to Ambani, How Alleged Over-Invoicing of Imported Coal Has Increased Power Tariffs', *The Wire*, 6 April 2016.

11. Rajiv Lall, 'Turn the PPP Model on Its Head', *Business Standard*, 3 January 2015.

12. Raghuram Govind Rajan, 'Essays on Banking', PhD thesis, Massachusetts Institute of Technology, May 1991.

13. Rajan and Zingales, 'Which Capitalism?'

14. Raghuram G. Rajan, 'Has Financial Development Made the World Riskier?', 2005.

15. 'Statement by Dr Raghuram Rajan on Taking Office on September 4, 2013', press release, Reserve Bank of India, 4 September 2013.

16. 'Report of the Committee to Review Governance of Boards of Banks in India', Reserve Bank of India, May 2014.

17. Lionel Barber and James Crabtree, 'Rajan Treads Different Path to More Circumspect Predecessors; RBI Governor', *Financial Times*, 19 November 2013.

18. 'Chairman of Syndicate Bank Arrested on Bribery Allegations', Reuters, 3 August 2014.

19. Tamal Bandyopadhyay, 'How Corrupt Are Our Bankers?', *Livemint*, 26 September 2016.

20. 'Annual Report 2016–17', State Bank of India, May 2017.

21. Rakesh Mohan, 'Transforming Indian Banking: In Search of a Better Tomorrow', Bank Economists' Conference 2002, Bangalore, 29 December 2002.

22. Ninan, *The Turn of the Tortoise*, p. 65.

23. 'PM's Remarks at Gyan Sangam: the Bankers' Retreat in Pune', Narendra Modi website, 3 January 2015.

24. 'Raghuram Rajan Not to Continue as RBI Governor after September', *Scroll*, 18 June 2016.

25. Luigi Zingales, 'RBI Governor Rajan's Fight against Crony Capitalism', Pro Market, 11 June 2016.

26. Rahul Shrivastava, 'Why IIT, Harvard Graduate Jayant Sinha Lost Finance Ministry', NDTV, 7 July 2016.

CHAPTER 9: THE ANXIOUS TYCOONS

1. 'Angul', Jindal Steel & Power website (accessed 28 December 2017).

2. Ashwin Ramarathinam and S. Bridget Leena, 'With Rs 73.4 Crore, Naveen Jindal Retains Top Paid Executive Title', *Livemint*, 23 September 2012.

3. Rahul Oberoi, 'How SC Ruling on Coal Blocks Will Impact Related Companies', *Money Today*, November 2014.

4. Rakhi Mazumdar, 'I Am Relieved We Could Finish Angul Project: Jindal Steel & Power Chairman Naveen Jindal', *Economic Times*, 29 May 2017.

5. Dillip Satapathy, 'Coal Fire 3: Jindal Steel & Power's Projects Worth Rs 80,000 Cr in Limbo in Odisha,' *Business Standard*, 2 November 2013.

6. 'Jindal Wins Government Nod for Flying Tricolour at Night', *Business Standard*, 24 December 2009.

7. Rakhi Mazumdar, '4-Way Split of Jindal Group Proposed', *Business Standard*, 27 August 1997.

8. *Partnering India's Aspirations*, Annual Report 2012–13, Jindal Steel and Power Limited.

9. Naazneen Karmali, 'Citizen Tycoon', *Forbes*, 25 September 2009.

10. Moinak Mitra, 'The Paladin of Power', *Economic Times*, 24 August 2012.

11. Sudheer Pal Singh, 'Navin Jindal's Toughest Hour', *Business Standard*, 14 November 2012.

12. James Crabtree and Avantika Chilkoti, 'Jindal Steel Shares Sink after Police Raid at Coal Mine', *Financial Times*, 20 October 2014.

13. 'Jindal Steel Defaults on Debenture Interest Payments', *Reuters*, 6 October 2016.

14. David Lalmalsawma, 'Zee News Editors Arrested in Jindal Extortion Case', Reuters, 27 November 2012.

15. Mehboob Jeelani, 'The Price of Power', *The Caravan*, 5 March 2013.

16. Myrdal, *Asian Drama*, p. 277.

17. 'The Bollygarchs' Magic Mix', *The Economist*, 22 October 2011.

18. Tarun Khanna and Krishna G. Palepu, 'Why Focused Strategies May Be Wrong for Emerging Markets', *Harvard Business Review*, July–August 1997.

19. Ninan, *The Turn of the Tortoise*, p. 93.

20. Martin Hirt, Sven Smit and Wonsik Yoo, 'Understanding Asia's Conglomerates', *McKinsey Quarterly*, February 2013.

21. *Asian Family Business Report 2011*, Credit Suisse, October 2011.

22. Aakar Patel, 'When Will the Brahmin-Bania Hegemony End?', *Livemint*, 28 August 2009.

23. Dasgupta, *Capital*, pp. 224, 225.

24. James Crabtree, 'Mumbai's Former US Consulate Sets Indian Record for Property Deal', *Financial Times*, 14 September 2015.

25. Samanth Subramanian, 'Breach Candy', *Granta*, 130, 2015.

26. James Crabtree, 'Mumbai's Towering Ambitions Brought Low by Legal Disputes', *Financial Times*, 10 October 2014.

27. 'Janardhan Reddy's Daughter's Wedding Invite!', News Minute/YouTube, 18 October 2016 (https://youtu.be/3TgCeDmE6UI) (accessed 29 December 2017).

28. Harish Upadhyay, 'Hampi Temple Replica, 50,000 Guests: A Wedding Bengaluru Is Talking About', NDTV, 15 November 2016.

29. Parul Bhandari, 'Inside the Big Fat Indian Wedding: Conservatism, Competition and Networks', *The Conversation*, 13 January 2017.

30. Amit Roy, '£30m Wedding Bill as Bollywood Comes to France', *The Telegraph*, 2 June 2004.

31. Preethi Nagaraj, 'Janardhan Reddy's Spending on Daughter's Wedding Is as Strategic as Extravagant', *Hindustan Times*, 16 November 2016.

32. James Crabtree, 'The Monday Interview: Prashant Ruia, Group Chief Executive of Essar', *Financial Times*, 17 March 2013.

33. 'The Essar Group' and 'Corporate Profile', Essar website, 2014.

34. Gupta et al., 'India Financial Sector: House of Debt Revisited'.

35. 'Default Options', *The Economist*, 3 February 2000.

36. Appu Esthose Suresh and Ritu Sarin, 'Essar Leaks: French Cruise for Nitin Gadkari, Favours to UPA Minister, Journalists', *Indian Express*, 27 January 2015.

37. Krishn Kaushik, 'Doing the Needful', *The Caravan*, 1 August 2015.

38. Kathrin Hille and James Crabtree, 'Rosneft Buys Stake in Essar Oil Refinery in India', *Financial Times*, 9 July 2015.

39. Naazneen Karmali, 'Road to Riches', *Forbes*, 4 December 2010.

CHAPTER 10: MORE THAN A GAME

1. Tim Wigmore, 'India–Pakistan Final: Will a Billion People Watch the Champions Trophy Final?', ESPN Cricinfo, 17 June 2017.

2. Raina and Chaudhary, 'Television Broadcasting in India'.

3. 'IPL Brand Value Doubles to USD 4.13 Billion', NDTV Sports, 23 March 2010.

4. 'Cricket, Lovely Cricket', *The Economist*, 31 July 2008.

5. Rahul Bhatia, 'Mr Big Deal', *Tehelka*, 20 May 2006.

6. Suveen Sinha, 'Lalit Modi: People like Mr Srinivasan May Come and Go but IPL Will Continue to Flourish', *Business Today*, 6 May 2014.

7. 'Documents: Lalit Modi's 1985 indictment, arrest warrant and guilty plea in US for drug possession and assault', AB Wire, 15 June 2015.

8. Samanth Subramanian, 'The Confidence Man', *The Caravan*, 1 March 2011.

9. Ibid.

10. Matt Wade, 'The Tycoon Who Changed Cricket', *The Age*, 8 March 2008.

11. Bhatia, 'Mr Big Deal'.

12. Astill, *The Great Tamasha*.

13. Hawkins, *Bookie Gambler Fixer Spy*, p. 52.

14. ' "Slapgate" a Thing of the Past for Sreesanth, Harbhajan', *Indian Express*, 25 October 2010.

15. Gideon Haigh, 'The Men Who Sold the World', *Cricket Monthly*, October 2015.

16. Rahul Bhatia, 'Beyond the Boundary', *The Caravan*, 1 August 2014.

17. Mukul Kesavan, 'An Emirate and Its Subjects', *The Telegraph*, 29 January 2015.

18. 'Srinivasan Promises Fair Investigation', ESPN Cricinfo, 26 May 2013.

19. Booth, *Wisden's Cricketers' Almanack 2012*.

20. 'Srinivasan Sticking on as BCCI Boss "Nauseating" ', *Hindustan Times*, 26 March 2014.

21. Ramachandra Guha, 'An Indian Century', *The Caravan*, 1 October 2014.

22. 'Frankly Speaking with N. Srinivasan: Part 1', Times Now/YouTube, 9 October 2013 (https://youtu.be/rXtWehl4J8k) (accessed 2 January 2018).

23. 'IPL 2013 Spot-Fixing Controversy: Full Text of N. Srinivasan's Press Conference in Kolkata', Press Trust of India, 26 May 2013.

CHAPTER 11: THE NATION WANTS TO KNOW

1. @NorthernComd.IA, '#JKOps Please Find a Statement Attached on the Operation at Uri in J&K', Twitter, 18 September 2016.

2. 'India Election Update: Last Week Tonight with John Oliver (HBO)', *Last Week Tonight*/YouTube, 18 May 2014 (https://www.youtu.be/8YQ_HGvrHEU) (accessed 30 January 2018).

3. A.A.K., 'Why India's Newspaper Business Is Booming', *The Economist*, 22 February 2016; 'Master List of Permitted Private Satellite TV Channels as on 31.05.2017', National Informatics Centre, 31 May 2017.

4. 'IRS 2014 Topline Findings', Readership Studies Council of India, 2014.

5. 'Mukesh Ambani Praises Arnab Goswami during Interview with Shekhar Gupta in NDTV', *Financial Express*, 1 November 2016.

6. Madhu Purnima Kishwar, 'When News Programs Become Kangaroo Courts, Part I: An Open Letter to Arnab Goswami', Manushi, 2012.

7. Painter, ed., *India's Media Boom*.

8. Rahul Bhatia, 'Fast and Furious', *The Caravan*, 1 December 2012.

9. Ninan, *The Turn of the Tortoise*, p. 106.

10. Bhatia, 'Fast and Furious'.

11. Rajdeep Sardesai, 'Life in a 24*7 Coop', *India Today*, 11 December 2014.

12. Ninan, 'Indian Media's Dickensian Age'.

13. 'India: Threat from Modi's Nationalism', Reporters without Borders, 2017. Pakistan ranks 139th and Bangladesh ranks 146th respectively, on the 2017 report.

14. Gaurav Laghate, 'TV Viewers in India Now Much More than All of Europe's', *Economic Times*, 3 March 2017.

15. Ken Auletta, 'Citizens Jain', *New Yorker*, 8 October 2012.

16. Ashish K. Mishra, 'Inside the Network18 Takeover', *Livemint*, 25 June 2014.

17. Harveen Ahluwalia, 'Times Group Serves Arnab Goswami Notice on Using "Nation Wants to Know"', *Livemint*, 18 April 2017.

18. 'This Is Arnab Goswami. I Am Here as Promised. Ask Me, What Redditors Want to Know!', Reddit, 27 April 2017.

19. Sadanand Dhume, 'A Tahrir Square Moment in India', YaleGlobal Online, 18 April 2011.

20. 'MP Rajeev Chandrasekhar Biggest Investor in Arnab Goswami's Republic?', *Business Standard*, 13 January 2017.

21. Ramanathan S., 'Arnab's Republic of Investors: Who Is Funding Goswami and What that Means', *News Minute*, 13 January 2017.

22. ANI, 'News Traders Dance on Congress's Tune: Modi', *Business Standard*, 30 April 2014.

23. 'PM Modi on Frankly Speaking with Arnab Goswami: Exclusive Full Interview', Times Now/YouTube, 27 June 2016 (https://youtu.be/892N6hiRpUM) (accessed 3 January 2018).

24. 'This Is Arnab Goswami'.

25. 'India: Threat from Modi's Nationalism'.

26. C. P. Surendran, 'India Is Arnab and Arnab Is India', *The Wire*, 28 July 2016.

CHAPTER 12: THE TRAGEDIES OF MODI

1. 'Iconic Race Course Road Renamed as Lok Kalyan Marg', Press Trust of India, 21 September 2016.

2. '#PMSpeaksToArnab: Read Full Text Here', Times Now, 27 June 2016.

3. In 2014, India's GDP per capita was $1,573 according to the World Bank. The GDP per capita for China and Malaysia was $7,683 and $11,184 respectively. 'GDP per Capita (Current US$): Data', World Bank, 2014.

4. Parag Gupta and Gaurav Rateria, 'Technology: The Millennials Series – The Disruptive Wave in the World's Seventh Largest Economy', Morgan Stanley, 19 February 2017. In 2017, India was classified by the World Bank as a lower-middle-income nation; see 'New Country Classifications by Income Level: 2017–2018', The Data Blog, World Bank, 7 January 2017.

5. 'Indian Economy to Reach $5 Trillion by 2025, Says Report', Livemint, 21 February 2017.

6. Phongpaichit, 'The Thai Economy in the Mid-1990s'.

7. Hausmann et al., 'Growth Accelerators'.

8. Asit Ranjan Mishra, 'India to See Severe Shortage of Jobs in the Next 35 Years', Livemint, 28 April 2016.

9. Mohan Guruswamy, '1.7 Billion Indians by 2050: Much Food for Thought', Deccan Chronicle, 31 May 2017.

10. 'Tryst with Destiny Speech Made by Pt Jawaharlal Nehru', Indian National Congress, 13 August 2016.

11. Kishore Mahbubani, 'One Year of Narendra Modi Govt: Bold Moves on World Stage', Indian Express, 29 May 2015.

12. McKean, Divine Enterprise, p. 71.

13. Devesh Kapur, 'And Now, (Modestly) Good News', Business Standard, 9 April 2012.

14. Mahim Pratap Singh, 'Jawaharlal Nehru Erased from Rajasthan School Textbook, Congress Angry', Indian Express, 26 May 2016.

15. 'Text of Prime Minister Shri Narendra Modi's Address to the Indian Community at Madison Square Garden, New York', Press Information Bureau, Prime Minister's Office, Government of India, 28 September 2014.

16. Poornima Joshi, 'The Organiser', The Caravan, 1 April 2014.

17. Patrick French, 'The "Shah" of BJP's Game Plan Who Wants to Alter India's Political Culture', Hindustan Times, 17 July 2016.

18. 'After 3 Months in Jail, Amit Shah Out on Bail', Indian Express, 30 October 2010.

19. Varshney, 'India's Watershed Vote'.

20. Mukul Kesavan, 'What about 1984? Pogroms and Political Virtue', The Telegraph, 26 July 2013.

21. 'PM Modi in Fatehpur: If There Is Electricity during Ramzan, It Should Be Available on Diwali Too', *Indian Express*, 20 February 2017.

22. Mihir Swarup Sharma, 'In Modi and Amit Shah Speeches, the 2 Sides of the BJP', NDTV, 16 June 2016.

23. 'General Election 2014: Partywise Performance and List of Party Participated', Election Commission of India website (http://eci.nic.in/eci_main1/GE2014/Party_Contested_GE_2014.xlsx) (accessed 3 January 2018).

24. Rupam Jain Nair, 'India's Modi to Observe Strict Fast during Maiden Trip to US', Reuters, 22 September 2014.

25. 'Rahul Gandhi Tears into Modi's "Suit-Boot Ki Sarkar"', *Times of India*, 21 April 2015.

26. Suryatapa Bhattacharya, 'Modi's Famous Pinstripe Suit Sells for $690,000 at Auction', *Wall Street Journal*, 20 February 2015.

27. Amy Kazmin, 'Narendra Modi Continues to Ride Wave of Popularity as India's PM', *Financial Times*, 16 November 2017.

28. Ellen Barry, 'Modi's Yoga Day Grips India, and "Om" Meets "Ouch!"', *New York Times*, 15 June 2015.

29. James Crabtree, 'Arvind Subramanian, Economic Adviser to Narendra Modi', *Financial Times*, 10 May 2017.

30. 'IT + IT = IT: PM Narendra Modi Devises New Equation', *Times of India*, 10 May 2017.

31. Suhasini Haidar, 'India for Israel, Says Modi; Force against Bad: Netanyahu', *The Hindu*, 6 July 2017.

32. Narendra Modi had thirty-seven million followers at @narendramodi in December 2017.

33. Zahir Janmohamed, 'The Rise of Narendra Modi', *Boston Review*, 28 June 2013.

34. '#PMSpeaksToArnab: Read Full Text Here'.

35. 'Dressing Down', *Business Standard*, 23 July 2014.

36. Price, *The Modi Effect*, pp. 247–8.

37. Mihir Sharma, 'Jobs Are Modi's Central Mission, and He's Failing', Bloomberg, 26 May 2017.

38. 'Doing Business in India', World Bank Group, 2017. India stood at 142nd in the rankings when Modi took office. By 2017 it had risen to 130th place.

39. P. Vaidyanathan Iyer, 'Modi May Be an Agent of Change, but He Has to Reshape an Entire Ocean', *Indian Express*, 22 December 2015.

40. 'Most of India's State-Owned Firms Are Ripe for Sale or Closure', *The Economist*, 1 June 2017.

41. Debroy et al., *Getting India Back on Track*, p. 41.

42. Khilnani, *The Idea of India*, ch. 1.

43. James Crabtree, 'If They Kill Even One Hindu, We Will Kill 100!', *Foreign Policy*, 30 March 2017.

44. James Crabtree, 'Forget Brexit. Rexit Is the Real Problem', *Foreign Policy*, 22 June 2016.

45. 'Tolerance and Respect for Economic Progress: Full Text of Raghuram Rajan's Speech at IIT-Delhi', *Times of India*, 31 October 2015.

46. 'Raghuram Rajan "Mentally Not Fully Indian", Sack Him, Subramanian Swamy Writes to PM Modi', *Times of India*, 17 May 2016.

47. Victor Mallet, 'India's Top Judge Thakur Pleads for Help with Avalanche of Cases', *Financial Times*, 25 April 2016.

48. 'Courts Will Take 320 Years to Clear Backlog Cases: Justice Rao', *Times of India*, 6 March 2010.

49. Michael Barbaro, 'Bloomberg's Bullpen: Candidates Debate Its Future', *New York Times*, 22 March 2013.

50. Ramachandra Guha, 'Are We Becoming an Election Only Democracy?', *Hindustan Times*, 29 November 2015.

51. Fareed Zakaria, 'The Rise of Illiberal Democracy', *Foreign Affairs*, November–December 1997.

52. Shashi Tharoor, 'Tharoor on Modi's Mid-Term: Parivar Haunts PM's Sabka Vikas Agenda', *The Quint*, 22 November 2016.

53. Crabtree, 'If They Kill Even One Hindu, We Will Kill 100!'

54. Gurcharan Das, 'Was Voting for the BJP a Risk Worth Taking? Three Years On, Jury's Out', *Times of India* blog, 4 June 2017.

CONCLUSION: A PROGRESSIVE ERA?

1. James Crabtree, 'Mumbai Takes to the Skies with New Airport Terminal', *Financial Times*, 10 January 2014.

2. Rajat Rai, 'Modi: The Rich Need Pills to Go to Sleep after Demonetisation Move', *India Today*, 15 November 2016.

3. Manjeet S. Pardesi and Sumit Ganguly, 'India and Oligarchic Capitalism', *The Diplomat*, 26 April 2011.

4. 'Data Shows Only 1% of Population Pays Income Tax, Over 5000 Pay More Than 1 Crore', Press Trust of India, 1 May 2016.

5. James Crabtree, 'Has Narendra Modi Cleaned Up India?', *Prospect*, 23 April 2015.

6. Coralie Pring, 'People and Corruption: Asia Pacific – Global Corruption Barometer', Transparency International, 2017.

7. Paul Collier, 'The C-Word: Paul Collier on the Future of Corruption', *Times Literary Supplement*, 11 July 2017.

8. James Crabtree, 'Modi's Money Madness', *Foreign Affairs*, 16 June 2017.

9. 'Global Infrastructure Outlook: Infrastructure Investment Needs – 50 Countries, 7 Sectors to 2040', Oxford Economics, July 2017.

10. Huntington, *Political Order in Changing Societies*, p. 1.

11. Klitgaard, *Controlling Corruption*, p. 24.

12. Ben W. Heineman Jr, 'In China, Corruption and Unrest Threaten Autocratic Rule', *The Atlantic*, 29 June 2011.

13. Pratap Bhanu Mehta, 'Seven Sins of Hubris', *Indian Express*, 5 June 2014.

14. Francis Fukuyama, 'What is Corruption?', Research Institute for Development, Growth and Economics, 2016.

15. For an excellent introduction to the topic of state capacity, see: Kapur et al., eds, *Rethinking Public Institutions in India*.

16. Huntington, *Political Order in Changing Societies*, p. 1.

INDEX

References to images are in *italics*.